D1521745

Primo Levi's Ordinary Virtues

Primo Levi's Ordinary Virtues

From Testimony to Ethics

ROBERT S. C. GORDON

OXFORD
UNIVERSITY PRESS

OXFORD
UNIVERSITY PRESS

Great Clarendon Street, Oxford OX2 6DP

Oxford University Press is a department of the University of Oxford.
It furthers the University's objective of excellence in research, scholarship,
and education by publishing worldwide in

Oxford New York

Athens Auckland Bangkok Bogotá Buenos Aires
Cape Town Chennai Dar es Salaam Delhi Florence Hong Kong Istanbul
Karachi Kolkata Kuala Lumpur Madrid Melbourne Mexico City Mumbai
Nairobi Paris São Paulo Shanghai Singapore Taipei Tokyo Toronto Warsaw

with associated companies in Berlin Ibadan

Oxford is a registered trade mark of Oxford University Press
in the UK and in certain other countries

Published in the United States
by Oxford University Press Inc., New York

British Library Cataloguing in Publication Data

Data available

Library of Congress Cataloging-in-Publication Data
Gordon, Robert S. C. (Robert Samuel Clive), 1966–
Primo Levi's ordinary virtues: from testimony to ethics/Robert S. C. Gordon.
p. cm.
Includes bibliographical references and index.
1. Levi, Primo—Ethics. I. Title.
PQ4872.E8 Z66 2001   853'.914—dc21   2001033991

ISBN 0–19–815963–3

1 3 5 7 9 10 8 6 4 2

Typeset in Bembo by
Cambrian Typesetters, Frimley, Surrey
Printed in Great Britain
on acid-free paper by
Biddles Ltd,
Guildford and King's Lynn

FOR BARBARA

ACKNOWLEDGEMENTS

I would like to thank Giulio Einaudi Editore for permission to reproduce extracts from Levi's work. During my work on this project, early drafts of chapters, parts of chapters, or sketches of the project as a whole have appeared in a number of books and journals and I am grateful to their editors and publishers for permission to make use of this material here: 'Etica', in M. Belpoliti, ed., *Primo Levi* (Milan: Marcos y Marcos, Riga 13, 1997), 315–30 (project); '*Per mia fortuna*. . . : Irony and Ethics in Primo Levi's Writing', *Modern Language Review*, 92/2 (Apr. 1997), 337–47 (Chapter 12); 'Primo Levi: On Friendship', in G. Bedani et al., eds., *Sguardi sull'Italia* (Leeds: W. S. Maney/Society for Italian Studies Occasional Papers 3, 1997), 284–94 (Chapter 10); 'Primo Levi: The Duty of Memory', in H. Peitsch, C. Burdett, and C. Gorrara, eds., *European Memories of the Second World War* (Oxford: Berghahn, 1999), 131–40 (Chapter 2); 'The Art of Listening: Primo Levi's Ethics of Storytelling', *Jewish Culture and History*, 3/1 (Summer 2000), 1–22 (Chapter 11); 'Per un'etica comune: le virtù quotidiane di Primo Levi', in E. Mattioda, ed., *Al di qua del bene e del male* (Milan: Franco Angeli, 2000), 87–108 (project).

The following institutions and their staff offered me valuable support which greatly facilitated the writing of the book: Pembroke College, the Taylor Institution Library, and the Modern Languages Faculty, University of Oxford; Gonville and Caius College and the Italian Department, University of Cambridge; the Arts and Humanities Research Board; the British Library; the Biblioteca nazionale, Florence. A large number of individuals have also helped me in ways both academic and personal and I would like to express my thanks to them here, in particular to: Carole Angier, Pierpaolo Antonello, Stefano Bartezzaghi, Tony Bayfield, Paola Benetti, Pat Boyde, Charles

Burdett, Ann Caesar, Michael Caesar, Alberto Cavaglion, Bryan Cheyette, Mirna Cicioni, Virginia Cox, Martin Crowley, Colin Davis, John Felstiner, Matthew Festenstein, Jason Freeman, Nadia Fusini, Paul Ginsborg, Sophie Goldsworthy, Jill Gordon, Lionel Gordon, Peter Hainsworth, Nick Harrison, Nancy Harrowitz, Robin Kirkpatrick, Giulio Lepschy, Laura Lepschy, Martin McLaughlin, Enrico Mattioda, David Mendel, Beniamino Placido, David Porter, Jackie Pritchard, Miri Rubin, Antony Rudolf, Anna Teicher, Frances Whistler, John Woodhouse. I owe a special debt to Marco Belpoliti, the animator behind a wave of new work on and interest in Levi in Italy, who has always been unfailingly generous and encouraging to me. The book is dedicated to Barbara Placido, with love.

R.S.C.G.

CONTENTS

x   *Contents*

ABBREVIATIONS

References to Primo Levi's works are from the two-volume Einaudi edition edited by Marco Belpoliti (P. Levi, *Opere*, vols. I–II, Turin: Einaudi, 1997) and are given by volume number followed by page number. I have left titles from Levi's work in Italian. For Levi's books as published in English, see section 1e of the Bibliography. All translations are my own unless otherwise stated.

I have mostly retained in English Levi's use of the German term *Lager* (camp) that has become commonplace in Italian as a way of referring to one or more concentration camp or, by extension, to the Final Solution as a whole. At other times I have used the phrase coined by David Rousset, *l'univers concentrationnaire*; but for the most part, I have used the term Holocaust, despite the very real problems associated with it, for reasons I explain in the Introduction (note 5).

INTRODUCTION

BEYOND TESTIMONY

Writing about the Holocaust, whether as survivor, chronicler, or mere glossator of the work of others, has become all but synonymous with 'bearing witness'. Adopting the language of testimony has become quite natural, almost an inevitable consequence of tackling this most fraught of subjects. And the reasons for this are compelling. Testimony brings with it a genuine rhetorical power. It taps into time-honoured traditions of memory and mourning; it gives voice to a mass of individuals who have little or no expertise in speaking or writing, only the authority of having been there, 'whose only claim to greatness is the greatness of their suffering', as Levi put it in a 1947 article (I. 1384).[1] Furthermore, it has the noble ring of collective, public action: testimony is a defiant deposition against crime, against evil. And the more testimonial narrative (spoken and written) has been used as a vessel for channelling unbearably painful and disorienting memories of the camps, the more it has acquired the characteristics, the markers, the structural and stylistic identity and variety of a genre, mixing elements of autobiography, the *Bildungsroman*, the historical novel, and others. As Elie Wiesel has put it, 'if the Greeks invented tragedy, the Romans the epistle and the Renaissance the sonnet, our generation invented a new literature, that of testimony'.[2] And through

---

[1] In this tapping into traditional rhetoric as a means to mourning, testimony echoes the forms of memorial practices after the First World War examined by Jay Winter in *Site of Memory, Sites of Mourning. The Great War in European Cultural History* (Cambridge: Cambridge University Press, 1995); see p. 5 and *passim* (although Winter is reluctant to draw direct parallels with the Second World War; see pp. 8–10, 228–9).

[2] E. Wiesel, 'The Holocaust as Literary Inspiration', in E. Wiesel et al., *Dimensions of the Holocaust. Lectures at NorthWestern University* (Evanston, Ill.: The University, 1977), 4–19 [9]. On the reversal of genres such as the *Bildungsroman* in Holocaust testimony, see L. Langer, *The Holocaust and the Literary Imagination* (New Haven: Yale University Press, 1975), 82, 84, 254–5. There are of course other generic shapes that have emerged from Holocaust writing: Richard Rubinstein and John Roth propose seven loose genres or styles (lamentation; resistance; endurance; survival; honesty; choice-making; protest) (*Approaches to Auschwitz* (Atlanta: John Knox, 1987), 254–89).

familiarization it has taken on something of a talismanic quality: to evoke testimony and to speak its language in describing a work need not mean dwelling on particular testimonial qualities or textures within it; it means staking a claim for it in that collective, noble position of defiance, like pinning on a commemorative badge.[3]

There is, then, no doubting the power of testimony understood both as a private vocabulary and as a public rhetoric and genre. Indeed, Primo Levi was one of its most eloquent advocates throughout his career as a writer about Auschwitz and in his public role as a survivor. He frequently and eloquently spoke as the proud, defiant witness, on both his own and others' behalf:

... che appunto perché il Lager è una gran macchina per ridurci a bestie, noi bestie non dobbiamo diventare; che anche in questo luogo si può sopravvivere, e perciò si deve voler sopravvivere, per raccontare, *per portare testimonianza*; ... (Steinlauf in *Se questo è un uomo*, I. 35; emphasis added)

(that precisely because the *Lager* is a great machine designed to bring us down to the level of animals, animals we must not become; that even in this place survival is possible, and so you have to want to survive, to tell the story, to bear witness)

Nello scrivere questo libro, ho assunto deliberatamente *il linguaggio pacato e sobrio del testimone*, non quello lamentevole della vittima né quello irato del vendicatore: pensavo che la mia parola sarebbe stata tanto piú credibile ed utile quanto piú apparisse obiettiva e quanto meno suonasse appassionata; solo *cosí il testimone in giudizio adempie alla sua funzione*, che è quello di preparare il terreno al giudice. I giudici siete voi. (Appendix to *Se questo è un uomo*, I. 175; emphases added)

[3] One example from many of the prevalence of testimonial language is found in the rich and varied collection edited by the Yale critic Geoffrey Hartman, *Holocaust Remembrance. The Shapes of Memory* (Oxford: Blackwell, 1994), made up of twenty essays (plus introduction) by leading scholars and writers in the field. The terms 'testimony' and 'memory' are far and away the lengthiest entries in the index; the 'testimony' entry refers the reader to nearly half of the 300 pages of the book and to fourteen of the essays (it is no coincidence that several of the others are by artists, writers, or architects rather than academics); 'testimony' or 'witness' appear in the title as a central concern of five essays. This does not make the book uniform or flat, but this is precisely the point: testimony is evoked constantly but is not necessarily the central object of analysis. The most influential recent work in this field has been S. Felman and D. Laub, *Testimony. Crises of Witnessing in Literature, Psychoanalysis and History* (London: Routledge, 1992), which makes remarkably brief reference to the preceding traditions testimony derives from (see pp. 204, 206–7), preferring to emphasize its status as what Wiesel calls ' "a new literature" ' (p. 6) and the complexities attached to that.

(In writing this book, I have deliberately taken on the calm and sober language of the witness, not the complaining voice of the victim, nor the angered tone of revenge: I thought my words would be all the more credible and useful the more they appeared objective and the less enraged; that is how the witness fulfils his function when summoned, preparing the ground for the judge. You are the judges.)

Hurbinek morì ai primi giorni del marzo 1945, libero ma non redento. Nulla resta di lui: *egli testimonia attraverso queste mie parole.* (*La tregua*, I. 216; emphasis added)

(Hurbinek died in the first days of March 1945, free but not redeemed. Nothing is left of him: he bears witness through these words of mine.)

[Auschwitz] mi ha segnato, ma non mi ha tolto il desiderio di vivere: anzi, me l'ha accresciuto, perché alla mia vita ha conferito uno scopo, quello di *portare testimonianza*, affinché nulla di simile avvenga mai più (1979; I. 1285; emphasis added)[4]

([Auschwitz] marked me, but it did not take away my desire for life: on the contrary, it stimulated it, because it gave my life a purpose, to bear witness so that nothing similar could ever happen again)

But the role of the witness does not exhaust Levi's resources by any means. Indeed, as an almost obsessive amateur linguistician, or better semiotician, Levi was acutely aware of the limitations imposed by the language of testimony on what he could achieve in his writing. And, taking off from Levi, there is a strong case to be made for reminding ourselves of the roots of testimony, of the fields from which it was borrowed, of its philology and etymology, so that we might not be constrained by the hidden assumptions that subtend it.[5] And the more the language of testimony can

---

[4] Most writers on Levi not surprisingly use the language of testimony without necessarily confronting it analytically *per se*. On the problematics of testimony and Levi's positioning within it, see G. Agamben, 'Il testimone', in *Quel che resta di Auschwitz. L'archivio e il testimone* (Turin: Bollati Boringhieri, 1998), 13–36 (a crucial essay for what follows, as will become clear); M. Lollini, 'Il caso Primo Levi e il problema della testimonianza', *Il piccolo Hans*, 72 (Winter 1991–2), 193–210.

[5] This is not to say that the language of testimony should be abandoned altogether, by any means. I am not proposing anything qualitatively different from the common and correct insistence that the term 'Holocaust' should be used with caution, with a full awareness of its origin and etymology. Levi disliked the term, like many others, but he acknowledged that its use was now inevitable ('the word cannot be avoided now', P. Levi, *The Voice of Memory. Interviews 1961–87*, ed. M. Belpoliti and R. Gordon (Cambridge: Polity, 2001), 269). I go along with his position in this book. On the term Holocaust, see Agamben, *Quel che resta di Auschwitz*, 26–9; A.-V. Sullam Calimani, 'A Name for Extermination (Hurban, Auschwitz, Genocide, Holocaust, Shoah)', *Modern Language Review*, 94/4 (Oct. 1999), 978–99.

be given its own specificity, its own strengths and weaknesses as a way of translating the experience of the Holocaust into writing, the more plausible becomes one of the underlying contentions of this book, that there are other languages in which to express the experience of the Holocaust, other vocabularies as flawed as but no more flawed than the language of testimony. Ethics is one of these vocabularies.

Testimony in Holocaust writing is a linguistic borrowing from another field, a metaphor. It has a dual origin, in theology and in jurisprudence, although it is the latter field and its associations that have dominated its usage in reference to the Holocaust and certainly loom largest in Levi's work.[6] Both areas contribute to the authority of the Holocaust witness's voice described earlier, but both also carry over into that other field certain of the constraints mentioned above. In Christian theology, bearing witness means bearing witness to the truth of the Word and of God, providing living proof of providence and of Revealed truth. As is often pointed out, the terms 'witness' and 'martyr' share the same etymology (the latter also deriving from a verb of memory), so that the martyr to the faith is, in suffering and dying, commemorating and bearing witness to its transcendental truth. The theology of testimony sets up the founding relation for the working of testimony, that between witnessing and truth, and also a corollary that is by no means obvious but which has powerful resonance in modern usage, the (redemptive) relation between suffering and truth.[7] In law, the witness—or to be more precise in analogy with the survivor of genocide, the eye-witness (since there are also expert witnesses, character witnesses, and so forth, who have quite different authorities and uses)—follows an elaborate set of

---

[6] On the closely related problems of moving between law and history (and, in passing, art) using the language of truth and proof that surrounds the witness, see Carlo Ginzburg's essay (dedicated to Primo Levi, who was a family friend through Ginzburg's mother, the writer Natalia), 'Unus testis. Lo sterminio degli Ebrei e il principio della realtà', *Quaderni storici*, 27/80 2 (Aug. 1992), 529–48 (also in S. Friedlander, ed., *Probing the Limits of Representation. Nazism and the Final Solution* (Cambridge, Mass.: Harvard University Press, 1992), 82–96). As S. L. Goldberg has pointed out, theology and law are also the two predominant sources of Western conceptions of morality: as we will see below, recent work on ethics has tried to escape the pattern of rigid, static codifications that they impose (S. L. Goldberg, *Agents and Lives. Moral Thinking in Literature* (Cambridge: Cambridge University Press, 1993), 6).

[7] See D. Tracy, 'Christian Witness and the Shoah', in Hartman, ed., *Holocaust Remembrance*, 81–9; Agamben, *Quel che resta di Auschwitz*, 24–5.

conventions and procedures which are guarantors of fidelity but also in a sense constraints on the witness's articulacy.[8] He or she also speaks the truth, indeed swears to do so, offers an account of a fact or event that he or she has seen that is both objective—it comes from this observer or bystander or participant who is not implicated but is present and has seen—and subjective—it comes from one person, and is valorized as testimony because of his or her individual presence. The witness in the court of law does not, indeed must not enter into dialogue, speculate, interpret, or draw conclusions from what he or she has seen. The witness should speak out loud, under oath, before the *res publica* represented by judge and jury, and the spoken testimony will supersede any earlier statement that has been recorded and signed in writing. The witness should not sit through other evidence, or know any related facts for fear of prejudicing his or her exquisitely objective and subjective contribution to the mosaic of truth. The mosaic is compiled in court, with the witness as a passive tool in the hands of the judge and jury, the processes of justice. And at the end of the process, the truth that the accumulation of testimony (and other evidence) will bring to fruition is of a very particular and inarticulate kind: it must answer a single, yes-no question: guilty or innocent? However subtle and elaborate the procedure and the mind of the judge or jurors, they are restricted in their endpoint to a binary epistemology, where justice is necessarily and quite properly summary. Judgement—in the sense of careful, nuanced, and sensitive understanding—is, at least in the endpoint of the process, discarded in favour of formal justice.

It should already be clear from this increasingly loaded description of the witness in theology and in law what sort of restrictions I have in mind on the scope for historical, philosophical, and moral enquiry contained within the metaphorical language of testimony. Judgements, nuances and gradations, complex questions and provisional answers, listening to and responding to others' evidence, being informed of contexts, circumstances, characters and destinies, interpretation and dialogue: without these— and we are implicitly without some or all of these if we are tied to

[8] Not all of these apply in all legal systems of course. The point here is rhetorical rather than legalistic: what are the residues of the legal practice of witnessing when the latter is translated elsewhere? (On US law, see E. Loftus, *Eyewitness Testimony* (Cambridge, Mass.: Harvard University Press, 1979)).

a jurisprudential mode with testimony at its centre—the texts we may have to relate the Holocaust will be markedly impoverished. At least, one might counter, they will be true (although, of course, truth is not the primary end of judicial process) and justice will be done and seen to be done; their poverty is perhaps not as important as their truth and their value for public justice, and others, readers, can do what they will to encourage their later evolution into fuller meaning (as Levi partly implied above with his invitation to judgement: 'I giudici siete voi'). But witnesses, especially witnesses who are victims, should surely have more than their day in court. They should be listened to as human beings, as subjects of suffering with elaborate, confused, and confounding stories to tell, as complex entities struggling to come to terms with events that have compromised their selfhood in many and varied ways, who demand a response.[9]

On the Christian theological origins and implications of testimony, most often more hidden than the legal connotations, it is easier still to see problems: as with the use of the word Holocaust, it is the redemptive residue that jars here, the possibility that the survival of the few and the death of the many could be for a purpose, perhaps even for salvation. This would certainly be startlingly inappropriate for a secular figure such as Levi, and is perhaps generally so. An important passage from *I sommersi e i salvati* should suffice to erect a barrier against any such residue:

Al mio ritorno dalla prigionia è venuto a visitarmi un amico piú anziano di me, mite ed intransigente, cultore di una religione sua personale, che però mi è sempre parsa severa e seria. Era contento di ritrovarmi vivo e sostanzialmente indenne, forse maturato e fortificato, certamente arricchito. Mi disse che l'essere io sopravvissuto non poteva essere stata opera del caso, di un accumularsi di circostanze fortunate (come sostenevo e tuttora sostengo io), bensì della Provvidenza. Ero un contrassegnato, un eletto: io, il non credente, ed ancor meno credente dopo la stagione di Auschwitz, ero un toccato dalla Grazia, un salvato. E perché proprio io? Non lo si può sapere, mi rispose. Forse perché scrivessi e scrivendo portassi testimonianza: non stavo infatti scrivendo allora, nel 1946, un libro sulla mia prigionia?

---

[9] The same could be said, at a different level, of the guilty witnesses, of the important testimony of the perpetrators, in some cases as complex and as morally challenging as those of the victims. See the extraordinary attempts to probe the character and motivations of Franz Stangl and Albert Speer made by Gitta Sereny (respectively, *Into that Darkness* (London: Deutsch, 1974); and *Albert Speer: His Battle with Truth* (London: Macmillan, 1995)).

Questa opinione mi parve mostruosa. . . . I 'salvati' del Lager non erano i migliori, i predestinati al bene, i latori di un messaggio: quanto io avevo visto e vissuto dimostrava l'esatto contrario. . . . Sopravvivevano i peggiori, cioè i piú adatti: i migliori sono morti tutti. (II. 1054–5)[10]
(On my return from imprisonment, I was visited by an older friend, who was both meek and hard-headed, a believer in a very personal religion that had always struck me as rigorous and serious. He was happy to see me alive and largely undamaged, perhaps even matured and strengthened, certainly enriched. He told me that my survival could not have been the work of chance, of a series of lucky circumstances (as I maintained and still maintain), but was rather the work of Providence. I was marked, chosen: I, the non-believer, even less of a believer after my season in Auschwitz, had been touched by Grace, saved. And why me particularly? There is no way of knowing, he replied. Perhaps so that I could write and by writing bear witness: indeed wasn't I writing at that very moment, in 1946, a book on my time in the camp?
This view struck me as monstrous. . . . The 'saved' in the camp were not the best, those predisposed to the good, the bearers of a message: all I had seen and lived through showed the exact opposite to be the case. . . . The worst survived, that is those who adapted most: the best all died.)

Of course, metaphorical origins and idioms are far more subtle and evolving than I have allowed for, so that it would be absurd to claim that the roots of the language of testimony in jurisprudence and theology imprison its later usage in the chains of the drily juridical and the piously Christian: metaphors are precisely the opposite of imprisonment, they are means to a flexibility of language and meaning. Furthermore, it is not unimportant to recall that judicial process and legal judgement in the form of the Nuremberg Trials and all their successor war-crime trials have been at the heart of political and public responses to the Holocaust and other calamities. Indeed, Levi himself at least once gave

---

[10] For an example of inappropriate 'redemptive' rhetoric applied to Levi, see N. Patruno, *Understanding Primo Levi* (Columbia: University of South Carolina Press, 1995), 6. The more general objection is made well by Judith Woolf: 'To be too moved by Levi's books can be to misread them, to experience a false catharsis' (J. Woolf, *The Memory of the Offence. Primo Levi's 'If This is a Man'* (Market Harborough: University Texts/Hull Italian Texts, 1996), 64). Levi was also keen to reject the (Christianizing) label of 'pardoner' applied to him by Jean Améry and others (see G. Poli and G. Calcagno, *Echi di una voce perduta. Incontri, interviste e conversazioni con Primo Levi* (Milan: Mursia, 1992), 194–8; Levi, *The Voice of Memory*, 111–12, 186). This is not to say, however, that Levi was always averse to drawing on Christian imagery or rhetoric: the very title of his first book, *Se questo è un uomo*, echoes the *Ecce homo* tradition.

evidence at the trial of a Nazi officer, Friedrich Robert Bosshammer, Eichmann's coordinator in Italy after January 1944.[11] So that there is clearly a certain interference in the use of legal idiom in Holocaust testimony, as if it passes through and is mediated by the fora of actual trials as much as any deeper tradition embedded in the language.[12] But whatever mitigation there might be, the language of formal justice, including testimony, has its problems when mapped onto the Holocaust; and Levi was acutely aware of them.

Across the range of his writing, we find him pointing up problems of haste, of scale, and of quality of judgement in law. In the preface to the Italian edition of Herman Langbein's *Menschen in Auschwitz* he warns against hasty and sweeping condemnation: 'giudicare è necessario ma difficile . . . A chi va la colpa . . . al singolo . . . o al regime . . .? . . . va giudicato con estrema cautela e caso per caso; e questo proprio perché totalitari non siamo' (I. 1248; 'to judge is necessary but difficult . . . who is to blame . . . the individual . . . or the regime . . . ? . . . it must be decided with extreme caution, and on a case-by-case basis: precisely because we are not totalitarians'). In a 1979 article, protesting at the idea of applying a statute of limitations to war-crimes cases, he writes of the sheer, monstrous scale of Nazi crimes which threatens traditional legal mechanisms with collapse:

Non sono un giurista, e per verità non ho mai meditato molto sulle origini e sulla giustificazione delle leggi, nostre o altrui: ma mi pare intuitivo

---

[11] The trial was held in West Berlin in 1971, when Bosshammer was accused of coordinating deportations from Romania, Bulgaria, Czechoslovakia, and Italy. On Levi's evidence to the trial, see L. Picciotto Fargion, 'Le informazioni sulla "soluzione finale" circolanti in Italia nel 1942–1943', *Rassegna mensile di Israel*, 55/2–3 (May–Dec. 1989), 351–6; L. Picciotto Fargion, *Il libro della memoria. Gli ebrei deportati dall'Italia (1943–1945)* (Milan: Mursia, 1991), 840–7.

[12] Several important responses to the Holocaust in literature and film have structured themselves around the trials, e.g. *Judgement at Nuremberg* (1961; directed by S. Kramer) and Peter Weiss's *The Investigation* (1965). On the latter, see J. Young, *Writing and Rewriting the Holocaust: Narrative and the Consequences of Interpretation* (Bloomington: Indiana University Press, 1990), 64–80. An interesting gloss on this aspect can be found in Domenico Scarpa's use of the South African Truth and Reconciliation Commission (a bold attempt to use law as a means to social and political resolution of injustice and response to collective trauma without the either-or, guilty-or-innocent endpoint) as a point of departure and comparison for discussing questions of law and judgement in Levi and other Holocaust writers (see D. Scarpa, ' "Tutto si confessa". Primo Levi e il grigiore del passato', in E. Mattioda, ed., *Al di qua del bene e del male. La visione del mondo di Primo Levi* (Milan: Franco Angeli, 2000), 47–58.

il concetto della giustizia, della necessità di una punizione per chi contravviene alle leggi, e della proporzionalità fra la punizione e la misura del delitto. Mi pare anche abbastanza intuitivo il concetto della prescrizione. . . . Ma mi pare che tutto questo abbia un valore, e sia ammissibile, quando si parla di reati che rientrano nell'immagine corrente, per cosí dire storica, della colpa . . . Ora, il caso dei crimini nazisti va oltre questa immagine, la oltrepassa in misura inimmaginabile e mostruosa, tanto che per essi ha dovuto essere coniato il nuovo termine di genocidio. La Germania nazista ha commesso delitti tali da far saltare l'edificio giuridico che in tutti i paesi civili, attraverso i secoli, era stato costruito per classificare e graduare i delitti 'normali'. (I. 1258)
(I am no jurist, and to tell the truth I have never dwelled much on the origins and justifications of laws, here or elsewhere: but the idea of justice seems to me an intuitive one, the need to punish those who break the laws and to fit the punishment in proportion to the scale of the crime. And the idea of a statute of limitations seems intuitively right also . . . But all this holds and is admissible when we are talking of crimes which reflect a commonly understood, or, so to speak, historical notion of guilt . . . Now, the case of Nazi crimes goes beyond this notion, takes us into unimaginable, monstrous territory, so much so that a new term, genocide, had to be coined to describe it. Nazi Germany committed crimes so grave as to make the whole edifice of justice, built up over centuries in all the civilized nations in order to classify and grade 'normal' crimes, fall apart.)

And, most importantly of all, the limitations of legal judgment are at the heart of Levi's mapping of the 'grey zone', the swathe of events and actions within the ambit of the Final Solution which cannot be understood as simply right or wrong, on the side of the innocent victim or on the side of the evil perpetrator. In the course of the chapter of that name in *I sommersi e i salvati*, he appeals several times for some other way of measuring out responsibility, for judging human actions:

La condizione di offeso non esclude la colpa, e spesso questa è oggettiva-mente grave, ma non conosco tribunale umano a cui delegarne la misura (II. 1023)
(Being a victim does not exclude all guilt, and often objectively serious guilt, but I know of no human court who might be asked to measure it)
chiedo che la storia dei 'corvi del crematorio' venga meditata con pietà e rigore, ma che il giudizio su di loro resti sospeso (II. 1037)
(I ask that the story of the 'crematorium crows' be meditated on with pity and rigour, but that our judgement on them be suspended)

la stessa 'impotentia judicandi' ci paralizza davanti al caso Rumkowski (ibid.)[13]

(the same 'impotentia judicandi' paralyses us in the case of Rumkowski)

The notion of the grey zone is not a plea for mitigation. Its power lies precisely in its acknowledgement that there *is* guilt and innocence at work, indeed that one of the aims of the Nazis was to confuse the two and that therefore verdicts do need to be applied wherever possible, but as part of a process of complex understanding, not as procedural output. They are necessary but not sufficiently sensitive tools to use to reach the level of judgement Levi wants. As Giorgio Agamben puts it, 'it is essential that law should not claim to exhaust the issue. There is a non-juridical consistency in truth, which means that the *quaestio facti* can never be reduced to the *quaestio iuris*.'[14]

One further example of Levi's attitude to the modes of formal justice can be found in his several responses to the 1961 trial in Jerusalem of Adolf Eichmann. In one of his most terrible and angry poems, 'Per Adolf Eichmann' (written after the abduction from Argentina and before the trial; II. 540), he imagines the Nazi functionary as a barren, death-circled man, and plays on the inadequacies of legalistic practice to try a man like him: even the oath is a problem—'Giurerai per un dio? Quale dio?' ('Will you swear by a god? Which god?'). Levi dreams of a punishment heavy with symbolism, far worse than mere execution ('giustiziare' in Italian): 'non ti auguriamo la morte. | . . . Possa tu vivere insonne cinque milioni di notti' ('we do not wish you death. | . . . May you live on awake for five million nights'). In pieces written during and after the trial, he accepts the procedure and the verdict wholeheartedly,[15] but in his most considered response, he acknowledges that this can only be a first step:

The Eichmann trial and historical documentation of Nazi crimes certainly have educational value, but they alone are not enough. Their effectiveness, the extent of their impact will not be great for as long as

---

[13] Chaim Rumkowski was the leader of the Łódź ghetto, who collaborated with the Nazis in an attempt to save or postpone the ghetto's liquidation but was also guilty of ceding to the (absurd) paraphernalia of power. Levi tells his story twice, once in *Lilít* ('Il re dei giudei', II. 67–74) and again here in *I sommersi e i salvati*.

[14] Translated from Agamben, *Quel che resta di Auschwitz*, 15.

[15] e.g., 'If I had had Eichmann before me, I would have condemned him to death', Levi, *The Voice of Memory*, 111.

there remains, in Germany but also in Italy, the ambiguous climate of moral vacancy that was instigated under Fascism and has survived it, in part through inertia, in part through foolish calculation. The moral restoration that we need can only come from schools. That Eichmann is guilty is easily shown; but every citizen, from schooldays onwards, needs to learn the meaning of truth and lies, that they are not exchangeable; that from the moment you abdicate your own conscience, as soon as you replace it with a cult of the leader 'who is always right', you risk becoming guilty of the gravest crimes.[16]

For such a trial to be of social, political, moral use, there needs to be a movement, an ideal sequence from formal justice to reflection and education; for the survivor such as Levi we might say from deposition as a witness to composition as a writer.[17] On the specific role of the witness, Levi is also acutely aware of complications and limitations. Alberto Cavaglion has pointed out that he felt little affinity for 'the cult of testimony as an end in itself'.[18] Indeed, the complications are often set at the heart of his work. The problems of judging within the 'grey zone' noted above are also problems of witnessing: from the

[16] From Levi's first published interview, 'La questione ebraica', *Storia illustrata* (June 1961), republished later in the English volume only of Levi, *The Voice of Memory*, (p. 182). The power and problems of trial procedure bring to mind Levi's fraught encounter, as translator, with Kafka's *The Trial*: see F. Kafka, *Il processo*, tr. P. Levi (Turin: Einaudi, 1983; and cf. II. 1208–10); 'Tradurre Kafka' (II. 939–41); Levi, *The Voice of Memory*, 155–60; and also M. Belpoliti, *Primo Levi* (Milan: Bruno Mondadori, 1998), 90–4.

[17] There is a parallel to this movement between testimony and reflection in the intense movement between psychopathology and reflection in the writing of *Se questo è un uomo* in 1946 (described in 'Cromo', *Il sistema periodico*, I. 867–77), suggesting an important parallel between testimony and trauma (to go beyond testimony is also to go beyond trauma). First, writing was cure or catharsis, 'le cose viste e sofferte mi bruciavano dentro; mi sentivo piú vicino ai morti che ai vivi, e colpevole di essere uomo, perché gli uomini avevano edifi-cato Auschwitz, ed Auschwitz aveva ingoiato milioni di esseri umani . . . Mi pareva che mi sarei purificato raccontando' (I. 870; 'what I had seen and suffered was burning within me; I felt nearer to the dead than to the living and guilty for being a man, because men had built Auschwitz and Auschwitz has swallowed up millions of human beings . . . I thought I would be purified by telling the story'). Then it transformed itself into lucid, probing enquiry, 'lo stesso mio scrivere diventò un'avventura diversa, non piú l'itinerario doloroso di un convalescente, non piú un mendicare compassione, e visi amici, ma un costruire lucido, ormai non piú solitario: un'opera di chimico che pesa e divide, misura e giudica su prove certe, e s'industria a rispondere ai perché' (I. 872–3; 'my very writing turned into a different adventure, no longer the painful itinerary of a convalescent, no longer a way of begging for compassion and friendly faces, but a lucid construction, no longer in solitude: the work of a chemist who weighs and divides, measures and judges by certain indices and works hard to reply to questions why').

[18] A. Cavaglion, 'Il termitaio', *Asino d'oro*, 4 (1991); now in E. Ferrero, ed., *Primo Levi: un'antologia della critica* (Turin: Einaudi, 1997), 76–90 [81].

Sonderkommandos (the prisoners chosen to man the crematoria), for example, 'non ci si può aspettare una deposizione nel senso giuridico del termine' (II. 1031) ('we cannot expect a deposition in the juridical sense of the term'). And in one of the most resonant and penetrating passages of *I sommersi e i salvati*, Levi himself abjures the privileges of the witness, because the true witnesses of the Holocaust are, in their millions, all dead:

Lo ripeto, non siamo noi, i superstiti, i testimoni veri . . . Noi sopravvissuti siamo una minoranza anomala oltre che esigua . . . chi ha visto la Gorgone, non è tornato per raccontare, o è tornato muto; ma sono loro, i 'musulmani', i sommersi, i testimoni integrali, coloro la cui deposizione avrebbe avuto significato generale. Loro sono la regola, noi l'eccezione. (II. 1056)
(I repeat, we the survivors are not the true witnesses . . . We are a small, anomalous minority . . . whoever looked at the Gorgon's head did not come back to tell the tale, or they came back dumb; but it is they, the 'Muselmänner', the drowned, the fully-fledged witnesses, whose evidence would have held as generally true. They are the rule, we are the exception.)

Levi's and other survivors' evidence is displaced, second-hand, circumstantial, all but hearsay; ' "per conto terzi" . . . per delega' (ibid.; ' "for a third party" . . . by proxy').[19] And so its valency is changed, complicated; a difficult field of relations and mediations is set up between the dead (or the silent), the survivor, and us the readers, between past, present, and future. Writing in this field entails passing through a stage of testimony, maintaining a relationship with testimony and all its associate mechanisms; but to navigate the field, languages beyond testimony are also needed.

LEVI THE MORALIST

Where to look for languages beyond testimony? Levi would seem an especially apt guide for two simple reasons. First, since he carried on his project of writing and speaking about the Holocaust over such an extended length of time (more than forty years) and

---

[19] See Agamben, *Quel che resta di Auschwitz*, 31–2 on this passage; and p. 15 for the dual Latin roots of testimony, 'testis' and 'superstes', both of which Levi echoes here in the terms 'terzi' (witness as third party) and 'superstiti' (witness as survivor). The same nexus is used by Derrida discussing Blanchot discussing testimony (see D. Del Giudice, 'Introduzione', in Levi, *Opere*, I. p. xvi).

in so many different forms and arenas, his work is an extraordinary resource for asking questions about how to approach this most difficult of subjects within and beyond testimony. Even within the preface to *Se questo è un uomo*, he declares a modest but also rather remarkable ambition for his book—'fornire documenti per uno studio pacato di alcuni aspetti dell'animo umano' (I. 5; 'to provide the material for a calm study of certain aspects of the human mind')—which has little or nothing to do with the aims of testimony, being rooted in his memories of Auschwitz but projected forward towards a hypothetical general study of the human mind. Secondly, Levi increasingly developed interests in subjects quite apart from the Holocaust, becoming an amateur enthusiast in fields of scientific research, anthropology, zoology, and linguistics (among others), and writing about them and much else besides as essayist, occasional journalist, science-fiction writer, and novelist. In other words, he also moved beyond testimony in the most straightforward sense of not writing exclusively about the camps.[20] Furthermore, crucially, these two aspects of his work are in close, rich, mutually illuminating dialogue. There is a constant to-and-fro rhythm of exchange between, on the one hand, the Holocaust written through testimony but also through other means, and, on the other hand, the larger world of his interests, written about with engaged curiosity but never quite forgetting analogies, echoes, points of contact with the Holocaust. The result is a flexible, sensitive, intelligent language that is perhaps the key defining characteristic of Levi's work (and a key reason behind his remarkable popularity). The contention running throughout this book is that that language is best understood as a language of ethics.[21]

Why ethics? Much of the general concern expressed above about the workings of testimony and the limitations of juridical or theological language suggests as a natural corollary a move towards

[20] In a 1963 interview he seemed quite convinced that he had nothing more to say, 'not another word', on Auschwitz (Levi, *The Voice of Memory*, 81).

[21] It has not been at all uncommon for writers on Levi to pepper their work with terms of ethics, morality, and virtue, but it has been much rarer for the terms to be substantially analysed or integrated into a reading of his work. Exceptions include B. Cheyette, 'The Ethical Uncertainty of Primo Levi', in B. Cheyette and L. Marcus, eds., *Modernity, Culture and 'the Jew'* (Cambridge: Polity, 1998), 268–81; M. Risk [Cicioni], 'Razionalità e coscienza etica di Primo Levi', *Italian Studies*, 34 (1979), 122–31; G. Varchetta, *Ascoltando Primo Levi. Organizzazione, narrazione, etica* (Milan: Guerini e Associati, 1991); Woolf, *The Memory of the Offence*, 77–8; and cf. note 23 below.

ethics. As Agamben points out, there is a natural confusion between the lexicon of law, theology, and ethics (guilt, responsibility, innocence, judgement, absolution, and so on),[22] a confusion which can be turned to advantage if ethics can be said to address similar fundamental issues, but without some of the negative baggage of the other two. But there is a more particular reason for reading Levi ethically than simply the notion that ethics is what is left when law and theology are bracketed out; a reason based on another distinguishing feature of his voice as a writer, its peculiarly old-fashioned, premodern (or premodernist) feel. One of the several characteristic ways in which Levi speaks anachronistically is when he adopts the voice of the 'moralist'.[23]

Levi is a moralist to the extent that he is an observer and analyser of habit and custom (hence his propensity for both anthropology and zoology or better, ethology) and that he brings to his observations a set of recognizable values, embodied in his writing. His values are constant companions along the way in his writing, even if, crucially, the form they take is anything but constant: the vicissitudes he and they go through, in memory or in fantasy, are the life-blood of his stories and essays. And precisely because these values, like characters in a fiction, seem at times buffeted by events, at others held firm, in an incessant putting to the test for survival, they could hardly seem further from the dry and dusty, conservative and unimaginative aura that the term 'moralist' might suggest. Indeed, by telling moral tales in the face of Auschwitz, Levi enacts a dramatic struggle to hold on to the very notion of value itself, however fragile or unsteady it may now be.

What is more, by biographical and cultural accident, there is

---

[22] Agamben, *Quel che resta di Auschwitz*, 16.

[23] See G. Macchia, ed., *I moralisti classici. Da Machiavelli a La Bruyère* (Milan: Garzanti, 1978), 7–20. The term is used somewhat tendentiously here, since it verges on the pejorative in current usage, casting a pall of gloom or moralizing superiority which would not do Levi justice. Levi himself fought shy of it (e.g. 'non volevo certo erigermi a moralista', 'I certainly had no wish to set myself up as a moralist', quoted in Poli and Calcagno, *Echi di una voce perduta*, 162); others have tried to tie him directly to earlier moralist traditions: see, for example, M. Forti, '*I sommersi e i salvati* di Primo Levi, dieci anni dopo', *Nuova antologia*, 131/2197 (Jan.–Mar. 1996), 203–17 (on Levi and 'dramatic' moralists from Sade to Manzoni to Dostoevsky); R. Massano, 'Moralità e stile di Augusto Monti. Resistenza senza era: la sua scuola dal carcere', in G. Tesio, ed., *Augusto Monti nel centenario della nascita*, conference proceedings (Turin: Centro studi piemontesi, 1982), 150 (on Levi, Pellico, and Monti); G. Tesio, *Piemonte letterario dell'otto-novecento. Da Giovanni Faldella a Primo Levi* (Rome: Bulzoni, 1991), 225, 230 (on Levi and Manzoni).

something about his personal mask as a moralist, something about the particular set of values through which he faces Auschwitz that makes their vicissitudes evoke a larger story. Levi's formative cultures and intelligences were several: an amateur grounding in classical and humanist high culture (taken in uncomfortably from his 'liceo' education); a passively absorbed, unpractised, half-forgotten Sephardic Jewishness (in occasional rituals and family stories);[24] an Enlightenment and positivist faith in reason, observation, and experimental science (from his father's science, from Turin's late nineteenth- and early twentieth-century positivist, socialist-leaning culture,[25] from his own degree in chemistry and physics); an eclectic bookish hinterland (again from his father, from an upbringing in a book-strewn, lay-Jewish household); a slowly crystallized sense of political justice (from his formation as an anti-Fascist and his brief time as a partisan Resistance fighter). Antony Rudolf summarizes the mix nicely:

Levi's morality is implied by and formed from an old-fashioned compound of reason, tolerance, trust in language, trust in silence, containment of anger, liberalism, cool Sephardi Jewishness, scepticism, good humour, wit and natural philosophy.[26]

[24] He described his Judaism as 'a small, happy anomaly' (*Il sistema periodico*, I. 770) until the Racial Laws of 1938. This integration or assimilation was typical of Italian Jewry as a whole in modern Italy after unification, even under Fascism at first. See L. Gunzberg, *Strangers at Home. Jews in the Italian Literary Imagination* (Berkeley and Los Angeles: University of California Press, 1992), 16–56; A. Momigliano, 'Gli ebrei d'Italia', in A. Momigliano, *Pagine ebraiche* (Turin: Einaudi, 1987), 129–42. On Italian Jewry under Fascism, see: M. Michaelis, *Mussolini and the Jews* (Oxford: Oxford University Press, 1978); M. Sarfatti, *Gli ebrei nell'Italia fascista. Vicende, identità, persecuzione* (Turin: Einaudi, 2000); J. Steinberg, *All or Nothing. The Axis and the Holocaust 1941–43* (London: Routledge, 1990); A. Stille, *Benevolence and Betrayal. Five Italian Jewish Families under Fascism* (London: Jonathan Cape, 1992); S. Zucotti, *The Italians and the Holocaust. Persecution, Rescue and Survival* (London: Peter Halban, 1987).
[25] On the immensely rich cultural and political history of Turin in the generations preceding Levi, see N. Bobbio, *Trent'anni di storia della cultura a Torino (1920–1950)* (Turin: Cassa di Risparmio di Torino, 1977) (for Levi, see pp. 100–6); A. D'Orsi, *La cultura a Torino tra le due guerre* (Turin: Einaudi, 2000); U. Levra and N. Tranfaglia, eds., *Torino fra liberalismo e fascismo* (Milan: Franco Angeli, 1987); and on Levi's father's participation in its positivistic circles, see 'Il mondo invisibile' (*L'altrui mestiere*, II. 800–1). It has become relatively commonplace to label Levi an Enlightenment figure (in Italian 'illuminista'): see, for example, D. Amsallem, 'Illuminista', in M. Belpoliti, ed., *Primo Levi* (Milan: Marcos y Marcos, Riga 13, 1997), 361–71; or Ernesto Ferrero's rather elegant description of Levi as 'un empirista settecentesco che ha letto Blake' (in P. Levi, *I racconti* (Turin: Einaudi, 1996), p. xvi); or P. V. Mengaldo, 'Ciò che dobbiamo a Primo Levi', in G. Folena, *Tre narratori: Calvino, Primo Levi, Parise* (Padua: Liviana, 1989), 89–98 [90].
[26] A. Rudolf, *At an Uncertain Hour. Primo Levi's War against Oblivion* (London: Menard

He was, in other words, almost an epitome of the educated (but not 'intellectual'), secular, modern subject, with many of the liberal, progressive, bourgeois values out of which modern Europe had grown in various stages, places, and times, from the Reformation and the Enlightenment onwards. It is a sweeping but nevertheless fascinating generalization, making Levi a test-case in that long-standing historical debate over what part of Nazism and the Final Solution was irrationalist mythology, jumbled ideology, and power-crazed idiocy, an aberrance from progress as conceived by the Enlightenment and its successors; and what part of it a perverse by-product of the hidden autocratic and inhumane assumptions of those very progressive movements.[27] To watch Levi work through questions of value, to read him as a modern moralist is, in other words, pregnant with the very deepest quandaries posed by the Holocaust, a necessary complement to his equally essential insight into the undoing of the modern, post-Enlightenment subject ('la demolizione di un uomo', I. 20) as the essential means and end of the death-camp system.[28]

The point is reinforced by comparison with other survivor-writers. Not for Levi a childhood of faith, Kabbala, Yiddish, and the 'shtetl' (Wiesel); nor elaborate literary, philosophical, psycho-logical, or political groundings (Améry, Antelme, Bettelheim,

Press, 1990), 4. Dominic LaCapra, remarkably, sees this cultural mix as damning evidence of an unexamined humanism (D. LaCapra, *Representing the Holocaust. History, Theory, Trauma* (Ithaca, NY: Cornell University Press, 1994), 120). For biographical information see I. pp. lxxiii–xcviii; or the poor biography M. Anissimov, *Primo Levi, ou la tragédie d'un optimiste* (Paris: Lattès, 1996) (cf. lengthy reviews by M. A. Bernstein, 'A Yes or a No', *New Republic*, 27 Sept. 1999; and T. Judt, 'The Courage of the Elementary', *New York Review of Books*, 46/9 (20 May 1999), 31–8).

[27] On Nazism's and the Holocaust's relationship to the Enlightenment, the necessary starting point is T. Adorno and M. Horkheimer's *Dialectic of Enlightenment* (London: Verso, 1997, 1st edition 1947), written during the war. See also Berel Lang's 'Genocide and Kant's Enlightenment' in his *Act and Idea in the Nazi Genocide* (Chicago: Chicago University Press, 1990), 165–206; V. Pecora, 'Habermas, Enlightenment and Antisemitism', in Friedlander, ed., *Probing the Limits of Representation*, 155–70. For a survey of responses to the Holocaust by writers, theologians, and historians, see M. Morgan, ed., *A Holocaust Reader* (Oxford: Oxford University Press, 2000) and L. Davidowicz, *The Holocaust and the Historians* (Cambridge, Mass.: Harvard University Press, 1981).

[28] The close and complex rapport between identity and morality in the history of the self is traced in C. Taylor, *Sources of the Self. The Making of Modern Identity* (Cambridge: Cambridge University Press, 1989), discussed further below. For an insightful reading of the mix of enlightened and darker, even neurotic impulses in Levi's work, see E. Gioanola, 'Diversità della letteratura. Letteratura della diversità', in P. Momigliano Levi and R. Gorris, eds., *Primo Levi testimone e scrittore della storia* (Florence: La Giuntina, 1999), 1–17.

Semprun).[29] Levi's writing is governed by other, more pragmatic tools of interpretation and analysis; and as a result, there is never quite the post-Holocaust ontological or moral void in Levi, never quite the radical silence conditioned by radical evil that others have evoked, only the terrible responsibility of now incorporating this too, even this, into the contours of the human.[30] His enlightened, liberal ethics survive Auschwitz, shaken at their very roots, dramatically displaced and reshaped by the trauma of the experience, but nevertheless intact. The fluid persistence of his 'moralism' along the forking, interlaced paths of his work is the core object of analysis in this book. The extent of its potential significance for our larger understanding of the Holocaust is captured quietly but forcefully in a passing footnote to Peter Novick's account of the strange role played by the Holocaust in post-war American life, *The Holocaust and Collective Memory*: 'Another unanswerable question: What would talk of the Holocaust be like in America if a skeptical rationalist like Primo Levi, rather than a religious mystic like Wiesel, had been its principal interpreter?'[31]

[29] See, for example, J. Améry, *At the Mind's Limits* (London: Granta, 1999; 1st German edition 1966); R. Antelme, *L'Espèce humaine* (Paris: Gallimard, 1978; 1st edition 1947); B. Bettelheim, *Surviving and Other Essays* (New York: Knopf, 1979); J. Semprun, *L'Écriture ou la vie* (Paris: Gallimard, 1994); E. Wiesel, *La Nuit* (Paris: Éditions de Minuit, 1958). All of these writers are touched on in subsequent chapters as points of comparison with Levi. For Levi's views on religion see Levi, *The Voice of Memory*, 261–78; on Bettelheim and psychoanalysis, ibid., 233–8; on his own naivety in politics as a young man and later declarations of a moderate socialism, see *Il sistema periodico*, I. 850–2, and Rudolf, *At an Uncertain Hour*, 33. For some interesting comments on Levi as a philosopher 'malgré lui', who absorbed Crocean idealist values even as he rejected them for science as a young man, see A. Cavaglion, *Primo Levi e 'Se questo è un uomo'* (Turin: Loescher, 1993), 22–4.
[30] On the weakness of 'apocalyptic' responses, see M. A. Bernstein, 'Narrating the Shoah', in his *Foregone Conclusions. Against Apocalyptic History* (Berkeley and Los Angeles: University of California Press, 1994), 42–73. Wiesel has often adopted an apocalyptic rhetoric (e.g. 'all that can be obtained through knowledge has to be recalled into question . . . Auschwitz negates all systems, destroys all doctrines', 'The Holocaust as Literary Inspiration', 6–7; or 'at Auschwitz not only man died, but also the idea of man', quoted by A. Rosenfeld, *A Double Dying* (Bloomington: Indiana University Press, 1980), 5). The Kantian phrase 'radical evil' is something of a refrain for Jorge Semprun in his *L'Écriture ou la vie*, 65, 98.
[31] P. Novick, *The Holocaust and Collective Memory* (London: Bloomsbury, 1999), 351. On Levi and Wiesel, see E. Wiesel, 'Io e Primo Levi', *Nuova antologia*, 127 (Apr.–June 1992), 204–8. On Wiesel, see C. Davis, 'Reviewing Memory: Wiesel, Testimony and Self-Reading', in H. Peitsch, C. Burdett, and C. Gorrara, eds., *European Memories of the Second World War* (Oxford: Berghahn, 1999), 131–40.

LITERATURE, ETHICS, VIRTUES

The turn towards ethics suggested here as a way of rereading Levi does not come out of a vacuum. It is informed and spurred by the enthusiastic embracing of ethics that took place in divergent fields of literary study over the last decade or so of the twentieth century, and by parallel moves to reshape ethics even within the traditional bounds of moral philosophy. Since one way of expressing what has been said so far about Levi's relationship with testimony would be to say that he is more literary, more of a writer than the label of witness will allow, the field where literature and ethics meet is bound to be a key context for what follows.[32]

Literature and ethics have converged in several distinct, if overlapping areas, each of which strikes intriguing chords with Levi's work.[33] Three are worth touching on briefly. Perhaps the furthest removed from Levi in terms of intellectual disposition or *forma mentis*, but also perhaps the most closely attuned to the Holocaust, is what we can loosely call the field of deconstruction. There have been several deconstructionist paths towards ethics, taken by Foucault, Hillis Miller, and Derrida among others,[34] but by far the most powerful and influential figure to emerge from within this area (in large part thanks to Derrida's dialogue with him) was the philosopher and Talmudist Emmanuel Levinas.

Levinas stood most simply and most significantly for the absolute primacy of the ethical: he set up the ethical as what he called 'first philosophy', prior to ontology and thus prior to the

---

[32] On this aspect of the testimony–literature relationship, see R. Gordon, 'Etica', in Belpoliti, ed., *Primo Levi* (Riga 13), 315–30 [315–16].

[33] For a clear survey of the field, on which I have drawn for parts of the following account, see L. Buell, ed., *Ethics and Literary Study*, special issue of *PMLA* 114/1 (Jan. 1999), 7–96 [7–19]. See also J. Adamson, R. Freadman, and D. Parker, eds., *Renegotiating Ethics in Literature, Philosophy and Theory* (Cambridge: Cambridge University Press, 1998); Goldberg, *Agents and Lives*; G. Harpham, *Getting it Right. Language, Literature, and Ethics* (Chicago: Chicago University Press, 1992); G. Harpham, 'Ethics', in F. Lentricchia and T. McLaughlin, *Critical Terms for Literary Study* (Chicago: Chicago University Press, 1995, 2nd edition only), 387–405; D. Parker, *Ethics, Theory and the Novel* (Cambridge: Cambridge University Press, 1994); J. Phelan, ed., *Reading Narrative. Form, Ethics, Ideology* (Columbus: Ohio State University Press, 1989); T. Siebers, *The Ethics of Criticism* (Ithaca, NY: Cornell University Press, 1988).

[34] See M. Foucault, *Ethics. Subjectivity and Truth*, ed. P. Rabinow (Harmondsworth: Allen Lane, 1994); J. Hillis Miller, *The Ethics of Reading* (New York: Columbia University Press, 1987); J. Derrida, *La Politique de l'amitié* (Paris: Galilée, 1994); and cf. S. Critchley, *The Ethics of Deconstruction* (Oxford: Blackwell, 1992).

very foundations of the Western philosophical tradition and its notion of the self, which he saw as always already forged in the encounter with the Other. This prior alterity establishes the ethical as an irreducible, ongoing process of responsibility rather than a vessel of codes and moral rules, rather than a single system. Because of this flexibility and acknowledgement of a plurality of positions, because of the strong bond between deconstruction and many forms of contemporary literary criticism, and because of the suggestively figurative and enigmatic language adopted by Levinas, much work on the ethics of literature has found Levinas a highly stimulating source.[35] In Chapter 1 below, we will see how elements of Levinas's ethics can, with a certain flexibility, be seen to chime with crucial motifs in Levi's record of Auschwitz, elements which allow Levi to trace out a possible ethical trajectory from his testimony into the wider world and back. This affinity is not so surprising, since, as many have noted, Levinas's work is constantly conditioned by and responsive to the Holocaust, which he rarely mentions but often seems to evoke.[36] More generally, Levi can be seen to share at least to a certain degree the type of open, other-directed, textured ethics proposed by Levinas and his epigones. At several points in what follows, for example, we will see Levi forging a metaethical capacity in his writing by conflating attention to others and attention to the movement of texts (in lexicon, syntax, rhythm) as channels of ethical effort. In this movement, we can recognize something of the dynamic ethical process of 'le dire' (the saying), opposed by Levinas to the static datum of 'le dit' (the said).[37]

---

[35] See, for example, A. Z. Newton, *Narrative Ethics* (Cambridge, Mass.: Harvard University Press, 1995), who mixes Levinas with Bakhtin and Stanley Cavell as his guiding influences. On the capacity of Levinas to be (almost) all things to all his readers, see C. Davis, *Levinas* (Cambridge: Polity, 1996), 139–40.

[36] He described his life as 'dominated by the presentiment and the memory of the Nazi horror' (quoted by Davis, *Levinas*, 143). But here and throughout the literature and ethics fields, it is worth noting a rather strange reluctance to treat in any but the most oblique or partial manner the single greatest modern challenge of all to our moral compass, the Holocaust. It is partly out of a conviction that the latter deserves a place in the former, and vice versa, that this study of Levi has been undertaken. (An exception to the rule is Zygmunt Bauman, whose work on ethics is profoundly linked to his influential work on the Holocaust, although he does not work with literature: see his *Modernity and the Holocaust* (Cambridge: Polity, 1989) and *Postmodern Ethics* (Oxford: Blackwell, 1993)).

[37] 'Ethics . . . signifies recursive, contingent, and interactive dramas of encounters and recognitions', Newton, *Narrative Ethics*, 12; on 'saying' and 'said', see pp. 5–6, 105–6.

Literature and ethics have also come together in a field that has been described (following Derrida) as 'paleonymic'. In other words, the turn to ethics has also been something of a return, a salvaging of an older, disused tradition in refashioned form (echoing Levi's moralism described above); in particular the notion of literature as a form of moral education.[38] This has meant not only, or not so much, a return to Arnold or Leavis (although elements of these surface on occasion), as a return to Aristotle and, with it, to an understanding of ethics as applied wisdom best acquired through social experience or narrative, and in any case not through abstract reasoning. This pragmatic, empirical, narrative-driven neo-Aristotelianism often seems to fit Levi like a glove. Its practitioners steer carefully clear of the patrician pedagogy of its forebears, however, preferring to see in literature precisely the lack of prescription and dogmatic assertion of truths that tarnishes moral philosophizing. Literature is ethical here because it is complex and shifting and able to encompass the many levels at which choice and action are formed and carried through in lived lives. Martha Nussbaum has been the most eloquent advocate of this cause:

My claim is that only the style of a certain sort of narrative artist (and not for example the style associated with the abstract theoretical treatise) can adequately state important [ethical] truths about the world, embodying them in its shape and setting up in the reader the activities that are appropriate for grasping them.[39]

She argues that ethical theory and literary theory and practice need to come together to produce a more nuanced, humanely responsive, and inclusive version of the founding Socratic ethical question, 'how to live?', than that offered by either side of modern moral philosophy, the Kantians or the utilitarians:

the question with which my projected literary-ethical inquiry begins is the question, 'How should one live?' This choice of starting point is

---

[38] On ethics as 'paleonymic', see Harpham, *Getting it Right. Language, Literature, and Ethics*, 1. Once again, although the writers in this field have hardly pondered it, the Holocaust is relevant: in a schematic history of literature's conception of itself, we might say that the classical-to-Enlightenment tradition of literature as moral guide was dealt a series of body blows in the post-Enlightenment epoch, but was dealt its death blow by the concentration camps: as Jean Améry put it, 'no bridge led from death in Auschwitz to *Death in Venice*' (*At the Mind's Limits*, 16).

[39] M. Nussbaum, *Love's Knowledge* (Oxford: Oxford University Press, 1990), 6.

significant. This question does not (like the Kantian question, 'What is my moral duty?') assume that there is a sphere of 'moral' values that can be separated off from the other practical values that figure in a human life. Nor does it assume, as does the utilitarian's focus on the question, 'How shall I maximize utility?' that the value of all choices and actions is to be assessed in terms of a certain sort of consequence that they tend to promote. It does not assume the denial of these claims either. So far it is neutral, leaving them for investigation inside the inquiry. The point is to state the opening question in a general and inclusive way, excluding at the start no major story about the good life for human beings.[40]

And the best way of stating the opening question in this way and then following possible answers in an aware and responsible manner is through novels (especially, for Nussbaum, the work of Henry James): as S. L. Goldberg puts it, literature is 'a distinctive and irreplaceable way of thinking about certain crucial aspects of Socrates' question'.[41]

Allied closely to Nussbaum in many respects, and much cited by her, has been the work of the eminent Chicago literary critic Wayne C. Booth, and especially his pragmatic analysis of the encounter between reader and book as a form of friendship, *The Company We Keep*.[42] And loosely comparable to both Nussbaum's and Booth's work in this area is Richard Rorty's collection of essays *Contingency, Irony, and Solidarity*.[43] Rorty, like Nussbaum or Booth, turns to novels and even to literary criticism as a model for what the philosopher (or in his terms the 'ironist') should be and do. Philosophy, he maintains, is close to useless when it insists on teasing out universals using casuistry and other forms of logical reasoning. Instead of investing in foundational beliefs or metaphysics of whatever kind, the ironist searches for 'redescriptions', alternative figures and vocabularies of ourselves, stories of our past, our present, and our possible futures, constantly comparing and revising our descriptions:

---

[40] Ibid. 173 (and cf. pp. 23–9).   [41] Goldberg, *Agents and Lives*, p. xiii.

[42] W. C. Booth, *The Company We Keep. An Ethics of Fiction* (Berkeley and Los Angeles: University of California Press, 1988); but see also his earlier *The Rhetoric of Fiction* (Chicago: University of Chicago Press, 1961) and *A Rhetoric of Irony* (Chicago: University of Chicago Press, 1974). For Nussbaum on Booth, see *Love's Knowledge*, 230–44. On friendship in Levi, see Chapter 10 below.

[43] R. Rorty, *Contingency, Irony, and Solidarity* (Cambridge: Cambridge University Press, 1989). The connection of Levi to Rorty (along with Gianni Vattimo's 'weak thought') is made in passing by Varchetta, *Ascoltando Primo Levi*, 35–41.

Such comparison, such playing off of figures against each other, is the principal activity now covered by the term 'literary criticism'. . . . Literary criticism does for ironists what the search for universal moral principles is supposed to do for metaphysicians.[44]

To show himself as an ironist, Rorty turns himself into a literary critic, reading Proust, Nabokov, and Orwell alongside Derrida, Foucault, and Habermas.[45] Rorty's ironist is permanently aware of the contingency of all her beliefs and vocabularies (of her language, selfhood, and membership of communities), cannot take them seriously as final beliefs (hence 'ironist'), and yet continues to work on them and refine them and make them fit their purpose better as what it is good to believe (not what is true).[46] Furthermore, Rorty's ideal is an ironist who is also, in his terms, a liberal; and he defines the liberal as someone whose primary aim is freedom not truth, as 'someone who believes that cruelty is the worse thing we do', who puts cruelty first.[47]

Levi's ethics touches Rorty's liberal ironism in interesting ways, but never quite goes over to his radical scepticism wholeheartedly. He is liberal, in terms of 'putting cruelty first', and also in more commonplace terms, in his investment in the shaping of the individual through and within various communities, various 'we's (see Part III below). He is also an ironist, both in a broad sense (see Chapter 12) and also to a degree in Rorty's terms, since he is acutely aware of the shifting of those communities, of the momentary connections that make a 'we' out of an instant and then dissolve it, nevertheless leaving it as fundamental to experience (see Chapter 10). He is also sensitive to the other contingencies—of language, of selfhood—that Rorty tries to establish. Finally, however, the Holocaust intervenes to complicate the alignment of

44 Rorty, *Contingency*, 80.

45 Ibid. 98–103, 141–88. His account of Orwell resonates with Levi particularly, if only because Rorty reads Orwell against the critical commonplace that he was a 'bad' or 'unliterary' writer because he had a truth or a moral message to tell pinned to a particular historical moment, an account that echoes with a clichéd view of Levi as unliterary, more of value as a witness than a writer. Rorty reads Orwell, especially *1984*'s account of cruelty and torture, as going beyond such arid distinctions, rendering them uninteresting. See also A. Margalit, *The Decent Society* (Cambridge, Mass.: Harvard University Press, 1996) which traces its notion of the 'decency' back to 'Orwell's socialism' (as opposed to 'Orwellian socialism'), p. 10.

46 Rorty, *Contingency*, 73; and cf. Parker, *Ethics, Theory and the Novel*, 15.

47 Rorty, *Contingency*, 146; he borrows the definition from J. Shklar, *Ordinary Vices* (Cambridge, Mass.: Bellknap Press, 1984), 43–4.

Levi with Rorty's 'liberal ironist', to dilute the complacency that sometimes emanates from the latter. Levi acquires his acute sense of contingency in Auschwitz and he experiences it as a loss—a loss of stability, of value—in a way that Rorty refuses to accept. Knowing he cannot fully return to the stable values he has lost, he moves back and forwards between a needed stability and a necessary contingency and looks to find ways for each to refine the other. The best illustration of how Levi's ethics works in this almost but not quite Rortian fashion (and is all the more interesting for it) is in Rorty's assault on common sense as complicit with the essential metaphysics he cannot stand: 'The opposite of irony is common sense. For that is the watchword of those who unselfconsciously describe everything important in terms of the final vocabulary to which they and those around them are habituated . . . The metaphysician is still attached to common sense.'[48] Levi, by contrast, is deeply attached to common sense, and is also an ironist: as we will see in Chapter 11 (but it is paradigmatic of the flexibility underpinning his ethics as a whole), he uses the shared vocabularies of common sense not as final vocabulary but as the starting point of a dialogue, a perspective (Chapter 7) from which to contemplate and change those vocabularies and establish new (contingent) ones. In a sense, he complements Rorty's scepticism with the critical, sympathetic friendship that runs through Nussbaum's and Booth's ethical-narrative encounters. It is as if Levi were staging a debate between the sceptic and the foundationalist and using it as the basis of conversation.

A final useful source of new directions in the literature and ethics debate has come more directly out of the professional field of British and American moral philosophy. It is at times indistinguishable from the second strand, since both Rorty and Nussbaum are philosophers by trade (Nussbaum especially bridges between the two), but it consists more of an internal self-questioning than a lunge for literature as a way out of traditional philosophy altogether. Nevertheless, it has had a key role to play within literary study also, and points us in the direction of the organizing principle behind the particular form of ethics examined in this book, a concept of virtue.

Starting from a dissatisfaction rather similar to Nussbaum's with

---

[48] Rorty, *Contingency*, 74.

the dead-end duality offered by post-Kantian moral philosophy (in the jargon, either deontological or consequentialist), philosophers such as Bernard Williams and Alasdair MacIntyre strove to revivify the field, both using a return of sorts to models of Ancient Greece as, paradoxically, an escape route from the cul-de-sac of modern responses to the moral problems of modernity.

Williams's *Ethics and the Limits of Philosophy*[49] develops the notion of 'thick ethical concepts',[50] which have something of the quality of ancient virtues, but which are more in the thick of actions and less objectively observed from the outside than the former, whilst also being less obsessed with origins or with futures than modern concepts. They are at one and the same time descriptive and prescriptive, 'world-guided and action-guiding';[51] and as a result are 'open to being unseated by reflection, but to the extent that they survive it, a practice that uses them is more stable in the face of the general, structural reflections about the truth of ethical judgements than a practice that does not use them'.[52]

MacIntyre starts his highly influential book *After Virtue*[53] with a sweeping narrative depicting our moral language in a state of unknowing collapse, pieced together from residues of a past which we misuse and misunderstand, if we listen to it at all.[54] Seeing the root of the collapse in the inevitable failure of the rational justification of morality attempted in the Enlightenment, MacIntyre proposes a return to Aristotelian virtue as an antidote to the mishmash of incommensurate, pseudo-objective, and historically blind moral positions of our age (illustrated by the historical drift from canonical virtues to competing lists of virtues to an ill-defined numberless category of 'virtue', used most restrictively as a concept to chain women, to what he calls 'after virtue').[55] The last figure to express saisfactorily an Aristotelian enquiry into virtues, based in practices and aware of traditions, in which virtues are

---

[49] B. Williams, *Ethics and the Limits of Philosophy* (London: Fontana, 1993; 1st edition 1985). On his work as a quarrel between ancient and modern, see pp. 197–202.

[50] Ibid. 129

[51] Ibid. 141; cf. the notion of 'thick description', a mode of interpreting cultures from both within and without, developed in anthropology by C. Geertz, *The Interpretation of Cultures* (London: Fontana, 1993; 1st edition 1973), 3–30.

[52] Williams, *Ethics*, 200.

[53] A. MacIntyre, *After Virtue* (London: Duckworth, 1985; 1st edition 1981).

[54] Ibid. 1–5.   [55] Ibid. 6–11, 146–64.

integrated with and integral to the unified narrative of a life, is for MacIntyre the 'ironic comedy' of Jane Austen.[56]

The detail of the debate between moral philosophers to which Williams and MacIntyre were contributing[57] is less interesting for our purposes here than the shape they suggest for ethical readings of lives and books: in particular they offer a way of opening up ethics through a return to virtue (or better to virtues), but to more flexible, narrative- and practice-driven virtues than in the past, at times descriptive, at others prescriptive, open to unseating through reflection (indeed virtuous by dint of such openness), but usefully rooted in an aspiration to stable values. The central claim of this book is that Primo Levi's writing, his narrative and other reflections, works its way around ethical issues by figuring out just such a practice of virtue(s), even in the face of the void of Auschwitz. This does not, of course, amount to a claim that Levi himself is virtuous, that he is a 'moral saint' of some kind (see Chapter 9 for his dislike of such terms), but that his writing marks out and maps a terrain whose coordinates can best be described as a catalogue of virtues. They are his way of reading and writing the world.

ORDINARY VIRTUES

> to know
> That which before us lies in daily life
> Is the prime wisdom.
>
> (Milton, *Paradise Lost*)

> Una delle lezioni di Auschwitz è, appunto, che capire la mente di un uomo comune è infinitamente piú arduo che comprendere la mente di Spinoza o di Dante.
>
> (Giorgio Agamben)

One persistent and fundamental feature of Levi's catalogue of virtues as they will be charted below remains to be set in the context of wider fields of ethical enquiry: their rather stubborn ordinariness. This is in part simply the product of a temperamental impulse in Levi to avoid the moral or rhetorical high ground,

---

[56] On Jane Austen, see ibid. 239–43 (the link MacIntyre makes in passing between Austen and James provides a bridge from his to Nussbaum's literary ethics); on practices, tradition, and the narrative unity of a life, see pp. 205–26.

[57] For a 'bibliography' and summary account, see P. Berkowitz, *Virtue and the Making of Modern Liberalism* (Princeton: Princeton University Press, 1999), 15–34, 193 note 3.

grand truths, and larger-than-life characters, to look instead for 'altre verità piú modeste' (I. 199; 'other more modest truths'). But it is symptomatic also of larger questions bound up with the nature of ethical enquiry, literature, and the Holocaust. An early version of the preface to *Se questo è un uomo* captures Levi's position pellucidly: 'ho cercato di mantenere l'attenzione sui molti, sulla norma, sull'uomo qualsiasi' (I. 1384; 'I tried to keep focusing on the many, on the norm, on the ordinary man'): the ordinary man is at the centre here, subject and object of Levi's attention.

Charles Taylor, in his magisterial account of the genesis of 'self-hood' and its relation to moral good, *Sources of the Self*, offers three overarching, conflicting historical 'frontiers' within modern identity: very roughly they can be labelled classical or theistic (Augustine to Montaigne), early modern (Reformation and Enlightenment), and modern (Romanticism and after). It is the middle of the three that interests us here. For Taylor the fundamental strands of our present identity and moral orientation which evolved in that middle, early modern period (underpinned by the theistic period, since Taylor's history is a rolling one) include 'freedom, benevolence . . . the demand for universal justice and beneficence . . . equality . . . the avoidance of death and suffering'.[58] All of these reach a sort of apotheosis in the Enlightenment, and are recognizable in the distinctly neo-enlightened secular culture of Levi's formation (see above). In particular, the avoidance of suffering or cruelty as a prime moral claim chimes with the liberalism of Rorty discussed above and will emerge at several points in Levi as a foundation for his ethical deliberations. But the most distinctive shift of the Protestant Reformation for Taylor, and the most suggestive feature of his account for our reading of Levi's ethics, is the move away from the 'heroism' of classical notions of the 'good life' as the ideal end of moral enquiry towards what he calls the 'affirmation of ordinary life'.[59] In this account, ordinary life—the life of marriage, the family, and the home, of work and production—became the proper centre of moral life for the first time, of notions of dignity and integrity, rather than being the banal backdrop against which the self struggled to a higher ideal. Ordinary life displaced the good life as the sphere of moral action. To use other terminologies, we might say that the active life had displaced

---

[58] Taylor, *Sources of the Self*, 495.   [59] Ibid. 13–16, 209–302.

the contemplative life; the democratic the oligarchic or elitist; the bourgeois the aristocrat. And with this shift a new taxonomy of perfections, and a new vocabulary for talking about them, was needed.

Taylor dedicates an important chapter of his book to Montaigne, the key figure of transition between his theistic stage and his two modern stages, the first voice fully to articulate a sense of self built in impermanence, uncertainty, and limit.[60] And Montaigne is also the core figure, the 'hero', of Judith Shklar's book *Ordinary Vices*, source of Rorty's definition of liberalism ('putting cruelty first') and of another attempt to import the 'ordinary' into the history of moral philosophy. Shklar's vices—cruelty, hypocrisy, snobbery, treachery, and misanthropy (in that order)—echo Taylor's notion of the ordinary in that they begin in minor character flaws and manifest themselves first in private or domestic settings and then also in public interactions.[61] She, like several others we have quoted, does not believe that philosophy has accounted for them adequately; indeed, she speculates that 'perhaps only stories can catch their meaning'.[62] But she is convinced of their importance for any liberal conception of the world, because they operate at the tricky borders between the private and the public good, and because they have their roots in questions of character and dispositions (once again, an Aristotelian notion). Building on Shklar, Peter Berkowitz has argued in *Virtue and the Making of Modern Liberalism* that such an account of vices is also necessarily a covert account of virtues, of ordinary virtues.[63] Indeed, Berkowitz's book fills an important lacuna by showing how conceptions of virtue persisted not far beneath the surface even through the philosophers of the liberal tradition, the very figures who had seemed to banish it from moral thinking according to MacIntyre and others (Hobbes, Locke, Kant, Mill). Crucially, Berkowitz performs this salvage operation by arguing that the central liberal notion of freedom ambivalently depends on (and struggles to facilitate) the cultivation of certain qualities of character or virtues of a lower order and of a less constant nature than previously understood;[64] much as, he says, a person on a diet

[60] Ibid. 177–84.
[61] Shklar, Ordinary Vices, 2.
[62] Ibid. 6; elaborated on pp. 228–31.
[63] Berkowitz, *Virtue and the Making of Modern Liberalism*, 29.
[64] Ibid. 9, 110, 172. And cf. p. 14 for an ironic anti-foundational gloss on this.

depends on food.[65] This hidden liberal conception of virtue is
neither Hobbesian self-interest nor Kantian moral law; it rather
'would take its bearing from ordinary language and everyday
experience and speculate in the space created by an open-minded
and self-aware skepticism'.[66]

Put simply, Berkowitz allows us to talk of virtue in Levi as
somehow simultaneously symptomatic of a certain neo-
Aristotelianism, of the premodern affirmation of the ordinary and
of liberal, post-Enlightenment values. In particular, Levi strikes a
chord with Berkowitz's account of Mill, with his belief in freedom, empiricism, and Benthamite utilitarianism combined with
Coleridgean sympathy, the exercise of human judgement through
corrigible error, the flexibility of received opinion.[67] All of these
will reappear as central features of the study of Levi's virtues
below.

If cruelty, hypocrisy, and the rest are 'ordinary' vices to be
contrasted with the dogmatic deadly sins of Christianity or the
vices by excess or deficiency in Aristotle, what would ordinary
virtues be, to contrast with heroic virtues or saintly virtues of
other, 'higher' traditions? We can begin to draw up a set of characteristics from all the strands touched on so far, in a studiedly
'loose and baggy'[68] manner since we know that contrasting traditions and shapes of ethical thinking will be overlaid in them; and
also since, above all else, ordinary virtues oppose 'higher' traditions
by being fluid, undogmatic, and anti-authoritarian (they are open
to unseating). So, without saying precisely what these virtues
might necessarily be, we can sketch out the features that might
generate them. Five stand out in what we have seen: first ordinary
virtues are rooted in dispositions or character, are commonly
recognizable and available to all; secondly, they begin at home or
at work, in Taylor's realm of 'ordinary life'; thirdly, they are
centred on a sort of low-level symbiosis between the individual
and his or her fellow (the other), that first borderline between

---

[65] Berkowitz, *Virtue*, 4.   [66] Ibid. 132.   [67] Ibid. 134–69.

[68] The phrase is used (proudly) in Goldberg, *Agents and Lives*, p. xiv, to describe how
literature thinks morally. Cf. Shklar's opening doubts about *Ordinary Vices* as not being
quite history, philosophy, or political theory, or even rational argument of any kind (p. 6);
or Berkowitz's comments on the advantages for the philosophical tradition of the fact that
the notion of virtue is almost inevitably 'imprecise and inconstant' (*Virtue and the Making of
Modern Liberalism*, 7).

public and private; fourthly, they act on a small scale, acknowledge their limits, and know their impermanence; and finally, they work themselves through in experience and in stories about experience, rather than in codes, and they use experience and stories to refine themselves. If we are looking for overarching labels, we would reach for terms such as responsiveness and responsibility, awareness (of self and others), pragmatism, uncertainty. We might also add that, in a metaethical sense, a language for training in these dispositions would also be 'virtuous' in its own right. Indeed it is crucial to an understanding of Levi as an ethical writer that he is always also a metaethical writer, implicitly asking through the very texture of his writing how best to approach and ask the question 'how to live?'

To bring all these considerations back towards Levi and the role of the Holocaust in an ethical reading of his work, we can usefully turn finally to two other figures: the first is Norberto Bobbio, eminent political theorist and jurist (and, as it happens, a friend of Levi's);[69] the second is Tzvetan Todorov.

Bobbio's elegant lecture *L'elogio della mitezza*[70] makes several of the same moves we have already seen, pointing out the strange eclipse in the modern age of talk of virtue and morals, and the consequent contempt or ridicule of the moralist.[71] He goes on to advocate his own 'favourite' virtue of meekness, and borrows a definition of it which sounds almost Levinasian in its axiomatic other-centredness ' "lasciare essere l'altro quello che è" ' (' "to let the other be that which he or she is" ').[72] More generally he draws a distinction between what he calls 'strong' and 'weak' virtues: the former are heroic, typical of the powerful, typical of politics and war; the latter are social virtues but of the private individual, especially the poor and the oppressed, those almost by definition beyond the trace of history (beyond the archive, the public record).[73] And he lists examples of weak virtues other than

---

[69] See among others N. Bobbio, 'Addio a Primo Levi', *Nuova antologia*, 122/557/2162 (Apr.–June 1987), 202–4; N. Bobbio, 'Primo Levi, perché', *Nuova antologia*, 123/559/2166 (Apr.–June 1988), 108–10.

[70] N. Bobbio, *L'elogio della mitezza e altri scritti morali* (Milan: Pratiche, 1998), 29–47. Domenico Scarpa has also suggested connections between this essay and Levi (Scarpa, ' "Tutto si confessa". Primo Levi e il grigiore del passato', 47–9).

[71] Bobbio, *L'elogio della mitezza*, 29–30.

[72] Ibid. 35.

[73] Ibid. 36–8.

'mitezza': 'humility, modesty, moderation, propriety, demureness, chastity, continence, sobriety, temperance, decency, innocence, ingenuousness, simplicity.'[74] This list (somewhat repetitive and uncomfortably close to a 'Victorian' sense of 'women's virtue', as Bobbio all but confesses when he labels them 'feminine') is less important in itself than in the quality of the distinction between weak and strong. Bobbio's weak virtues are clearly a possible version of what we are calling ordinary virtues, and their rooting in the experience of the poor and private is related to Taylor's ordinary lives. Furthermore, Bobbio ends by linking meekness to a modern form of subaltern resistance to politics, power, and war: non-violence.[75] Levi's ordinary virtues too are both private but fundamentally social, responsive to the other; and they are also beyond heroism, politics, and even history in a crucial sense, since they are virtues which have emerged from (changed by but not quite destroyed by) the Holocaust, that is by a system which cut its victims out of public history, precluded the dynamics of politics, war, or heroism. And even the association with non-violence—although not a channel of defiance available to the camp inmate—has some antithetical resonance in Levi, since his analysis of the nature of Nazi violence ('useless violence', as he calls it) will be crucial to the ethics emerging from the camps (see Chapter 4 below).

From here the link to Todorov is direct: his 1991 work *Face à l'extrême*[76] explicitly sets aside the traditional 'aestheticizing' heroisms of war as one-dimensional and irresponsible (in the etymological sense) in the face of the pseudo-battles of the Warsaw ghetto and the camps.[77] Instead, a response to suffering centred on dignity, altruism and resistance, often only sustained from within or between individuals, leads Todorov to oppose everyday virtues (*vertus quotidiennes*) and heroic virtues, and parallel vices. Like Bauman in *Modernity and the Holocaust*, Todorov is linking the shift in ethics in the modern epoch discerned by figures such as MacIntyre, Taylor, and others with a sort of apotheosis of the

---

[74] Translated from ibid. 37.   [75] Ibid. 46–7.

[76] T. Todorov, *Face à l'extrême* (Paris: Seuil, 1991).

[77] Ibid. 11–36. Cf. Levi's comment in *Il sistema periodico*: 'quei nuovi personaggi [Gramsci, Salvemini, Gobetti, i Rosselli] rimanevano "eroi" . . . non avevano spessore né sostanza umana' (I. 851; 'those new characters remained as "heroes" . . . they had no human density or substance').

modern in the Final Solution. But crucially, Todorov rejects the apocalyptic temptations of such a vision of modernity as implying the death of morals: he argues that multiple forms of morals, of ethical action and resistance to violence, were constantly on display within the ghettos and the camps, and, what is more, that these can be read and used today.[78] Levi figures largely in Todorov's account—indeed is rather the 'hero' of his book, the best embodiment of his argument, as Montaigne was for Shklar's *Ordinary Vices*—above all as an instance of how to read and use the morals within the Holocaust and accounts of it today, by making them into an instrument to sharpen our judgement and to blunt indifference.[79]

Bobbio and Todorov show us how we might probe specific ordinary virtues and, more or less directly, they also bring us closer to the context of the Holocaust from which Levi's writing emerged. They help position an account of virtues in relation to other grand discourses around them (history, politics, the *univers concentrationnaire*, and, we can add, law or justice), to suggest what might be gleaned from such an account that is not available to those other discourses. They do not write the list of Levi's ordinary virtues, but then almost by definition we cannot expect them to be handed to us on a plate: their very ordinariness, as we have seen, would make every list for every individual home-made, eccentric. Levi himself noted as much, in a crucial passage from his second book, *La tregua*:

nessuno nasce con un decalogo in corpo, e ciascuno si costruisce invece il proprio per strada o a cose fatte, sulla scorta delle esperienze proprie, o altrui assimilabili alle proprie; per cui l'universo morale di ognuno ... viene a identificarsi con la somma delle sue esperienze precedenti, e rappresenta quindi una forma compendiaria della sua biografia. (I. 242)
(no one is born with a ready made rulebook, rather we all build our own on the way or in retrospect, in the wake of our experiences or those of others we have taken on board; in this way, every person's moral universe ... comes to coincide with the sum of their previous experiences and so represents a summary form of their biography.)

We know Levi's biography in simple outline—home, Auschwitz,

---

[78] Todoror, *Face à l'extrême*, 36, 40–6.
[79] Ibid. 268–86 (although this section dedicated specifically to Levi is less convincing or original than the use made of Levi throughout the rest of *Face à l'extrême*).

home again (eventually), work (as chemist, writer, survivor)[80]—
and we know the outlines of his cultural formation. What geography did his 'moral universe', his own 'ten commandments'
('decalogo') acquire, on the way or as a result, 'per strada o a cose
fatte'. What is left of his (and our) ordinary life and how to live it
beyond Auschwitz?

The book is divided into four parts and thirteen chapters. Each
chapter investigates one of Levi's 'ordinary virtues' as it appears
and is modulated, questioned, and probed across Levi's *œuvre*, from
his Holocaust writing to his science-fiction stories, from his autobiography to his fiction, from his poetry to his journalism. Some
chapters and even some parts naturally dwell more on certain
corners of the *œuvre* than others, but this is in itself a resource Levi
opened for himself; the capacity to move between different genres
and forms to probe away at distinct aspects of the ethical questions
that persistently concerned him. Each part groups together a
number of virtues under collective headings which in themselves
stand as overarching ordinary virtues in their own right. The list
made up of the thirteen chapter headings and four part headings is
neither exhaustive nor definitive, nor could it be, given what has
been said above about the working of Levi's ethics. Virtues overlap and intertwine one with the other by their very nature, and
certain qualities recur in ways that cut across chapters and parts. So
that although it is part and parcel of the process of a virtue-led
reading, part of its elegance and aptness for Levi, to think in terms
of single labels for each virtue, it is also part and parcel of his
refashioned virtue ethics that those labels should amount to
temporary settlements, to feints towards fixed value which turn
out to contain an acknowledgement of their contingency.

Part I (Chapters 1 to 4) concentrates on Levi's Holocaust writing,
and in particular *Se questo è un uomo*, in order to show how the
founding movements in Levi's ethics emerge out of an antithetical

---

[80] There is an important thread of imagery and geography of 'the home', both literal and
metaphorical, that runs throughout Levi's work and reinforces (or perhaps even inaug-
urates) the 'ordinariness' under discussion here. See, among many other instances, the
nostalgia for home that runs throughout *La tregua* and *Se non ora, quando?* (in the latter case,
Mendel's nostalgia is for a home town and a family life that no longer exists); the imagery
of 'la casa' in the poem-epigraphs to both *Se questo è un uomo* (I. 3) and *La tregua* (I. 203);
the essays 'La mia casa' and 'Le parole fossili' in *L'altrui mestiere* (II. 633–6, 819–22).

response to the dynamics of camp experience and his first camp writings. It identifies four dynamics of the camp world and its representation which lay the groundwork for an ethical enquiry into the working of the ordinary world outside the *Lager*. Part II (Chapters 5 to 8) is rooted more firmly in that ordinary world and the practical virtues Levi deploys to make sense of it. It is guided by multifaceted forms of reasoned, responsive, and creative intelligence that look to analyse, measure, observe, and solve the problems of living. Part III (Chapters 9 to 11) examines the ways in which the private virtues of practical intelligence of Part II are complemented by others which build knowledge and responsibility in exchanges with others of various kinds, in communities. Finally, Part IV (Chapters 12 and 13) shows how Levi punctures the sobriety of his own ethical enquiries by investing in diversions from the 'useful' or the right-minded and from the threats made by Auschwitz and other calamities to them, making humour and play necessary ordinary virtues in their own right, the building-blocks of freedom.

PART I

THE ETHICAL TURN

It is a cardinal contention of this book that Levi arrives at a fine-tuned and complex dynamic of ethical enquiry by way of a centrifugal impulse towards the 'ordinary', driving outwards from the 'black hole of Auschwitz' (as he called it in a late article, II. 1321–4), against its deadening, centripetal weight. What is more, the ethics he arrives at is never a settled system of values, but is always open and uncertain, precisely because these centripetal and centrifugal forces continue to struggle with each other at every step and turn of his work. For this reason, whereas much of the analysis of Levi's work offered in Parts II–IV will move flexibly between his Holocaust-based work and his other creative projects, in an attempt to underscore the evolving subtle investment in a number of 'ordinary virtues', here in Part I the focus will be on the origins or prehistory of those virtues as sketched out in *Se questo è un uomo*. This is not to say straightforwardly that Levi's virtues have their origins antithetically in the vices or more starkly the evil of Auschwitz, but rather that in his bewildering experience of the camp and his memory of it later, there are intimations of an anti-ethical system, one that threatens to preclude the very possibility of making the ethical moves that will characterize his work. At several different levels, each with its own powerful resonance in the rest of his *œuvre*, Levi seems to take that system and turn it towards the ethical, to reimagine it in relation to an ethics which stands against the *Lager* but can never forget the *Lager*. The ethical turn shapes and conditions the nature and quality of Levi's virtues. Chapter 1 shows how the look and the look denied—literally the eyes turned away—is one of the deepest, most essential patterns in the dehumanizing, desubjectivizing mechanism of the camps; Chapter 2 examines Levi's attempts to turn memory from an instinctive, traumatic response into a deliberate, and thus potentially ethical choice; Chapter 3 demonstrates the efficacy of the ethical turn by arguing that even silence, even the refusal to testify can at times be turned into a marker of ethical reflection; and finally, Chapter 4, moving more widely beyond *Se questo è un uomo*, and therefore bridging between Part I and Parts II–IV to come, synthesizes the dynamic behind Chapters 1, 2, and 3 in a 'utilitarian' movement from uselessness to use.

I

LOOKING

> Ethics is an optics.
> (E. Levinas)

Again and again, in reading Levi's work, we find ourselves turning back to its founding text, *Se questo è un uomo*, and indeed to the first, stark pages of that text where the seeds of so much of his later work are sown. The first three chapters of the book, 'Il viaggio', 'Sul fondo', and 'Iniziazione' (I. 7–35), offer founding 'lessons' in physical violence and humiliation related with especial acuity and intensity; and alongside the fear and confusion of entering the *univers concentrationnaire* come founding moments in the denial of the ethical. In this transition towards horror, subsequently echoed and extended in the remainder of the book, the denial of one element of human interaction emerges as a devastating means of depersonalization, as the core of the camps' 'anti-ethics': the excruciating refusal to answer the questions or even to return the look of the newcomer on the part of the SS, the Kapos, the other prisoners, and the rest. The response denied, the look denied—and conversely the possible foundation of an ethics in the acknowledgement of the look—is the subject of this first chapter.

To bind ethics to an act of looking almost inevitably evokes the work of Emmanuel Levinas, as the epigraph to this chapter neatly illustrates.[1] Levi, whose way of thinking was in many ways

---

[1] For the source of the epigraph, see E. Levinas, *Totalité et infini. Essai sur l'extériorité* (The Hague: Martinus Nijhoff, 1971; 1st edition 1961), 8. Levinas's work is notoriously slippery and difficult to decipher and I, like many others, have found it useful to force his terminology into service in imprecise ways (for instance, I have over-literalized his notion of the 'face to face'). The consonance with Levi is, nevertheless, striking (see Introduction). On some of the terms used below (the other, the face to face) and on Levinas in general, see C. Davis, *Levinas* (Cambridge: Polity, 1996); and for selections of his work, see S. Hand, ed., *The Levinas Reader* (Oxford: Blackwell, 1989), especially the essay 'Ethics as First Philosophy', 75–87. See also Z. Bauman, *Postmodern Ethics* (Oxford: Blackwell, 1993), *passim*.

profoundly alien to the philosophical tradition that Levinas represents, nevertheless seems to coincide in his ethics with a Levinasian
notion that the look instigates human relations that in turn insti-
gate the demands of the ethical. For Levi as for Levinas, the roots
of the ethical lie in the encounter between two people, each looking at the other, acknowledging and recognizing the other, in
particular acknowledging the 'otherness' of the other.[2] Two
subjects enter the realm of the ethical in the act of facing each
other, of facing up to each other and their own ethical subject-
hood, of asking for a mark of the self in the other and vice versa:
what Levinas calls the 'face to face'. And this vocabulary seems
remarkably apt in the context of the struggle to understand the
profound 'otherness' of the Final Solution. We will see its relevance to the opening chapters of *Se questo è un uomo* below, but it
is worth noting first how a pattern of one-on-one dialogue and
encounter after the Event, between victims and survivors or
between the innocent and the guilty, in Levi and in others, has
seemed especially resonant in the literature of the Holocaust and
the history of our understanding of it. One need only think of the
exemplary instances of Gitta Sereny's dark investigations of Franz
Stangl and Albert Speer, or of the enigmatic meeting between
Martin Heidegger and Paul Celan after the end of the war, to recall
the weighty moral complexity loaded onto such encounters and
their capacity to stand metonymically for our need to interrogate
this difficult history.[3] Levi too, in his life and his writing, marks out
his journeys in comparable symbolic encounters, setting more store
by them than perhaps any other writer-survivor: think, for example, of his meeting with Jean Samuel ('il Pikolo' of the 'Canto di
Ulisse' chapter in *Se questo è un uomo*, I. 105–11) in 1946, both
miraculously alive but forced as 'non-persons' to meet in no-man's

---

[2] Here and throughout the chapter, I use the term acknowledgement as an important
marker of ethical interaction, both as self-knowledge and knowledge of the other. Stanley
Cavell has written influentially on this notion: see, for example, S. Cavell, 'Knowing and
Acknowledging', now in S. Mulhall, ed., *The Cavell Reader* (Oxford: Blackwell, 1996),
46–71.

[3] See G. Sereny, *Into that Darkness* (London: Deutsch, 1974) and *Albert Speer: His Battle
with Truth* (London: Macmillan, 1995). On Celan's visit to Heidegger, see the poem
'Todtnauberg', in P. Celan, *Selected Poems*, tr. M. Hamburger (Harmondsworth: Penguin,
1990), 292–4, and J. Felstiner, *Paul Celan: Poet, Survivor, Jew* (New Haven: Yale University
Press, 1995), 244–7.

land between France and Italy;[4] or of the extraordinary face-to-face meeting-that-never-was between Levi and the German Buna chemist Müller as related in 'Vanadio' in *Il sistema periodico* (I. 922–33), which Müller tortuously asks for as a means of testing himself and the extent of his guilt, and which Levi ambivalently resists for fear that it might seem like an act of false and impossible absolution.[5] These and other instances show us a sort of mutual questioning, a request for reciprocal acknowledgement and on occasion confession only available, it seems, in the direct face-to-face encounter; and a cluster of terms they throw up—the look, the face, the request, the question—are useful pointers to the origin and ethical resonance of this dynamic, for Levi at least, in those first hours in Auschwitz as related in *Se questo è un uomo*.

Again and again, in the opening pages of the book, the image and the bitter, confusing experience of the expectant look and the unanswered question emerges alongside the bombardment of impressions and bewildering experiences of the journey and arrival at Auschwitz as defining features of this chaotic 'brave new world'. Each instance marks a further step towards the nadir suggested by the phrase 'Sul fondo' (the chapter from which most of the extracts below are taken), each question an end to dialogue or an interruption of human relations, even of human thought itself. The effect is cumulative and numbing, as perhaps only a bare listing can suggest:

Qui ricevemmo i primi colpi: e la cosa fu cosí nuova che non provavamo dolore, nel corpo né nell'anima. Soltanto uno stupore profondo: come si può percuotere un uomo senza collera? (I. 10–11)
(Here we received the first blows: and it was so new that we felt no pain, either in our bodies or our souls. Only a deep sense of astonishment: how can you strike a man with no anger?)

[4] See the account by Samuel himself, in J. Samuel, 'Depuis lors, nous nous sommes revus souvent', in A. Cavaglion, ed., *Primo Levi. Il presente del passato* (Milan: Franco Angeli/ANED, 1991), 23–8 [27]. The importance of sites of transition for Levi is discussed further below: see P. Pauletto, 'Frontiere', in M. Belpoliti, ed., *Primo Levi* (Milan: Marcos y Marcos, Riga 13, 1997), 336–47.
[5] Levi's biographer, Myriam Anissimov, has pointed out how he manipulated the sequence and some of the facts of the exchange with 'Müller' (a pseudonym) in 'Vanadio' (see M. Anissimov, *Primo Levi, ou la tragédie d'un optimiste* (Paris: Lattès, 1996), 288–307), but this only goes to underline the emblematic importance of the episode for Levi. For slightly differing accounts, see II. 873–7 and *The Voice of Memory*, 243–4.

Come pensare? Non si può piú pensare, è come già essere morti (I. 16)
(How to think? We can no longer think, it is like being already dead)

Rubare [le scarpe] da chi? perché ci dovrebbero rubare le scarpe? e i
nostri documenti, il poco che abbiamo in tasca, gli orologi? Tutti
guardiamo l'interprete, e l'interprete *interrogò* il tedesco, e il tedesco
fumava e *lo guardò da parte a parte come se fosse stato trasparente, come se
nessuno avesse parlato.*(I. 17; emphasis added)
(Who would steal [our shoes]? Why should they steal them? And our
papers, whatever meagre things we have in our pockets, our watches?
We all look at the interpreter, and the interpreter asked the German, and
the German went on smoking and looked at him from one side to
another as if he were invisible, as if no-one had said a word.)

Noi facciamo *molte domande*, loro invece ci agguantano e in un momento
ci troviamo rasi e tosati. Che *facce* goffe abbiamo senza capelli! (I. 17;
emphasis added)

(We ask many questions, but they grab hold of us and in an instant we
are shaven and sheared. What strange faces we have with no hair!)

E allora perché ci fanno stare in piedi, e non ci danno da bere, e nessuno
ci spiega niente, e non abbiamo né scarpe né vestiti ma siamo tutti nudi
coi piedi nell'acqua, e fa freddo ed è cinque giorni che viaggiamo e non
possiami neppure sederci.
    E le nostre donne?

    L'ingegner Levi mi chiede se penso che anche le nostre donne siano
cosí come noi in questo momento, e dove sono, e se le potremo rivedere.
Io rispondo che sí, perché lui è sposato e ha una bambina; certo le rive-
dremo. (I. 18)
(And why then do they make us stand up and not give us anything to
drink, why does no one explain anything to us, we have no shoes and no
clothes and are all naked with our feet in water and it's cold and it's five
days we've been travelling and we cannot even sit down.
    And our women?
    Levi the engineer asks me if I think our women are in the same state
as us at this moment, where they are, if we will see them again. I say yes,
because he is married and has a baby girl; of course we will.)

Lo preghiamo di chiedergli che cosa aspettiamo, quanto tempo ancora
staremo qui, delle nostre donne, tutto: ma lui [Flesch] dice di no, che non
vuol chiedere. . . . sa che è inutile. (I. 18)
(We beg him to ask what we are waiting for, how long we have to stay
here, about our women, everything: but [Flesch] says no, that he does-
n't want to ask. . . . he knows that it's useless.)

entrò uno vestito a righe. Era diverso dagli altri, . . . un viso piú civile

. . . cerca di rispondere a tutte le nostre domande. . . . Noi gli facciamo molte domande, lui qualche volta ride, risponde ad alcune e non ad altre . . . Qualcuno si sente rinfrancato, io no, io continuo a pensare che anche questo dentista, questo individuo incomprensibile, ha voluto divertirsi a nostre spese, e non voglio credere una parola di quanto ha detto. (I. 19–20)
(a man dressed in stripes came in. He was different from the others, . . . had a kinder face . . . he tries to answer all our questions. . . . We ask him many questions, sometimes he laughs, he answers some and not others . . . Some of us feel relieved, but I do not, I keep thinking that even this dentist, this incomprehensible individual, has been amusing himself at our expense and I don't want to believe a word he has said.)

è entrato un ragazzo dal vestito a righe, dall'aria abbastanza civile, piccolo, magro e biondo. Questo parla francese, e gli siamo addosso in molti, tempestandolo di tutte le domande che finora ci siamo rivolti l'un l'altro inutilmente.
    Ma non parla volentieri, nessuno qui parla volentieri. (I. 22–3)
(a boy in a striped outfit came in, looking fairly polite, small, thin, and blond. He speaks French and a large number of us lunge at him, submerging him with all the questions that we have been asking each other up to that point, to no avail.
    But he does not speak willingly, no-one here speaks willingly.)

Warum?—gli ho chiesto nel mio povero tedesco.—Hier ist kein Warum, (qui non c'è perché), mi ha risposto, riccacciandomi dentro con uno spintone. (I. 23)
('Warum?, I asked him in my poor German. 'Hier ist kein Warum' (there is no why here), he answered, pushing me back inside with a shove.)

Uno dei due, mentre passiamo, mi chiama, e mi pone in tedesco alcune domande che non capisco; poi mi chiede da dove veniamo.—Italien, rispondo; vorrei domandargli molte cose, ma il mio frasario tedeco è limitatissimo . . .
    Poi mi dice:—Ich Schlome. Du?—Gli dico il mio nome, e lui mi chiede:—Dove tua madre?—In Italia—. Schlome si stupisce:—Ebrea in Italia?—Sì,—spiego io del mio meglio,—nascosta, nessuno conosce, scappare, non parlare, nessuno vedere—. Ha capito; ora si alza, mi si avvicina e mi abbraccia timidamente. L'avventura è finita, e mi sento pieno di una tristezza serena che è quasi gioia. (I. 24–5)
(As we pass by, one of the two calls me and asks me some questions in German that I do not understand; then he asks me where we are from. 'Italien', I reply; I want to ask him many things, but my German vocabulary is tiny . . .
    Then he says, 'Ich Schlome. Du?' I tell him my name and he asks,

'Where your mother?' 'In Italy.' Schlome is amazed: 'Jew in Italy?' 'Yes', I do my best to explain, 'hidden, no one knows, escape, keep quiet, no one see.' He has understood. Now he gets up, comes over to me, and embraces me shyly. The adventure is over, and I feel full of a calm sadness that is almost joy.)

. . . E fino a quando? Ma gli anziani ridono a questa domanda: a questa domanda si riconoscono i nuovi arrivati. Ridono e non rispondono. (I. 30)

(. . . Until when? But the older inmates laugh at this question: you can tell the new arrivals from a question like this. They laugh and they do not reply.)

Ho troppe cosa da chiedere. Ho fame, e quando domani distibuiranno la zuppa, come farò a mangiarla senza cucchiaio? e come si può avere un cucchiaio? e dove mi manderanno a lavorare? Diena [compagno di cuccetta] ne sa quanto me, naturalmente, e mi risponde con altre domande. Ma da sopra, da sotto, da vicino, da lontano, da tutti gli angoli della baracca ormai buia, voci assonanti e iraconde mi gridano:—Ruhe, Ruhe!

Capisco che mi si impone il silenzio . . . Qui nessuno ha tempo, nessuno ha pazienza, nessuno ti dà ascolto . . .

Rinuncio dunque a fare domande, e in breve scivolo in un sonno amaro e teso. (I. 32)

(I have too many things to ask. I am hungry, and when they give out the soup tomorrow, how will I manage to eat with no spoon? and how can I get a spoon? and where will they send me to work? Diena [who shares my bed] knows as much as I do, of course, and he replies with questions of his own. But from above, below, nearby, and far off, from every corner of the barracks which is now in pitch black, angry echoing voices shout at me, 'Ruhe, Ruhe!')

I understand I'm being told to stay silent . . . Here no one has any time, no one has any patience, no one listens to you . . .

So I give up asking questions, and soon I slip off into a bitter, nervous sleep.)

This avalanche of unanswered, on occasion unanswerable questions is to a degree disguised by being interwoven with passages of informative description of the *Lager*, in what amounts to the retrospective answers to many of the questions.[6] Indeed, they are also

---

[6] 'Domanda' is one of the key lexical items to emerge from a computer analysis of the text of *Se questo è un uomo*: see J. Nystedt, *Le opere di Primo Levi viste al computer. Osservazioni stilolinguistiche* (Stockholm: Acta Universitatis Stockholmiensis/Almquist and Wiksell, 1993), 59–60.

set alongside another form of questioning, not by the prisoners as they arrive, but by the survivor-writer addressing his reader ('Se dovessero uccidervi domani col vostro bambino, voi non gli dareste oggi da mangiare?', I. 9; 'If they were going to kill you tomorrow with your child, would you not give him food to eat today?') and thereby inaugurating another ethical dynamic in the texture of Levi's writing which will be crucial for other aspects of his ethics. But the first form of truncated enquiry, illustrated in the list above, is a primary vehicle for the evocation of the subjective impact of deportation there and then, of the bewilderment and incomprehension, of the enforced dishonesty and mistrust of oneself and others; and finally, as represented by the final passage in the list, taken from the start of 'Iniziazione', of the abjuration of questioning—'Rinuncio dunque a fare domande'—and the descent into silence—'Ruhe, Ruhe!' Here lies the anti-ethical moment *par excellence*, the abjuration of both the means and the end of ethical enquiry, the turning away from the encounter of an 'I' with a 'you' and vice versa and thus from subjectivity itself.

This is the moment of the 'demolizione di un uomo' Levi had referred to some paragraphs earlier (I. 20), and indeed, from 'Iniziazione' onwards, *Se questo è un uomo* will take on a static, ahistorical, and atemporal quality ('Per noi, la storia era fermata', I. 113; 'For us history has stopped'), after the perverse destructive 'progress' towards the void of these first chapters. The register will now turn towards the reiterative and the abjuration of the question will become internalized. The prisoners survive—the few that do survive—by not thinking. We learn, for example, that the prisoners do all they can to avoid talking directly about death, the selections, and the crematoria—'tutti ne parlano indirettamente, per allusioni, e quando io faccio qualche domanda mi guardano e tacciono' (I. 46; 'they all refer to it indirectly, by allusion, and when I ask some direct questions, they look at me and fall silent')—and even Levi himself, in the very last days of his imprisonment, as the Germans frantically prepare their retreat, replays as his own the weary refusal to answer questions, here of recently arrived and so naive French inmates eager to know more of the imminent and total evacuation of the camp:

Mi coprirono di domande:—Verso dove? A piedi? . . . e anche i malati? quelli che non possono camminare?—Sapevano che ero un vecchio

prigioniero e che capivo il tedesco: ne concludevano che sapessi sull'argomento molto di piú di quanto non volessi ammettere.
Non sapevo altro: lo dissi, ma quelle continuarono colle domande. Che seccatura. Ma già, erano in Lager da qualche settimana, non avevano ancora imparato che in Lager non si fanno domande. (I. 149)
(They assailed me with their questions: 'Where to? On foot? . . . the sick also? those that can't walk?' They knew I was an old prisoner and that I understood German: they assumed from this that I must know much more on the matter than I was letting on.
But I knew nothing more: I said so, and the questions kept on coming. What a pain. But of course, they had only been in the camp a few weeks, they had not yet learned that in the *Lager* you don't ask questions.)

In this way, the end of the book echoes the beginning, as though the lesson of not asking questions, of not acknowledging the other, frames the entire camp world described in the central chapters. The lapidary, self-evident truth of the final phrase ('in Lager non si fanno domande') underscored by the sarcastic colouring ('Che seccatura. Ma già . . .') seems to leave little room for any exception to the rule, for any return to the humane responsiveness precluded in the camps. But, as we shall see again and again with Levi, there are indeed exceptions, rules never quite hold watertight; indeed it is a guiding principle of his writing and his ethics that the complex truth of any question lies in the dynamic interaction between rules and exceptions, between the general and the particular. In *Se questo è un uomo*, this pattern is established forcefully in the narrative structure of the book: Levi's reflections on what Auschwitz has made of him reach peaks, at times excruciating peaks of intensity at moments of transition or change of routine—from the barracks to the camp hospital, from outside work to the laboratory, from day to night and from sleep to waking, from German rule to liberation—as well as at brief 'moments of reprieve', such as that provided by a chance extra bowl of soup or some hours of warm sunshine (I. 66–72). At these moments, a certain scrap of humanity returns, the assuefaction to the numbing rules of camp routine cracks for an instant, and along with a crowd of forgotten human impulses—nostalgia for home, shame, altruism, and the suffering caused by their return—comes the impulse towards questioning, looking, acknowledging the other and a renewed sense of anguish at their denial. In other words, the motif of the look denied returns at points throughout the book, as if to install it as a founding principle of the world of the *Lager*, a metonymy of its anti-ethical system.

The key examples of the motif in the body of *Se questo è un uomo* come from the two transitional spaces of the hospital, the 'Ka-Be', on the one hand and the Buna laboratory, where Levi is allowed to work for a period of his imprisonment, on the other. In the former, we find Levi once more unsure as to what is about to happen to him, as he was on arrival in the camp. As there, he asks for help, here turning to his non-Jewish, Polish neighbour for some idea of what to expect:

Lui si è voltato all'infermiere, che gli somiglia come un gemello e sta in un angolo a fumare; hanno parlato e riso insieme senza rispondere, come se io non ci fossi: poi uno di loro mi ha preso il braccio e ha guardato il numero, e allora hanno riso piú forte. . . .

L'infermiere indica all'altro le mie costole, come se io fossi un cadavere in sala anatomica; accenna alle palpebre e alle guance gonfie e al collo sottile, si curva e preme coll'indice sulla mia tibia e fa notare all'altro la profonda incavatura che il dito lascia nella carne pallida, come nella cera.

Vorrei non aver mai rivolto la parola al polacco: mi pare di non avere mai, in tutta la mia vita, subito un affronto piú atroce di questo. . . . si rivolge a me, e in quasi-tedesco, caritatevolmente, me ne fornisce il compendio: – Du Jude kaputt.' (I. 42–3)

(He turned to the nurse, who looked rather like his twin standing in a corner smoking; they spoke and laughed together without replying, as if I were not there. Then one of them took me by the arm and looked at my number and they let out an even louder laugh. . . .

The nurse points my ribs out to the other, as if I were a corpse in an anatomy theatre; he mentions my eyelids and my swollen cheeks and thin neck, he bends down and presses my tibia with his index finger and points out the deep dent his finger leaves in my pale flesh, like in wax.

I wish I had never spoken a word to the Pole: I don't think I have ever been so insulted in all my life. . . . he turns to me, in his almost-German, and charitably offers his summing up: 'Du Jude kaputt.')

The affront, the offence dealt to Levi by his neighbour—and the term 'affronto' used here is closely reminiscent of Levi's resonant term for the Event of the Holocaust in general, 'l'offesa' (II. 1006 ff.)—lies in not answering the question and instead turning to talk to a third party, cutting him out of the circuit of human communication. The Pole and the nurse humiliate Levi by laughing at him and discussing him as a sub-human specimen. But perhaps the essence of the affront, the refusal to acknowledge the question and thus the mutual responsibility of questioner and respondent, is already there in the very first, instinctive move of the Pole, to turn away: 'Lui si è voltato.' And the emblematic force of this anti-ethical turn is only underscored by the caricatural, grotesque, and sarcastic return to dialogue at the end of the passage: 'si rivolge a me ...' The 'face to face' is abjured.

The same image, the same dynamic of turning away is extended in the early part of the following chapter, 'Le nostre notti', as Levi reflects on the next moment of transition for the prisoner, out from the hospital and back into the camp, vulnerable and supposedly cured:

l'uomo che esce dal Ka-Be, nudo e quasi sempre insufficientemente ristabilito, si sente proiettato nel buio e nel gelo dello spazio siderale. I pantaloni gli cascono di dosso, le scarpe gli fanno male, la camicia non ha bottoni. *Cerca un contatto umano, e non trova che schiene voltate.* (I. 51; emphasis added)
(a man who leaves the Ka-Be, naked and almost always insufficiently cured, feels thrust out into the dark and the freezing cold of the starry outside. His trousers are falling off him, his shoes are hurting, his shirt has no buttons. He looks for some human contact and finds only backs turned.)

In 'Le nostre notti', of course, Levi will go on to describe the shared dream of every prisoner of returning home and not being listened to, not being looked at: and he evokes it again in the preface to *I sommersi e i salvati*: 'l'interlocutore *si voltava* e se ne andava in silenzio' (II. 998; emphasis added; 'the interlocutor would turn and walk away in silence').

Moving forward to Levi's weeks in the Buna laboratory, we find another powerful, shameful instance of the same dynamic. In the lab, Levi comes into contact with 'normal' workers, including the Müller of 'Vanadio' referred to earlier and also a series of young German, Polish, and Ukrainian women (I. 138–40). Levi and his companions are mortified with embarrassment at the way they look and smell, and the girls seem to show off the normality and relative comfort of their lives with ostentation. Once more, it is the rejected question, the turn away, and the denied look that embodies their inhumane ignorance:

Una volta ho chiesto una informazione a Fräulein Liczba, *e lei non mi h risposto, ma si è volta* a Stawinoga con viso infastidito e gli ha parlato rapidamente. Non ho inteso la frase ma 'Stinkjude' l'ho percepito chiaramente, e mi si sono strette le vene. (I. 139; emphasis added)

(Once I asked Fräulein Liczba about something, and she did not reply, turning instead to Stawinoga with an irritated look and saying something quickly. I didn't catch the sentence in full, but I clearly heard the word 'Stinkjude', and my blood froze.)

The example of the girls, as with Müller, is important because they are in a sense figures of the reader, of those of us who live in an ordinary world coming into contact with the extraordinary degradation of the camps. They are also, of course, figures of complicity, like the Germans Levi sees in Munich on his way home at the end of *La tregua*:

Mi sembrava che ognuno avrebbe dovuto interrogarci, leggerci in viso chi eravamo e ascoltare in umiltà il nostro racconto. Ma nessuno ci guardava negli occhi, nessuno accettò la contesa: erano sordi, ciechi e muti (I. 393)

(I thought that each one of them should have asked us questions, should have read in our faces who we were and listened in humility to our story. But no one looked us in the eye, no one took on the challenge: they were deaf, dumb, and blind.)

The girls, like the Germans, offer a testing ground for our own resistance and ethical responsibility in the face of others' suffering, a test the girls fail callously. The same charged encounter of the ordinary and the perverse permeates one of the most quoted and intense episodes of *Se questo è un uomo*, Levi's encounter with Pannwitz, the Nazi doctor who tests Levi's chemistry as a condition of his entry into the Buna laboratory. Here too, we are confronted with a perversion of a dynamic of human enquiry, in this case the formal oral examination or 'interrogation' of a student by a professor typical of the Italian education system. On top of ethical enquiry, then, there is a form of pedagogical exchange turned sour here. And once again, the perversion of the look is at the very core of the offence Levi feels. In the pause before the exam begins, Levi reflects on the meaning of the encounter, of Pannwitz's look from another world on 'Häftling 174517', and his reflections carry him to the greatest question of all those posed by the Holocaust:

Quando ebbe finito di scrivere, alzò gli occhi e mi guardò.

Da quel giorno, io ho pensato al Doktor Pannwitz molte volte e in molti modi. Mi sono domandato quale fosse il suo intimo funzionamento di uomo. . . . soprattutto, quando io sono stato di nuovo un uomo libero, ho desiderato di incontrarlo ancora, e non già per vendetta, ma solo per una mia curiosità umana.

Perché quello sguardo non corse fra due uomini; e se io sapessi spiegare a fondo la natura di quello sguardo, scambiato come attraverso la parete di vetro di un acquario tra due esseri che abitano mezzi diversi, avrei anche spiegato l'essenza della grande follia della terza Germania. (I. 101–2)

(When he had finished writing, he looked up at me.

From that day, I have thought of Dr Pannwitz many times and in many different ways. I have wondered about his innermost workings as a man . . . above all, once I had regained my freedom, I wished to meet him again, not for revenge but just out of human curiosity.

Because that look did not run from one man to another; and if I could get to the bottom of that look, exchanged as if across the glass of an aquarium between two beings living in two different worlds, I would have found also the essence of the great folly of the Third Germany.)

The figure of Levi is here something other than human, but so too, in the perverse refusal to recognize the human in him, is the look of Pannwitz. Conversely, the voice of Levi the survivor who wishes to encounter Pannwitz again, to look him in the eye, in order to plumb the depths of motivation behind the Third Reich is a voice of salvaged humanity and ethical enquiry, the same voice as Gitta Sereny's mentioned above.

There is, then, a sort of language or semantics of looking within the camp. In a world where communication through words is truncated or scrambled by cacophony, other idioms evolve to mark positions of power and to articulate conditions and actions. It is thus no surprise to note that looks, or looks denied, are pregnant with meaning not only between the guards or outsiders and the abject inmates, but also between the prisoners themselves. Earlier we saw how initiation into the camp entailed learning silence, learning not to ask questions. Later, that very silence becomes an articulation of the same shame as experienced before Pannwitz or the Pole in the 'Ka–Be'. For example, when Levi and Walter are faced with the selection and inevitable death of their neighbour Schmulek, a threefold withdrawal occurs, of questions, of looks, and of words themselves:

Io guardo ora Schmulek, e dietro di lui ho visto gli occhi di Walter, e *allora non ho fatto domande.* . . . Quando Schmulek è partito, mi ha lasciato cucchiaio e coltello; Walter e io *abbiamo evitato di guardarci* e siamo rimasti a lungo *silenziosi*. (I. 47; emphases added)
(Now I am looking at Schmulek; behind him I have seen Walter's eyes and so I ask no questions. . . . When Schmulek left, he gave me his spoon and his knife; Walter and I avoided each other's gaze and remained silent for a long while.)

In the silence and the inability to sustain the look of the other in the face of the death of another, there is a minimal residue of the human weight of the look. Similarly, as the last act of the camp tragedy before the German evacuation, Primo and Alberto and all the other thousands of remnants of men witness the execution of one of the Birkenau rebels who managed to blow up one of the crematoria:

Distruggere l'uomo è difficile, quasi quanto crearlo: non è stato agevole, non è stato breve, ma ci siete riusciti, tedeschi. Eccoci docili sotto *i vostri sguardi*: da parte nostra nulla piú avete da temere: non atti di rivolta, non parole di sfida, *neppure uno sguardo giudice*.

Alberto ed io siamo rientrati in baracca, e *non abbiamo potuto guardarci in viso*. (I. 146; emphases added)
(To destroy a man is difficult, almost as much as to create one: it has not been easy, nor has it been swift, but you Germans have managed it. Here we are, subdued beneath your eyes: from our part you have nothing more to fear, no acts of revolt, no words of defiance, not even a judging look.
Albert and I returned to the barrack and we could not look each other in the eye.)

In all these instances, there is in Levi's responses of anger and shame an important trace of humanity that denies his declarations of his definitive and complete bestialization even as he makes them. His work on the shame of the survivor, developed in the chapter 'La vergogna' of *I sommersi e i salvati* (II. 1045–58) but already a key feature of his account in *Se questo è un uomo* and *La tregua*, is based on the paradox of shame and guilt over the loss of human dignity being proof of the human dignity of the survivor, and in particular of the immediate returning humanity during the moments of reprieve in camp life or during the transition after liberation. If we return to the scene of Levi and the laboratory girls, we find a telling confirmation of the dynamic of shame as a sort of mirroring:

Di fronte alle ragazze del laboratorio, noi tre ci sentiamo sprofondare di vergogna e di imbarazzo. Noi sappiamo qual è il nostro aspetto: ci vediamo l'un l'altro, e talora ci accade di specchiarci in un vetro terso. Siamo ridicoli e ripugnanti. Il nostro cranio è calvo il lunedí, e coperto di una corta muffa brunastra il sabato. Abbiamo il viso gonfio e giallo, segnato in permanenza dai tagli del barbiere frettoloso, e spesso da lividure e piaghe torpide; . . . (I. 138)

(Before the laboratory girls, the three of us felt ourselves submerged in shame and embarrassment. We know what we look like: we see each other and sometimes we catch a reflection of ourselves in a clear glass. We are ridiculous and repugnant. Our skulls are bald on Mondays and covered with a brownish, short mould by Saturday. Our faces are swollen and yellow, permanently scarred by the marks of the hasty barber and often also with hardened bruises and wounds; . . .)

What is fascinating here is the emphasis on the head and face as the primary source of degradation and dehumanization. So too is the notion of reciprocal looking, of self- and mutual mirroring in a world emblematically without mirrors. This is an ambivalent sign, on the one hand of 'human contact', seeing oneself in the other, but on the other hand of facelessness, of the other and the self reduced literally to indistinguishable shells of individuals. We are back to a Levinasian image of the denial of the other in the denial of, the literal destruction of the face. The same image recurs in Levi's description of the most abject prisoners of all, the category of the so-called *Muselmänner*, in camp jargon, or the 'sommersi' in Levi's vocabulary, those who have abandoned all physical and mental will to live and remain as void, waiting for inevitable death:

Essi popolano la mia memoria della loro presenza *senza volto*, e se potessi racchiudere in una immagine tutto il male del nostro tempo, sceglierei questa immagine, che mi è familiare: un uomo scarno, dalla fronte china e dalle spalle curve, *sul cui volto e nei cui occhi non si possa leggere traccia di pensiero*. (I. 86, emphases added)[7]

---

[7] This image of the faceless *Muselmann* as in some sense the distinguishing essence of the system of degradation in Auschwitz, the voiceless and to some degree inaccessible core of the Event, has been analysed with acuity by Giorgio Agamben, drawing on Levi quite substantially (see G. Agamben, *Quel che resta di Auschwitz* (Turin: Bollati Boringhieri, 1998), 37–80). It is perhaps worth noting here, in the context of the strange pairing of Levi and Levinas, that there is an intermediary figure with profound connections to both, that of

(They people my memory with their faceless presence, and if I wanted to capture in a single image all the evil of our time, I would choose this one, which I know so well: a bony figure of a man, his forehead hanging low, his shoulders bent over, with not a trace of thought on his face or in his eyes.)

To be faceless means to deny and be denied one's very essence, to be denied even the slimmest chance of survival or of life embodied in the ethical 'eye contact' between human beings.

It is worth, finally, returning to the poem that stands as an epigraph to *Se questo è un uomo* (later published with the title 'Shemà'; I. 3; II. 525), where the image of the face, barely noted by most readers of the poem, takes on a tone of considerable awe and fear, weighed down with the freight of association we have seen here between the face, the look, the question, and the dynamics of human acknowledgement. In 'Shemà' Levi translates the face into a token of what might happen if we forget Auschwitz. The warmth of the face is first an index of human happiness and companionship; but, warns Levi in his Mosaic anger, the face turned away, the denial of suffering and of acknowledgement, risks stirring up catastrophe.

> Voi che vivete sicuri
> Nelle vostre case,
> Voi che trovate tornando a sera
> Il cibo caldo e *visi amici*:
>> Considerate se questo è un uomo . . .
>> Considerate se questa è una donna . . .
>
>> O vi si sfaccia la casa,
>> La malattia vi impedisca,
>> *I vostri nati torcano il viso da voi*.(I. 3; emphases added)

Robert Antelme. On the links between his 1947 account of deportation, *L'Espèce humaine*, and *Se questo è un uomo*, see Alberto Cavaglion's preface to the 1997 Italian edition (R. Antelme, *La specie umana* (Turin: Einaudi, 1997), pp. v–xiv); D. Scarpa, 'La specie umana negli anni del silenzio', *L'indice dei libri del mese*, 7/14 (July 1997), 31–2. See also S. Cesari, *Colloquio con Giulio Einaudi* (Rome: Edizioni Theoria, 1991), 73–4. Antelme, like Levi, is eloquent on the face: 'on en était venu à faire soi-même un effort de négation de son propre visage, parfaitement accordé à celui du SS. Niée, deux fois niée, ou alors aussi risible et aussi provocante qu'un masque . . . la figure avait fini pour nous-mêmes par s'absenter de notre vie' ('We ended up making the same effort of denial of our own faces, in perfect harmony with the SS. Denied, twice over, or else as laughable and provocative as a mask . . . our faces have for us finally been removed from our lives', *L'espèce humaine* (Paris: Gallimard, 1978), 57).

(You who live secure | in your houses, | you who come home in the evening to find | hot food and friendly faces: | Consider if this is a man | . . . | Consider if this is a woman | . . . || Or may your house crumble, | illness impede you | your children turn their faces from you)

In the movement from ordinary human lives to the terrifying consequences of the Holocaust within the single image of the face, ethics and testimony meet and merge.

The charting in *Se questo è un uomo* of the suppression within the *Lager* of human or humane looking, and its occasional bittersweet reflowerings, lays the groundwork for a whole series of Levian virtues which will emerge in the course of future chapters in Parts II to IV. The search for an apt way of looking at the world and at others, shot through with the anxiety in memory of the degraded and denied looking of the camp world, runs throughout what follows. In specific instances, the search throws up values, duties, or virtues we could name variously as acknowledgement, attention, attentiveness, care (attending to), patience, listening, dialogue, sensitivity, a sense of proportion and perspective, an ability to see and draw lines of connection—all forms of apt or right looking. Some of these will be the subject of chapters in their own right below (e.g. Chapter 7 on 'Perspective'), others will emerge as undercurrents to chapters with ostensibly quite different concerns (e.g. Chapter 11 on 'Storytelling' which is to a significant degree a study in the virtue of listening), and others still permeate all of what follows, resurfacing in several chapters under different guises. Indeed, it is characteristic of the nature of Levi's ordinary virtues that their names are not fixed but fluid and often interchangeable, since they are neither proscriptive nor prescriptive, but rather parabolas of lived and acted out enquiry into the world. Many, if not all of them have an origin and an unsettling undertow in the non-looking, the blindness seen in Auschwitz.

2

MEMORY

Remember that you were a slave in the land of Egypt.
(Deuteronomy 24: 22)

No other Holocaust survivor has written down and reflected on his memories of the camps over such a long period of time—from 1944/5, when he wrote scraps of notes in the Buna lab at Monowitz, until his death in 1987, weeks after the publication of an article for *La stampa* on the revisionism debate in Germany—and with as much persistent and lucid intelligence as Levi. It is hardly surprising, then, that in the course of his writing, it is not only the camps that come in for a forensic and difficult scrutiny, but also the very processes of memory itself. But, as we shall see, the forms and uses of memory that interest Levi are relatively unusual in the field of Holocaust writing where, in recent years, the term has (like testimony itself) become something of a talisman, almost *de rigueur* in evoking the aporia of 'coming after', in signalling an entry into the realm of testimony. As Lawrence Langer, a doyen of the field, noted in 1995:

One of the most striking events in Holocaust studies in recent years has been the proliferation of titles focusing on a single theme: memory. Saul Friedländer's *When Memory Comes* (1979), Pierre Vidal-Nacquet's *The Assassins of Memory* (1985), Charlotte Delbo's last work, *Days and Memory* (1985), Sybil Milton's *In Fitting Memory: The Art and Politics of Holocaust Memorials* (1991), my own *Holocaust Testimonies: The Ruins of Memory* (1991), a collection of essays on the convent controversy at Auschwitz called *Memory Offended* (1991), another set of essays on Elie Wiesel called *Between Memory and Hope* (1990) . . . James Young's study of Holocaust monuments called *The Texture of Memory* (1993) and Geoffrey Hartman's edited volume of Holocaust essays *The Shapes of Memory* (1993).[1]

---

[1] L. Langer, *Admitting the Holocaust* (Oxford: Oxford University Press, 1995), 13.

Quite clearly, such a proliferation carries risks, above all the risk of dilution and devaluation of the term into little more than a vapid marker of piety, or worse still, simply a marketing device. Speculating on the reasons for this obsession, Langer offers a more optimistic and substantive explanation, seeing the phenomenon as symptomatic of a shift in the relation of history and memory as competing modes of capturing the past in work on the Holocaust:

Perhaps this means we have finally begun to enter the second stage of Holocaust response, moving from what we know of the event (the province of historians), to how to remember it, which shifts the responsibility to our own imaginations and what we are prepared to admit there.[2]

The formulation of a wholesale shift from history to some more intimate engagement is obviously over-simplified, since it is self-evident that history, imagination, and memory have interlaced with each other throughout the post-war period in charting aspects of the Holocaust, as even the troubled publication history of *Se questo è un uomo* shows.[3] And indeed, for all the proliferation of work on memory, there is little to suggest that at the same time work within 'the province of historians' has not continued apace, equalling if not outstripping the former. But in its suggestion that these modes of writing have different valencies at different moments and that their relations are symptomatic of larger issues in our evolving understanding of the Holocaust, Langer's notion is a useful starting point for an examination of memory in Levi. This chapter examines Levi's own uses of memory in a way that

[2] Langer, *Admitting the Holocaust*, 13. In this context, an influential work has been Yosef Yerushalmi's *Zakhor* (Seattle: University of Washington Press, 1982), which charts relations in Judaism between history or historiography (or rather the lack of it in the Jewish tradition over nearly two millennia until the 18th century), memory, and myth. Yerushalmi only briefly touches on the Holocaust (pp. 97–9).

[3] The book was famously turned down by Einaudi in 1946–7, in all probability on the advice of both Natalia Ginzburg and Cesare Pavese, before being accepted in a 1955 contract, only to be delayed and published in 1958 in a series of essays rather than narrative (see I. 1376–416). Belpoliti has argued strongly against overplaying the 'scandalous' side to that first rejection (M. Belpoliti, 'Il falso scandalo', *La rivista dei libri*, 10 (1 Jan. 2000), 25–7). On the history of post-war responses to and representations of the Holocaust in various countries, see A. Bravo and D. Jalla, eds., *Una misura onesta. Gli scritti di memoria della deportazione dall'Italia 1944–93* (Milan: Franco Angeli, 1994); T. Kushner, *The Holocaust and the Liberal Imagination* (Oxford: Blackwell, 1994), 205–69; P. Novick, *The Holocaust and Collective Memory* (London: Bloomsbury, 1999); A. Wieviorka, *Déportation et génocide* (Paris: Plon, 1992).

provides a bridge between subjective imagining and documentary history, drawing on elements of both, by reading memory as ideally turned towards the ethical, reclaimed as a 'virtue' to be inserted alongside the other ordinary virtues examined in this book. To do so, it charts a movement in Levi—which, like Langer's phases, is less a chronology than a constant transversal oscillation—between memory as impulsive, solipsistic, and traumatic and memory as deliberate, open to dialogue, and constructive; between memory as psychopathology and memory as duty.

In this pattern, memory is figured as a duty both for the survivor and for the non-survivor who acquires a form of collective memory of these events from the survivor: as Levi says in the afterword to *Se questo è un uomo*, 'meditare su quanto è avvenuto è un dovere di tutti. Tutti devono sapere, o ricordare . . .' (I. 198; 'to meditate on what has happened is a duty for everyone. Everyone must know or remember').[4] And the slippage of terms here is particularly telling: 'meditare'—a verb familiar from Levi at his most lapidary, testimonial, and memorial in 'Shemà', 'meditate che questo è stato' ('meditate that this has been')—becomes a more pliable form of duty, as it overlaps with 'sapere' and 'ricordare', becoming a form of knowledge or memory transmitted from the single to the shared ('tutti'). In other words, what might seem to belong exclusively to Langer's first stage—the province of historians who record what happened—also works as a basis for reflection on the meaning and difficulties of recording what happened, the processes of its becoming past, its re-emergence as memory and history in some projected future. Levi makes both the act of remembering and its consequences of value and thus instils a 'duty of memory' in himself and in his readers; and by enveloping his readers in this sort of collective meditation, he returns in some fashion to the historical dimension and to a historical consciousness of the Holocaust. In this sense, Langer's 'shift to

---

[4] The phrase the 'duty of memory' was used as the title of a French version of a long interview with Levi carried out as part of an oral history project in Turin, 1982–3: P. Levi, *Le Devoir de mémoire* (Paris, Éditions Mille et une nuits, 1995) (now in Levi, *The Voice of Memory*, 218–49). The very notion of 'deontic' duty has been moot in debates on postmodern ethics: Zygmunt Bauman has argued against the association of postmodernity with a 'twilight of duty', preferring to see in it a renaissance of duty and morality in a different guise (Z. Bauman, *Postmodern Ethics* (Oxford: Blackwell, 1993), 2–3). On collective memory, see the influential M. Halbwachs, *On Collective Memory* (Chicago: Chicago University Press, 1992; 1st edition 1950).

our imaginations and what we are prepared to admit there' is not against history but part of a process of inserting memory into history.

The processes and representation of memory are already richly present in the pages of *Se questo è un uomo*, for all that the book itself will become an object of memory for Levi over the course of the decades to come, blocking at times his access to the direct memories of his experiences themselves.[5] In that first book, memory runs along the two distinct parabolas that characterize all first-person narratives, one governed by the author–character (Levi in the *Lager*) and another governed by the author–narrator (Levi the survivor writing in Turin). The former traces echoes from Auschwitz back to his life before deportation in Turin and Milan (evoked, for example, in the early chapters of *Il sistema periodico*, I. 757–859); the latter moves from the perspective of the survivor back towards the terrifying contemplation of Auschwitz. The structure of first-person narrative is such that the two axes tend to merge as the author–character becomes the author–narrator. Holocaust memoirs, however, centred on an unassimilated trauma, tend to tell the story instead of a radical rupture between these two lines of memory and the two selves behind them. In part this is true of Levi also, as he notes in *La tregua*: 'la cesura di Auschwitz . . . spaccava in due la catena dei miei ricordi' (I. 375; 'the caesura of Auschwitz . . . split in two the chain of my memories'). Indeed, at times the very testimonial project seems on the edge of collapse: 'Oggi, questo vero oggi in cui sto seduto a un tavolo e scrivo, io stesso non sono convinto che queste cose sono realmente accadute' (I. 99; 'Today, this very day as I sit at a table and write, I myself am not convinced that these things really happened').[6] But Levi is a 'normalizer', even as he contemplates the abnormal, and he expends much energy in building bridges between the two axes of memory. In Chapter 9, we will see how one of the most crucial of these bridges is the interrogation of the

[5] On the history of *Se questo è un uomo* as a 'wandering nomad . . . leaving a long, intricate trail behind it for forty years', see II. 1124, and on Levi's art of repeating camp stories, see Levi, *The Voice of Memory*, pp. x, xix, 218. And cf. Alberto Cavaglion's thesis that all Levi's work is a gloss on that first book (A. Cavaglion, 'Il termitaio', *Asino d'oro*, 4 (1991), 117–21).

[6] Even the syntax contributes to the difficulty here: one might expect the doubts expressed to lead to a subjunctive 'siano realmente accadute', but of course, for all his strange, self-threatening inner doubts, they did indeed happen.

ethical data of common sense as it persists and alters before, during, and after Auschwitz. But there is also a bridge in Levi's understanding of the mechanics of memory itself as it moves along its parabolas. In particular, Levi charts vividly the constant negotiations between sensory and intellective, involuntary and voluntary acts of memory. To adapt Langer's formulation slightly, understanding memory means not only understanding 'what we are prepared to admit' to our imaginations, but also that which cannot be erased from them.

For a so-called calm, rationalist writer, it is remarkable how frequently and with what power sensory or involuntary memory erupts into Levi's work. In his Holocaust-centred writing, it has three principal vehicles: dreams, smell, and music. Dreams play a central role in Levi's depiction of the subjective experience of the camps. In the momentary pause of sleep, the memory of being human returns, alongside the deepest fears of the here and now contaminating the world known before. In a famous and much-quoted passage of *Se questo è un uomo*, he explains how every prisoner shared two dreams, each bound up with such processes of memory and fear: first a terrible dream of return, in which they tell the tale of their suffering only to be met with indifference even by their closest family; and then an intense dream of food and drink, always unreachable at the last (I. 54–5). Memories of food and of home (of ordinary worlds)—'cibo caldo e visi amici', as 'Shemà' has it (I. 3; 'hot food and friendly faces')—emerge to crack the protective, numbing shell of forgetting and denial that surrounds the prisoner when awake; conversely, the perverse reality of the camp infiltrates even their subconcious dreamworld of memory and desire, so that the food eludes them, tantalizingly, and the family ignores or 'forgets' them. In other words, the dreams blur terrifyingly what is past, present, and future, what is conscious and subconscious, just as they blur the boundary between the ordinary and the perverse. The same cluster of elemental fears and desires expressed by dreams re-emerges with greater power still at the end of *La tregua* in a dream that picks up on elements of his camp dreamworld—friends, family, food—only to turn into one of the most powerful moments of despair in all his work:

Sono a tavola con la famiglia, o con amici, o al lavoro, o in una campagna verde ... eppure provo un'angoscia sottile e profonda, la sensazione definita di una minaccia che incombe. E infatti, al procedere del sogno, a poco a poco o brutalmente, ogni volta in modo diverso, tutto cade e si disfa intorno a me. . . . Tutto è ora volto in caos: sono solo al centro di un nulla grigio e torbido, ed ecco: io *so* che cosa questo significa, ed anche so di averlo sempre saputo: sono di nuovo in Lager, e nulla era vero all'infuori del Lager. Il resto era breve vacanza, o inganno dei sensi, sogno: la famiglia, la natura in fiore, la casa. Ora questo sogno interno, il sogno di pace, è finito, e nel sogno esterno, che prosegue gelido, odo risuonare una voce, ben nota: una sola parola, non imperiosa, anzi breve e sommessa. È il comando dell'alba in Auschwitz, una parola straniera, temuta e attesa: alzarsi, 'Wstawac'. (I. 395)

(I am at the table eating with my family or friends or at work, or in a green countryside . . . and yet there is a subtle, deep anxiety, the definite feeling of a threat hanging over me. And indeed, as the dream goes on, either slowly or bluntly, each time in a different way, everything collapses and disintegrates around me. . . . Now everything has changed to chaos; I am alone in the centre of a grey and turbid nothing, and now I *know* what this means, and I also know that I have always known it; I am in the *Lager* once more, and nothing is true outside the *Lager*. All the rest was a brief pause, a deception of the senses, a dream; my family, nature in flower, my home. Now this inner dream, this dream of peace, is over, and in the outer dream which continues, gelid, a well-known voice resounds, a single word, not imperious, but brief and subdued. It is the dawn command of Auschwitz, a foreign word, feared and expected: get up, 'Wstawac'.)

The former reality resurfaces and obliterates the present, inverting its relation with memory and the past, making the present into a dream and the unbearable past into reality. This is the agony that returns 'at an uncertain hour', an agony of an involuntary memory that not only constitutes or reconstitutes the self, but threatens its dissolution. There is no ethical content or value to this memory, no virtue in its enactment or contemplation, only the oppression of the senses.

Sensory memory of another kind, that of olfactory memory, also emerges as important for Levi as for other survivors. Indeed, there is a strange and rather horrific prominence given to the sense of smell as a means of evoking the most obscene symbol of the camps, the crematoria. In Jorge Semprun's 1994 memoir *L'Écriture ou la vie*, for example, the author reflects on returning to Buchenwald after the war:

J'ai pensé que mon souvenir le plus personnel, le moin partagé . . . celui

qui me fait être ce que je suis . . . qui me distingue des autres . . . qui me
retranche même tout en m'identifiant, de l'espèce humaine . . . qui brûle
dans ma mémoire d'une flamme d'horreur et d'abjection . . . d'orgueil
aussi ... c'est le souvenir vivace, entêtant, de l'odeur du four crématoire:
fade, écœurante . . . l'odeur de chair brûlée sur la colline d'Ettersberg.[7]
(It struck me that my most personal, least shared memory . . . which
made me what I am . . . which sets me apart from others . . . which cuts
me off from, whilst identifying me with the human race . . . which burns
in my memory with a flame of horror and abjection . . . and of pride too
. . . is the hardy, heady memory of the smell of the crematorium: flat,
sickening . . . the smell of burnt flesh over the Ettersberg hill.)

Levi too is struck by the intensity of his olfactory memory of
Auschwitz and, like Semprun again, the reflection coincides with
a return journey to the camp. In a 1984 essay in *L'altrui mestiere*
with the title 'Il linguaggio degli odori' (II. 837–40), he follows the
traces of smell and memory, dutifully quoting Proust's madeleine,
along both the axes of recall discussed above: on his return to
Poland,[8] the sights leave him moved, but with a sort of reverent
distance, whereas the smells,

l' 'odore di Polonia', innocuo, sprigionato dal carbone fossile usato per il
riscaldamento delle case, mi ha percosso come una mazzata: ha risvegliato
a un tratto un intero universo di ricordi, brutali e concreti, che giacevano
assopiti, e mi ha mozzato il respiro. (II. 840)
(the smell of Poland, innocuous, unleashed by the carbon fossil used for
heating in the homes, struck me like a blow: it reawoke in an instant a
whole world of memories, brutal and concrete, that were lying dormant,
and it took my breath away.)

Although Levi carefully specifies that his 'smell of Poland' is a
sweet one, it nevertheless evokes a smell of burning, and the
violence of his language in describing its effects suggests a parallel
with Semprun's horrific 'odeur'. But these involuntary processes
are violent by their very nature: Levi offers a parallel movement
along the other axis of memory, that from the camp itself back to
the normal world of his Italian youth:

Con altrettanto violenza, 'laggiú', ci fervivano gli occasionali odori del

---

[7] J. Semprun, *L'Écriture ou la vie* (Paris: Gallimard, 1994), 302.
[8] Levi returned to Auschwitz first as part of an official party in 1965 and then, with
much greater personal impact, in June 1982, during which he was filmed and interviewed
for RAI television by Daniel Toaff and Emanuele Ascarelli. The interview is now in Levi,
The Voice of Memory, 208–17.

mondo libero: il catrame caldo, evocatore di barche al sole; il fiato del bosco, odoroso di funghi e muschio, veicolato dal vento dei Beschidi; il profumo di sapone nella scia di una donna 'civile' incontrata sul lavoro. (ibid.)[9]

(With the same violence, 'down there', occasional smells from the free world agitated us: hot tar, the smell of boats in the sun; the breath of the woods, with the smell of mushrooms and musk, sent our way by the Carpatian wind; the perfume of soap in the wake of a 'civilian' woman met during work.)

Through the aggressions of dreams and smells, the two universes of here and there collide. And the same process is found, nuanced by a complex movement between the dual axes of memory, in an intense page of *Se questo è un uomo* where music is the trigger of a dissolution of the self more immediate and destructive than any dream. Levi is in the hospital and he is woken (for once from a dreamless sleep) by the distant rhythm of the camp band:

Noi ci guardiamo l'un l'altro dai notri letti, perché tutti sentiamo che questa musica è infernale. . . . Esse [marce e canzoni] giacciono incise nelle nostre menti, saranno l'ultima cosa del Lager che dimenticheremo: sono la voce del Lager, l'espressione sensibile della sua follia geometrica, della risoluzione altrui di annullarci prima come uomini per ucciderci poi lentamente.

Quando questa musica suona, noi sappiamo che i compagni, fuori nella nebbia, partono in marcia come automi: le loro anime sono morte e la musica li sospinge, come il vento le foglie secche , e si sostituisce alla loro volontà. . . . Alla marcia di uscita e di entrata non mancano mai le SS. Chi potrebbe negare loro il diritto di assistere a questa coreografia da loro voluta, alla danza degli uomini spenti, squadra dopo squadra, via dalla nebbia verso la nebbia? (II. 44–5)

(We look at each other from our beds, because we all feel that this music is sent from hell . . . The [marches and songs] are cut deep into our minds, they will be the last aspect of the *Lager* that we will forget: they are the voice of the *Lager*, the felt expression of its geometric folly, of the resolution by others to annihilate us first as men and then to kill us slowly.

When this music plays, we know that our companions, out in the fog, are marching off like automata: their souls are dead and the music is pushing them like dried leaves in the wind; it has replaced their will. . . . The

---

[9] On Levi's encounter with the ordinary women working in the Buna laboratory, see also Chapter 1 above.

SS never miss the exit and entry marches. Who could deny them the right to be present at this choreography, willed by them, this dance of spent men, squad after squad, away from fog towards other fog?)

Involuntary memory is violent and inarticulate, self-centred and also decentring; and yet it is also resonant with a certain truth, for Levi. It throws up talismans, symbols of unacknowledged, forgotten, or repressed realities, circumventing external or internal processes of censorship, and these are a precious, if tricky resource in confronting the many manipulations to which memory is subject. In *I sommersi e i salvati*, Levi confronts the possible failures, manipulations and processes of denial of memory, on the part of both victims (or their families) and oppressors, in his most extended meditation on the subject, the essay 'La memoria dell'offesa' (II. 1006–16). There, he is fascinated by the vacillation of memory on the borderline of conscious and subconscious control, noting how a false account can become 'true' even for its creator simply through repeated 'recollection', whether the motivation for deception was fear of trauma or fear of prosecution. There is something of the desensitizing rhythm of the work-music in the camps quoted above, in the falsification of memory through almost ritual denial. There is also a dim echo here of a short story by Levi called 'I mnemagoghi' (I. 401–8), published in *Storie naturali* in 1966 but, crucially, written in 1946, just as he was writing *Se questo è un uomo*. The short story tells of an old provincial doctor Montesanto who has withdrawn into a secluded, strange world where he embodies and captures his memories in chemical compounds, each preserved in a flask to prevent it fading: 'non posso pensare che con orrore all'eventualità che anche uno solo dei miei ricordi abbia a cancellarsi' (I. 405; 'I can only think with horror of the possibility of even one of my memories being lost'). But Montesanto's flasks have become an addiction and a foggy barrier between himself and lived experience: he has come to exist only as he is embodied in his perfumes: 'si potrebbe dire che [questi mnemagoghi] *sono* la mia persona' (ibid.; you could say that these 'mnemagogues' *are* my very self). The young visitor Morandi is at first seduced by the game of identifying the different smells, as though entering into Montesanto's being, but he comes away strangely disturbed, needing fresh air and contact with his friends as though to cleanse himself of some poison.

'I mnemagoghi' amounts to a filtered, fictional meditation on how best to preserve and use the memories burning within Levi in 1946. Montesanto's 'chemical' method is prodigious but flawed; his memories preserved perfectly but somehow also desensitized to the present and to lived reality. Like Montesanto's flasks, Levi notes more than once that his (and others') memories of his time in the camps are intensified, as if ineradicable, and not only because of their origin in the senses. This intensification is well illustrated by Levi's discussion in 'Comunicare' (*I sommersi e i salvati*, II. 1059–72) of what he calls 'mechanical memory' (II. 1069), and the example is of particular interest since it hinges on the relationship between memory, language, and writing. Mechanical memory is what Levi calls his and other prisoners' tendency to etch automatically and irremovably into their memories whole strings of foreign words (Polish, German, Yiddish, Russian, Dutch) heard in the Babel of the camp, without having the slightest idea of their meaning. He calls these snatches 'frammenti indistinti strappati all'indistinto: frutto di uno sforzo inutile ed inconscio di ritagliare un senso entro l'insensato' (II. 1064; 'indistinct fragments torn from the indistinct reality; the product of a useless and unconscious effort to forge meaning where there is none'). Later these form the basis of many key moments of his written accounts. By extension, Levi constantly casts himself as immune to the fading of memory when dealing with the camps, as though he had lived his time there on a higher, ineradicable plane of existence: for example, he ends 'La memoria dell'offesa', a chapter dedicated entirely to the fallibility and self-serving distortions of memory, with a disclaimer: despite all he has said, his own memories seem to him 'indenni dalle derive che ho descritte' (II. 1016; 'untouched by the slippages I have described'). Similarly, in the preface to *Racconti e saggi*, he portrays himself, with typical modesty, as 'un uomo normale di buona memoria che è incappato in un vortice' (II. 859; emphasis added; 'a normal man *with a good memory* who happened to get caught up in a whirlwind').[10] But as with his favorite literary role

---

[10] Oral historians Anna Bravo and Daniele Jalla use this phrase as the starting point for a discussion of memory and history of the Holocaust in A. Bravo and D. Jalla, 'Primo Levi: un uomo normale di buona memoria', *Passato e presente*, 18 (Sept.–Dec. 1988), 99–108 (later in A. Cavaglion, ed., *Primo Levi: Il presente del passato* (Milan: Franco Angeli, 1991), 67–78). On the image of the 'vortice', another centripetal image for the Holocaust, see A. Cavaglion, 'Asimmetrie', in M. Belpoliti, ed., *Primo Levi* (Milan: Marcos y Marcos, Riga 13, 1997), 222–9 [226].

model, the Ancient Mariner, this condition of heightened memory is a curse and an intolerable burden. In an article called 'Un "giallo" del Lager' (II. 909–12), he is presented with a photo of a fellow deportee whom he had hardly known at all, but finds he remembers him without hesitation:

a volte, ma solo per quanto riguarda Auschwitz, mi sento fratello di Ireneo Funes, 'el memorioso' di Borges, quello che ricorda ogni foglio di ogni albero che avesse visto, e che 'aveva piú ricordi da solo, di quanti ne avranno avuti tutti gli uomini vissuti da quando esiste il mondo'. (II. 911)
(At times, but only in dealing with Auschwitz, I feel like a brother of Ireneo Funes, Borges's 'memorioso', who remembers every leaf of every tree that he has ever seen, and who 'had more memories himself than all the men who had ever lived since the world began'.)

In Borges's story 'Funes el memorioso',[11] Funes is ultimately overwhelmed by his infinitely detailed memory. He cannot communicate in normal language, since language requires categorization by similarities, whereas he is swamped by infinite differences (he tries to invent an infinite, asystemic language). He tries to explain his condition to the narrator by saying that our normal perceptions of reality are to his as our dreams are to our waking reality (a reversal perhaps at the root of Levi's inversion of dream and reality at the end of *La tregua*). Eventually he dies, aged only 22.

Montesanto, the Ancient Mariner, Funes are all enslaved by inescapable memory. To preserve memory without succumbing to it, to become sensitive to its falsifications and to avoid its addictive obsessions, involuntary memory needs to be put to measured, conscious work. The data of involuntary memory must not be abandoned, but must be filtered and transformed. The dilemma Levi implicitly sets himself is to move from a pathological testimony, where memory is solipsistic and crushing, towards an ethical memory, in which a conscious, voluntary awareness and acknowledgement of the past (memory and history) can communicate a sort of collective sense of value for writer and reader. This is memory's ethical turn.[12]

---

[11] J. L. Borges, 'Funes el memorioso', in *Prosa completa*, vol. II (Barcelona: Bruguera, 1985), 177–84.

[12] The same impulse lies behind Levi's passionate rejection of notions of incommunicability in *I sommersi e i salvati* (II. 1059–60). See Chapter 3 below.

How, then, to reclaim memory, how to establish a turn towards a deliberate, ethically aware memory out of the triggers of the senses? Some of the *loci* of involuntary memory that we have cited thus far help suggest ways towards an ethical memory. Returning to the essay 'Il linguaggio degli odori', for example, we find that the bulk of the essay is a light-hearted reflection on the insensitivity of humans to smell, with certain exceptions such as chemists, for whom smell is a precious and necessary workmate. Of course, many if not all of Levi's readers (following Levi himself) have noted the affinities between his writing, his testimony, and his chemistry: 'Il linguaggio degli odori' offers another point of analogy showing a raw material or matter in the form of smell pinpointed in the careful language and formulae of the chemist, then transformed, combined, or analysed by chemistry into a solution or a product, just as the writing of memory might transform the raw data of involuntary memory into a useful, communicable awareness of the past. It suggests a Montesanto set aright.

Another means to a transformation of sensory data is also adumbrated in the page quoted above from *Se questo è un uomo* on music. Levi's reflections come as he lies in his Ka-Be sick-bed, one of those moments of transition or reprieve mentioned in Chapter 1 as so crucial for Levi's ethical reflections. From there, he struggles to listen carefully to but also to stand beyond the numbing effect of the music as he will do—and the analogy is made explicitly—after liberation in recalling the sounds. The struggle amounts to a model attempt to position himself between the necessarily horrific memory and the cognitive and ethical dividends paid by holding on to that memory with awareness:

bisognava uscire dall'incantamento [del ritmo], *sentire la musica dal di fuori, come accadeva in Ka-Be e come ora la ripensiamo, dopo la liberazione e la rinascita, senza obbedirvi, senza subirla, per capire che cosa era*; per capire per quale meditata ragione i tedeschi avevano creato questo rito mostruoso, e perché oggi ancora, quando la memoria ci restituisce qualcuna di quelle innocenti canzoni, il sangue ci si ferma nelle vene, e siamo consci che essere ritornati da Auschwitz non è stata piccola ventura. (I. 45; emphases added)

(we had to break the spell [of the rhythm], hear the music from the outside, as we heard it from the Ka-Be and as we hear it now, after our liberation and rebirth, without obeying it, without submitting to it, in order to understand what it was; to understand for what studied reason the Germans had created this monstrous ritual, and why still today, when memory takes us back to some of those innocent songs, our blood freezes and we are acutely aware that to have come back from Auschwitz was no mean fortune.)

The same pattern of holding on to the involuntary but reclaiming it as a vessel of difficult understanding and of communication pertains for Levi's 'mechanical memories' and other indelible marks of the *Lager*, which are not only a token of that 'useless and unconscious effort to forge meaning where there is none' referred to above, but also, perhaps, a preliminary to something of greater value:

O forse, questa memoria inutile e paradossa aveva un altro significato e un altro scopo: era una inconsapevole preparazione per il 'dopo' per una improbabile sopravvivenza in cui ogni brandello di esperienza sarebbe diventato un tassello di un vasto mosaico. (II. 1064)
(or perhaps this useless and paradoxical memory had another meaning and another aim: it was an unconscious preparation for 'after' for an improbable survival in which every scrap of experience would become a piece of a vast mosaic.)

The after, the vast mosaic to which those fragments might contribute, is not, however, simply an explication of what was inexplicable before. The foreign phrases can perhaps be translated afterwards but they also remain, as they must remain, fragments of a senseless universe. Levi goes on to explain in 'Comunicare' how he has made a conscious effort to retain his bastardized camp accent and the jargon of his German, even after learning standard German in the post-war years, for the same reason that he has kept his tattooed number on his arm: to turn the imposed and unchosen into a chosen and thus ethically determined act of memory, still fragmentary, and rooted in trauma, but with the power to communicate with and to disturb his interlocutors (II. 1068). Furthermore, it is noteworthy that in both these examples (his German and his tattoo) scraps of language or symbols are his point of departure, the sources for the vast, complex mosaic of after, where his writing is developed into a fuller, ethically acute medium. A comparable example of this same impulse could be found in the scraps of notes Levi made in the Monowitz lab— quite 'uselessly', since he had to destroy them at once, and quite foolishly, since he risked punishment and even death if he was discovered writing—as markers, literal and symbolic, of a future mosaic of memory.[13]

This central role played by language and writing is crucial for Levi, not only because his entire *œuvre* is permeated by a keen fascination for the workings of languages and systems of meaning generally, but also because it sets him apart so sharply from other survivors. Once more, the comparison with Semprun is instructive, since despite the profound affinities the latter feels with Levi, his book *L'Écriture ou la vie* revolves around his absolute inability to fulfil his intention to write down his experience in Buchenwald until more than fifteen years after the event. He chooses life over what he feels as the death, the asphyxia of writing memory, surviving by achieving what Ireneo Funes had failed to achieve, oblivion: 'j'étais revenu dans la vie. C'est-à-dire dans l'oubli. . . . j'avais choisi une longue cure d'aphasie, d'amnésie délibérée, pour survivre' (I had come back to life. That is to oblivion. . . . I had chosen a long course of treatment with aphasia, deliberate amnesia, in order to survive).[14] Levi, by contrast, had managed to write his memory, as 'deliberate memory' rather than 'deliberate amnesia', and to turn it towards life. One might say that Levi reinstates the *aut aut* of the original title of Semprun's book, *L'Écriture ou la mort*.

Two important moments of Levi's work evoke powerfully the ethical and communal value of acts of memory, whilst developing the link between these acts and writing and language. The first is perhaps the best known of all the episodes in *Se questo è un uomo*, the chapter 'Il canto di Ulisse' (I. 105–11). With an hour to spend fetching and carrying soup, Levi and Jean il Pikolo enter into another of those rare moments of reprieve when human communication is still possible and their humanity and their memories—of homes, cities, studies, of their mothers—return together. When Jean asks to be taught some Italian, Levi starts off for no apparent reason—and thus, initially, as if involuntarily—reciting the famous canto of Ulysses in Dante's *Commedia* (*Inferno* XXVI). The lines come to him, partially, with gaps and leaps and inversions and he struggles to translate them into his rough, paraphrasing French.

---

[13] For one of several versions of his note-taking, see Levi, *Le Devoir de mémoire*, 26–7. On writing in the camps, see Bravo and Jalla, eds., *Una misura onesta*, 46–50.

[14] Semprun, *L'Écriture*, 205.

The rest of the chapter comes in a sort of stream of consciousness as Levi strains to recapture the lines he learned at school, finding in them personal memories—seeing, for example, the mountain of Purgatory glimpsed by Ulysses in the image of the mountains between Milan and Turin—and other, intuited meanings and interpretations, for himself and Jean, for the camp world and for all humanity. Spiralling out from the half-recalled text, the act of memory is thus only indirectly significant for the content of Dante's 'canto' (although Levi's appeals to Jean are in part a degraded, inverted, and yet somehow equally heroic version of Ulysses' appeal to his companions). It is rather the rote-learned relic that is being put to use here, in building a bridge of humanity to Jean and to the outside world. A spontaneous impulse is being transformed into an act of ethical value.

Forty years later, in *I sommersi e i salvati* (II. 1100–3), Levi would gloss this episode in his essay on the 'Intellectual in Auschwitz', setting his own uses of culture against Jean Améry's damning aphorism 'no bridge led from death in Auschwitz to *Death in Venice*'.[15] Levi agrees in large part with Améry here, confirming that cultural baggage was indeed of little practical use in orienting oneself or understanding: 'La ragione, l'arte, la poesia non aiutano a decifrare il luogo da cui esse sono state bandite' (I. 1103; 'Reason, art, poetry cannot help to decipher a place from which they have been banished'). Thus such residues were to be set alongside those resurgent, involuntary memories of home and family which one could never entirely suppress but which it was wise to avoid. However, following the pattern established above, Levi sees a duty in using these memories to forge a displaced, oblique route to some sort of value and understanding: 'A me, la cultura è stata utile; non sempre, a volte forse per vie sotterranee ed impreviste, ma mi ha servito e forse mi ha salvato' (I. 1100; 'culture was of use to me: not always, and perhaps in subterranean and unpredictable ways, but it served a purpose, and maybe even saved me'). Remembering Ulysses was a path to both a renewal of

---

[15] J. Améry, *At the Mind's Limits* (London: Granta, 1999; 1st German edition 1966), 16. On Levi and Améry, see N. Wood, 'The Victim's Resentments', in B. Cheyette and L. Marcus, eds., *Modernity, Culture and 'the Jew'* (Cambridge: Polity, 1998), 257–67; A. Stille, 'Introduction', in J. Améry, *At the Mind's Limits* (New York: Schocken, 1990), pp. vii–xv; F. Molino Signorini, ' "Uomini fummo". . . Riflessioni su Primo Levi e Jean Améry', *Rassegna mensile di Israel*, 57/3 (Sept.–Dec. 1991), 463–78.

a sense of selfhood—'salvandolo [il passato] dall'oblio e fortifi-
cando la mia identità . . . un modo insomma di ritrovare me stesso'
(I. 1100–1; 'saving [the past] from oblivion and strengthening my
identity . . . in short, a way of rediscovering myself')—and to at
least a mirage of communal understanding and memories: thus
Jean il Pikolo is the real human hero of the episode, since his intuition that there is something more than Dante being evoked here
charges the episode with poignant value.

The core of Ulysses' speech which, almost by accident, seems
to provide a momentary revelation for Levi and Jean links with a
second, seminal instance in Levi's work of the conjunction
between ethics, memory and writing. Not surprisingly, perhaps,
one of the terzinas from Dante that Levi manages to remember
perfectly is the most famous of them all, Ulysses' appeal to the
moral dignity and prowess of being human: 'Considerate la vostra
semenza: | Fatti non foste a viver come bruti, | Ma per seguir
virtute e conoscenza' ('Consider well the seed that gave you birth.
| You were not made to live your lives as brutes, | but to be
followers of worth and knowledge') (*Inferno* XXVI. 118–20; tr. A.
Mandelbaum). The incitement speaks directly to the two prisoners who have all but lost their human dignity, all but become
'bruti'. But it also represents an appeal to an atavistic humanity
('considerate la vostra semenza'). And both this idea and the very
term 'considerate' take us back once more to the poem 'Shemà',
where the same imperative (and its cognate 'meditate') is,
precisely, an imperative that sets up the communication between
text and reader, or humanity at large, as an ethical obligation. By
comparison with the prayer on which 'Shemà' the poem is closely
based, we can see that the obligation shared between reader and
writer is also, indeed is always, an obligation to memory.

The source of the poem is the prayer at the heart of the Jewish
faith, taken initially from Deut. 6: 4–7. The prayer opens with the
central monotheistic declaration: 'Hear O Israel, the Lord is Our
God, the Lord is One.' But the rest is taken up almost entirely with
an injunction to memory, to the recording and passing down of this
single truth: paraphrasing, 'write these words on your heart, teach
them to your children and repeat them when you are in your house,
and when you are walking, when you are in your beds [dreams] and
when you rise. And bind them on your arm and between your eyes
to remember. And write them on the door-posts of your home and

on your gates.' Levi's poem too moves from the quiddity of 'this has been' (the equivalent of the declaration of God's unity, the founding truth) to the hard tangible incision of its setting down and our obligation to integrate it with our everyday, 'ordinary' lives:

> Vi comando queste parole.
> Scolpitele nel vostro cuore
> Stando in casa andanda per via,
> Coricandovi alzandovi;
> Ripetelele ai vostri figli.

(I command these words to you. Etch them into your heart | at home walking down the street, | going to bed getting up; | Repeat them to your children.) (I. 3)[16]

The ethical turn from involuntary to voluntary memory is built in part on another, even more familiar dyad, that of body and mind. Levi is far from unique amongst Holocaust survivors in feeling particularly traumatized by the absence of the victims' bodies, and thus the radical difficulty of any act of mourning or memorial. In 'Nel parco', a short story from *Vizio di forma* (I. 671–80),[17] Levi addresses the absence of the body and its relation to memory obliquely, through a fantasy treatment of literary fame: he imagines all fictional characters living in a park where they survive only as long as they remain in the collective memory of the real world. At the end of the story, the protagonist, Antonio Casella, finds his body slowly but inexorably fading away, until it is all but dispersed into light and wind, 'la sua memoria estinta e la sua testimonianza compiuta' (I. 680; 'his memory extinguished, and his testimony complete'). Literary memory, like historical memory, is a sort of afterlife founded on the transmission of memory to others. Memory's duty is to preserve itself and transmit itself and to link itself to a present beyond the fading of physical traces. The problematic point at which memory meets history—hinted at at the start of this chapter—ultimately emerges as a defining endpoint for the ethical memory Levi strives for in his work.

---

[16] On memory as incision, see also the imagery of wax in the poem 'Agli amici' (II. 623), discussed in Chapter 10 below.
[17] On 'Nel parco' and Levi's Holocaust work, see F. Cereja, 'Contre l'oubli', in Levi, *Le Devoir de mémoire*, 73–81; I. Rosato, 'Primo Levi: sondaggi intertestuali', *Autografo*, 6, NS 17 (June 1989), 31–43 [32–4].

The same issue governs a masterly work of Holocaust mourning and melancholy, Giorgio Bassani's *Il giardino dei Finzi Contini*:[18] the author and narrator of that book is thrown back upon his memories of his childhood love Micol Finzi Contini during an innocuous Sunday afternoon outing to some Etruscan tombs near Rome. Why, asks a young child in the car on the way home, are we less sad about the dead Etruscans than about other dead people? Because we see the tomb, and their homes and way of life preserved in it, but not them. But, reflects the author, what about the almost empty and forgotten family tomb of the Finzi Contini, all killed in some unknown camp? Levi returns to the same issue in his 1978 poem 'La bambina di Pompei' (II. 549), in which the famous preserved, incinerated body of a girl in Pompeii allows the visitors to relive her fear and anguish. But, Levi reflects, no body remains to help us remember Anne Frank or a girl from Hiroshima. He ends with a plea to politicians to pause before destroying the world in a nuclear holocaust, echoing both 'Il canto di Ulisse' and 'Shemà': 'Prima di premere il dito, fermatevi e considerate' ('Before you push the button, pause and consider well'). The appeal is to a consciousness of history and to a recognition of the humanity of the individual and the individuality of the human being, even in her exemplarity. In the broad sweep of its uses of history, the poem forges a bond between Levi's ethical uses of memory and the historical consciousness contained within his work: history returns as itself prone to trauma and loss, to fading along with memory, as in 'Nel parco'. The duty of memory for Levi is to invent the possibility of a collective history after the loss of testimonial memory, through and beyond the evidence of the senses, since, as Semprun puts it: 'Un jour prochain, pourtant, personne n'aura plus le souvenir réel de cette odeur: ce ne sera plus qu'une phrase, une référence littéraire, une idée d'odeur. Inodore, donc' ('One day soon, no one will any longer have the real memory of that smell: it will be no more than a phrase, a literary reference, an idea of odour. And so, odourless').[19]

---

[18] G. Bassani, *Il giardino dei Finzi Contini* (Milan: Mondadori, 1980; 1st edition 1962), 7–13. On Levi and Bassani, see D. Camilleri, 'Écriture et responsabilité: Giorgio Bassani et Primo Levi', in P. Momigliano Levi and R. Gorris, eds., *Primo Levi testimone e scrittore della storia* (Florence: La Giuntina, 1999), 111–31.

[19] Semprun, *L'Écriture*, p. 302.

3

DISCRETION, OR LANGUAGE AND SILENCE

A time to stay silent and a time to speak.

(Ecclesiastes 3: 7)

Chapter 2 began with a recent tendency in Holocaust writing to draw on a rather clichéd topos of memory as a marker of solemnity, arguing that Levi enacts a form of memory that is made denser and more difficult by its ethical dimension. We can usefully begin this chapter in much the same manner. There is a related, perhaps even more solemn topos about the experience of the Holocaust and the writing of it which, like all such topoi, contains a kernel of truth but also a deadening and simplifying reduction of the truth.[1] It relates to the very real and profound difficulty in finding words and images to convey the sheer extremity of horror realized in the Final Solution and experienced by each individual who fell victim to it. At its noblest, it has been shaped by rhetoricians like George Steiner into a ritual lament for the dead:

As in some Borges fable, the only completely decent 'review' [of books such as Wiesel's *La Nuit*] would be to re-copy the book, line by line, pausing at the names of the dead and the names of the children as the orthodox scribe pauses, when recopying the Bible, at the hallowed name of God. Until we know many of the words by *heart* (knowledge deeper than mind) and could repeat a few at the break of morning to remind ourselves that we live *after*, that the end of the day may bring inhuman trial or a remembrance stranger than death.[2]

---

[1] See Levi on 'Stereotypes' (*I sommersi e i salvati*, II. 1109–23) and Chapter 9 below, on 'common sense'.

[2] George Steiner, 'Postscript', in *Language and Silence* (London: Faber and Faber, 1985; 1st edition 1967), 180–93 [193].

Steiner's copyist has not quite surrendered to silence, but the topos in its more vacuously pious usages has moved in that direction. It is perhaps most familiar to us by now in its pithy paradoxical forms: to write about the Holocaust is to (attempt to) 'express the inexpressible', 'say the unsayable', to step beyond the bounds of meaningful communication in language.[3] One can imagine Levi's response to the paralysis induced by the bare assertion of such oxymorons would be akin to his reformulation of Adorno's over-quoted and distorted dictum that there can be no poetry after Auschwitz: 'dopo Auschwitz non si può fare poesia se non su Auschwitz' ('after Auschwitz there can be no poetry except poetry about Auschwitz').[4] But Levi's relationship to questions of language and silence in Holocaust writing is more complex than this might suggest. There are moments when Levi leans towards a Steineresque theological rhetoric, just as there are Adornian moments also; and indeed, Levi at times acknowledged a core of truthfulness even to the most inertia-inducing and insurmountable of paradoxes of ineffability. This chapter looks once again at questions of language and silence in Levi, not in order to rehash worn topoi, but rather, as with memory, to see Levi sensitizing us to the ethical dimensions of the question, probing the limits to language and also the value of silence in what this chapter will read as an exercise in discretion.

Ineffability has, of course, a long pedigree as a rhetorical resource in transcendental and visionary literature, a tradition epitomized in the European canon by Dante's *Commedia*—'Trasumanar significar per verbo | non si porìa' (*Paradiso* I. 70–1)—and revisited in a modernist, nihilistic idiom by figures such as Samuel Beckett—'nothing to express . . . no power to

---

[3] For a recent example, A. Leak and G. Paizis, eds., *The Holocaust and the Text. Speaking the Unspeakable* (London: Macmillan, 2000) and the hostile review attacking the tendency by Michael Bernstein, 'Unspeakable no more', *Times Literary Supplement*, 5061 (3 Mar. 2000), 7–8 (and subsequent correspondence on 14 and 21 Apr. 2000). Gillian Rose has eloquently attacked this tendency as 'Holocaust piety', which needs to be replaced by 'Holocaust ethnography' (G. Rose, 'Beginnings of the Day: Fascism and Representation', in *Mourning Becomes the Law. Philosophy and Representation* (Cambridge: Cambridge University Press, 1996), 41–62 [41–8]). See also P. Haidu, 'The Dialectics of Unspeakability: Language, Silence and the Narratives of Desubjectification', in S. Friedlander, ed., *Probing the Limits of Representation* (Cambridge, Mass.: Harvard University Press, 1992), 277–99.

[4] P. Levi, *Conversazioni e interviste 1963–1987*, ed. M. Belpoliti (Turin: Einaudi, 1997), 137.

express, no desire to express, together with the obligation to express'.[5] Despite the network of connections that might bind all three of Levi, Dante, and Beckett together—Dante's impact on both the others was immense, and conversely, Beckett's mapping of the void has been read convincingly as at the very least inconceivable without the Holocaust[6]—Levi, always the antimodernist, is closer to a Dantesque rhetoric of silence than to Beckett's, even if only to that part of Dante's rhetoric that can be secularized and put to use as rhetoric. Dante's *Paradiso* moves in a crescendo of ever more rapt images of the unsayability, the paradoxical inexpressibility of the Godhead, the circle that cannot be but is squared (*Paradiso* XXXIII. 133–4). But, crucially, Dante knows that he is both stating a truth and creating its rhetorical opposite. He is saying God and reaching for transcendence even as he erases Him in human language: his rhetoric is meant to leave us on the threshold of exactly what it seems to deny us. Dante's *secular* mission, after all, is to share his goal, his journey with his reader. Similarly (in rhetorical terms at least) with writing about the extreme suffering of the Holocaust in Levi: to some extent the experience is unsayable, but in truth to say as much alongside narratives of events, experiences, and histories of it is to bring us to a point where it is imaginable, even if we do not quite imagine it precisely and wholly as it was. It is made imaginable even if not imagined. It is only by acknowledging the rhetorical force of this paradox stripped of its theologizing bent (Beckett's version is in reality more mystical than Levi's) that we can properly unmask the defining difficulty of the Holocaust, otherwise shrouded in mysticism: not in the telling of it but in the living of it, as Jorge Semprun neatly expresses it: 'Non pas que l'expérience vécue soit indicible. Elle a été invivable, ce qui est tout autre chose' ('Not that the experience lived through is unsayable. It was unlivable which is quite a different matter').[7]

[5] S. Beckett and G. Duthuit, 'Three Dialogues' (1949), in M. Esslin, ed., *Samuel Beckett* (Englewood Cliffs, NJ: Prentice Hall, 1965), 16–22 [17].
[6] See, for example, P. Hawkins and A. Howland Schotter, eds., *Ineffability. Naming the Unnamable from Dante to Beckett* (New York: AMS Press, 1984).
[7] J. Semprun, *L'Écriture ou la vie* (Paris: Gallimard, 1994), p. 23; and cf. 'On peut toujours tout dire, en somme. L'ineffable dont on nous rebattra les oreilles n'est qu'alibi. Ou signe de paresse' (ibid.; 'One can always say everything, in the end. The ineffable they will harp on about is merely an alibi. Or a sign of laziness'). G. Agamben compares the notion of 'unsayability' to a form of mysticism, a form of 'silent worship, as of a god' (*Quel*

Levi, then, has little time or patience for the more grandiose and all-encompassing declarations of ineffability—language is rooted in failure; it is always saying the unsayable; the Holocaust, like the human condition, is beyond words; communication is impossible—and he does not hesitate to say so, in a much-quoted passage from the essay in *I sommersi e i salvati* on, precisely, 'Communication':

Salvo casi di incapacità patologica, comunicare si può e si deve. . . . Negare che comunicare si può è falso: si può sempre. Rifiutare di comunicare è colpa. (II. 1059–60)
(Except in cases of pathological incapacity we can and must communicate. . . . To deny that we can communicate is false: we always can. To refuse to communicate is [morally] wrong.)

At the same time, there is a real rhetorical force to be felt in the deployment of the paradox in a qualified mode, one that sees language as ordinarily a practical, working product of and means to human communication creating dialogue and community as it goes, which was violently disabled both in the camps and in speaking about them afterwards. In this second sense, the Holocaust is seen as having shattered communities of language, whether between victims or between victim and bystander or reader. Levi, who, perhaps more than any other writer-survivor of the Holocaust, put language at the centre of his account of the camps,[8] embraces this form of crisis in language from the very earliest pages of *Se questo è un uomo*—with, however, a rider that is crucial for our understanding of his ethics, that its foundation in rhetoric be acknowledged. To say that aspects of the *Lager* lie beyond expression in language is more rhetorical topos, more a form of hyperbole, than a moral topos or a watertight statement of a truth. It is designed to produce a powerful response and a heightened alertness

che resta di Auschwitz (Turin: Bollati Boringhieri, 1998), 30). On the 'unsayable' as a vector of transmission, rather than a literal obligation to silence, see J. M. Chaumont as quoted in A. Bravo and D. Jalla, eds., *Una misura onesta* (Milan: Franco Angeli, 1994), 36.

[8] A. Epstein, 'Primo Levi and the Language of Atrocity', *Bulletin for the Society for Italian Studies*, 20 (1987), 31–8; S. L. Gilman, 'To Quote Primo Levi: "If You Don't Speak Yiddish, You're Not a Jew" ', in *Inscribing the Other* (Lincoln: University of Nebraska Press, 1991), 293–316; J. Woolf, *The Memory of the Offence. Primo Levi's 'If This is a Man'* (Market Harborough: University Texts/Hull Italian Texts, 1996), 29–38. On Levi's extraordinarily rich fascination with languages and symbols and the games that can be played with them, see S. Bartezzaghi, 'Cosmichimiche', in M. Belpoloti, ed., *Primo Levi* (Milan: Marcos y Marcos, Riga 13, 1997), 267–314.

in an addressee—in us—even as it denies the possibility of saying what it wants to say.

There are three essential, climactic moments in *Se questo è un uomo* when Levi has recourse to a concise and powerful rhetoric of ineffability. Indeed, these moments are climactic by very dint of their declaration of language's failure, such is the rhetorical force of the topos. But in each case, the rhetoric is there to point to another dimension of language, in which communication can occur, in which dialogue and ethical meditation can be instigated and sensitivities honed. The first and briefest of the three comes at the dramatic peak of the terrible sequence describing the arrival of Levi's train at Auschwitz and its impact on the bewildered and exhausted 'passengers':

per la prima volta ci siamo accorti che la nostra lingua manca di parole per esprimere questa offesa, la demolizione di un uomo. (I. 20)
(for the first time we realized that our language has no words to describe this offence, the demolition of a man.)

The declaration is a moving and lapidary one, but there are hints that it is more than the surrender to silence that it might seem. The phrase 'la demolizione di un uomo' is a clinical and lucid statement of the book's very core mission (announced also in its title); and the term 'offesa' will become a seminal term in Levi's lexicon and one that others have adopted as a simple, powerful, and unburdened word for expressing the inhumanity of the Holocaust.[9] In other words, the topos of ineffability that precedes these terms serves as a marker, a heightener and even qualifier of their impact; it is true to a degree and felt as such, but not quite a self-standing truth and certainly not an invitation to a Wittgensteinian silence ('whereof one cannot speak thereof one must be silent').[10] It alerts

---

[9] See, for example, *La tregua*, I. 206 or 'La memoria dell'offesa' in *I sommersi e i salvati*, II. 1006–16; and, beyond Levi (but of the many influenced by him), A. Bravo and D. Jalla, eds., *La vita offesa. Storia e memoria dei Lager nazisti nei racconti di duecento sopravvissuti* (Milan: Franco Angeli, 1986); or M. Amis, *Time's Arrow. Or The Nature of the Offence* (London: Jonathan Cape, 1991).

[10] *Tractatus Logico-Philosophicus* (1922). In his discussion in 'Stereotipi' of why more Jews did not flee Germany in the 1930s (II. 1118–23), Levi sees in part a typical Germanic rigidity as captured by the proverb 'Nicht sein kann, was nicht sein darf', but also in part a human resistance to upheaval in the face of imminent catastrophe. Similarly with silence, Levi rejects the rigid exclusions of language's limits, but accepts another, more humane form of silence (see below).

us to the problems of communication and language, but also traces paths towards possible solutions, in language.

Similarly, in the second instance—an extraordinary passage from the chapter 'Ottobre 1944'—we find Levi simultaneously declaring the failure of language and struggling to render or translate the 'inexpressible' reality into descriptive detail:

> Come questa nostra fame non è la sensazione di chi ha saltato un pasto, cosí il nostro modo di aver freddo esigerebbe un nome particolare. Noi diciamo 'fame', diciamo 'stanchezza', 'paura', e 'dolore', diciamo 'inverno', e sono altre cose. Sono parole libere, create e usate da uomini liberi che vivevano, godendo e soffrendo nelle loro case. Se i Lager fossero durati piú a lungo, un nuovo aspro linguaggio sarebbe nato; e di questo si sente il bisogno per spiegare cosa è faticare l'intera giornata nel vento, sotto zero, con solo indosso camicia, mutande, giacca e brache di tela, e in corpo debolezza e fame e consapevolezza della fine che viene. (I. 119–20)

(Just as our hunger is not the feeling of having missed a meal, so our way of being cold would require a new term to describe it. We say 'hunger', we say 'tiredness', 'fear' and 'pain' but they are something else. They are free words, created and used by free men who lived in their own homes, in happiness and in suffering. If the camps had lasted longer, a new harsh language would have been born; and that is what is needed to explain what it means to labour for a whole day in the wind, below freezing, with nothing on but a shirt, pants, a jacket and canvas trousers, and nothing inside but weakness and hunger and the knowledge that the end is near.)

Confronted with the inadequacy of our banal lexicon of everyday life, Levi reaches for distinctions, qualifications, and details, moves towards a 'new language' rather than towards silence. To combat the ghost of the 'bitter new language' almost born from the *Lager*, Levi reinvents or stretches our own language to accommodate a new awareness of horror. Not, it should be said, by an aping of the grotesque chaos of language and languages in the camps, as some have done, but rather by a direct return to that everyday language, to refine it with simple detail and descriptive concision, with a realization that every word and phrase is more extreme and less recognizable than it might seem.[11]

---

[11] Levi's difficult encounters with both Paul Celan and Franz Kafka, as reader and, in the latter case, as translator, could be said to have revolved around precisely this issue: does one adopt the language of fear and chaos to render them, or does one figure them in as

The conjunction between this rhetorical topos and Levi's ethics is clearer still in the third, much-quoted, climactic declaration of language's inadequacies, from the end of a chapter whose (ironic) title announces its importance to the ethical dimension of the book, 'Al di qua del bene e del male':

> Vorremmo ora invitare il lettore a riflettere, che cosa potessero significare in Lager le nostre parole 'bene' e 'male', 'giusto' e 'ingiusto': giudichi ognuno, in base al quadro che abbiamo delineato e agli esempi sopra esposti, quanto del nostro comune mondo morale potesse sussistere al di qua del filo spinato. (I. 82)

(We would now like to invite the reader to reflect on what our words 'good' and 'evil', 'right' and 'wrong' could possibly mean in the *Lager*; let each of you judge, on the basis of the picture we have sketched and of the examples given above, how much of our shared moral world could survive on this side of the barbed wire.)

The rhetorical power of pushing at the limits of language, questioning its capacity to express our core values, is fully in place here. But the dynamic in the detail of the sentence—the invitation to careful reflection and judgement, the call for thoughtful adjustment of our knowledge in the light of new data, the appeal to a fluid notion of a 'shared moral world'—is at one with Levi's open, outward-projected, and far from mute or inexpressible ethics. The consequence of this exhortative sentence is not the abandonment of the terms 'good' and 'evil', 'just' and 'unjust', but their sensitive readjustment. Our shared moral world is shaken, changed forever, but intact. And we have the right, the duty to reflect upon it and reshape it, in language. The sentence is an invitation to flex and stretch the ethical muscles of our language, not an invitation to the silent inertia of actual ineffability.

In this aspect of *Se questo è un uomo* we can see the origin of Levi's commitment to speaking in public about his experiences after his return to Italy, as part of a determination to encourage dialogue and considered historical awareness of the Holocaust. As Marco Belpoliti has argued, Levi's career as a public speaker and later interviewee stands as a crucial third strand with his other careers as

precise, sensitive, and accessible a language as possible? Levi felt distinctly uneasy about the former (modernist) solution: see his reservations on Kafka and Celan (and Ezra Pound) in 'Tradurre Kafka' (II. 939–41) and 'Dello scrivere oscuro' (II. 676–82); and A. Rudolf, *At an Uncertain Hour. Primo Levi's War against Oblivion* (London: Menard Press, 1990), 41–9.

chemist and as writer, interacting with and conditioning both of these.[12] As Levi says in *I sommersi e i salvati*, survivors fall generally into two categories, 'quelli che raccontano' and 'quelli che tacciono' (II. 1109; 'those who tell their story . . . those who stay silent'), and he is decidedly one of the former. His rejection of silence as constituting a position from which to understand or respond to the Holocaust is a cardinal feature of his ethical universe, since working out and working through problems in language are part and parcel of his belief in practice, in the active life, and his distrust of passivity and turning a blind eye. Furthermore, it is what makes his 'ordinary virtues' work both ethically and metaethically, since he is constantly concerned with, fascinated by the problem of what language to use to tackle problems, ethical and practical. As with the ethical turn in his uses of memory (Chapter 2), this commitment to language is part of a resistance to the pathologizing of the survivor, to seeing himself as subject to rather than actively engaged with his experiences and their significance for all of us. However, his relation to silence is also more complicated than this one-way hostility might suggest. At certain times and in certain ways, precisely because it has been banished as a catch-all response, silence is able to return as a part of that active, practical universe to work in a local sense as an ordinary virtue in its own right. There is, in other words, 'a time to stay silent and a time to speak', and the capacity to choose between these (and by extension to make other ethical–linguistic choices) is what we might call discretion.

One further feature of the passages from both 'Ottobre 1944' and 'Al di qua del bene e del male' quoted above can help elucidate this secondary relation to silence in Levi. In both cases, silence is banished and language reclaimed by way of a typically Levian move away from the general and towards the particular and concrete, or rather an expressionistic evocation of the latter. In the first passage, these take the form of flashes of concrete details—the wind and frozen temperature, the clothes, the mix of emotions and physical sensations –that are not so particular as to be idiosyncratic but nor are they the bland categories of the previous sentence—hunger, tiredness, fear, pain, winter. The second passage exhorts us to see the answer in the details almost in the

[12] See M. Belpoliti, 'Io sono un centauro', in Levi, *Conversazioni*, pp. vii–xix.

form of a moral commandment: 'giudichi ognuno, *in base al quadro che abbiamo delineato e agli esempi sopra esposti.*' The unsayable is dismantled by the 'said' (or the 'told', that is, narrative: see Chapter 11). And within the ambit of the 'said', in all its local specificity, the 'unsaid', silence, changes its moral valency. At the level of the particular, the individual, of lived experience and stories, the unspoken can be a necessary token of respect and restraint, a declaration of ethical control over what should and should not be laid bare for all to see.[13]

As in Chapters 1 and 2 above, the founding examples of this virtue of discretion come early on in *Se questo è un uomo*. In particular, three solemn moments in the first chapter, 'Il viaggio', each literally or symbolically marking a mournful farewell to life, show us Levi's discretion at work.

First, at dawn on the day of deportation from Fossoli towards Auschwitz, Levi describes the end of reason, the sort of collective madness brought on by the realization that the journey towards the unknown, towards death is about to begin. Resignation, rebellion, fear, desperation, and nostalgia all jostle in the prisoners' hearts and minds, leading to strange and disturbing results, but here Levi cuts short his account, as if ostentatiously editing himself, ending the sequence in a hanging silence: 'Molte cose furono allora fra noi dette e fatte: ma di queste è bene che non resti memoria' (I. 10; 'Many things were said and done between us at that time: but of these it is right that no memory remains').[14]

Shortly afterwards, as the train crosses the Alps and leaves Italy (with Levi's typical attention for borders, sites of transition), a silence descends, as though a bell were tolling or a rite being enacted, an acknowledgement of the inadequacy of words at such a time of symbolic passage into exile, beyond life itself: 'Passammo il Brennero alle dodici del secondo giorno, e tutti si alzarono in piedi, ma nessuno disse parola' (I. 12; 'We crossed over the

---

[13] Alberto Cavaglion points out a parallel between Levi's coded silence and the notion of 'writing between the lines' in Leo Strauss's *Persecution and the Art of Writing* (1952) (A. Cavaglion, *Primo Levi e 'Se questo è un uomo'*, 80–5); see also A. Momigliano, 'Ermeneutica e pensiero politico classico in Leo Strauss', in his *Pagine ebraiche* (Turin: Einaudi, 1987), 189–99.

[14] It is worth noting another Dantesque echo here, from early on in the journey of the *Commedia* where Virgil instructs Dante in one of his first stern lessons to ignore the souls of the 'ignavi', too passive to enter either heaven or hell, and pass on: 'non ragionam di loro ma guarda e passa' (*Inferno* III. 151).

Brenner at noon of the second day; everyone stood up, but no one said a word'). At analogous moments of loss of identity later in the book, as explored in Chapter 1, a shared silence and a looking away will mark the passage to new levels of degradation, with the incomprehension and shame that accompanies them.

Finally, as the train journey ends, Levi writes briefly and movingly of his rapport with a woman-friend deported alongside him, who was to die in the camp:

Accanto a me, serrata come me fra corpo e corpo, era stata per tutto il viaggio una donna. Ci conoscevamo da molti anni e la sventura ci aveva colti insieme, ma poco sapevamo l'uno dell'altra. Ci dicemmo allora, nell'ora della decisione, cose che non si dicono fra i vivi. Ci salutammo, e fu breve; ciascuno salutò nell'altro la vita. Non avevamo piú paura. (I. 13) (Next to me, huddled like me between other bodies for the whole journey, had been a woman. We had known each other for many years and misfortune had thrown us together, but we knew little one of the other. At that time, at the moment of truth, we told each other things that living beings do not tell. We said our farewells and it was soon over; we each said farewell to life in the other. We were no longer afraid.)

There is more than one dimension to Levi's discretion here. First he chooses not to name the woman and to do no more than hint at an uncertain intimacy, perhaps desire, in the face of fear. Both these features run through his *œuvre*. Levi was much concerned with the problems of naming real names in his autobiographical writings, with the risks of offending people by turning them into 'characters' or misremembering them and with choosing the time and the place to tell the stories of the living.[15] Similarly, as several critics have pointed out, Levi exercises extreme caution in crossing the boundary into areas of emotional and sexual intimacy, in part as a result of a personal inclination to timid reserve on such matters,[16] but also—and certainly in the case of the 'donna' of 'Il

[15] See, for example, Levi, *The Voice of Memory*, 82, 148–51. The woman in the train was Levi's close friend Vanda Maestro. On Vanda, Primo, and the group deported together with them from Fossoli, see Luciana Nissim's account, 'Ricordi della casa dei morti', in L. Nissim and P. Lewinska, *Donne contro il mostro* (Turin: Vincenzo Ramella Editore, 1946), 18–58; later in *Diario*, 4/14 (7–13 Apr. 1999) and 15 (14–20 Apr. 1999); and cf. A. Guadagni, 'La memoria del bene. Luciana Nissim', *Diario*, 2/8 (26 Feb.–4 Mar. 1997), 14–19.

[16] On Levi's reserve and shyness, see G. Poli and G. Calcagno, *Echi di una voce perduta* (Milan: Mursia, 1992), 216–18; *The Voice of Memory*, 16, 140–1; M. Cicioni, *Primo Levi. Bridges of Knowledge* (Oxford: Berg, 1995), 72; *Il sistema periodico*, I. 845–8. Levi was much less inhibited in some of his science-fiction stories which at times vividly evoke magically or bio-scientifically altered forms of sexuality (see Chapter 8 note 13).

viaggio'—as a further instance of showing due respect when dragging others into his written world. But there is a larger dimension to the discretion displayed here: Levi also refuses—part in shame and part in defiance—to articulate the 'language of the dead' brutally acquired in the course of the train journey, just as he will refuse later to articulate the 'new bitter language' of the *Lager*, preferring instead to mark the human consequences of its acquisition, in resignation but also with a certain courage, tapping into an archetypal language found also in his poetry. Similarly, in *Se non ora, quando?*, he will have the narrator explicitly refuse to describe the massacre at Novoselki: 'Non è per descrivere stragi che questa storia sta raccontando se stessa' (II. 283; 'It is not to describe massacres that this story is telling itself').

In these ways, Levi achieves an extraordinary rhetorical feat through economy of language, at one and the same time touching us with the profound intimacy of the memory and terrifying us with the universal resonance of the moment. The same power achieved through marking silence and shame is found at another defining moment of transition, before and after the liberation of the camp by Russian soldiers: before, Levi reaches a new nadir of degradation, forced to sleep next to a corpse—'non è uomo chi, *perso ogni ritegno*, divide un letto con un cadavere' (I. 168; emphasis added; 'he who, all restraint lost, shares a bed with a corpse, is not a man'); afterwards, in the first pages of *La tregua*, the soldiers' silence is eloquent:

Non salutavano, non sorridevano; apparivano oppressi, oltre che da pietà, da *un confuso ritegno, che sigillava le loro bocche*, e avvinceva i loro occhi allo scenario funereo. Era la stessa vergogna a noi ben nota . . . quella che il giusto prova davanti alla colpa commessa da altrui, e gli rimorde che esista, che sia stata introdotta irrevocabilmente nel mondo delle cose che esistono. . . . (I. 206; emphasis added)[17]
(They neither greeted us, nor smiled; they seemed to be suffering not only from pity but also from a confused restraint that sealed their lips and drew their eyes to the funereal scene. It was that shame we knew so well . . . the shame of the just man when faced with the guilt committed by others, whose existence he regrets, the fact that it has irrevocably entered the world and all that exists in it. . . .)

---

[17] The term 'il giusto' recalls André Schwarz-Bart's powerful Holocaust novel *Le Dernier des justes* (Paris: Seuil, 1959).

The three moments of discreet silence from 'Il viaggio' set up a sort of ethical-rhetorical right to silence, both at moments of suffering and as one recalls it. And this silence stands for more than mere questions of language, however central the latter might be. They preserve, or offer a token of the humane right to preserve the privacy and intimacy of the individual. In this way, they amount to another form of resistance against the dissolution of the individual inherent within the camp system. Thus, when in *La tregua* Levi meets again by chance Flora, a prostitute who had helped him and Alberto in the camp, he is moved *not* to speak to her, in order not to reawaken the humiliations of that time: 'Non mi feci riconoscere da Flora, per carità verso di lei e verso me stesso' (I. 352; 'I didn't show Flora who I was, out of a sense of charity both for her and for myself'). In the very act of Levi's discretion, the relations between two individuals or a group of individuals are preserved as properly private (indeed, for Levi, the integrity of the individual depends on the encounter with others, as we saw in Chapter 1). And of course, in the camp, such relations are worn away. Respect for privacy is null and the individual is subsumed in a faceless mass. The indiscreet and indiscriminate practice of exposure and making public is a cardinal feature of the camp system: the nudity (in showers, in latrines, and in the ultimate violation, of the dead body) (II. 1079–80), the complete elimination of intimacy and private space of any kind, the indistinct physical features of every starved, shaven, numbered, tattooed, deindividualized prisoner are among its most horrific aspects, all first recorded in the opening chapters of *Se questo è un uomo*. Similarly the bawled, babelic languages of the camps, so acutely recorded by Levi, leave little room for discreet silence, and all too much time for shameful, head-bowed wordlessness. All these leave no space and no time for discretion, indeed they leave no distinct, discrete selfhood at all.

In taking the significance of moments of discretion beyond issues of language to the core questions of selfhood, we can see larger resonances for the notion of discretion itself. Above, the *Lager* was described as both 'indiscreet and indiscriminate' and this pairing points us to a bond between two related, near homonymous 'virtues' figured in Levi: discretion as prudence or tact, on the one hand, and discreteness or discrimination, on the other, as the acknowledgement of difference and the capacity to distinguish that is at the core of our engagement with others and with the world, of our capacity to make judgements, moral and otherwise.[18] This bond allows us to find paths out of the tortuous and tortured field of language and memory of the Holocaust, towards the interrogation of the ordinary world that also subtends Levi's work. As with other Levian virtues founded in a dialectical encounter with their utter antithesis in Auschwitz, Levi's discreet silence looks forward to an extended parabola of enquiry into individual, human choices and actions in the rest of his work. Discrimination is another term to synthesize Levi's practical, fine-tuned ethics or intelligence, which will be at the heart of Part II below, just as it also is at the heart of his vision of chemistry. Here, in anticipation of later chapters, we can follow one strand of his investment in practical intelligence that maintains the bond between it and a certain form of restrained silence.

There is a series of (male) characters in Levi's work, in both his fiction and his autobiographical memoirs, who win his admiration by embodying those virtues of ordinary, practical wisdom, the essence of his applied ethics. They each display flaws and seem to resist resolutely, in their very characters, his tendency to idealize them (the resistance is part and parcel of why Levi admires them); but in so far as Levi has heroes, they are to be found in these patient, restrained, instinctively discriminating figures. Given what we have seen above, it might now seem more than mere coincidence or cliché that each of these men is also taciturn, quick to act and slow to talk, given to silence. Perhaps the two most important of the series are Sandro and Lorenzo: Sandro, or 'Sandro il taciturno' as Levi calls him, is Primo's chemistry and mountaineering companion during his university years ('Ferro', *Il sistema periodico*, I. 771–81), a young man hidden behind an 'involucro di ritegno' (I. 773; 'shell of reserve') who nevertheless imparts a series of lessons in inner determination, self-realization, and maturity that makes him an object of moving admiration for Levi. Integral to Sandro's 'heroism' is his instinctive anti-rhetoricism: 'non era della razza di quelli che fanno le cose per poterle raccontare (come me): non amava le parole grosse, anzi, le parole . . . parlava come nessuno parlava, diceva solo il nocciolo delle cose' (I. 777; 'he

---

[18] On distinction as a form of intelligence, moral and otherwise, in Levi, see E. Ferrero, 'Introduzione', in *Primo Levi: un'antologia della critica* (Turin: Einaudi, 1997), pp. xix–xx.

wasn't the kind to do things so that he could talk about them later (like me): he disliked big words, in fact words in general . . . he talked unlike anyone else, he only ever said the nub of the matter'). Similarly, Lorenzo, the Italian manual worker in Monowitz to whom, Levi says, 'debbo di essere vivo oggi, non tanto per l'aiuto materiale, quanto per avermi costantemente rammentato . . . che ancora esisteva un mondo giusto al di fuori del nostro' (*Se questo è un uomo*, I. 117–18; 'I owe my being alive today, not so much for the material help he gave me, as for his constant reminder . . . that there was still a just world out there beyond our own'), crowns his unassuming, modest heroism with blunt silence:

Lorenzo non parlava quasi mai. Sembrava che di parlare non avesse bisogno; il poco che so di lui l'ho ricavato solo in piccola parte dai suoi scarsi accenni . . . era stato muratore al suo paese e nei dintorni, cambiando spesso padrone perché non aveva un carattere facile; se un capomastro gli faceve un'osservazione, anche con il migliore dei modi, lui non rispondeva, si metteva il cappello e se ne andava. . . .
   Non parlava, ma capiva. Non credo di avergli mai chiesto aiuto . . . Lorenzo faceva tutto da solo.[19]
(Lorenzo almost never said a word. It was as though he did not need to talk; the little that I know about him I picked up only in small part from his scarce comments . . . he had been a bricklayer in his village and the nearby area, always changing boss because he wasn't an easy character to deal with; if a master-builder made an observation, even with the best of intentions, he would not reply, put on his hat, and move on . . .
   He did not speak, but he understood. I don't think I ever asked him for help . . . Lorenzo did everything on his own.)

Elsewhere, Levi sensitizes his characters to know when to speak and when to stay silent, building dialogue and friendship (see Chapter 10) on this form of recognition: for example, Levi himself as a character-interlocutor in *La chiave a stella* who tactfully listens to Faussone's often repetitive, ill-told tales and tells his own stories of Auschwitz and of his chemistry in the interstices of the book;[20]

---

[19] From Levi's moving account of Lorenzo's unhappy return to Italy after the war, 'Il ritorno di Lorenzo', in *Lilìt e altri racconti* (II. 59–66, [61]). Lorenzo's 'pure and uncontaminated' humanity leads Levi to pinpoint this moment as containing 'il senso intimo del libro' ('the intimate meaning of the book') (1973 schools edition of *Se questo è un uomo* (Turin: Einaudi, 1973), edited with notes by Levi himself, p. 161).

[20] See Chapter 11 below on the 'hidden' testimonial dimension of *La chiave a stella* and on the virtue of listening to other people's stories.

or Mendel, whose tortured rapport with the mysterious, haunted Leonid in *Se non ora, quando?* develops falteringly, as each struggles with the traumas of silence, loss, and dislocation:

Mendel non rispose: si rendeva conto che il suo compagno [Leonid] non era di quelli che si guariscono con le parole; forse nessuno che avesse sulla schiena una storia come la sua sarebbe guarito a parole. . . . Per aiutarlo, bisongava capirlo, per capirlo bisognava che lui parlasse, e lui non parlava che cosí, quattro parole e poi silenzio, con lo sguardo che sfuggiva il suo sguardo. . . . Ci vuole pazienza. (II. 256)

(Mendel said nothing: he realized that his companion [Leonid] was not one of those people who gets better with words; perhaps no one carrying around on his back a story like his could be cured with words. . . . To help him, you needed to understand him and to understand him he had to talk, and he only talked like that, a few words and then silence, with his eyes avoiding other eyes. . . . You needed patience.)

As a final example of the wise, taciturn type in Levi, who shuns confession and display and retains a dignified separateness and a capacity to weigh up and judge action discriminatingly, we might cite the leader of the Arunde tribe in 'Verso occidente', one of Levi's 'anthropological' stories in *Vizio di forma* (I. 578–87), who nobly rejects the offer from a Western scientist of a chemical substance that might remove the Arunde instinct to choose suicide over an unfulfilled life. The refusal is clipped and laconic: 'preferiamo la libertà alla droga, e la morte all'illusione' (I. 587; 'we prefer freedom to drugs, and death to illusion').

Finally, it is worth noting Levi humorously turning to the very opposite of discreet silence on occasion. In something of an ironic reprise of the division in *I sommersi e i salvati* between 'quelli che tacciono' and 'quelli che raccontano', he offers us not only strong, silent types like Sandro and Lorenzo but also a series of characters, variously tolerated or mocked, who cannot contain themselves or quite explain themselves, who cannot sustain a dialogue or tell a good story (see Chapter 11). And in an extension with which we are now familiar, this lack of discretion and precision often comes accompanied by a lack of judgement. Faussone in *La chiave a stella*, or one side of him, falls into this category, as do several of the over-zealous scientists in Levi's science fiction (including Walter, the scientist in 'Verso occidente'); but perhaps the most resonant cases of all are several of the German readers of *Se questo è un uomo* whose letters are presented in the last essay of *I sommersi e i salvati*,

'Lettere di tedeschi' (II. 1124–48). These readers, whose reactions Levi realizes he needs above all others, frequently evoke ambivalence in him because they are either too confessional or too keen to elaborate a tortuously forced defence in mitigation. As a result he struggles to enter into dialogue with them. That this lack of discretion and discrimination should be expressed in the writing of letters is a potent reminder of the origin of our discussion in questions of language and the written word. Ethics begins in dialogue, in language, but the value of discretion/discrimination lies in the space it gives beyond or before language, to a constant and careful reflection on whether or not and how to express what we have to express.

4

USE

utile per una vita migliore.
(Manzoni)

In both his ethics and his personal make-up, Levi invariably strikes us as a pragmatist. When he tackles problems, encounters the unfamiliar, follows passions, or simply invents for pleasure, we can almost always trace in the shape of his thinking a pragmatic, constructive, solution-led *Weltanschauung*. A practical, engaged sense of living, working, and writing exudes from his every page and from it emerges a defining feature of his ethics, the commitment to various forms of practical intelligence, what Aristotelians would call 'practical wisdom' or *phronesis*. Aspects of this 'wisdom' will be analysed in some detail in Part II. But prior to it and in many respects parent to it is another characteristic dynamic of his ethics: a penchant found on page after page of his *œuvre* for judging according to the categories of the useful and the useless. As we will see, use turns out to be a flexible and complex value in its own right, but also a tool for measuring the ethical efficacy of other actions and experiences, both in Auschwitz and beyond. This chapter sets out to explore Levi's 'utilitarianism'.

As was noted in the Introduction, Levi inherited a swathe of intellectual values founded in the rationalist Enlightenment and its heirs, a tradition that could be said to include the utilitarianism developed by Bentham, Mill, and others. Indirectly, at least, even his literary affinities confirm this: a great deal links Levi to Alessandro Manzoni (the grandson of Cesare Beccaria, legal philosopher and precursor of Bentham), among whose mottoes for the aim of literature (even as he defended Romanticism) was the phrase 'il vero, *l'utile*, il buono e il *ragionevole*' ('the true, the useful, the good, and the reasonable').[1] And although there is no sense in sticking labels from the history of philosophy on a writer like Levi, who was quite alien to such thinking, there are nevertheless fascinating pointers from within the utilitarian tradition towards Levi's investment in the value of use. Utilitarian ethics revolves around two all-embracing determinants of human action, pain and pleasure, balanced and calculated to achieve its prime goal, maximal happiness (the greatest happiness of the greatest number). In Bentham's words:

Nature has placed mankind under the governance of two sovereign masters, *pain* and *pleasure*. It is for them alone to point out what we ought to do, as well as to determine what we shall do . . . They govern us in all we do, in all we say, in all we think. . . . The *principle of utility* recognizes this subjection and assumes it for the foundation of that system, the object of which is to rear the fabric of felicity by the hands of reason and law.[2]

In the course of his work, Levi is constantly fascinated by the key terms in the utilitarian lexicon—pain, pleasure, happiness, and the more or less 'scientific' calculations to be made between them. From early on in *Se questo è un uomo*, the suffering of the *Lager* is understood and in a sense contained by a crucial insight into the nature of happiness and the human mind:

Tutti scoprono piú o meno presto nella loro vita, che la felicità perfetta non è realizzabile, ma pochi si soffermano invece sulla considerazione opposta: che tale è anche una infelicità perfetta. I momenti che si oppongono alle realizzazioni di entrambi i due stati-limite sono della stessa natura: conseguono dalla nostra condizione umana, che è nemica di ogni infinito. (I. 11)[3]

(Everyone discovers sooner or later in life that perfect happiness is not achievable, but few pause to think also about the opposite consideration:

---

[1] A. Manzoni, 'Sul romanticismo', in *Opere*, vol. II. ed. M. Barbi and F. Ghisalberti (Florence: Sansoni, 1942), 619. For parallels between Levi and Manzoni, see M. Belpoliti, *Primo Levi* (Milan: Bruno Mondadori, 1998), 111–14; G. Borri, *Le divine impurità* (Rimini: Luisé, 1992), 48–9; G. Tesio, *Piemonte letterario dell'otto-novecento* (Rome: Bulzoni, 1991), 230. On Beccaria, it might be worth noting that *I sommersi e i salvati* has an often-forgotten and rather strange subtitle, *I delitti, i castighi, le pene, le impunità*, echoing Beccaria's famous treatise of 1764, *Dei delitti e delle pene*.

[2] J. Bentham, *An Introduction to the Principles of Morals and Legislation* (Oxford: Oxford University Press, 1996, 1st edition 1789), 11.

[3] The terminology of happiness and unhappiness linked to notions of limit and infinity inevitably evoke connections with Leopardi: see Belpoliti, *Primo Levi*, 102–3; M. Lollini, 'Golem', in M. Belpoliti, ed., *Primo Levi* (Milan: Marcos y Marcos, Riga 13, 1997), 354–7.

that so too is perfect unhappiness. The moments which prevent the realization of both these limit-states are of the same nature: they derive from our human condition which is hostile to all extremes.)

A sense of the complicated balance of happiness and unhappiness leads Levi here to a fundamental statement of an 'Aristotelian' ethical principle—the rejection of extremes—as we will see further below and in Chapter 5. Similarly, when he turns his attention to the balance of pain and pleasure, Levi elucidates some of his most important ethical concerns. If we return to the Arunde tribe of the short story 'Verso occidente', mentioned near the end of the previous chapter, we find them living and ultimately choosing not to live on the basis of, precisely, a clinical weighing up of the pros and cons, the pleasures and pains of life:

Ognuno di loro veniva educato, fin dall'infanzia, a stimare la vita esclusivamente in termini di piacere e di dolore, valutandosi nel computo, naturalmente, anche i piaceri e i dolori provocati nel prossimo dal comportamento di ognuno. Quando, a giudizio di ogni singolo, il bilancio tendeva a diventare stabilmente negativo, quando cioè il cittadino riteneva di patire e produrre piú dolori che gioie, veniva invitato ad un'aperta discussione davanti al concilio degli anziani, e se il suo guidizio trovava conferma, la conclusione [la morte] veniva incoraggiata e agevolata. (I. 585)

(Each one of them was educated, from childhood, to weigh up life exclusively in terms of pain and pleasure, feeding into the calculation, of course, also the pleasures and pains caused to others by their behaviour. When, in the judgement of each individual, the balance tended steadily towards the negative, that is when the citizen felt he was suffering, producing more sorrow than joy, he would be invited to open a debate before the council of the elders, and if his judgement was confirmed, the conclusion [death] was encouraged and facilitated.)

This system of deciding the outcome of individual lives has a certain nobility for Levi, and its clarity of thinking and consequentialist action is clearly something he sets in contrast with the hubris of Walter, the scientist who thinks he can cure unhappiness in them through a chemical substance. But in a sense, both the Arunde and Walter share a flaw, which complicates the picture of Levi as either the pure calculating utilitarian or the pure, rationalist scientist: both are rigid and absolutist in their attitudes, too systematic, lacking any element of doubt. In the story, both face annihilation as a result. Between them stands its real heroine,

Walter's companion Anna, who has a more humane and vulnerable belief in the provisional means of our own making that we all find to combat the onset of despair. This points us towards a vital general principle in Levi: a consistent hostility to rigid systems and certainties, to summary calculations even when, as in this case, they are pointed in the direction of values he tendentially would share.[4] As so often, it is a principle established first in *Se questo è un uomo*, in this instance in the intense initiatory encounter with the officer Steinlauf. Steinlauf, like the Arunde, is proud and noble: he teaches Levi a precious lesson on the need to wash—even in filth, even if one has no energy to stand—in order to retain a core human dignity, 'per non cominciare a morire' (I. 35; 'so as not to begin to die'). Levi takes the lesson in good faith, but he is also mistrustful of it for its inflexibility:

Queste cose mi disse Steinlauf, uomo di volontà buona: strane cose al mio orecchio dissueto, intese e *accettate solo in parte*, e mitigate in *una più facile, duttile e blanda dottrina*, quella che da secoli si respira al di qua delle Alpi, e secondo la quale, fra l'altro, *non c'è maggior vanità che sforzarsi di inghiottire interi i sistemi morali elaborati da altri, sotto altro cielo*. No, la saggezza e la virtù di Steinlauf, buone certamente per lui, a me non bastano. Di fronte a questo complicato mondo infero, le mie idee sono confuse; sarà proprio necessario elaborare un sistema e praticarlo? o non sarà più salutare *prendere coscienza di non avere sistema*? (I. 35; emphases added)[5]

(These things Steinlauf said to me, a man of good will: but they were strange to my unaccustomed ears, taken in and accepted only in part, and mitigated by an easier, more flexible and milder doctrine, found in the air on this side of the Alps for many centuries, according to which there is no greater vanity than to struggle to swallow entire moral systems constructed by others, in far off worlds. No, Steinlauf's wisdom and virtue, doubtless ideal for him, were not enough for me. Faced with this complicated, infernal world, my ideas are muddled: is it really necessary to have a system and to put it into action? Wouldn't it be healthier to take stock of the fact that there is no system?)

---

[4] Cf. Bernard Williams on utilitarianism as weakened by its reliance on whatever is 'momentarily quantifiable' and 'commensurable' to facilitate calculation (*Morality* (Cambridge: Cambridge University Press, 1993; 1st edition 1972), 89–90).

[5] See B. Cheyette, 'The Ethical Uncertainty of Primo Levi', in B. Cheyette and L. Marcus, eds., *Modernity, Culture and 'the Jew'* (Cambridge: Polity, 1998), 268–81; and on Steinlauf, see A. Cavaglion, 'La scelta di Gedeone: appunti su Primo Levi e l'ebraismo', *Journal of the Institute of Romance Studies*, 4 (1996), 187–98.

Pain and pleasure shape the moral universe we inhabit for Levi, but not in any systematic or wholly controllable way. Indeed, they are in ambiguous relation to each other, the boundaries between them are blurred. This complex nexus is explored by Levi in some of his most remarkable short stories, such as 'Versamina' (I. 467–76).[6] Emblematically set in the chaos of post-war Germany and echoing in its theme the upturned world of the Nazi camps, 'Versamina' tells of the disastrous scientific experiments of a certain Kleber who discovered a way to convert pain ('il guardiano della vita', 'life's guardian') into pleasure ('lo scopo e il premio della vita', 'life's purpose and prize'), thereby scrambling all the basic instincts of human (and animal) identity in his subjects and all coordinates of their moral compass. The story suggests there is no simple, zero-sum calculation to be made between pain and pleasure, but rather a constant oscillating, a merging and demerging balance between them; and the examination of their movement can lead to insight into our ethical choices and actions, to knowledge and praxis.

As with happiness and unhappiness, pleasure and pain, so with use and uselessness. Levi's utilitarian mindset is never a pure calculation between binary extremes, but it uses a binary shape 'ironically', to show its limitations and to refine it non-systematically. A flexible redefinition of the useful acts as a gateway into and a path through a field of ethical reflection, without laying down any 'ex cathedra' prescriptive lessons or formulae: as he says in his 1986 poem 'Delega', 'Non chiamarci maestri' (II. 624; 'Do not call us teachers'). And 'Versamina' points us to the most common dynamic by way of which Levi works through these reflections, a dynamic of reversal: how can one term turn into the other, pain into pleasure, the useless into the useful? There is a sort of imaginary alchemy at work here (Kleber himself was something of a scientist-cum-magician), through which a certain understanding of utility might transform even the most morally vacant or immoral base metal into a source for ethical reflection. And here, of course, we are drawn back to the source of Levi's ethics in his experience of Auschwitz, the basest metal of all: one could say that the defining limit of Levi's utilitarianism is contained in the

---

[6] See also 'Trattamento di quiescenza' (I. 548–67), 'Knall' (I. 647–50), 'Un testamento' (II. 144–8), and the essay 'Contro il dolore' (II. 673–5), discussed below.

implicit, dangerous question, 'what use (if any) can we make of Auschwitz?' Or rather 'what was or is Auschwitz useful *for/*good *for?*' The question is all the more charged and important because Levi himself, in one of the most powerful essays in *I sommersi e i salvati*, defined the very essence and uniqueness[7] of the Nazi Final Solution as its uselessness, its 'useless violence'.

The essay is worth considering in some detail. 'Violenza inutile' (II. 1073–90)[8] takes us vividly back to the reality of the camps as described in *Se questo è un uomo*. Indeed, in its immediacy, it stands apart from some of the other essays in the book, many of which address issues of *a posteriori* response and retrospection (on memory, shame, the letters from German readers) or mechanisms of the mind and the intellect (communication, shame, the role of the intellectual, stereotypes). 'Violenza inutile' deals directly in suffering, specifically in the peculiar nature of Nazi violence at Auschwitz. Nazi violence is in the first instance to be understood as a cocktail of, on the one hand, specifically German ideology and cultural tradition (II. 1074) and, on the other hand, the mechanisms of power, subjection and oppression characteristic of all systems of coercion. That much might be expected: the true focus of interest of the essay, however, lies in the way Nazi violence displayed a terrible quality quite different from general apparatuses of ideology and power, a quality Levi calls 'uselessness'. Nazi violence was all too often 'useless', Levi maintains, in that it served no purpose above and beyond violence itself; it was '. . . una diffusa violenza fine a se stessa, volta unicamente alla creazione di dolore; talora tesa ad uno scopo, ma sempre ridondante, sempre fuor di proporzione rispetto allo scopo medesimo' (II. 1073; '. . . a widespread violence as an end in itself, aimed only at the creation

    [7] See Z. Bauman, *Modernity and the Holocaust* (Cambridge: Polity, 1989), 83–116; A. Margalit and G. Motzkin, 'The Uniqueness of the Holocaust', *Philosophy and Public Affairs*, 23/1 (Winter 1996), 65–83; M. Marrus, *The Holocaust in History* (New York: New American Library, 1987). For a polemical rejection of the 'uniqueness' tag, see N. Finkelstein, *The Holocaust Industry. Reflections on the Exploitation of Jewish Suffering* (London: Verso, 2000), 39–78.

    [8] The core idea of the essay is already in place in an article of 1959, 'Monumento ad Auschwitz', 'È dell'uomo operare in vista di un fine: la strage di Auschwitz, che ha distrutto una tradizione e una civiltà, non ha giovato a nessuno' (I. 1116–19 [1117]; 'It is proper to mankind to act with an end in mind: the massacre at Auschwitz, which destroyed a tradition and a civilization, benefited nobody'). Levi later reworked some of the issues in 'Violenza inutile' in a disturbing story of unmotivated violence and humiliation, 'Forza maggiore' (*Racconti e saggi*, II. 906–8).

of pain; sometimes it had an aim, but it was always redundant, always out of all proportion to the aim itself'). Many of the most distinctively barbaric and often unpredictably perverse features of camp life fall naturally into this working definition of 'useless violence': a violence absurd in its excess, redundant with respect to whatever deluded 'purpose' was imagined for it, always the cause of pain and humiliation and, furthermore, a facilitator of other forms of pain, in what Levi calls later in *I sommersi e i salvati* a 'genealogy of violence' (II. 1151).

Levi makes a point of explaining that the examples he has chosen to illustrate the useless violence of the camps—from the train journey[9] through all the emblematic stages of camp brutality and humiliation—recur in all or most survivors' memoirs, making the case for the fundamental explanatory power of the notion. In each case Levi is keen to preserve the dual aspect noted earlier: a root in the rational practice of coercion (however perverse the end served by the means) or in ideology and cultural tradition (for example, Prussian militarism); and then a threshold crossed into excess, disproportion, senselessness, and absurdity; all tokens of uselessness. To preserve this balance, Levi forces himself into extreme forms of identification, doggedly adopting Nazi 'logic' in order best to see the point where even that logic fails: with typical wit he calls this process of identification 'fare violenza (utile?) su se stessi per indursi a parlare del destino dei piú indifesi' (II. 1085; 'to perform an act of (useful?) violence on oneself to force oneself to speak of the fate of the most defenceless'). Thus, for example, he 'sees the purpose' in destroying Jewish women and children as well as the men, since the elimination of all Jews was a stated aim of Nazi ideology and women and children would represent the future of the Jewish 'race'. But there is a point where even this logic fails:

Ma perché, nelle loro razzie furiose, in tutte le città e i villaggi del loro impero sterminato, violare le porte dei morenti? Perché affannarsi a

---

[9] 'Non c'è diario o racconto, fra i molti nostri, in cui non compaia il treno, il vagone piombato, trasformato da veicolo commericale in prigione ambulante o addirittura in strumento di morte' (II. 1075; 'There is no diary or narrative, amongst the many written by us, without the train, the sealed carriages, turned from commercial vehicles into moving prisons or even instrument of death'). In one interview, Levi explains that he does not trust Bruno Bettelheim's writings on the camps in part because the latter did not go through the trauma of deportation across Europe by train (*The Voice of Memory*, 238).

trascinarli sui loro treni, per portarli a morire lontano, dopo un viaggio insensato, in Polonia, sulla soglia delle camere a gas? Nel mio convoglio c'erano due novantenni moribonde, prelevate dall'infermeria di Fossoli: una morì in viaggio, assistita invano dalle figlie. Non sarebbe stato piú semplice, piú 'economico', lasciarle morire, o magari ucciderle, nei loro letti, anziché inserire la loro agonia nell'agonia collettiva della tradotta? (ibid.)
(But why, in their insane round-ups, in all the cities and villages of their boundless empire, break down the doors of the dying? Why struggle to drag them onto the trains to carry them far away to die, after a senseless journey, in Poland, at the threshold of the gas chambers? In my convoy there were two dying 90-year-olds, taken away from the infirmary at Fossoli: one died during the journey, vainly cared for by her daughters. Wouldn't it have been simpler, more 'economical', to leave them to die, or even to kill them, in their beds, instead of including their agony in the collective agony of the transport?)

   The violence of adopting such a rebarbative logic is 'useful' for pinpointing one of the insuperable barriers where Nazi violence transcends any conceivable direct, causal utility—where it is good for nothing. Two consequences flow from this uncomfortable thought experiment. First, it gives a vivid sense of uselessness as a form of tautology or solipsism, of violence as tending only towards the suffering it by definition causes and then causes to multiply: 'veramente si è indotti a pensare che, nel Terzo Reich, la scelta migliore . . . fosse quella che comportava la massima afflizione, il massimo spreco di sofferenza fisica e morale' (ibid.; 'truly one is led to think that, for the Third Reich, the best choice . . . was the one that brought the maximum affliction, the greatest waste of physical and moral suffering'). Secondly, it reveals an important ambiguity to the term 'useless' in Levi's essay: this violence may not have any direct, organic utility, but it might be said to have an indirect, 'alienated' utility within the Nazi conception. The deportation of the dying, for example, can have no specific, pragmatic use; it can serve symbolically, however, to reaffirm and represent with every new deportation the total and irreversible nature of the Final Solution, to control even the mode and place of death of the Jews and thus deny them even that last refuge of freedom and self-definition. Indeed, the primary uselessness of such acts could be seen as precisely what opens up the possibility of this secondary, symbolic, and appallingly immoral use. This is what Levi calls 'moral violence' added to and growing out of the physical violence.

As with the blind inclusiveness of the dying in the deportation convoys, so with other instances detailed in Levi's essays: the humiliating and, for orthodox Jews, profane tattooed numbers, rendered quite redundant by the numbers already sewn on the prisoners' uniforms; the chronic lack of spoons, so crucial for survival, even though on liberation thousands of spoons were found piled up in storage-rooms; the back-breaking work, on occasion consisting solely of carrying piles of sand round in circles from team to team; the appalling experiments, such as those testing the boiling point of blood using human guinea pigs, when the information was readily available either from a simple test-tube experiment or from published tables (II. 1075–89). In all these cases, useless physical violence is in varying but pointed relation to moral violence, but the more these examples accumulate, the more apparent it becomes that this combination coincides with and accounts for the core processes of dehumanization of the camp system. As we saw in Chapter 3, these processes often worked by shattering the moral cordon around the body, denying the social, civilized selfhood guaranteed by privacy, physical modesty, and taboo. In 'Violenza inutile', Levi's paragraph on nakedness is one of the focal points of the essay:

In Lager si entrava nudi: anzi, più che nudi, privi non solo degli abiti e delle scarpe (che venivano confiscati) ma dei capelli e tutti gli altri peli. Lo stesso si fa, o si faceva, anche all'ingresso in caserma, certo, ma qui la rasatura era totale e settimanale, e la nudità pubblica e collettiva era una condizione ricorrente, tipica e piena di significato. Era anche questa una violenza con qualche radice di necessità (è chiaro che ci si deve spogliare per una doccia o per una visita medica), ma offensiva per la sua inutile ridondanza. La giornata del Lager era costellata di innumerevoli spogliazioni vessatorie: per il controllo dei pidocchi, per le perquisizioni degli abiti, per la visita della scabbia, per la lavatura mattutina; ed inoltre per le selezioni periodiche, in cui una 'commissione' decideva chi era ancora atto al lavoro e chi invece era destinato alla eliminazione. Ora, un uomo nudo e scalzo si sente i nervi e i tendini recisi: è una preda inerme. Gli abiti, anche quelli immondi che venivano distribuiti, anche le scarpacce dalla suola di legno, sono una difesa tenue ma indispensabile. Chi non li ha non percepisce più se stesso come un essere umano, bensì come un lombrico: nudo, lento, ignobile, prono al suolo. Sa che potrà essere schiacciato ad ogni momento. (II. 1079–80)
(You entered the *Lager* naked; indeed, more than naked, deprived not only of clothes and shoes (which were confiscated) but of all your hair,

on head and body. Of course, the same thing happens, or happened, when you go into the army, but here the shaving was total and repeated weekly, and public, collective nudity was a recurrent condition, typical and full of meaning. This too was a form of violence, with some root in necessity (of course you have to strip for a shower or for a medical examination), but made offensive by its useless redundancy. A day in the *Lager* was studded with numerous oppressive strippings: to control lice, to search clothes, to check for scabies, to wash each morning; and otherwise for the occasional selections when a 'committee' decided who was still capable of working and who was instead ready for elimination. Now, a naked, barefooted man feels as if his nerves and tendons have been cut: he is defenceless prey. Clothes, even the filthy clothes they gave out, and the rough, wooden-soled shoes, are a tenuous but indispensable form of defence. Whoever is without them no longer thinks of himself as a human being, but feels more like a worm: naked, slow, base, prone to the ground. He knows he can be crushed at any moment.)

As so often in Levi, the recourse to animal imagery marks a moment of acute ethical reflection.[10] The individual, any individual (and the opening out from the specifics of a camp selection into a zoological contemplation of 'un uomo' is itself a typical ethical move on Levi's part, turning from the particular to the generic and back again), is placed in a position of readiness for his or her own destruction by being stripped naked. To be and feel *like* prey is to be ready to be crushed. The symbolic power of the analogy *is* the very stuff of the moral violence inflicted, of the immoral uses of useless violence. The same paradox provides Levi with the crucial closing thought of 'Violenza inutile' when he quotes Franz Stangl, commandant of Treblinka, replying to Gitta Sereny's question in *Into that Darkness* about the purpose of all the unnecessary cruelty and the humiliation he presided over, when he knew the victims were to die anyway:

'Per condizionare quelli che dovevano eseguire materialmente le operazioni. Per rendergli possibile fare ciò che facevano'. In altre parole, prima di morire, la vittima dev'essere degradata, affinché l'uccisore senta meno il peso della sua colpa. È una spiegazione non priva di

[10] M. Belpoliti, 'Animali', in Belpoliti, ed., *Primo Levi* (Riga 13), 157–20. And cf. 'Quante sono le virtù che sono state simboleggiate con un animale!' ('How many virtues have been symbolized with an animal!', N. Bobbio, *L'elogio della mitezza e altri scritti morali* (Milan: Pratiche, 1998), 44).

logica, ma che grida al cielo: è l'unica utilità della violenza inutile. (I. 1090)[11]
('To condition those who had materially to carry out the operations. To make what they were doing possible for them.' In other words, before dying the victim must be degraded, so that the killer is less weighed down by his guilt. It is an explanation not without its own logic, but which cries out to the heavens: it is the only use of useless violence.)

'Violenza inutile', like all the essays in *I sommersi e i salvati*, illuminates and refines our understanding of the Holocaust. In terms of our understanding of utility as an ethical tool, it is strikingly important for at least three reasons. First, the very pairing of the title takes us back to Levi's utilitarian interest in pain and sets a limit to it. By exploring violence at its unjustifiable extreme, an extreme where pain is no longer a counterbalance to pleasure but a suffering beyond utilitarian calculation, 'Violenza inutile' sets a limit on the consequentialism in Levi's ethics. In other words, it acknowledges a space for fixed laws that overrides a morality based on results. This (Kantian) side to Levi is made generally explicit near the beginning of 'Violenza inutile', where he identifies Nazism's folly as, at root, the abandonment of moral law:

[sono] usciti progressivamente dalla realtà a mano a mano che la loro morale si andava scollando da quella morale, comune a tutti i tempi ed a tutte le civiltà, che è parte della nostra eredità umana, ed a cui da ultimo bisogna pur dare riconoscimento. (I. 1074)
([they] progressively left reality behind, bit by bit, as their morals sloughed off the morals shared by all ages and all civilizations, which are part of our human inheritance and which in the end we must indeed recognize.)

It is there too in one of his favourite proverbial turns of phrase, from Kant, that pops up in several essays and articles: 'Emanuele Kant riconosceva due meraviglie nel creato: il cielo stellato sopra il suo capo, e la legge morale dentro di lui' (II. 786; 'Immanuel Kant recognized two wonders in creation: the starry sky above his head and the moral law within'). And it is there with most direct relevance for the question of suffering in the short, but fascinating

---

[11] Michel Foucault came close to a similar formulation in his *Discipline and Punish* when he characterized the workings of the prison or penitentiary as a form of 'carceral excess' which imposes disciplinary order on its subjects (M. Foucault, *Discipline and Punish* (Harmondsworth: Penguin, 1979), 248).

essay 'Contro il dolore' (*L'altrui mestiere,* II. 673–5), where Levi posits something close to a universal moral law on cruelty (although notice the utilitarian calculation sneaked in here too): 'non creare dolore, né in noi né in alcuna creatura capace di percepirlo . . . è ammissibile soffrire (e far soffrire) solo a compenso di una maggior sofferenza evitata a sé o ad altri' (II. 674; 'not to create pain, neither in ourselves nor in any other creature able to perceive it . . . suffering (and causing suffering) is acceptable only if it is to avoid a greater suffering in oneself or others').[12]

Having set a limit to his utilitarianism, we can now move back to note how supple and flexible the notion of use is within those limits. 'Violenza inutile' shows the simple explanatory power of asking the question 'What use is X? What is X good for? What purpose does X serve?' To ask such questions of Nazi violence is to force strange, but compelling projections (Levi thinking as a Nazi would think) and to watch when the projections reach a limit and use spills over into uselessness. At the same time, as we have also seen, this spilling over into uselessness in reality opens up a space of another notion of use, an alienated, perverse, immoral use, breaking the utilitarian link between the useful and the good. Indeed, the very opening statement of the essay is built on just such a break: 'Il titolo di questo capitolo può apparire provocatorio o addirittura offensivo: esiste una violenza utile? Purtroppo sì' (I. 1073; 'The title of this chapter might seem provocative or even offensive: is there such a thing as useful violence? Unfortunately there is'). Implicit in these processes is a powerful reinforcement for one of the assumptions behind this book, that Levi works at his ethics by shuttling between the Holocaust and the ordinary, here asking an ordinary, banal question of an extraordinary event and watching the terms of the question falter. Use fails in its function as a simple ethical criterion of judgement, but in its flawed application

---

[12] Cf. 'La tortura . . . è il male massimo, peggiore ancora della pena di morte', 'I collezionisti di tormenti' (II. 1200–2; 'torture . . . is the worst evil, worse even than the death penalty'). This emphasis on cruelty as the blackest vice (and the use of animals to show this) provides one of the strongest links between Levi and Montaigne: see M. de Montaigne, 'On Cruelty', in *The Complete Essays*, tr. M. A. Screech (Harmondsworth: Penguin, 1991), 472–88; and cf. J. Shklar, 'Putting Cruelty First', in *Ordinary Vices* (Cambridge, Mass.: Bellknap Press, 1984), 7–44. See also R. Rorty, *Contingency, Irony, and Solidarity* (Cambridge: Cambridge University Press, 1989), 141–98; and Cavell, for whom the key test-case for his notion of 'acknowledgement' is the phrase 'I know he is in pain' (S. Mulhall, ed., *The Cavell Reader* (Oxford: Blackwell, 1996), 60, 68, 71).

it takes on that role as gatekeeper or guide to a minefield of ethical questions, as suggested at the start of this chapter. The movement between use and uselessness becomes a facilitating metaethical movement, offering a language in which to think through the problems of Auschwitz and the everyday.

The third element to take from 'Violenza inutile' is the most fertile in extending our enquiry into Levi's *œuvre* as a whole and testing out the role of use and uselessness there. As it picks out its various examples from Auschwitz, the essay formulates a number of cognates for uselessness which can help us to draw a map of Levi's understanding of the notion in and beyond testimony. Each cognate or working definition could be traced through to other moments in Levi's work to show how a modified notion of use (and its opposite) lays the foundations for more than one of the ordinary virtues in this book.

As we saw above, to be useless was variously understood in 'Violenza inutile' as to be purposeless or aimless, inappropriate or absurd, solipsistic or tautologous, extreme, redundant or excessive, senseless, rigidly generalized or abstract. To start with purposelessness, Levi is persistently worried throughout his *œuvre* by the possibility that life might be without purpose or by the consequences of thinking as much. The story 'Verso occidente' is once more important here: the dispute between the two zoologists-cum-anthropologists, Walter and Anna, revolves around the former's speculation that the life instinct, the sense that life has a purpose ('scopo'), might be the mere product of a chemical substance in whose absence life is unveiled as pointless, purposeless, not worth clinging on to. Anna, instinctively hostile to this view, admits to having felt as much during a period of post-natal depression, which she describes as:

Quel buco. Quel vuoto. Quel sentirsi... *inutili*, con tutto *inutile* intorno, annegati in un *mare di inutilità*. Soli anche in mezzo a una folla: murati vivi in mezzo a tutti murati vivi. (I. 580; emphases added)
(That hole. That void. That sense of being... useless, with uselessness all around, drowning in a sea of uselessness. Alone even in the middle of a crowd: buried alive in the middle of all the others buried alive.)

The chain of associations is powerful indeed: uselessness is a void, a token of lifelessness, a form of imprisonment and solitude. Conversely, a life of purpose or meaning must be, or a life must gain purpose and meaning by being, full, free, humanly sociable, useful. As if foreshadowing the tension in 'Violenza inutile' between good and bad uses of the useful, Walter and Anna are torn between his view that sees an artificial, chemical supplement as an appropriate weapon with which to defeat the 'mare di inutilità' and her view which sees the need to fight one's own battles ('combattere coi propri mezzi, senza l'aiuto esterno', I. 583; 'to fight with one's own means, without outside help') to strengthen one's hold on life. The vocabulary of this debate—the aim of life, death and living, struggle—recurs throughout Levi's *oeuvre*, reflecting as in this story his Darwinian mindset. Perhaps the last and most resonant instance comes at the very end of his essay on Jean Améry in *I sommersi e i salvati*, 'L'intellettuale ad Auschwitz', where he stands against suicide in a phrase that moves with typical climactic verve between Auschwitz and the everyday: 'Gli scopi della vita sono la difesa ottima contro la morte: non solo in Lager' (II. 1108; 'The aims of life are the best defence against death: not only in the *Lager*').[13]

As well as considering repeatedly the strength and source of the assumption that life has a purpose, a use, as a foundation of all his reflections on 'how to live', Levi also uses the notion of purpose and purposelessness to fix a guiding rule of apt proportion in his view of the world: thus, he justifies his capture as a partisan on the opening page of *Se questo è un uomo* by confessing that he was too young to know the 'doctrine' according to which 'il primo ufficio dell'uomo è perseguire i propri scopi con mezzi idonei' (I. 7; 'the first office of man is to pursue his own ends with apt means'). Importantly, he tells us that this was a doctrine he was to learn in the *Lager*: a useful lesson from a world of 'inutilità'. This (Aristotelian) rule of proportion, of 'idoneità' or means fitting the ends, closely allied to the eschewal of excess, redundancy, and extremes, will be an important part of the ethics of 'measure' examined in Chapter 5 below. But there is also another sense in which the useless is to be identified with the inapt or inappropriate: in 'Violenza inutile', a good example was the militaristic discipline and cleanliness of the Nazi regime imposed absurdly on the chaos and filth of the camps. Another example follows in 'L'intellettuale ad Auschwitz', where Levi wonders what uses (if

---

[13] See Chapter 9.

any) culture had in Auschwitz. As we saw in Chapter 3, Levi accepts that 'culture' was largely useless, because inapt: '[la cultura] certo *non era utile* a orientarsi né a capire. . . . cercar di capire, là, sul posto, era *uno sforzo inutile* . . . *uno spreco di energie* che *sarebbe stato più utile investire* nella lotta quotidiana contro la fame e la fatica' (II. 1103; emphases added; '[culture] was certainly not useful in orienting oneself or in understanding . . . to try to understand, there, on the spot, was a useless effort . . . a waste of energies that would have been better invested in the daily struggle against hunger and exhaustion'). But he also holds on to the occasional powerful uses of culture, even there:

La cultura poteva *servire*: non sovente, non dappertutto, non a tutti, ma qualche volta, in qualche occasione rara, preziosa come una pietra preziosa, *serviva* pure, e ci si sentiva come sollevati dal suolo . . . *mi ha servito e forse mi ha salvato*. (II. 1099–100; emphases added)
(Culture could be useful: not often, not everywhere, not for everyone, but sometimes, on certain rare occasions, precious as a rare gem, it did still have its purpose, it could make you feel as though you were flying above the ground . . . it served a purpose and maybe even saved me)

In this essay, Levi works to mark the boundary between the uses and uselessness of culture and, by doing so, he also works simultaneously to redefine culture, the intellectual, and his own position in relation to it. This movement itself becomes an embodiment of the intellectual's flexible cognitive-ethical enquiry as Levi sees it and practises it.

Another feature of uselessness encountered above was solipsism. In 'Trattamento di quiescenza' (I. 548–67), a short story about 'virtual reality' *avant la lettre*, the protagonist displays a distaste at the experience of pain and pleasure in swift, meaningless 'video' sequences that echoes Anna's distaste in 'Verso occidente' for artificial solutions to the struggles of life:

Ma di qui, da questo giochetti frigidi alla spese del dolore, che cosa si può spremere se non un piacere in scatola, fine a se stesso, solipsistico, da solitari? Insomma mi sembrano una diserzione: non mi sembrano morali. (I. 563)
(But what can you get out of this, out of these frigid little games played with pain, except for an artificial pleasure that's just an end in itself, solipsistic, solitary? At heart, they seem cowardly to me, immoral.)

This form of solipsism has its converse in an ethics of active 'civic' consideration of others, stepping beyond self-regard and egoism, as already encountered in Chapter 1. In the squalor of the abandoned camp hospital at the end of *Se questo è un uomo*, Levi's first emblematic step towards rebirth as a human being comes in his sharing some bread with others (I. 156) and in labouring successfully to set up a heater in the ward to give the eleven patients some hope of survival: 'Eravamo rotti di fatica, ma ci pareva, dopo tanto tempo, di avere finalmente fatto qualcosa di utile; forse come Dio dopo il primo giorno della creazione' (I. 157; 'We were broken with exhaustion, but, after so long, it seemed that we had finally done something useful; perhaps like God after the first day of creation'). The final, typically ironic touch evoking the Creation seals a sense of worth rediscovered in working for a purpose: and if there were any doubt of Levi's association of the useful with the moral here, one need only recall the verse of Genesis that lies behind his closing phrase, 'And God saw everything he had made, and behold, it was very good' (Gen. 1: 31) (see Chapter 8).

An analogous concern with solipsistic introspection and lack of dialogue governs another *locus classicus* of reflexive self-commentary in Levi's work, the much-quoted essay 'Dello scrivere oscuro' in *L'altrui mestiere* (II. 676–81) where writing which speaks only to itself, which is indecipherable to its reader, is damned (although Levi is careful to point out that he is not setting himself up as legislator, 'dar legge al narratore è almeno inutile', II. 676; 'to set up laws for the narrator is at best useless'):

a chi scrive nel linguaggio del cuore può accadere di risultare indecifrabile, ed allora è lecito domandarsi a che scopo egli abbia scritto: infatti . . . la scrittura serve a comunicare . . . sta allo scrittore farsi capire da chi desidera capirlo: è il suo mestiere, scrivere è un servizio pubblico . . . (II. 677)

(if you write in the language of the heart, you risk being indecipherable, and then it is a valid question to ask to what purpose you were writing: indeed . . . the purpose of writing is to communicate . . . it is up to the writer to make himself understood by whoever wishes to understand him: it's his job, writing is a public service . . .)

The final aspect of uselessness listed above was the rigidly generalized or abstract, whose converse is the practical, specific, and concrete world-view that, as stated at the start of the chapter, permeates Levi's every word. Much of Levi's writing on science is concerned with the borderline between pure theory, with its concomitant dangers, and applied science, the field of his own work career.[14] In this context, the contrast he draws is not so much between the useless and the useful—since he respects pure scientific research greatly—but between pure use and what was called above the 'useful for . . .', in itself a more concrete, applied notion. *Il sistema periodico* is in many respects a manual of this anti-theoretical, concrete ethics—allied to work (see Chapter 6) and to problem-solving intelligence—as summed up in a moment of the chapter 'Zinco' where Levi compares chemistry to hunting (via Pavese and Melville): 'Prendi e parti, quando il momento è giunto gli aruspici e gli àuguri non hanno luogo, *la teoria è futile e si impara per strada*, le esperienze degli altri non servono, l'essenziale è misurarsi (I. 766; emphasis added; 'You get up and go, when the moment has come oracles and omens are out of place, theory is futile, you'll learn as you go, others' experiences are useless, the important thing is to test yourself'). Similarly the story of the heater in the hospital is one of ingenuity and problem-solving, a form of useful intelligence set against the predominant absurdity, even stupidity that was yet another defining feature of Nazi useless violence.

The workings of Levi's utilitarianism can take us in many different directions simultaneously, reinforcing the sense of it as a flexible vessel for the elucidation of other ethical values as much as a core value in its own right. Areas of Levi's ethics that will concern us later, especially those explored in Part II, have emerged organically, as it were, from a discussion of use. On a local, banal level, it is a dynamic that allows him to see small, compromised goods even in flawed objects or practices: thus, for example, with the infamous American television drama *Holocaust*, broadcast in Italy in 1979, in which Levi sees profound problems and risks of misuse, but also very real uses for the dissemination of awareness of the past;[15] or in his discussion of stereotypes in *I sommersi e i salvati*, where he is careful to acknowledge the partial usefulness of such simplifications even as he combats them (II. 1018, 1117). Use is

[14] See essays such as 'Covare il cobra', *Racconti e saggi*, II. 990–3. On Levi and science in general see the important essay by Mario Porro, 'Scienza', in Belpoliti, ed., *Primo Levi* (Riga 13), 434–75; and also Borri, *Le divine impurità*; M. Petrucciani, 'Tra algebra e metafora: la scienza nella cultura letteraria italiana 1945–1975', in V. Branca et al., eds., *Letteratura e scienza nella storia della cultura italiana* (Palermo: Manfredi, 1978), 273–330 [322–4].
[15] See the three articles Levi wrote on *Holocaust*, I. 1264–80.

thus the opposite of fixed or rigid. It is an efficient, flexible tool for the extraction of good from the hybrid, volatile compound of experience. This combination of efficient extraction and strange transformation is best captured by two idioms that could be said to govern Levi's investment in utility.

The first of these is the idiom of economics, worth and exchange, never far beneath the surface of Levi's utilitarianism (nor indeed of historical utilitarianism). There are innumerable examples: earlier, Levi was quoted as seeing culture as a 'precious gem'; in a 1976 article, he reiterates his belief in writing clearly, because only in that way is writing 'redditizio' (I. 1204; 'profitable'); in an essay from *L'altrui mestiere* on leadership and the nuclear question, he settles on the need to 'suggerire, proporre, imporre poche idee chiare e semplici agli uomini che ci guidano, e sono idee che ogni buon mercante conosce: che l'accordo è l'affare migliore, e che a lungo termine la buona fede reciproca è la piú sottile delle astuzie' ('I padroni del destino', II. 785; 'to suggest, to propose, to impose a few simple, clear ideas on the people who lead us, ideas that any good merchant knows: that agreement is the best deal and that in the long run, reciprocal good faith is the subtlest form of cunning'); and in another piece in *L'altrui mestiere*, he characterizes Eastern European Jewish culture as a culture in which 'l'istruzione era considerata il valore supremo della vita: "la miglior merce", come si diceva proverbialmente' ('La miglior merce', II. 815–18 [816]; 'education was considered the highest value in life: "the best goods", as the proverb had it'). A chain leads from this investment in exchange value as a measure of worth, moral and cultural, to the notion of utility in part simply because the Italian noun 'l'utile' can mean both the useful and also profit (just as in English terms such as value and worth are both moral and mercenary), but also because the balances and dues of fair exchange are at the heart of what is flouted in the excesses and imbalances of the useless camp system: indeed, a key focus of attention for Levi in *Se questo è un uomo* is the bizarre economic system of exchange that is thrown up by the perverted disorder of the *Lager*.[16] And as the persistent cultural dimension of Levi's

---

[16] See the entire chapter 'Al di qua del bene e del male', I. 73–82; and large parts of *La tregua* where Levi's fascination with the tricks of trade ('astuzie', to use one of his most cherished, ethically charged terms) is on constant, exuberant display.

economics of value suggests, the very processes of his moral enquiry through narrative are also themselves a form of recognition and exchange: as Walter Benjamin points out in his essay on 'The Storyteller', the narrator in the oral tradition is one who offers something of use, something profitable in his tales. His or her 'good counsel' is useful and good at one and the same time.[17]

Alongside the often sober language of economics, however, the nature of use is also bound up with a transformative impulse— turning raw material into something of use—which, as was hinted at earlier, is almost alchemistic in origin. In one story in *Il sistema periodico*, 'Azoto', this is made explicit: Levi's bond to chemistry and its bond to nature in turn is directly identified with the transformative alchemy of both. His task in 'Azoto'—a commercial task, it should be noted—is to extract cosmetics from excrement:

lungi dallo scandalizzarmi, l'idea di ricavare un cosmetico da un escremento, ossia aurum de stercore, mi divertiva e mi riscaldava il cuore come un ritorno alle origini, quando gli alchimisti ricavavano il fosforo dall'urina. Era un'avventura inedita e allegra, e inoltre nobile, perché nobilitava, restaurava e ristabiliva. Cosí fa la natura: trae la grazia della felce dalla putredine del sottobosco, e il pascolo dal letame; . . . (I. 895–6) (the idea of extracting a cosmetic from excrement, *aurum de stercore* so to speak, far from scandalizing me amused me and warmed my heart like a return to our origins, when alchemists extracted phosphorus from urine. It was a new, happy, and even noble adventure, because it ennobled, restored, retrieved. Just like nature, who draws out the grace of the fern from the rotting undergrowth and the pasture from manure; . . .)

As with nature so with human experience: our task is transformative, to convert the useless into the useful. The vitality and joy of this passage locates part of the value of the transformation in sheer, unexpected discovery—a use for uselessness *qua* uselessness which itself will be explored as an unexpected but integral part of Levi's ethics in Part IV below—but it also epitomizes Levi's more direct end-focused utilitarianism that has been the subject of this chapter. Shortly before the passage, Levi traced the origin of his penchant for alchemy to two familiar sources: '*Il mestiere di chimico* (fortificato, nel mio caso, *dall'esperienza di Auschwitz*) insegna a superare,

[17] W. Benjamin, 'The Storyteller. Reflections of the Works of Nikolai Leskov', in *Illuminations*, ed. H. Arendt, tr. H. Zohn (London: Jonathan Cape, 1970), 86. See Chapter 11.

anzi ad ignorare, certi ribrezzi, che non hanno nulla di necessario né di congenito: la materia è materia, né nobile né vile, infinitamente transformabile . . .' (I. 895; emphases added; 'A career as a chemist (fortified in my case by the experience of Auschwitz) teaches you to overcome, even to ignore, certain forms of disgust, which are neither necessary nor inborn: matter is matter, neither noble nor vile but infinitely transformable . . .'). In chemistry and after Auschwitz, Levi aims to transform formless matter, good for nothing, into matter 'good for' something. The lesson is easily translated into a language of ethics: turn the useless to good use. This holds true even with Auschwitz, whether *in* Auschwitz— where in the very early, desperate days, Levi tells us, 'Abbiamo imparato che *tutto serve*' (I. 27; emphasis added; 'We have learned that everything has its uses')—or *after* Auschwitz: 'anche dalle sciagure (un pessimista direbbe: specialmente dalle sciagure) si possono imparare molte cose' (II. 1302; 'even from disasters (a pessimist would say, especially from disasters) we can learn many things'). 'Pessimism of the intellect, optimism of the will', we might say: another version of the ethical turn.

PART II

WIT, OR PRACTICAL INTELLIGENCE

The basic building-block of Levi's understanding of the world is his practical intelligence. In the camps and beyond, he seems to say, intelligent engagement with the world and with others will clarify and humanize experience, will solve problems where they are soluble or at least bring growth and self-knowledge when they prove insoluble. In the Italian tradition, one perhaps has to go as far back as Boccaccio's *Decameron* (1349–51) to find a work so firmly rooted as Levi's in shrewd, flexible intelligence and pragmatism. The comparison is not as far-fetched as it may seem. Although writing in quite different contexts, both Boccaccio and Levi could be said to chart the morality of a world doubtful of the practical applicability of traditional virtues (Boccaccio's secular mercantile world, Levi's secular, sceptical post-Holocaust world). The praise of intelligence is a core element of their different narrative universes.[1] Pursuing the parallels a little further, in both Boccaccio and Levi this aspect of their world-view is comic, in the generic sense of the word: that is, it posits and expects resolution; it uses human means, whether successful or not, to pursue it; and the world—the localized interactions, commerces, intimate encounters and dramas that constitute experience—are assumed to be malleable to those means.[2] This comic dynamic is also responsive: intelligence is valuable and good as a shrewd, creative response to events, to fortune or misfortune, and here too, for both authors, it represents an alternative to classical, heroic virtues of strength, courage, honour, and the like. Furthermore, in their different ways, both are also comic in the straightforward sense of the term, and although Levi's humour will be dealt with separately in Part IV, it is worth noting here that the two senses of the term have underlying affinities as well as superficial ones: Levi's humour is itself a form of his intelligence and both humour and intelligence are virtues in his ethical vision. For this reason, a key term for his ethics and for this book as a whole—because it captures homonymically the identity between humour and intelligence in Levi—is the term 'wit'.

---

[1] On intelligence in Boccaccio, see, for example, R. Hastings, *Nature and Reason in the Decameron* (Manchester: Manchester University Press, 1975); on Boccaccio as mercantile, see V. Branca, *Boccaccio medievale* (Florence: Sansoni, 1991). Levi mentions Boccaccio in more than one interview: see Levi, *The Voice of Memory*, 100, 133.

[2] On medieval notions of comedy, see Z. Baranski, 'Comedia: Notes on Dante, the Epistle to Cangrande and Medieval Comedy', *Lectura Dantis*, 8 (Spring 1991), 26–55.

There is a final, essential link between Boccaccio and Levi: their comic worlds of wit are darkened by the shadows of tragedy. In both, the comedy of problem and resolution is always under-pinned by the tragedy of unresolvable suffering and death. Boccaccio's terrible opening description of the 1348 Black Death in Florence and Levi's descriptions of Auschwitz both frame and condition all they have to say on the ordinary virtues of wit and, indeed, it is this framing more than anything else that gives them both their ethical density. It is striking and apt to note, therefore, that the term 'wit' lies at the etymological root of the term 'witness', both derived from verbs of seeing ('videre'): in other words, to explore Levi's wit as Part II sets out to do is also an alter-native way of exploring his witnessing from that which begins in the solemn, legal-vocational language of testimony.

5

MEASURE, OR A SENSE OF LIMIT

Two things fill my mind with ever new and increasing
wonder and awe . . . the starry heaven above and the moral
law within.

(Kant)

The wonder is, not that the field of the stars is so vast, but
that man has measured it.

(Anatole France)

This second Part examines four virtues of wit or practical intelligence at work in Levi. The first of these is what I have called
'measure'. The word is deliberately intended as multivalent (multi-
valency is itself an active virtue for Levi and many of his values are
best expressed by terms with overlapping, plural—although not
endless—meanings). Its meanings and uses branch out in several
directions yielding further dividends in helping to shape Levi's
ethics. The chapter focuses on three particularly important senses
of the term. The first two, picking up on aspects encountered in
both Chapters 3 and 4 above, are measure as restraint, the opposite of excess, and measure as accuracy and aptness, the opposite of
mismeasure; the third is measure as self-measure, as the struggle for
knowledge and self-knowledge by 'measuring oneself' against the
world. All three, as we shall see, depend in no small degree on
limits, on a sensitivity to boundaries and trangressions and the
possible benefits and harm these bring. Ultimately this perception
of limit reveals the endpoint of the value of measure, not only
because to measure a phenomenon—and thus to know it properly—is necessarily to measure out its boundaries, the limit where

it no longer applies; but also because the sense of a limit points us towards a (Socratic) definition of human enquiry.[1]

RESTRAINT

The first meaning of measure, as restraint and the rejection of excess, is the most frequently recognizable in Levi. Restraint has already featured as an aspect of the exploration of issues of language and silence in Chapter 3; similarly, in Chapter 4, redundancy and excess were core features of the 'uselessness' of Nazi violence. More familiarly still, Levi's most famous declarations of intent regarding his writing on Auschwitz embrace a deliberate, calm restraint, a 'measured' tone wholly bound up with his core, Enlightened[2] values of reason, progress, and justice:

io non sono un fascista, io credo nella ragione e nella discussione come supremi strumenti del progresso, e perciò all'odio antepongo la giustizia. Proprio per questo motivo, nello scrivere [*Se questo è un uomo*], ho assunto deliberatamente il linguaggio pacato e sobrio del testimone, non quello lamentevole della vittima, né quello irato del vendicatore . . . (I. 175)

(I am not a fascist, I believe in reason and in discussion as the highest instruments of progress, and so before hatred I place justice. Precisely for this reason, in writing [*Se questo è un uomo*], I have deliberately taken on the calm and sober language of the witness, not the complaining voice of the victim, nor the angered tone of revenge . . .)

Here we are in territory so familiar as to be perhaps clichéd. Levi's noble restraint in the face of the horrors of Auschwitz has, for many, been the defining cause of his remarkable success with the reading public.[3] But just as his claims to objectivity are dented by moments when he is anything but 'pacato e sobrio', just as the assumptions behind his vocabulary of testimony (also prominent in

---

[1] Thinking about limits and the perception and temptations of the limitless links this aspect of Levi to Leopardi also: see Chapter 4 note 3.

[2] On measure, in this sense and others, as a product of the Enlightenment, cf. Foucault's characterization of the shift in Enlightenment reforms of punishment as a move towards 'measured' and 'man-measured' systems of punishment as a restraint on the potentially infinite power of the state (*Discipline and Punish* (Harmondsworth: Penguin, 1979), 74, 90–1).

[3] See, for example, E. Roditi, 'The Jewish Contribution to Post-war Italian Literature', *Jewish Quarterly*, 28/1/102 (Spring 1980), 20–3 [20–1]; S. Woolf, 'Primo Levi, Drowning and Surviving', *Jewish Quarterly*, 34/3/127 (1987), 6–9 [7]; C. James, 'Last Will and Testament', *New Yorker* (23 May 1988), 86–92 [88].

this quotation) are open to refinement and integration within a larger ethics (see Introduction),[4] so his defence of calm becomes more interesting when read as a rhetorical pointer to a broader-based ethics of measured restraint as a response to experience. Measure is at the Aristotelian heart of this most Aristotelian of writers. Eschew the extremes, he seems to say, and inhabit and understand the middle ground, the mean. Extremes are dangerous and foolish, even when driven by good intentions: as one of Levi's talking animals in *Lilít* bluntly puts it, 'È stolto eccedere, come è stolto ogni eccesso' ('Le sorelle della palude', II. 143; 'to exceed is foolish just as every excess is foolish'). Indeed, the twin historical catastrophes that dominate Levi's world-view—the Holocaust and the threat of a nuclear apocalypse—are in certain respects both products of virtues he would call his own—respectively, order and scientific enquiry—taken to extremes. Furthermore, excess is qualitative as well as quantitative. The Nazis were guilty not only of taking a sense of Prussian discipline and national pride[5] too far but also of doing so to the perverse exclusion of all other considerations. For Levi the sin of excess is to indulge not only in 'too much of X' but also in 'X and only X'. It is totalitarian in shape. Along with it comes a loss of scale or perspective against which to measure or judge one's actions (see Chapter 7). This means that, conversely, the middle ground, the measured, broad centre is more than simply a contained version of the extremes; it is rather a messy mix, a 'grey zone' (*I sommersi e i salvati*, II. 1017–44), a hybrid compound where ambiguity and uncertainty reign.[6] This is what allows Levi to be a much more subtle ethicist than the

---

[4] More useful in this respect is the closely related definition of *Se questo è un uomo* in its preface as 'uno studio pacato di alcuni aspetti dell'animo umano' (I. 5), with its emphasis on the value of careful reflection and study as a token of measure in Levi.

[5] Levi not uncommonly uses the category of national character to understand actions and events, and Germans in particular seem to represent the key test-case for this practice, and a key means to analysing the Holocaust. On Germans and Russians, see *inter alia La tregua*, I. 250, 263, 268. He associates Germans with a certain 'mancanza di misura'. He has a German term for it, '*Masslosigkeit*' (II. 1104), which he uses to tease gently one of his younger and more open German correspondents in *I sommersi e i salvati* who condemns her nation's excessive zeal only to reply to Levi's intrigued enquiry with a 23-page research document. In *La chiave a stella*, Faussone has developed clear views on various nations on his travels (see, e.g., I. 1049, 1070). Elsewhere, Levi associates measure, among other things, with the character of both the Piedmontese and the British: see ' "Bella come una fiore" ' (*Racconti e saggi*, II. 986–99).

[6] See B. Cheyette, 'The Ethical Uncertainty of Primo Levi', in B. Cheyette and L. Marcus, eds., *Modernity, Culture and 'the Jew'* (Cambridge: Polity, 1998), pp. 268–81.

commonplace assertions (including his own) of his calm and sobriety would suggest. He is able to see the worth and the attraction of extremes; indeed the mean only takes on its true ethical value if you have flirted with or touched on the extremes. The much-quoted rejection of hatred and victimhood given above is tellingly preceded by the following:

Devo confessare che davanti a certi visi non nuovi, a certe vecchie bugie, a certe figure in cerca di rispettabilità, a certe indulgenze, a certe convivenze, la tentazione all'odio la provo, ed anche con una certa violenza: ma io non sono un fascista . . . (I. 175)
(I have to confess that before certain familiar faces, certain old lies, certain figures looking for respectability, certain indulgences and alliances, I do feel the temptation to hate, and at times the temptation is quite strong: but I am not a fascist . . .)

That the list is so long and so pregnant with political and historical associations is itself eloquent. Levi is constantly pulled towards hatred only then (ethically) to choose restraint. In this he enacts an essentially humane straining for civilized restraint which elsewhere, in a crucial passage of the chapter 'I sommersi e i salvati' in *Se questo è un uomo*, he identifies with the essential task of human society:

una sensibile azione di smorzamento è esercitata dalla legge, e dal senso morale, che è legge interna; viene infatti considerato tanto piú civile un paese, quanto piú savie ed efficienti vi sono quelle leggi che impediscono al misero di essere troppo misero, e al potente di essere troppo potente (I. 84)
(a noticeable muffling effect is achieved by laws and by our moral sense, which is inner law; indeed, a country is considered all the more civilized the more wise and efficient its laws for preventing the weak from being too weak and the powerful from being too powerful)

The concentration camp was not so much a place where the human became bestial (although at times it was that too) as a place where no effort at 'smorzamento' was effected, where there was no law, internal or external, to draw back from extremes. It is this perception which led Levi to his binary categories of prisoners—the 'drowned' and the 'saved'—which are not inhuman extremes, but rather untempered human impulses latent in all society: 'una terza via esiste nella vita, dove è anzi la norma: non esiste in campo di concentramento' (I. 86; 'there is a third way in life, indeed it is the norm: it does not exist in concentration camps'). And else-where, this same pattern—two extremes to which people escape in extreme conditions, fleeing from the complicated middle-ground of ordinary reality—repeats itself persistently in Levi's reflections on the camp world and its relations to our world.[7] It is there in his frequent negation of survivors as saints rather than normal people: 'Fummo di nuovo soltanto giovani: | Non martiri, non infami, non santi' ('Cantare', II. 522; 'We became young people once more: | Not martyrs, not criminals, not saints'). It is also there in his subtle meditations on probability and our tendency to simplify the many possible futures before us into all-or-nothing extremes, as he shows in *Se questo è un uomo* (I. 30), where fear and danger prompt many to an absurd certainty over what awaits them; and later in the essay 'Eclissi dei profeti' in *L'altrui mestiere* (II. 853–6), picking up on and quoting the former at length:

... esiste una tendenza, irrazionale ma osservata da secoli, e bene evidente nelle situazioni di pericolo, ad avvicinare la probabilità di un evento terribile ai suoi valori estremi, zero e uno, impossibilità e certezza. (II. 854)
(... there is an irrational but centuries-old and well-observed habit, which emerges especially in situations of danger, of nudging the prob-ability of a terrible event to its extreme values, zero or one, impossibility or certainty.)

Thus pessimism and optimism are two sides of the same coin, two extreme hiding places from the varying, elusive probabilities and possibilities that define the future, that make us blind but also responsible, individually and collectively: 'il domani dobbiamo costruircelo noi, alla cieca, a tentoni' (II. 856; 'it is up to us to

---

[7] There is a large psychological and psychoanalytical literature on the extreme condi-tions of the concentration camps and their effect on character and action: see, for example, B. Bettelheim, *Surviving and Other Essays* (New York: Knopf, 1979); T. Des Pres, *The Survivor* (New York: Oxford University Press, 1976); A. Devoto, *Il comportamento umano in condizioni estreme. Lo psicologo sociale e il lager nazista* (Milan: Franco Angeli, 1985); V. Frankl, *Man's Search for Meaning* (New York: Washington Square Press, 1985; 1st edition 1946); M. Martini, *Il trauma della deportazione. Ricerca psicologica sui sopravvissuti italiani ai campi di concen-tramento nazisti* (Milan: Mondadori, 1983. There are echoes of this literature in T. Todorov, *Face à l'extrême* (Paris: Seuil, 1991), *passim*. For an attempt to use Levi as a prime source for such psychological literature, see C. Volpato and A. Contarello, *Psicologia sociale e situazioni estreme. Relazioni interpersonali e intergruppi in* Se questo è un uomo *di Primo Levi* (Quaderni di psicologia, 20, Bologna: Patron Editore, 1999) (a shorter version is in *European Journal of Social Psychology*, 29, 1999: 239–58).

build our tomorrow, groping our way in the dark'). A sense of measure, of accepting the grey zone that is reality and fleeing extremes of action or reaction, contains within it the prime moral responsibilities of individual and personal action. To accept this messy reality and its responsibilities is to be what Levi calls both rational and 'reasonable' ('se fossimo ragionevoli . . .', I. 30; 'if we were reasonable . . .'), to have reasonable doubt. And in this scepticism about the certainties of the future, we can hear echoes of Levi's often stated distrust of prophets and political utopias, of all the temptations of 'radical' thinking ('la radicalità . . . è fonte di male', II. 855; 'radicality . . . is the source of evil'), and his embracing instead of smaller, less certain but cherished truths and aspirations, of a precisely sustainable and realizable kind, what he calls in the 'Afterword' to *Se questo è un uomo*:

altre verità piú modeste e meno entusiasmanti, quelle che si conquistano faticosamente, a poco a poco e senza scorciatoie, con studio, la discussione e il ragionamento, e che possono essere verificate e dimostrate. (I. 199)

(other more modest and less exciting truths, of the sort that are won with hard work, bit by bit, with no cut corners, through study, discussion, reasoning, which can then be checked and shown to be true.)

A final marker of measured restraint in Levi is to be seen in his persistent attachment to patience. Patience prevents hasty, excessive, unreasoned, and unreasonable response. It leaves a space for careful ethical engagement with the world and is thus perhaps the most useful, recurrent form of holding back that Levi knows. We have already seen it at work in Chapter 1 above as a form of attention and looking sorely missed in the camps: 'qui [nel campo] nessuno ha tempo, nessuno ha pazienza, nessuno ti dà ascolto' (I. 32; 'here no one has any time, no one has any patience, no one listens to you'). It is characteristic of his calmly noble and forbearing companion, Leonardo (I. 252); and of his watch–maker protagonist of *Se non ora, quando?*, Mendel (II. 235, 256). We find it in Levi's praise of distillation in *Il sistema periodico*: 'Distillare è bello. Prima di tutto, perché è un mestiere lento, filosofico e silenzioso, che ti occupa, ma ti lascia tempo di pensare ad altro' (I. 789; 'Distillation is beautiful. Above all because it is a slow, philosophical, and silent job, which occupies you but lets you think of other things'). It is also there, hand in hand with a general praise of shrewd intelligence, in one of the key sites in the whole *œuvre* for Levi's practical ethics, the article 'Trenta ore sul *Castoro sei*' in *L'altrui mestiere* (II. 704–10).[8] The article tells of Levi's time on a mini-submarine, seeing at first hand the problem-solving ingenuity of the crew. He is prompted to recall his seafaring literary heroes—Conrad, Melville, Verne—but ends on the father of all literary seafarers, Homer's Ulysses:

nelle loro parole, frenate, educate, precise e prive di enfasi, ho riconosciuto l'eco della voce di un altro navigatore e raccontatore le cui avventure remote sono oggi poesia eterna: quello che aveva navigato per dieci anni per mari strani, e le cui virtù prime, piú assai del coraggio che pure non gli mancava, furono la pazienza e l'ingegno molteplice. (II. 710)[9]
(in their words, restrained, polite, precise, and without rhetoric, I heard the echo of the voice of another navigator and storyteller whose far-off adventures are today eternal poetry; who sailed strange seas for ten years and whose prime virtues, before courage (although he was hardly lacking in that), were patience and many-layered wit.)

Notice the explicit contrast here between the heroic virtue of courage and Levi's more ordinary virtues, here represented by the dyad of patience and wit. We cannot help but compare the echo of this Ulysses with that of Dante's Ulisse half-remembered by a starving Levi in Auschwitz ('Il canto di Ulisse', I. 105–11). The two Ulysses here seem to stand in emblematic contrast: both are searchers for knowledge and shrewd actors in the world and Levi is drawn to them both; but the former follows a path of measured patience and wit, the latter a 'mad flight' of transgression, pride, *démesure*. In the pairing, we can see a model of the possible virtues and limits of Levi's fundamental project, the search for knowledge.

Patience is also a characteristic virtue of Levi's salaried path to knowledge or better to 'know-how', his chemistry. In another piece in *L'altrui mestiere*, entitled 'Il segno del chimico' (II. 810–14), Levi makes just such a distinction between 'knowing something' and 'knowing how to do something' (II. 814), the latter produced by the strange phenomenon of the university chemistry lab where, unlike in school, mere academic intelligence

[8] See also an earlier version of this essay, 'Ospite del capitano Nemo', I. 1323–7.
[9] Compare Levi's comments on *The Odyssey* in *La ricerca delle radici* (II. 1381); and the use of Jonah, biblical 'seafarer' and precursor of Melville and others, in 'Il cantore e il veterano' (*Lilít*, II. 37–42).

was not enough. Failing an experiment was felt by the group as more serious than failing an exam:

Qui [nel laboratorio] occorevano altre virtù: umiltà, pazienza, abilità manuale; ed anche, perché no? buona vista ed olfatto, resistenza nervosa e muscolare, resilienza davanti agli insuccessi. (II. 812)
(Here other virtues were needed: humility, patience, manual dexterity; and also (why not?) good senses of sight and smell, strength of nerve and muscle, resilience in the face of failure.)

Once again, note how Levi explicitly builds up his taxonomy of practical virtues in contrast to other traditional 'virtues'. And note also how, for Ulysses, for the submarine crew, and for the lab, the complementary pair of intelligence (exams) and patience et al. (lab) indicates how Levi's wit is always an applied, experimental intelligence, of the mind and of the senses, as its etymological origin in vision might suggest.

MEASUREMENT

Chemistry demands intelligence and patience, then, perspicacity of mind and body, but it also demands that a premium be set on a second sense of measure, at least as important and as ethically weighted as the first. This is measure in its more literal sense of accurate, precise, proportionate and appropriate measurement, of quality or quantity; measurement as describing, weighing, judging; measurement as distinction, careful acknowledgement of similarity and difference. If the first sense was the opposite of *démesure*, this is measure as the opposite of 'mismeasure'.[10]

Levi's impatience with imprecision is apparent and declared: for example, in a piece on a 1985 scandal concerning toxic additives in Austrian wine (II. 962–5), he drily exhorts journalists to use 'un linguaggio adeguato e preciso' ('an appropriate and precise language'), to be well informed, and to inform their readers so that the latter can be allowed to make a reasoned judgement of the case in hand. In part, this is made all the more urgent because the workings of the law in Italy are so slow and so abstruse that no juridical verdict will be available to guide public opinion. Thus the

[10] The same image is used by S. J. Gould's study of the strange history of the idea of intelligence as a measurable quantity, *The Mismeasure of Man* (Harmondsworth: Penguin, 1997; revised edition).

journalist has a sort of civic duty to be expeditious and accurate, 'chiaro e corretto' (II. 963; 'clear and correct'). Much the same advice is given to writers in a series of essays in *L'altrui mestiere*— 'Perché si scrive?', 'Dello scrivere oscuro', 'A un giovane lettore' (II. 659–62, 676–81, 845–7)—where writing clearly is also seen as a moral duty to the reader as a fellow human being and object of communication and exchange. A favourite phrase in these writings is the utilitarian-sounding formula, 'il massimo di informazione con il minimo ingombro' (II. 847; 'the maximum information with minimum baggage'), where precision is a means of avoiding excess. A similar affinity marks Levi's comments on Marco Polo's *Milione*, the account of his journeys to China, in *La ricerca delle radici*, Levi's fascinating anthology of his favourite books: 'le fatiche e i pericoli sono accennati con sobrio riserbo, e le meraviglie viste e udite sono descritte col buon senso del mercante attento alle frodi, ai prezzi e ai guadagni, e con la precisione divertita dell'uomo curioso' (I. 1461; 'the travails and dangers are referred to with sober reserve and the wonders seen and heard are described with the common sense of a merchant who is alert to fraud, prices, and profits, and with the amused precision of the curious man'). Indeed, it is worth noting in passing that alongside two senses of measure here ('sobrio riserbo' and 'precisione') there are also several of the other ordinary virtues at work in Levi, the wit of the senses ('meraviglie viste e udite'), common sense ('buon senso', see Chapter 9), commercial wit (see Chapter 4 and comments on Boccaccio above), diversion, and curiosity (see Chapter 13). Here, however, our focus is on precision and we can take this one step further if we move on from precision as clarity and economy to precision as an art of careful separation and distinction, a 'Scheidekunst', in other words the essential and primordial form of chemistry (I. 556; see Chapter 3).

This association directs us at once to two key points in Levi's *œuvre*, one concerning chemistry and the other the camps. The former is in 'Potassio' (*Il sistema periodico*, I. 782–91), a fable with a moral that resonates throughout the book and through all Levi's exploration of difference, whether material, cultural, or racial. Foolishly taking potassium as a plausible substitute for its almost identical twin sodium, Levi's lab experiment has literally gone up in flames. Wiser after the event, he offers us the moral:

... occorre diffidare del quasi–uguale (il sodio è quasi uguale al potassio: ma col sodio non sarebbe successo nulla), del praticamente identico, del pressapoco, dell'oppure, di tutti i surrogati e di tutti i rappezzi. Le differenze possono essere piccole, ma portare a conseguenze radicalmente diverse, come gli aghi degli scambi; il mestiere del chimico consiste in buona parte nel guardarsi da queste differenze, nel conoscerle da vicino, nel prevederne gli effetti. Non solo il mestiere del chimico. (I. 791) (... we must be suspicious of the almost-the-same (sodium is almost the same as potassium, but with sodium nothing would have happened), of the practically identical, the near-as-you-like, the this-or-that, of all surrogates and patched-up replacements. Differences can be small but lead to radically different outcomes, like pointers on a scale; the work of the chemist consists in large part in watching out for such differences, getting to know them close up, predicting their effects. And not only the work of the chemist.)

As if following this moral, Levi sets the task of comparing and distinguishing, of fitting the tools to the task, at the heart of *I sommersi e i salvati*. Hence in 'La vergogna', explaining his hostility to psychoanalytical accounts of camp inmates and survivors (Bruno Bettelheim above all), he says:

Le loro interpretazioni ... mi sembrano approssimative e semplificate, come di chi volesse applicare i teoremi della geometria piana alla risoluzione dei triangoli sferici. I meccanismi mentali degli Häftlinge erano diversi dai nostri; curiosamente, e parallelamente, diversa era anche la loro fisiologia e patologia. In Lager, il raffreddore e l'influenza erano sconosciuti, ma si moriva, a volte di colpo, per mali che i medici non hanno mai avuto occasione di studiare. Guarivano (o diventavano asintomatiche) le ulcere gastriche e le malattie mentali, ma tutti soffrivano di un disagio incessante, che inquinava il sonno e che non ha nome. Definirlo 'nevrosi' è riduttivo e ridicolo. (II. 1057)[11] (Their interpretations ... seem to me vague and simplistic, like someone applying plane geometric theorems to the resolution of spherical triangles. The mental mechanisms of the Häftlinge were different from our own; curiously, in a parallel way, so too were their physiology and pathology. In the camps, colds and flus were unknown, but you could die, sometimes at a stroke, from illnesses that doctors have never had the

---

[11] This passage draws on Levi's first piece of writing on Auschwitz, pre-dating even *Se questo è un uomo*, a report on medical conditions in the *Lager* co-authored with his fellow survivor Leonardi Debenedetti, published in a medical journal in 1946: P. Levi and L. Debenedetti, 'Rapporto sull'organizzazione igienico-sanitaria del campo di concentramento per ebrei di Monowitz (Auschwitz—Alta Silesia)', *Minerva medica*, 37 (July–Dec. 1946), 535–44 (now at II. 1339–60). For Levi's hostility to Bettelheim, see *The Voice of Memory*, 233–8.

chance to study. Gastric ulcers and mental conditions were cured (or became asymptomatic), but everyone suffered from an incessant unease which polluted our sleep and has no name. To label it 'neurosis' is reductive and absurd.)

The passage is an exemplary illustration of how the extreme contingent conditions of the camps upturned cognitive tools and assumptions.

Beyond incompetence, there is a moral dishonesty for Levi in explanations like Bettelheim's which fail to distinguish properly, to measure with the right tools, a dishonesty that reaches extremes in collaborators and negationists who after the war, as he explains in 'La memoria dell'offesa', came to believe their own lies: 'tenere distinte la buona e la mala fede è costoso: richiede uno sforzo continuo, intellettuale e morale' (II. 1010; 'to keep good faith and bad faith distinct is costly: it requires continual moral and intellectual effort'). But even within the category of the guilty, there are distinctions to be made, as the extraordinary essay on 'La zona grigia' elucidates (II. 1017–44). There is no end to the work of moral distinction and the moral work of distinction to be done.

The criticism of psychoanalysis in 'La vergogna' verges on being a methodological one. Levi's complaint is that the analysis has been done with the wrong cognitive equipment; and this way of thinking recurs elsewhere, both in *I sommersi e i salvati* and in figurative form in his science fiction. His most common term for the apt tool to measure and thus understand is 'metro' (ruler, tape measure), although on occasion he uses related terms for 'code', 'compass', even 'thermometer'. In *I sommersi e i salvati*, he uses 'metro' to explain why everyday embarrassment or shame was all but absent in the camps: 'Il nostro metro morale era mutato' (II. 1049; 'our moral measure had changed'). He also is acutely aware of the price to be paid when such a change is forced upon us—'cambiare codice morale è sempre costoso' (II. 1054; 'to change moral code always comes at a price')—and how hard it is to judge at all when different rules or codes govern the judge and the judged:

bisogna guardarsi dall'errore che consiste nel giudicare epoche e luoghi lontani col metro che prevale nel qui e nell'oggi: errore tanto più difficile da evitare quanto più è grande la distanza nello spazio e nel tempo. (II. 1122; see Chapter 7)
(we must be careful to avoid the error of judging distant places and eras with the scales of the here and now: an error that is all the more difficult to avoid the further away we are in time and space.)

In the science-fiction collections *Storie naturali* and *Vizio di forma*, there is a small group of stories which play games with measuring or testing.[12] In 'Lumini rossi', for example, Levi imagines a bland but oppressive near-future in which the working day of an office-worker husband is filled by small red lights, his car journeys, lift journeys, and home mod cons, even down to his wife's state-imposed 'fertility light', which lights up to prevent them conceiving a third child (I. 626–9). Sexual dystopia aside, the husband is depressed and wearied by his life 'measured out' in small red lights, three and a half million of them, he calculates, in a working life. A similar, muted, and wrily comic dystopia of mismeasuring is to be found in 'La misura della bellezza' (I. 495–504), which follows the invention of a 'Calometro' or beauty-measuring machine, which proves to be little more than a measure of conformism or vanity.

A third story, 'Le nostre belle specificazioni' (I. 661–70), plays games with a very specific language of testing that intrigues Levi, the language of technical patents and product-testing. So fascinated is Levi by this field that he includes in *La ricerca delle radici* the text of a specification by the American Society for Testing Materials (ASTM) for testing the resistance of adhesive tape to cockroaches (II. 1493–5). He introduces the piece comparing today's measurement of atomic emissions to Lorenzo Spallanzani in the eighteenth century who measured in units of one or more Credo recital, commenting that: 'le fondazioni della nostra civiltà tecnologica devono essere consolidate da misure e definizioni precise' (II. 1493; 'the foundations of our technological civilization must be consolidated by precise definitions and measurements'). At the same time, however, he notes anxiously the increasing tidal wave of minute measurement that risks turning scientific knowledge into a 'mostruoso reticolo delle specificazioni' (ibid.; 'a monstrous network of specifications'). The double edge is clear, and will be ironized and explored in the story: precision and careful measurement against the oppression of over-specification.

'Le nostre belle specificazioni' is set in a Testing Centre much

[12] On Levi's science fiction in general, see G. Grassano, ' "La musa stupefatta" di Levi. Note sui racconti fantascientifici', in G. Ioli, ed., *Primo Levi: memoria e invenzione* (San Salvatore Monferrato: Edizione della Biennale 'Piemonte e lettaratura', 1995), 164–89; E. Ferrero, 'Introduzione', in P. Levi, *I racconti* (Turin: Einaudi, 1996), pp. vii–xx.

like the ASTM. The hero Renaudo encounters the mysterious, pedantic figure Peirani who explains the supreme importance of technical specifications as a measure for all functions, actions, even values:

'. . . il mondo di oggi riposa sulle specifiche, e cammina bene se queste sono rigorose, male se non lo sono, o se mancano affatto. Non ha mai avuto il dubbio che l'evidente divorzio fra le dottrine techniche e quelle morali, e l'altrettanto evidente atrofia di queste ultime, siano dovuti propio al fatto che l'universo morale manca finora di definizioni e tolleranze valide? Il giorno in cui non solo tutti gli oggetti, ma anche tutti i concetti, la Giustizia, l'Onestà, o anche solo il Profitto, o l'Ingegnere, o il Magistrato, avranno la loro buona specifica, con le relative tolleranze, e ben chiari i metodi e gli strumenti per controllarle, ebbene, quello sarà un grande giorno. E neppure dovrebbe mancare una specifica delle specifiche: ci sto pensando da tempo.' (I. 663)

('. . . today's world rests on specifications, and it progresses well as long as these are rigorous, badly if they are not or if they are missing altogether. Have you never suspected that the clear divide between technical and moral notions and the equally clear atrophying of the latter might be due to the fact that the moral universe has until now been quite without proper definitions and tolerances? The day in which not only all objects, but all concepts, Justice, Honesty, or even just Profit, or the Engineer, the Magistrate, will have their decent specifications, well, that will be a great day. And no one should forget the need for a specification for specifications: I've been working on it for some time.')

Here, as always in his science fiction, Levi is ironizing the reductive simplification of genuine and complex moral problems. Peirani is hoist with his own petard in the remainder of the story: Renaudo discovers a dusty old specification for Man, penned by Peirani and then shelved by the 'company'. When it is put into practice, Peirani fails his own test and resigns. And the story ends on a dystopian note, as the narrator opens out onto a world increasingly overrun by 'la normalizzazione, l'unificazione, la programmazione, la standardizzazione, e la razionalizzazione della produzione' (I. 670; 'normalization, unification, planification, standardization, and the rationalization of production'). In other words, measurement can be a root cause of social control, hierarchy, and exclusion, another form of the potentially totalitarian legacy of Enlightenment progress of which Levi, devotee of Enlightened values, is all too starkly aware.

Peirani's principles are corrupt in their excess, then, but the problem of measurement, judgement, of how to measure moral issues without a scale on which to measure them, is a deep and recurrent concern of Levi's. The paradoxical bind is that we must work as if there were indeed such specifications for morality, humanity, identity, and the like, whilst not falling into the trap of actually believing they could ever crystallize into simple formulae or facts and figures such as those tried out by Peirani. It is the same bind that makes the nuclear question so testing and so anxious, as Levi discusses in 'Eclissi dei profeti': with no precedent to the risk of global annihilation against which to judge our dealing with it now, our responsibilities are more complex and weighty than ever. Precision of measurement demands precise acknowledgement of when precise measurement is impossible.

One final, more general aspect of the practice of measurement as an ethically weighted process concerns chemistry once again, and specifically the language of weighing itself as an idiom of careful judgement. Two moments, from *Il sistema periodico* and *I sommersi e i salvati* respectively, best illustrate Levi's credo of chemistry as a means to knowledge, judgement, and writing through weighing. The first comes in the midst of one of the most moving descriptions Levi gave of his rebirth to life after his return, upon finding work and meeting his future wife:

lo stesso mio scrivere diventò . . . un costruire lucido, ormai non piú solitario: un'opera di chimico che *pesa e divide, misura e giudica* su prove certe, e s'industria di rispondere ai perché. . . . Era esaltante cercare e trovare, o creare, la parola giusta, cioè commisurata, breve e forte; ricavare le cose dal ricordo, e descriverle col massimo rigore e il minimo ingombro. (I. 872–3; emphasis added)
(my very writing turned into . . . a lucid construction, no longer solitary: the work of a chemist who weighs and divides, measures and judges by certain indices and works hard to reply to questions why. . . . It was uplifting to look and to find, or to create, the right word, that is, proportionate, brief, and strong; to dig things out of my memory and describe them with the maximum rigour and the minimum baggage.)

The process of moving from weighing up to dividing ('pesa e divide'; chemistry as 'Scheidekunst' again) is equivalent to that process that moves from measurement to judgement ('misura e giudica'), a sequence that perhaps defines once and for all our topic here. And notice, again, how recurrent features of the practice of measure are gathered together in this passage— measure as process and struggle, not necessarily as solution ('s'industria di rispondere ai perché'), as restraint and economy (here of language, 'commisurata, breve e forte', 'col massimo rigore e il minimo ingombro').

The second example comes from Levi's response to Jean Améry, 'L'intellettuale ad Auschwitz', a key locus both because Améry's notion of the intellectual was a humanist one—thus calling Levi to defend his scientific formation with its values of precision, among other things—and because Améry's guiding mode of response to Nazi violence and torture was to 'return the blow', to resent so as not to flatten the guilt of the guilty.[13] Levi's restraint is thus called into sharp critical question by Améry. In this context, Levi tellingly defends but also acknowledges the risks of his 'scientific' practice of considering people as 'esseri umani ma anche "campioni", esemplari in busta chiusa, da riconoscere, analizzare e pesare' (II. 1102; 'human beings, but also "samples", models in a sealed envelope, to identify, analyse, and weigh'), and therefore of learning from Auschwitz the measure of man, how to 'misurare gli uomini' (ibid.).

SELF-KNOWLEDGE

If the first two meanings of measure frequently go hand in hand— to be restrained and proportionate, to follow the mean whilst watching the extremes *is* in a sense to be precise in one's measurements and distinctions and to know the limits of measurement— the third is more loosely related but no less important, carrying the weight of the first two meanings into new and newly intense territory. The third ethical meaning of measure emerges when it is turned reflexively in on the self, in the verb 'misurarsi'. In Levi's value-laden vocabulary, 'misurarsi' has few rivals for the sheer power assigned to it for defining the proper purpose of experience and action.

Before looking at the moments where Levi expounds his notion of 'misurarsi' and its sources, it is worth noting that none of these instances is in either *Se questo è un uomo* or *I sommersi e i salvati*, as though Levi were operating a distinction between the

---

[13] On Levi and Améry, see Chapter 2 note 15.

undoubtedly testing, probing extremes of experience in Auschwitz, where however the tests could not be read as active engagement with experience, and the measuring of oneself against the vicissitudes of life beyond the camps, which could and should be read in precisely that way. There is a clear parallel here with his attitude to work, an ennobling and properly human activity, but one which he refused to see in even reduced form in the so-called 'work' enforced on him in Auschwitz (see Chapter 6). With that important proviso, which speaks volumes about Levi's practice of careful distinction in his crucial switching from the camps world to the everyday world and back, we can turn to the two principal sources of Levi's notion of self-testing, both rooted in memories from his youth: Joseph Conrad and mountaineering.

Conrad was a hero for the young Levi (as he was for his contemporary Italo Calvino, and others of their literary generation in Italy). He is one of a group of writers of a certain 'strong' kind who forge a key side of Levi's identity (others include Jack London and Melville—in Pavese's translation—later supplemented by Vercel, Rigoni Stern, and so on).[14] In Conrad, Levi admires the world of the professional seaman, the intimate knowledge of and respect for the sea as a powerful enemy and master of life; but he also admires his capacity to go against the grain, in life and writing, to chart the struggles of a life without ceding to the anxious need to talk in the first person ('l'angoscia di dire "io"', *La ricerca della radici*, II. 1414; 'the anxiety of saying "I"'), to create adventure through the challenges of the seafarer. 'Misurarsi' or 'provarsi' are the terms he uses to describe this package of qualities in Conrad and it is clearly from him that he adopts it as a guiding practical end for experience. His first opportunity to hone his own life as a form of adventure came in the mountains near Turin.

In the chapter 'Ferro' in *Il sistema periodico*, Levi relates his friendship with Sandro, the taciturn, thick-skinned, but immensely generous and adventurous fellow student referred to in Chapter 3. Levi and Sandro seal their friendship through climbing mountains and mountaineering becomes a powerful life-lesson for Levi, inculcating in him the value of risk, of challenging the physical, natural

---

[14] On Levi, Calvino, and Conrad, see G. Bertone, 'Italo Calvino e Primo Levi', in *Il castello della scrittura* (Turin: Einaudi, 1994), 177–211 [203–4]. Conrad and the others mentioned all end up in *La ricerca delle radici*.

world and emerging unscathed (or indeed emerging scathed, which brings its own lessons), of setting out reliant only on oneself and one's wits to judge the way ahead. Ultimately, this challenge becomes a crucial route to self-knowledge through testing and stretching one's limits. This is what Levi encapsulates in the term 'misurarsi': '[A Sandro] importava conoscere i suoi limiti, misurarsi e migliorarsi' (I. 778; '[For Sandro] the important thing was to know his limits, to test himself and better himself'). The phrase sets up the three stages as congruent: to measure oneself *is* to know one's limits which in turn *is* to improve oneself. Levi finds the same nexus in a book by Bertrand Russell, *The Conquest of Happiness*, in which to be judged, to be challenged, and especially to fail certain challenges are crucial stages in self-knowing. Not to be judged, by contrast, 'è come pilotare una barca senza bussola, o come pretendere di mantenere costante una temperatura senza consultare un termometro' (II. 934; 'is like sailing a ship without a compass, or like trying to keep a constant temperature without consulting a thermometer').[15] Once again, the instruments of measurement—the compass and the thermometer—are central figures for self-knowledge.

The same qualities of restraint and self-sufficient reflection found in Sandro's actions are echoed in his reflections, years later, on the resources that chemistry has brought him as a writer:

le cose che ho viste, sperimentate e fatte nella mia precedente incarnazione sono oggi, per me scrittore, una fonte preziosa di materie prime, di fatti da raccontare, e non solo di fatti: anche di quelle emozioni fondamentali che sono il misurarsi con la materia (che è un giudice imparziale, impassibile ma durissimo: se sbagli ti punisce senza pietà), il vincere, il rimanere sconfitti (II. 641–2)
(the things I saw, tried out, and did in my previous incarnation are today, for me as a writer, a precious source of primary material, of events to narrate, and not only events: also those fundamental emotions which come from testing oneself against matter (an impartial judge, impassive but extremely harsh: if you make a mistake it punishes you pitilessly), from winning and losing)

Both mountaineering and chemistry are constituted by the trials of

---

[15] B. Russell, *The Conquest of Happiness* (London: Allen and Unwin, 1930) is included in *La ricerca delle radici* (II. 1484–90) and is praised in an article in *Racconti e saggi* ('Lotta per la vita', II. 933–4).

the natural world, the confrontation with Matter or *hyle* (I. 767). And we might add here, in the light of earlier parts of this chapter, that there is an honesty and nobility in this form of trial with nature that stands in stark contrast to the artificial static trials and tests of efficiency against dry technical specifications satirized in 'Le nostre belle specificazioni' and the like.

In retrospect, Levi also senses in Sandro's eccentric, but prematurely wise guidance in the mountains a darker presentiment: 'piú oscuramente [Sandro] sentiva il bisogno di preparasi (e di prepararmi) per un avvenire di ferro, di mese in mese piú vicino' (I. 778; 'in some more obscure way [Sandro] felt the need to prepare himself (and me) for a future of iron, coming closer by the month'). If, then, there is something obscene about looking for self-improvement in the trials of the camps, as suggested above, Levi can nevertheless see a bridge leading from his lessons in the mountains near Turin (in physical survival but also in moral resistance) and his ordeal or indeed Sandro's fighting and death in the Resistance, shot in the back by a Fascist child-killer in 1944 (I. 781). Levi too, in later describing his own choice to go into the hills and fight in the Resistance—a decision which swiftly led to his capture and deportation—again returns to this defining purpose and motive:

dopo la lunga ubriacatura di parole, certi della giustezza della nostra scelta, estremamente insicuri dei nostri mezzi, con in cuore assai piú disperazione che speranza, e sullo sfondo di un paese disfatto e diviso, siamo scesi in campo per misurarci. (I. 852)
(after the long delirium of words, sure of the rightness of our chosen path, extremely unsure of our means, with much more despair than hope in our hearts, and against the backdrop of a defeated and divided country, we entered the fray to test ourselves.)

The continuing Sandro-like (and indeed anti-Fascist) suspicion of words is worth noting here, since the trials of self-measure are constantly accompanied in Levi by praise of action and suspicion of mind. This is a crucial and seldom acknowledged facet of Levi, who so often appears on the contrary and wrongly as cerebral, rationalist to the last. Every step he takes in *Il sistema periodico* away from bookish and humanistic study towards first science in books, then science in student labs, and then science in the world of work and real problems to be solved, is accompanied by joyous reflection on the concrete, useful, and fallible vitality of the new challenge:

per la prima volta dopo diciassette anni di carriera scolastica, di aoristi e di guerre di Peloponneso, le cose imparate incominciavano dunque a servirmi. L'analisi quantitativa, così avara di emozioni, greve come il granito, diventava viva, vera, utile, inserita in un'opera seria e concreta. Serviva: era inquadrata in un piano, una tessera di un mosaico. Il metodo analitico che seguivo non era più un dogma libresco, veniva ricollaudato ogni giorno, poteva essere affinato, reso conforme ai nostri scopi, con un gioco sottile di ragione, di prove e di errori. (I. 801)
(for the first time after seventeen years of a school career, of aorists and Peloponnesian wars, something I had learned was beginning to come in useful. Quantitative analysis, so spare in its emotions, dense as granite, was coming alive, true, useful, part of a serious concrete task. It was useful: part of a plan, the tile of a mosaic. The analytic method I was following was no longer some bookish dogma, but was tested out every day, could be refined, adapted to our aims, through a subtle game of reason, trial and error.)

The role of error in this process will be taken up in Chapter 6 below, but it is worth pausing on this passage and noting the sheer brio with which Levi enacts in his writing the vital process of flexible, experimental reaching towards knowledge, usefulness, and understanding that is the very process he is describing. Added to this is the very real instinctive, almost physically primitive (indeed masculine—Sandro is one of those strong, solitary, silent men noted in Chapter 3) connotations in this wordless struggle with nature. Nowhere is this clearer than at a point earlier on in *Il sistema periodico* where Levi offers us another figure for that struggle, the hunter: as a hunter, you are on your own, 'prendi e parti . . . le esperienze degli altri non servono, l'essenziale è misurarsi. Chi vale vince' (I. 766; 'you get up and go . . . the experiences of others are useless, the essential thing is to measure yourself. The worthy will win'). In later formulations, Levi softens this pitiless version by feeding into the process of 'misurarsi' a human dimension, such as the bond of experience forged between himself and Sandro, but a residue of the solitary path of the hunter remains even there. It is there too in the character of Faussone in *La chiave a stella*, clearly in part a fictional descendant of Sandro's. In *La chiave a stella*, in a pivotal chapter entitled 'Tiresia', the narrator (Levi) and Faussone agree that their three métiers—Levi's writing and chemistry and Faussone's engineering—share a great deal in common: all three find in the objects they create and see growing and existing before them '[il] vantaggio di potersi misurare, del non dipendere da altri nel misurarsi, dello specchiarsi nella propria opera' (I. 989; 'the advantage of being able to test oneself, of not depending on others in testing oneself, of being reflected in one's own work'). In its solitary nobility, 'misurarsi' begins to seem at these moments as not only or not so much a virtue to be proactively chosen as a means to self-improvement, as a form of destiny, to be suffered and survived: in finishing the account of his choice to join the partisans quoted above, Levi says as much: 'siamo scesi in campo per misurarci. Ci separammo per seguire il nostro destino, ognuno in una valle diversa' (I. 852; 'we entered the fray to test ourselves. We split to follow our destiny, each in a different valley').

A final point to underline in tracing the multivalent virtue of measure in Levi is its persistent dependency on a (Socratic) notion of limit, a limit to what is human. This sensitivity to boundaries has emerged more than once above, in this chapter and others: in Levi's probing the limits of human language, of happiness, pleasure and pain, of the scope of man's knowledge and self-knowledge, of physical strength and survival. In Dante's Ulisse, we have a figure of knowledge as a striving after limits and then transgressing its boundaries. And, despite the virtue of measured restraint that permeates his work, Levi also has in him a fascination with excess, 'la virtù dell'eccesso', as he labels it in Rabelais (II. 646). Several of his strangest science-fiction stories explore the disturbing, often erotically charged possibility of the interpenetration of bodies, surfaces, channels of fertility (e.g. 'Disfilassi', *Lilìt*, II. 93–9); others chart the boundary between what is human and what is or could be of the machine, and tease out a series of moral quandaries from the mapping involved. Several of these will be explored further in future chapters. Here it will suffice to have established in Levi's simultaneous sense of measure (restraint, precision and self-knowledge) and of limit—and the possible transgression of both—a fundamental constellation of his ethics of practical intelligence.

6

PRACTICE, OR TRIAL AND ERROR

Si enim fallor sum.
(Augustine)

A great deal has been written about Levi's championing of a certain work ethic.[1] Indeed, for anyone attempting a reading of his *oeuvre* from an ethical perspective, his ideas on work, expressed especially in books from the 1970s such as *Il sistema periodico* and *La chiave a stella*, would seem to constitute one of the most evident and weighty anchors of all. In both those books, Levi champions a vision of work as an intelligent, individual, and immensely fulfilling endeavour in contrast to a certain strand of pessimistic left radicalism of the 1960s and 1970s which saw all work as necessarily alienating, deindividualizing, and, ultimately, complicit with 'the system'; all of this set against the memory of the genuinely alienating, deindividualizing—we might say, useless—work of the *Lager* ('Arbeit macht frei').[2] A less than generous reader might add

---

[1] For Levi himself on work, see *La chiave a stella*, especially 'Batter la lastra' (I. 1015–16) and his interview with Giuseppe Grassano in Levi, *The Voice of Memory*, 121–35 [122–4]. Others who have discussed this aspect include G. Varchetta, *Ascoltando Primo Levi. Organizzazione, narrazione, etica* (Milan: Guerrini, 1991); M. Strata, 'Primo Levi: un uomo al lavoro', *Critica letteraria*, 20/11/75 (1992), 369–84; M. Cicioni, *Primo Levi* (Oxford: Berg, 1995), 84–5, 94; M. Belpoliti, *Primo Levi* (Milan: Bruno Mandadori, 1998), 100–2; D. Del Giudice, 'Introduzione' in Levi, *Opere*, I. pp. xlii–lii. For an interesting attempt to link Levi's Faussone to post-industrial work practices, see G. Lerner, 'I legionati dell'ex città-fabbrica', *La stampa* (3 Nov. 1997), 7.

[2] See Levi's 1959 article ' "Arbeit macht frei" ', I. 1120–1; and Rudolf Höss's autobiography which includes a paean to the moral value of work (R. Höss, *Comandante ad Auschwitz* (Turin: Einaudi, 1985), 55–7; Levi wrote a preface to this edition, now at II. 1276–83). Another *locus* of Levi's meditation on work is in *La tregua* where the contrast between his two wily guides and companions, Mordo Nahum and Cesare, is to a significant degree based on a difference of spirit in their approach to work: see I. 237–8.

that his comments on work at times offer evidence of the thin dividing line that separates moral reflection from moralistic preaching in Levi. Partly for this reason, and partly out of a simple desire not to go over well-worn territory, there is no chapter on 'Work' in this book. However, if we take Levi's investment in the value of work as a starting point of ethical reflection rather than a *fait accompli*, we find that more subtle and more interesting ethical trajectories emerge. If we move away from his sometimes dour defence of solid professions, of skill and its handing down between the generations, of self-sufficiency and self-employment, and see them as symptoms of a broader and more flexible notion of practice, we can see a larger defence of human autonomy, human craft and creativity and engagement with the world (leading to knowledge). This opens a field of reflections closely attuned to the other ordinary virtues under discussion in Part II. 'Practice' in this sense implies both action and training in a set of actions; it suggests processes of testing, trying out, probing, and experimenting, all propelled and given ethical weight for Levi by the possibility, indeed the fundamental necessity of getting things wrong along the way. This chapter looks at the 'uses of error' in Levi's ethics.[3]

We can begin to approach the question of error by way of its epistemological aspect. For whether in his chemistry, his writing, or his life's experience, Levi pursues knowledge through testing out hypotheses and probing for the limits of error. Umberto Eco writes about the epistemology of error in his 1999 collection of essays *Serendipities*, in an essay entitled 'The Force of Falsity'.[4] Looking at some of the most portentous errors in history—from Ptolemaic astronomy to the Donation of Constantine to the *Protocols of the Elders of Zion*—he makes several points that are useful as a basis for examining error in Levi. First, serendipity itself: error can transform the world, for better or for worse, leading from a mistaken notion to the discovery of something true either in a chain of pure chance or by the realization of why that mistaken notion was in error but contained a kernel of truth. Such half-truths, says Eco, 'exist in a twilight zone between common

---

[3] The phrase is taken from F. Kermode, *The Uses of Error* (London: Collins, 1990).

[4] U. Eco, *Serendipities* (London: Weidenfeld and Nicolson, 1999), 3–21. S. J. Gould's *The Mismeasure of Man* (Harmondsworth: Penguin, 1997), mentioned in Chapter 5, is a case study in the scientific uses of error, and of the historical process of recognizing error as such: Gould calls it 'a chronicle of deep and instructive fallacies' (p. 26).

sense and lunacy, truth and error, visionary intelligence and what now seems to us stupidity, though it was not stupid in its day and we must therefore reconsider it with great respect' (p. viii). Secondly, the 'politics' of error: errors survive tenaciously for as long as they serve a useful purpose as models of the truth. They are only abandoned when another, equally useful model (perhaps even the truth itself) emerges at the right moment (p. 18), not simply when the truth appears. Thirdly, errors are fictions, myths and tales that are immensely powerful and dangerous *because* they are myths and tales, and we need to be alert readers of narrative to control the borders between truth and error, to distinguish (p. 19).

Eco is, in effect, suggesting a sort of adapted Popperian approach to the history of knowledge, installing error and falsifiability as core principles.[5] Levi has much in common with both Eco and Popper as philosophers of science in this respect, although, as we shall see, he affords far greater importance than either to a form of *self*-knowledge also forged in a process of practice, or trial and error. Levi, like Eco, is an advocate of serendipity, not least in his wandering ('vagabondaggio', II. 631) through 'other people's trades' in *L'altrui mestiere* (see Chapter 13); and a keen analyst of the power of error and chance in transforming the world and individual destiny, and in acquiring knowledge. He is also fascinated by the persistence of error in the face of contrary evidence (see, for example, his astronomical story 'Una stella tranquilla', I. 78–9); and he sees the narrative power of stories of trial and error, turning the epistemology of error into an offshoot of narrative. Finally, he like Eco is doggedly intent on distinguishing truth from falsity even where the task is fraught and near-impossible. All of these could be illustrated out of Levi's Holocaust experiences: the terrible chance of being 'caught up in a whirlwind' (II. 859), the self-deceiving errors of memory amongst the perpetrators ('La memoria dell'offesa', II. 1006–16), his numberless *distinguo*'s in his dissection of the *Lager* world. However, the strongest affinities between Levi and the sort of epistemology sketched by Eco is found, as one might expect, in his writings on science.

---

[5] See K. Popper, *The Logic of Scientific Discovery* (London: Hutchinson, 1959), 40–2, 78–92 (for other aspects related to Levi, see pp. 18, 22 (scientific knowledge as 'common sense knowledge writ large'), 112–35 ('testability'), 136–45 ('simplicity')).

A good starting place is Levi's 1985 review of the autobiography of Salvador Luria, the American-based Italian geneticist and Nobel laureate, 'Roulette dei batteri' (*Racconti e saggi*, II. 950–3). Levi and Luria had much in common—both were Turin-born and Jewish, both attended the legendary liceo Massimo d'Azeglio (Luria several years before Levi), both were scientists who worked with molecules, even if one was carrying out pure research on immensely complex genes and the other was working for commercial ends with simple synthetic polymers. From Luria's autobiography Levi recognizes and admires something of a philosophy of scientific research or simple problem-solving that chimes with his own.

Levi takes his cue from the two images in Luria's title, in English *A Slot Machine, a Broken Test Tube*,[6] two images that help him restate his understanding of the struggle of the scientist in the laboratory as he reaches forward towards new discoveries. The slot machine is for Luria a personal token of the irrational and individual element in scientific progress: rather than working by rational induction or deduction, Luria arrived at a sudden intuition or conjecture (to use Popper's terminology) about the genetic workings of bacteria through a casual observation of a colleague playing at a slot machine. From the anecdote Levi and Luria draw out certain prerequisites for innovation and understanding, such as intuition, flexibility, and the ability to make connections and see analogies across wide gulfs, the interpretation of symbols, the alert mind of the lone 'adventurer'-scientist.

The second image complements the first: Luria recounts how he replaced a broken test-tube in haste with another that contained a slightly different type of bacteria, thereby leading by chance to a result that led directly to the development of modern genetic engineering. In this sequence serendipitous error has a dual role to play: first there is error as random accident, as the pure chance of the broken test-tube; then there is the scientific 'error' of assuming that one kind of bacteria would serve much as well as another (in itself not so much an error, since the experiment did work in its own terms: the crucial point was that secondary differences created unexpected secondary results, leading to a sort of displaced or transversal epistemological leap noted also by Eco). As

---

[6] S. Luria, *A Slot Machine, a Broken Test Tube* (New York: Harper and Row, 1984).

with the slot machine, however, the scientist must have the ability to assimilate and respond to the unexpected result thrown up by the errors, through both scientific reason and all the irrational qualities of the adventurer: Levi is reminded of a famous Machiavellian topos, 'la vittoria è dei forti aiutati dalla fortuna' (II. 952; 'victory goes to the strong helped by fortune'). Images of victory and implicitly of struggle, but also of error and chance, are intertwined and interdependent.[7]

The review ends with comment on the recurrent 'primitive' imagery of science as agonistic struggle, as 'conflittuale, intessuta di battaglie, sconfitte e vittorie' (II. 952; 'conflictual, interwoven with battles, defeats, and victories'). Levi qualifies the image, noting that according to the optimistic Luria, the battle is conducted against 'the unknown' rather than against fellow scientists—'non si tratta mai di una guerra civile . . . gli scienziati discutono fra loro, competono, ma non combattono' (ibid.; 'it is never a civil war . . . scientists discuss amongst themselves, compete, but they do not fight'). Luria's idealistic vision is poised between, on the one hand, struggle, the confrontation of mind and 'the unknown' matter around it; and, on the other hand, cooperation, the balance between the individual and the community of scientists in the prosecution of that struggle. Both elements—struggle and cooperation—are carefully calibrated features of Levi's sense of scientific and also larger ethical practice. Furthermore, the vocabulary of struggle, of battle, victory and defeat, translates directly into a vocabulary of error, of trial, error, and resolution, since to be 'defeated' by the unknown or by brute matter is to be proved wrong in an experiment, in an attempt to analyse, manipulate, or refashion the world. And there are strong echoes here of the dynamics of 'misurarsi' examined above in Chapter 5. As Levi states in his preface to *La ricerca delle radici*, there are fundamental and parallel tensions inscribed in the very fabric of our destiny as thinking beings: '*errore/verità*, riso/pianto, senno/follia, speranza/disperazione, *vittoria/sconfitta*' (II. 1365; emphases added; 'error/truth, laughter/tears, wisdom/folly, hope/despair, victory/defeat'). And the parallels go further still, beyond our

---

[7] Already in *La tregua*, Levi was ironically describing Cesare's con of injecting fish with water to increase their weight and value in these terms: 'Come avviene per molte scoperte scientifiche, la pensata della siringa era scaturita da un insuccesso e da una osservazione fortuita' (I. 331).

knowledge and self-knowledge into the very workings of Darwinian evolution and adaptation, described by Levi more than once as a form of Nature's intelligence ('astuzia') applied through a process of trial and error (II. 728).

From 'Roulette dei batteri', we can take three fundamental figures at work within Levi's philosophy of science: science as a struggle with the unknown towards victory and defeat; scientific discovery as intuitive adventure, almost heroically open to the unexpected and the irrational; and scientific discovery as a product of instructive error, chance, and the capacity to recognize and seize the opportunity they present. Not surprisingly, the same elements recur frequently whenever Levi talks about his own experience of chemistry, both as a career and as a system of knowledge about the world. In *L'altrui mestiere*, for example, we have already come across two essays—'Ex chimico' and 'Il segno del chimico'—where Levi looks back over his career and training as a chemist, and the vocabulary of struggle, irrational adventure, and error pervades them both.

'Ex chimico' traces the bonds between his chemistry and his second métier, writing, and one of these is, precisely, the experience of failure:

... il misurarsi con la materia (che è giudice imparziale, impassibile ma durissimo: se ti sbagli ti punisce senza pietà), il vincere, il rimanere sconfitti. Quest'ultima è un'esperienza dolorosa ma salutare, senza la quale non si diventa adulti e responsabili. Credo che ogni mio collega chimico lo potrà confermare: si impara piú dai propri errori che dai propri successi. Ad esempio: formulare un'ipotesi esplicativa, crederci, affezionarcisi, controllarla (oh, la tentazione di falsare i dati, di dar loro un piccolo colpo di pollice!) ed infine trovarla errata, è un ciclo che nel mestiere del chimico si incontra anche troppo spesso 'allo stato puro', ma che è facile riconoscere in infiniti altri itinerari umani. Chi lo percorre con onestà ne esce maturato. (II. 641–2)

(... to test oneself against matter (an impartial judge, impassive but extremely harsh: if you make a mistake it punishes you pitilessly), winning and losing. The latter is a painful but salutary experience, without which no one becomes adult and responsible. I believe that every fellow chemist can confirm that you learn more from your mistakes than from your successes. For instance: to formulate an explanatory hypothesis, to believe in it, to grow to like it, to check it (oh, the temptation to falsify the data, to give them a little tweak!), and in the end to find it wrong, is a cycle that a chemist will encounter in its pure form all too often, but which is easy to recognize in countless other human paths also. Travel the path with honesty and you will emerge maturer for it.)

Similarly, but with different emphases, in 'Il segno del chimico' Levi returns to his days as a student, recalling the initiatory rites of passage of his first laboratory adventures. One of these rites was the scarring of the hand by shattered test-tubes, an accident or error that the students were not forewarned about, since the rite was in the error and the mark it left in blood and scars. Another rite was getting basic practical analyses of unknown elements wrong. A failed exam was unfortunate, but was also 'una disavventura da raccontare con una certa allegria' (II. 812; 'a misadventure to relate with a certain pleasure'); to fail in the 'primary scene' of one's first contact with 'matter' was, by contrast, a source of shame:

sbagliare un'analisi era brutto: forse perché, inconsciamente, ci si rendeva conto che il giudizio degli uomini (in questo caso dei professori) è arbitrario e contestabile, mentre il giudizio delle cose è sempre inesorabile e giusto: una legge uguale per tutti. (ibid.)
(to get an analysis wrong was unpleasant: perhaps because, unconsciously, we realized that the judgement of men (in this case of professors) was arbitrary and debatable, but the judgement of things is always inexorable and right: a law that is the same for all.)

As both extracts make clear, Levi is interested in far more than chemistry here. We might have suspected as much, since they are in any case only two in a rich collection of essays centred on *other people's* trades, and thus interested in the bridges between different human activities, crafts, or professions. The move beyond the laboratory is clear in a typically Levian stylistic (and metaethical) slippage between the particular and the general: in 'Ex chimico', as he talks of his unique personal make-up as a writer, the impersonal carefully emerges ('quelle emozioni fondamentali', 'non si diventi adulti', 'infiniti altri itinerari umani', 'Chi lo percorre'); in 'Il segno del chimico' similarly, a university anecdote swiftly transforms itself into a comparison between the human ('il giudizio degli uomini') and the material ('il giudizio delle cose'). Furthermore, in both extracts quoted above, his experiences of failure are markers of the ritual passage into adult maturity and responsibility, suggesting an idealized moral-biographical aspect to this question—error as a vessel of ethical *Bildung*—which will prove fundamental as we move on to works such as *Il sistema periodico*. Finally, both forge a link between error and storytelling ('di fatti da raccontare, e non solo di fatti'; 'una disavventura da raccontare'), a crucial ethical and metaethical dimension underpinning this and many other ordinary virtues in Levi. The (mocklegal) title of one of Levi's science-fiction collections seals the connection: *Vizio di forma*. Its stories are made from tracing the scientific and human consequences of a flaw or formal defect. Error makes for ethical narrative (see Chapter 11).

All the elements we have seen in 'Roulette dei batteri' and other essays are brought into compelling synthesis in *Il sistema periodico*, where practice and problem-solving, training and trial and error give the book its very narrative drive and its autobiographical shape. The opening chapters especially amount to a condensed *Bildungsroman* constructed around the noise of Levi's first experiments and errors both in chemistry—the explosion of glass in 'Idrogeno' or the shutters set on fire in 'Potassio'—and in a life moving from adolescence to adulthood—the timid victory of grasping fellow student Rita's arm ('Mi pareva di aver vinto una battaglia . . . contro il buio, il vuoto, e gli anni nemici che sopravvenivano', I. 770; 'I felt I had won a battle . . . against darkness, the void, and the hostile years that were coming'); or the taste of 'bear's meat' during hours stuck up in the freezing mountains with Sandro ('il sapore di essere forti e liberi, liberi anche di sbagliare, e padroni del proprio destino', I. 781; 'the taste of being strong and free, free even to make mistakes, and masters of our own destiny'). Later in the book, stories of chance, serendipity, and the inventive capacity to exploit them come to the fore, in the shape of the intuitive flash ('l'idea mi venne come si accende una lampada', I. 805; 'the idea came to me like a bulb lighting up') or the chance discovery (e.g., of a supply of cerium in the camp laboratory, exploited by Alberto's ingenuity in 'Cerio', I. 862–6) or lateral thinking (trying out chicken excrement to make cosmetics in 'Azoto', I. 890–7).

Levi is never averse to drawing moral lessons from his experience and his stories, and many of these episodes come accompanied with morals, on grand questions such as difference, impurity, freedom, the need to 'misurarsi', and the nobility of matter transformed. Indeed, several of these *loci* are recognizable as foundation-stones of the ordinary virtues that we have discussed elsewhere:

chi va in caccia non ha che da prendere il fucile, anzi meglio la zagaglia
e l'arco, e mettersi per il bosco: il successo e l'insuccesso dipendono solo
da lui. . . . l'essenziale è misurarsi. Chi vale vince, chi ha occhio o brac-
cia o fiuto debole ritorna e cambia mestiere . . . ('Zinco', I. 766)
(to go hunting you need only take a rifle, or better a spear and bow, and
head off into the woods: success and failure depend only on you . . . the
essential thing is to test oneself. The worthy will win, whoever has weak
sight, arm, or instinct should return and change profession . . .)

la nobiltà dell'Uomo, acquisita in cento secoli di prove e di errori, era
consistita nel farsi signore della materia, e . . . io mi ero iscritto a Chimica
perché a questa nobiltà mi volevo mantenere fedele. ('Ferro', I. 774)
(Man's nobility, acquired over a hundred centuries of trial and error, had
consisted in making oneself the master of matter, and . . . I had enrolled
for Chemistry because I wished to keep faith with that nobility.)

Il metodo analitico che seguivo non era piú un dogma libresco, veniva
ricollaudato ogni giorno, poteva essere affinato, reso conforme ai nostri
scopi, con un gioco sottile di ragione, di prove e di errori. Sbagliare non
era piú un infortunio vagamente comico, che ti guasta un esame o ti
abbassa il voto: sbagliare era come quando si va su roccia, un misurarsi,
un accorgersi, uno scalino in su, che ti rende piú valente e piú adatto.
('Nichel', I. 801)
(The analytic method I was following was no longer some bookish
dogma, but was tested out every day, could be refined, adapted to our
aims, through a subtle game of reason, trial and error. To make a mistake
was no longer a vaguely comic accident, which spoils an exam or lowers
a mark: it was like going climbing, testing oneself, noticing, moving one
step up which leaves you worthier and more adept.)

Ma non è piú tempo di folletti, di niccoli e di coboldi. Siamo chimici,
cioè cacciatori: nostre sono 'le due esperienze della vita adulta' di cui
parlava Pavese, il successo e l'insuccesso, uccidere la balena bianca o sfas-
ciare la nave; non ci si deve arrendere alla materia incomprensibile, non
ci si deve cedere. Siamo qui per questo, per sbagliare e per correggerci,
per incassare colpi e renderli. Non ci si deve mai sentire disarmati: la
natura è immensa e complessa, ma non è impermeabile all'intelligenza;
devi girarle intorno, pungere, sondare, cercare il varco e fartelo. I miei
colloqui settimanali col Tenente sembravano piani di guerra. ('Nichel', I.
804)
(But this is not a time of elves, sprites, and pixies. We are chemists, that
is hunters: ours are 'the two experiences of adult life' that Pavese talked
of, success and failure, to kill the white whale or destroy the ship; we
must not surrender to unfathomable matter, we must not give in. This is
why we are here, to err and put right, to take blows and return them.

You must never feel defenceless: nature is immense and complex but not impermeable to intelligence; you must circle around her, prick her, take soundings, search for a breach and open it. My weekly discussions with the Lieutenant were like councils of war.)

The last two extracts, both from 'Nichel', are worth dwelling on a little. 'Nichel' is a doubly pivotal story in *Il sistema periodico*. As it opens, in late 1941, 'Primo Levi, di razza ebraica' (as his degree certificate has it) has graduated 'cum laude'; at home, his father is slowly dying from a tumour, while the Germans are triumphant across Europe and Pearl Harbor is days away; 'il mondo precipitava alla catastrofe' (I. 792; 'the world was plunging towards catastrophe'). All these elements point to a symbolic moment of passage in Levi from adolescence to adulthood, an invasion of reality, history, of that world of action and consequence so crucial to Levi's ethics of work and error. It is time to put away childish things. As if to underline this, the arrival of the mysterious Tenente, who appears on his doorstep to offer him his first practical job in a strange, secret mine outside Turin, strikes the young Primo as a sort of annunciation:

io non tardai a ravvisare in lui la figura del messaggero, del mercurio che guida le anime, o se vogliamo dell'angelo anunciatore: di colui insomma che ognuno attende, lo sappia o no, e che porta il messaggio che ti fa cambiare la vita . . . (ibid.)
(I did not hesitate to see in him the figure of the messenger, of Mercury guiding the souls or if you wish of the anunciating angel: in short, the one we all wait for, knowingly or not, who carries a message that will change our lives)

The story of his attempts to extract nickel from the rocks at the mine is one of ingenuity, naive excitement, failure, and success; and both the magic of the place and the moment in his life and in Europe's history load these attempts with meaning for Levi. Even the rocks are the same Alpine rocks that meant so much to him and Sandro: 'quei rovi e quelle pietre che erano la mia isola e la mia libertà, una libertà che forse presto avrei perduta. . . . con essa [quella roccia] avevo contratto un duplice legame, prima nelle imprese con Sandro, poi qui, tentandola come chimico per strapparle il tesoro' (I. 803; 'those briars and those stones which were my island and my freedom, a freedom that I would perhaps soon lose. . . . with [the rock] I had forged a double bond, first from my exploits with Sandro and then here, testing it out as a chemist to find a way of stripping it of its treasure'). And the youthful freedom that the rocks and mountains represented, now slowly slipping from Levi as this strange adventure progresses with war raging around him and his own catastrophe not far away, was of course the freedom to err ('la libertà di sbagliare', I. 781).[8]

The link from 'Nichel' to Levi's catastrophe is more than chronological. It is intriguing to note that key problems thrown up by the Holocaust are adumbrated as he comments in 'Nichel' on error, struggle with brute matter, victory, and defeat. The problem of incomprehensibility—so charged in the context of the Holocaust, as we saw in Chapter 3—is here inserted into the broader struggles of human intelligence: 'la natura è immensa e complessa, ma non è impermeabile all'intelligenza; devi girarle intorno, pungere, sondare, cercare il varco e fartelo.' More tellingly still, the dilemma of resistance or defiance, the problem of 'returning the blow' as dissected by Jean Améry and reflected on by Levi in *I sommersi e i salvati* and elsewhere, here seems turned on its head. Levi for once seems to stand with Améry—'Siamo qui per questo, . . . incassare colpi e renderli. Non ci si deve mai sentire disarmati'—but we should recall a distinction made by Levi through Salvador Luria in 'Roulette dei batteri': struggle with the unknown does not mean, indeed should preclude struggle between individuals. Levi will 'return the blow' against misfortune or the stubborn uncooperativeness of matter, not against other men, not even his own torturers.[9]

There are other ways in which, as with so many of the virtues we are discussing, a complex mirroring with the strange, inverted world of the camps is at work in the shaping of Levi's general sense of the uses of error. Three principal lines of intersection suggest themselves, one related to the system of annihilation in the Nazi camps, another to modes of death and unlikely survival for the victims, and finally a slightly oblique connection concerned with the issue of written testimony afterwards.

---

[8] See Levi's interview on mountaineering with Alberto Papuzzi in Levi, *The Voice of Memory*, 59–64; and A. Cavaglion, *Primo Levi e 'Se questo è un uomo'* (Turin: Loescher, 1993), 54–6. The link between youth and this freedom to get things wrong is confirmed wearily in 'Stagno' later in *Il sistema periodico*: 'la licenza di sbagliare si restringe con gli anni' (I. 902; 'our licence to make mistakes shrinks as we grow older').

[9] See Chapter 2 note 15.

First, it is obvious that any minimal error or failure, in the terms laid down within the camp system of work and torture (failure to follow orders, failure to understand orders, failure to work beyond physical collapse, the error of assuming any identity or the barest human rights, etc.), was synonymous with death, rather than with the dense, meaningful life or freedom that Levi likes to associate with error in his youth and early work stories. The system, like the self-important Prussian ethic at its origins, like the blind obedience of its practitioners, was rigid in this respect.[10] The flexibility, the capacity to respond to serendipitous chance, the probing experimentalism of Levi's ethics of error are anathema to this rigidity. In contrast, Levi is careful ironically to puncture the self-importance and potential rigidity of his own paeans to trial and error, victory and defeat. In each one of the stories quoted above—'Zinco', 'Ferro', and 'Nichel'—the young Levi's excitement at the prospect of heroic struggle is contained and even mocked: in 'Zinco', the hunter praised by Levi is the rather detached and sadistic Professor P., hardly a role model of humane flexibility; in 'Ferro' Sandro gently ridicules Primo for his high-flown dreams of the nobility of chemistry; and even in 'Nichel', Levi's hard-won victory over the stones of the mine proves chemically flawed and commercially useless.[11]

A second link between error and Auschwitz is found in Levi's 'Machiavellism'. As we saw earlier, error and chance overlap in the epistemological sense in which Levi uses the terms, reflecting the Machiavellian bond between 'virtù' and 'fortuna'. Levi's practical intelligence is in part synonymous with those qualities—or 'virtù'—needed to respond to and use the results of error and good or bad luck. In Auschwitz, the balance between 'virtù' and 'fortuna' was distorted beyond recognition. This is reflected in

---

[10] Levi quotes Rudolf Höss, the commandant of Auschwitz, who was fond of the English patriotic slogan 'right or wrong, my country' (I. 668), to encapsulate this rigidity (and its absurdity). We saw in Chapter 4 how the otherwise admirable Steinlauf, teacher of an important lesson in human dignity in the camp, was also somewhat guilty of this vice, for Levi (I. 35).

[11] A similar exercise in deflation of his own myths is seen in 'Un testamento' (*Lilít*, II. 145–8), a will in which a conman-dentist passes on the secrets of the trade to his son, in a parody of Levi's noble line of travelling artisans, passing skills on from father to son. See also a short dystopian radio-play by Levi and Carlo Quartucci in which children inherit genetically the factory skills of their parents (P. Levi and C. Quartucci, *Intervista aziendale* (Turin: RAI radiodramma, [1968?]); not included in *Opere*).

other distortions, such as the destruction or perversion of the
ethics of work, but also in the distortions of scale and value so that
the loss of a shoe can lead swiftly to illness and death, whereas the
loss of life passes almost unnoticed. The ironic (mis)use by Levi of
the term 'fortuna' is related to this inversion of scale. It starts with
the extraordinary first words of the preface to *Se questo è un uomo*,
'Per mia fortuna, sono stato deportato ad Auschwitz solo nel 1944
. . .' (I. 5; 'It was my good fortune to be deported to Auschwitz
only in 1944 . . .'; see Chapter 12) and stretches forward at least as
far as the 1985 piece 'Pipetta da guerra' (*Racconti e saggi*, II. 886–9)
where Levi narrates for the first time exactly how it happened that
he was left behind to die in the camp when the Nazis evacuated
Auschwitz whereas his 'alter ego' Alberto and almost the entire
camp with him was not. A chain of chance, what he calls 'piccole
cause', was the difference between life and death for Primo and
Alberto, although at the time, events seemed to be conspiring for
the opposite—Primo's death and Alberto's survival. Shortly before
evacuation, Levi and Alberto came into contact with scarlet
fever—Levi fell almost fatally ill, but Albert had had the disease as
a child and was immune. Levi survived, 'Alberto fu vittima della
piccola causa, della scarlattina da cui era guarito bambino' (II. 889;
'Alberto was the victim of the minor cause, scarlet fever, which he
had been cured of as a child'). The logic and scale of cause and
effect was all skewed, chance determined life and death with a
force overwhelmingly beyond the capacity (or 'virtù') of individuals to try out means to circumvent it. There was no room for
trial, let alone error.[12]

Finally, it is worth noting briefly a muted but tantalizing link
between the modes of Holocaust testimony in Levi and the ethical
practice of trial and error, by way of lexicon. One of the key technical terms for the latter, encountered in stories such as 'Le nostre
belle specificazioni' (I. 661–70) and in *La chiave a stella*, is 'collaudo',
control or test. As Faussone tells us: 'per me un uomo che non ha
abbia mai avuto un collaudo negativo non è un uomo, è come se
fosse rimasto alla prima comunione. . . . se uno non li prova non
matura' (I. 1083; 'for me a man who has not been judged negatively
is not a man, as if he was still at his first communion. . . . if you

---

[12] On 'virtù', 'fortuna', and survival, see also Levi's preface to a survivor's account, M.
Herman, *Diario di un ragazzo ebreo* (Cuneo: L'Arciere, 1984: preface now at II. 1242–4).

don't experience them [failures] you don't mature'). The mechanisms of controlling and testing new machinery, inventions, scientific or technical solutions in Levi are rich and varied, and, as we have seen, the complications that ensue when they fail frequently provide the narrative spring for work stories (Faussone again: 'Le storie di lavoro sono quasi tutte così', I. 1095, 'almost all work stories are like that'). One of the techniques of testing entails trying out one solution whilst running a parallel placebo or control test alongside it. A good example is the story 'Tantalio' (*Lilìt*, II. 136–41) which plays science-fiction-cum-chemical games with the question of luck and misfortune (thus already echoing what was said above about the issue of fortune in and out of the camps). The protagonist is testing the qualities of a paint that apparently protects what it covers from bad luck. The control samples for his tests are called 'testimoni' (I. 138). Although an unusual use of the term,[13] its implications are suggestive, since it offers another way out of narrow, legalistic notions of testimonial writing. Just as the terms 'trial' or 'process' can be removed from the juridical field and read, as they have been in this chapter, as symptomatic of practical, fallible, applied engagement with the world, so the term 'testimone' seems to have momentarily in 'Tantalio' a less rigid role than the courtroom eye-witness. Here the 'witness' is the control, an observer partially within and partially without (after all, as Levi famously reminds us in *I sommersi e i salvati*, no survivor saw the system through to its necessary end, death; II. 1055–6), that allows us to probe, delimit, and validate our understanding.

There is, then, a multi-layered mirroring of the ethics of error and trial in the anti-ethics of Auschwitz. As in all such mirroring in Levi, however, the point is not to argue that there is a sort of cryptic Holocaust key to his entire work, there to be unlocked by an ideal reader, but rather to see how he can move between his work-life and the Holocaust, between the ethics of the ordinary and the duties of testimony, in order to forge an evolving dialectic of understanding of his own world. To return to 'Nichel' and

[13] 'testimone, *s.m.* . . . 3. Cosa, oggetto, manifestazione, aspetto che rappresenta un indizio o una prova . . .; nella tecnica, elemento o macchina presa come termine di confronto', *Vocabolario della lingua italiana*, vol. IV (Roma: Istituto della Enciclopedia italiana, 1994), 826–7.

the two reflections on error quoted from it earlier, it is therefore important to note that, echoes of the camps and of testimony aside, both quotations also resonate with what Levi sees as a universal experience of coming of age and a general sense of that Levian process of probing, flexible, intelligent engagement with our world—the phrase 'un gioco sottile di ragione, di prove e di errori' (I. 801) captures it nicely. In this respect, the reference in the second of those quotations to Pavese is fundamental.[14] As a matter of biographical and cultural historical fact, the figure of Pavese cast a long shadow over a younger generation that included Levi and Calvino among others, and we can see Levi absorbing Pavesian elements (and with him, a line from Coleridge to Melville, Conrad, London, etc.) and moulding them to his own experience. In Pavese's translation of *Moby Dick* (a fundamental stagepost in Levi's youth), in Pavese's own narrative, even in the epigraph of his final novel *La luna e i falò*, taken from *King Lear*— 'ripeness is all', 'la maturità è tutto'—we can see the origin of Levi's concentration on work, failure and success, and maturity.[15] Pavese himself lived the fracture between success and failure, between effort and the world, in a profoundly traumatic and neurotic fashion, and this in itself should be enough to warn us off any pacific, pious understanding of the role success and failure play in Levi. All the stories from *Il sistema periodico* we have mentioned have been stories of growing up based on a sort of failure; even Faussone, hardly one to dwell analytically on remembered childhood, connected the value of the 'collaudo negativo' above to becoming a man, to leaving behind first communion, to maturity. Levi's ethics, an ethics of responsibility and responsiveness, of sensibility and sobriety, could indeed be described as an ethics of a difficult maturity.

Practice, or trial and error, in Levi is a process of living and of learning from living. It is fallible by definition, but it is inscribed in the very system of life from the natural evolving universe down to the human individual, as it is in the writing of works of literature

---

[14] The remembered quotation about 'the two experiences of adult life' is probably from *Il mestiere di vivere* (Turin: Einaudi, 1981; 1st edition 1952), p. 381, 15 Dec. 1949 entry: 'Le due esperienze adulte—successo e importanza, smarrimento e nullità', mixed in with memories of Pavese's work on *Moby Dick*. Thanks to Bart Van den Bossche for suggesting this source.

[15] C. Pavese, *La luna e i falò* (Turin: Einaudi, 1990; 1st edition 1950), 3.

and the telling of stories. Responding to it is a practised constituent of his writing. Not that this should imply a dry dogma, any more than any other of the virtues at work in Levi's *œuvre*. Indeed, the virtue of trial and error is in its very nature a virtue of incoherence, of human flaw, shared with nature and compounded by our machinations, but also a virtue of immense potential resource. Maturity is in the knowing (and therefore coherent) incoherence of being human: as he says of what he looks for when trying to create a fully rounded fictional character out of thin air, '[il personaggio] dev'essere incoerente come tutti noi lo siamo, avere umore vario, sbagliare, perdersi, crescere' (II. 777; '[the character] must be incoherent like all of us, have changeable moods, get things wrong, get lost, grow').

7

PERSPECTIVE, OR LOOKING AGAIN

> Eppure, i pittori sanno bene che in un quadro messo a testa in giù si mettono in evidenza virtù e difetti che prima non si erano osservati.
>
> (Primo Levi)

Practical intelligence in Levi entails looking at and understanding the world responsively, flexibly, critically: it is a form of 'good' or 'right' looking, looking at the world anew. And such quality of vision depends, among other things, on where one is looking from and on knowing where one is looking from: in other words on perspective. This chapter explores Levi's subtle attention to perspective, his fascination with the tricks it can play, his awareness of the nature of his own perspective and the coexistence of different perspectives and their respective claims to being right. It focuses on a rich cluster of stories and essays from Levi's science fiction and journalism where these concerns come strongly to the fore, but as always these are taken to be in taut moral relation to the core problems of the Holocaust and Holocaust writing in his *œuvre*.

The most suggestive axis connecting the two spheres of perspective and testimony is the language of the visual. We saw in Chapter 1 how moments of looking, or of the look denied, constituted intense focal points in the narrative of dehumanization of *Se questo è un uomo*; and we saw at the start of Part II how both wit and witnessing have a shared etymology in verbs of vision. We can take this further by returning to the role of the eye-witness as the agent of testimony discussed in the Introduction: the eye-witness is dependent on and defined by his or her position or perspective on what was seen. The eye-witness has *seen* an event or an action from a position of proximity but also, most often, of personal detachment (or at least presumed lack of complicity): both the vision and the position juridically guarantee a privileged value to his or her account. At the same time, however, the specificity of any single perspective is as much a guarantor of subjectivity as of objectivity. The witness tends towards a third-party position, a position of corroboration (of the victim, say, or of another eye-witness), so much so that in certain traditions of thinking about legal evidence, one witness alone cannot constitute proof. This is the so-called '*unus nullus* rule': the testimony of one witness is equivalent to the testimony of none.[1]

When the vocabulary of testimony is translated into the arena of Holocaust survivor narrative, the *unus nullus* rule resurfaces. It is there in Levi's open declaration at the start of *I sommersi e i salvati* that 'per una conoscenza del Lager, i Lager stessi non erano sempre un buon osservatorio' (II. 1001; 'to know about the *Lager*, the *Lager* themselves were not always the best observatory'), a phrase glossed by the poem 'Plinio' (II. 548) about the dangers of the observer falling victim to what he is observing (like Pliny the Elder at Pompeii). It is also there in the form of the tragic bind forged quite deliberately by the Nazi system of extermination: the system protected itself by consciously going to unbelievable extremes (hence the taunt that even if some did survive no one would believe their stories, since they beggared belief; *I sommersi e i salvati*, II. 997), and by reducing and isolating each individual prisoner, as if he or she were ever 'unus nullus'. The bases of negationism lie in this bind, in the testimonial weaknesses of the position of the survivor.[2]

Levi, perhaps more eloquently than anyone else, articulated the partial, third-party perspective of the witness-survivor. He knew that the position of the eye-witness does not always guarantee an understanding of the mechanisms at work in front of your eyes, as

---

[1] See entry on 'Unus nullus rule' in *Jowett's Dictionary of English Law*, 2nd edition, ed. J. Burke, vol. II (London: Sweet and Maxwell, 1977), 1836, which also refers to a contrasting principle in English law of which Levi would surely have approved: '*ponderantur testes, non numerantur*', witnesses should be weighed not counted (quality not quantity).

[2] Carlo Ginzburg takes up this issue in 'Unus testis. Lo sterminio degli Ebrei e il principio della realtà', *Quaderni storici*, 27/80/2 (Aug. 1992), 529–48. Ginzburg points out that both Jewish and Roman Law share a tradition of distrust of the single witness. The problem this creates is similar in certain respects to the 'double-bind' of the survivor-victim discussed by Lyotard (J.-F. Lyotard, *Le Différend* (Paris: Éditions de Minuit), 1983, 19 ff.).

the phrase quoted above suggests ('Per una conoscenza dei Lager
. . .'). And he also knew that, as a 'third party', no survivor could
be a true witness to the essence of the Final Solution:

Noi toccati dalla sorte abbiamo cercato, con maggiore o minore sapienza,
di raccontare non solo il nostro destino, ma anche quello degli altri, dei
sommersi, appunto; ma è stato un discorso 'per conto di terzi', il racconto
di cose viste da vicino, non sperimentate in proprio. La demolizione
condotta a termine, l'opera compiuta, non l'ha raccontata nessuno, come
nessuno è tornato a raccontare la sua morte (II. 1056)[3]
(We who were touched by ill-fate have tried, with more or less wisdom,
to relate not only our destiny but also that of the others, the drowned;
but it has been a 'third-party' report, the story of things seen close up,
not experienced in the first person. The demolition carried to its conclusion, the finished job, has not been related by anyone, just as no one has
returned to relate their own death)

Levi bears witness as a third party, as a proxy, away from the dark
centre of the Event. And, as if modulating this voice into another,
more ordinary tone and mode of experience, he conceives of his
position as an eclectic essayist and writer as in some sense similar.
Compare the previous passage to the following, from the preface to
L'altrui mestiere, where he makes a virtue of the pleasures and possibilities of looking at the world from the near margin:

Se si sta in gruppo serrato, come fanno d'inverno le api e le pecore, ci
sono vantaggi: ci si difende meglio dal freddo e dalle aggressioni. Però *chi
sta al margine del gruppo*, o addirittura è isolato, ha altri vantaggi, può
andarsene quando vuole e *vede meglio* il paesaggio. Il mio destino, aiutato
dalle mie scelte, mi ha tenuto lontano dagli assembramenti: troppo chimico, e chimico per troppo tempo, per sentirmi un autentico uomo di
lettere; troppo distratto dal paesaggio, variopinto, tragico e strano, per
sentirmi chimico in ogni fibra. Ho corso insomma da isolato, ed ho
seguito una via serpeggiante, annusando qua e là, e costruendomi una
cultura disordinata, lacunosa e saputella. A compenso, mi sono *divertito a
guardare il mondo sotto luci inconsuete, invertendo per cosí dire la strumentazione:
a rivisitare le cose della tecnica con l'occhio del letterato, e le lettere con l'occhio del
tecnico* (II. 631; emphases added)

---

[3] See G. Agamben, *Quel che resta di Auschwitz* (Turin: Bollati Boringhieri, 1998), 31–2;
and cf. Levi in *Storia vissuta. Dal dovere di testimoniare alle testimonianze orali nell'insegnamento
della storia della seconda guerra mondiale* (Milan: Franco Angeli, 1988), 113 (now at II. 1351–2):
'Fin dal mio primo libro . . . ho sempre desiderato che i miei scritti . . . fossero letti come
opere collettive' ('From my first book . . . I have always wanted my writings . . . to be read
as collective works').

(Staying in a close group, like bees and sheep in winter, has its advantages, such as protection from the cold and from aggression. But being on the edge of the group, or even being isolated, has other advantages; you can leave when you choose and you see more of the landscape around. My destiny, aided by my choices, has kept me distant from groupings: too much and for too long a chemist to feel an authentic man of letters; too distracted by the richly coloured, tragic, and strange landscape to feel myself a chemist in every sinew. I have in short always run out on my own, following my meandering course, sniffing here and there, building up a disordered, patchy, and fake-learnèd culture. On the plus side, though, I have enjoyed looking at the world in an unusual light, reversing the perspective, as it were: reviewing aspects of technology with the eye of the *littérateur* and literature with the eye of the scientist)

The isolated position of the survivor-witness and the binds and inadequacies that position brings in testimony are here translated and valorized (with a melancholic residue of that origin, in the phrase 'il mio destino', for example) as a worthy cognitive mode: eccentric, idiosyncratic, and upturned perspectives are seen as a means to pleasure but also to a 'better vision' ('vede meglio il paesaggio').

Levi's sensitivity to perspective can be charted in his exploration of four distinct if overlapping modes of remapping reality or seeing unseen realities. Each is founded on forms of distance or difference.[4] The four modes are distance in time, distance in space, difference in scale, and difference in language and culture. As a group, the four cover a spectrum characteristic of Levi's mindset, since two are geometrical (space and scale), an idiom he frequently used as a way of figuring both knowledge and sentiment (see Chapter 10), another (time) is bound up with history and memory, and the fourth with both his persistent, at times obsessive interest in language and with his anthropological outlook.

TIME[5]

As a first instance of Levi's penchant for playing with perspectives of time, we might take his open letter to the Latin poet and satirist

4 For a suggestive philosophical-aphoristic meditation on the theme of distance, which echoes several of the themes of this chapter, see E. Tadini, *La distanza* (Turin: Einaudi, 1998); and for a study of moments in the history or genealogy of ideas on distance, see C. Ginzburg, *Occhiacci di legno. Nove riflessioni sulla distanza* (Milan: Feltrinelli, 1998).

5 On time in Levi, see P. Valabrega, '*Il segreto del cerchio*: la percezione del tempo nella

Horace, 'Caro Orazio', written for *La stampa* in 1985 (II. 946–9). In a vague echo of Petrarch's proto-humanist epistles, the *Familiares* and *Seniles*, Levi's letter tries to explain the modern world to Horace, what has changed between his time and now. To do so, he imagines ways of translating the world of today into a language that would make sense from the perspective of Rome two thousand years earlier. The sequence of material he chooses is emblematic: first he explains how Latin evolved into Italian; then he skims over two millennia of history, from the fall of Rome to the rise of Christianity, to the end of slavery and the waging of 'many wars', to nuclear weapons ('many things have happened', he comments bathetically); then he dazzles Horace with tales of modern '*mirabilia*' (the discovery of America, self-propelling ships and cars, cities, tourists, cameras, moon-travel, contraception, drugs, etc.); and finally, he ends in melancholy on what has not changed since Horace wrote of them (flattery and corruption, the seasons and nature, our quest for happiness and death). Knowingly forced and playful as a conceit, the letter allows Levi to muse on the continuities and discontinuities of history, on what is universally human and what is contingent to time and place; and to invite us to reflect, through these, on the present. As he says apologizing to Horace, 'La prego di scusarmi, scrivo non solo a Lei e per Lei ma anche per i miei lettori d'oggi, e non vorrei snaturare troppo il nostro linguaggio' (II. 947; 'I beg your indulgence, since I am writing not only to you and for you but also for my readers of today, and I do not wish to distort our language unduly').

Distance in time also emerges as a motif in Levi's science stories and poems, in part in a Wellesian vein of speculation about time travel and in part in a vein of reflection on the subjective, inner processes of time. A good example is the playlet 'La bella addormentata nel frigo', an ironic and deflationary reworking of both the fable Sleeping Beauty and a familiar topos of 'biomedical' science fiction, cryogenics (*Storie naturali*, I. 477–94). The protagonist Patricia has been cryogenically preserved and remains frozen for all but a handful of days in each year, tended to by the same

opera di Primo Levi', *Rassegna mensile di Israel*, 55/2–3 (May–Dec. 1989), 281–8; G. Santagostino, 'Primo Levi e le facce nascoste del tempo', in G. Ioli, ed., *Primo Levi: memoria e invenzione* (San Salvatore Monferrato : Edizione della Biennale 'Piemonte e letteratura', 1995), 190–206; E. Mattioda, *L'ordine del mondo. Saggio su Primo Levi* (Naples: Liguori, 1998), 37–50.

family that has done so for generations. As a result, she is in effect a time-traveller: when we meet her, she has lived over 160 years and she is intent on reaching as far into the future as possible in as young a bodily state as possible, although as the story also reveals, the cost has been high: hers has been a life without control and although she has literally lived or survived through generations, she has hardly *experienced* those years at all, spent largely in a comatose state. Worse still, with the passage of time, Patricia has become something of an object, a family heirloom, as her keeper Peter Thürl explains: 'fa parte, per cosí dire, dell'asse ereditario dealla nostra famiglia . . . è un simbolo, ecco' (II. 484; 'she is, so to speak, part of our family heritage . . . a symbol, you see'). The distinction between a life lived in a reduced, objectified state of consciousness and a life experienced fully is a crucial one for Levi, as we shall see. Patricia comes to long for the latter over the former.

Baldur, a guest at the Thürl family home for Patricia's birthday defrosting, is drawn to her like a moth to a flame, anxious to see the world through her eyes:

Signorina, perdoni il mio ardire, ma so che il suo tempo è misurato, vorrei che mi descrivesse il nostro mondo visto con i suoi occhi, che mi parlasse del suo passato, del suo secolo a cui tanto dobbiamo, delle sue intenzioni per il futuro . . . (II. 488)
(Miss, forgive me my excitement, but I know your time is limited and I'd like you to describe our world seen through your eyes, to talk about your past, your century which means so much to us, your plans for the future . . .)

In reply Patricia explains the relativity of her experience of time in the world: two months ago for her, Peter was thirty years younger and five months ago he was not even born. Baldur is overcome. In Patricia, his notion of time collapses; she is eternity and youth all in one, she flies where others crawl (II. 490). But Patricia's experience of living on her lofty time-scale is quite different. Far from being ecstatic, her existence is close to unbearable: 'tre sono i miei doni, non due. L'eternità, la giovinezza e la solitudine. E quest'ultima è il prezzo che paga chi ha osato quanto io ho osato' (ibid.; 'my gifts are three, not two. Eternity, youth, and solitude. This last is the price paid for daring what I have dared').

Patricia and the reaction of Baldur and others sensitize us to the ironic advantages and disadvantages of time's relativity and suggest what a different world ours would be if lived through another time-scale, if time passed differently. The otherworld Patricia inhabits contains echoes of another world where time passed differently, which elevate and complicate the whimsical tone of the play: she is alone and imprisoned in a world where, with a few exceptions, time stands still. She is only ever awake enough to suffer, in her case the abuse or rather rape by Peter Thürl that is revealed as the play proceeds. Compare the stasis and suffering of *Se questo è un uomo*:

> per noi, ore, giorni e mesi si riversavano torpidi dal futuro nel passato, sempre troppo lenti, materia vile e superflua di cui cercavamo di disfarci al piú presto . . . il futuro ci stava davanti grigio e inarticolato, come una barriera invincibile. Per noi, la storia era fermata.' (I. 113)
> (for us, days and months passed numbly from the future to the past, always too slow, vile and superfluous matter which we tried to get rid of as soon as possible . . . the future lay before us grey and inarticulate, like an immovable barrier. For us, history had stopped.)

Furthermore, as Peter himself explains, 'non c'è mai stata una esistenza piú intensa di quella di Patricia. La sua vita è concentrata: non contiene che l'essenziale' (II. 485; 'there has never been an existence more intense than Patricia's. Her life is concentrated: has nothing but the essential'), which seems only a tonal modulation away from Levi's oft-repeated sense that he and others lived some moments in Auschwitz on a plane of heightened sensibility, in 'technicolor' compared to a routine there and here lived in 'black and white'.[6] Moreover, since one of Levi's pieces of evidence for this counterintuitive assertion is precisely his hyper-intense mechanical memory of his time in the camps (see Chapter 2 above), a link might be posited between a changed perception of time and a different, intensified relation with memory.

'La bella addormentata nel frigo' offers no lesson or resolution, despite its fable-like title, nor could it given the somewhat tawdry array of abusive, resentful, and selfish characters it contains. But it probes the implications of different perspectives on time and as such is paradigmatic of the way Levi opens up different ways of looking in general. The field it opens takes on an ethical shape

---

[6] See *The Voice of Memory*, 251; M. Dini and S. Jesurum, *Primo Levi: le opere e i giorni* (Milan: Rizzoli, 1992), 89.

when it is read as a thought experiment on different ways to live in relation to time and on the relation of human identity and value to technologies that mediate our rapport with time.

Other cognitive and ethical implications of temporal perspective emerge when Levi probes the subjectivity of temporal perception. In 'Scacco al tempo' (II. 913–16), for example, a drug called 'Paracrono' endows the recipient with the power to control and alter subjective flows of time, speeding up useless or unpleasant activities and lengthening moments of pleasure (one of the test-cases describes slowing down an orgasm to last 36 hours). As discussed in Chapter 4, Levi is consistently interested in the relation and perception of pain and pleasure, which in turn are at the heart of a particular aspect of his ethics, his oblique utilitarianism. 'Scacco al tempo' shows how that very experience of pleasure and pain conditions and is conditioned by subjective perceptions of time. The subjective control offered by 'Paracrono' (of pain and pleasure, and of time) inverts the situation in 'La bella addormentata' where Patricia had little to no control over her fate when frozen.

Much more solemn meditation on time's shifting perspectives and on history and memory, with once again direct links back to Levi's Holocaust work, is found in the 1978 poem 'La bambina di Pompei' (II. 549), discussed briefly at the end of Chapter 2 above. The poem is an extended play on temporal distance and perspective, on what survives of the past into the present and what effects those residues (or lack of them) have on our historical and affective relationship to the past. Of the three girls evoked in the poem, the girl from Pompeii is present physically in her incinerated body, Anne Frank is lost, her body only ashes, but her diary stands as a lost presence projecting her as an individual into history and memory, and finally the girl from Hiroshima is wholly lost, absent, forgotten. Levi's imagination is captured by the inversion here: under normal circumstances, history and memory would have forgotten Pompeii (or at least the individuals within it) and remembered the girl from Hiroshima, by a simple rule of proximity, but the inversion thrown up by circumstance challenges our modes of forgetting in each case. That Anne Frank stands in the middle only goes to underscore the complexity of grasping a perspective of any kind on the Holocaust, historical and affective. The poem turns on the most burning moral question shared between the Holocaust and questions of perspective and distance: the question of indifference. And as was suggested at the end of Chapter 1, much of Levi's ethical thinking could be epitomized in opposites of indifference such as attention or attentiveness (to the world and to others).[7]

SPACE

Distance in space naturally shares many of the dynamics and characteristics of distance in time as a mode of looking differently in Levi. The two are interdependent. For example, just as Levi uses the letter form in 'Caro Orazio' to play games with distance in time, so in another, even simpler instance, ' "Cara mamma" '(*Lilít*, II. 126–30), he uses the same form to signal distance in space (and time). Here a soldier of the Roman Empire writes home to his mother from a posting on Hadrian's Wall. He describes the odd customs of the natives (anticipating Levi's anthropological vein, of which more later) and tells his mother about his new wife and the like. Connecting space and time, Levi makes much play in " 'Cara mamma" ' of the different rhythms of communication of the period, so that this is the son's first letter in a year, even though the mail is described as swift. It is worth noting also that a scribe writes the letter for the soldier (and indeed interrupts at one point to protest at his mocking of the local sport of caber-tossing), echoing that crucial 'third-party' role so important to Levi the survivor-writer.[8]

The epistolary form is by no means the only marker of Levi's fascination with distances, however. During the 1960s especially, the significance of spatial perspective is given an extra impetus for Levi by space travel and the first moon-landings which he observes

[7] See Levi's open letter on *Close Encounters of the Third Kind* (I. 1233–4), where he points out how much harder it is to love one's neighbour than a far-off 'alien'. Several of the essays in Ginzburg's *Occhiacci di legno* address issues of distance, perspective, and indifference, drawing on a vast tradition from Aristotle to Montaigne to modern art theory and much else: see in particular 'Straniamento', 'Distanza e prospettiva', and 'Uccidere un mandarino cinese' (pp. 15–39, 174–209). Calvino also made distance and social commitment the key motifs of his 1957 fable *Il barone rampante*.

[8] For another instance of Levi's use of the epistolary form, see the story-cum-letter written to the popular scientist Piero Bianucci from another planet, 'Le fans di spot di Delta Cep.', II. 1297–300. The novel he was working on at his death, variously titled 'Il doppio legame' or 'Chimica per signore', was also epistolary (M. Cicioni, *Primo Levi* (Oxford: Berg, 1995), 170; M. Belpoliti, *Primo Levi* (Milan: Bruno Mondadori, 1998), 47).

with genuine fascination and awe. In this period, the paradigmatic spatial point of view turned to cognitive or ethical use by Levi is that of looking back on the earth from the moon (e.g. 'La luna e noi', II. 648–50; 'La luna e l'uomo', II. 926–8). One of the most suggestive stories in this vein, 'Visto di lontano' (*Vizio di forma*, I. 600–8), was written shortly before the first moon-landings and it opens declaring itself as a last homage to the poets and fantasists of the moon ('Luciano di Samosata, Voltaire, Swedenborg, Rostand, E. A. Poe, Flammarion ed H. G. Wells', I. 600) before the new 'poetry' of scientific fact takes over. The story then takes the form of a technical report by a lunar native (a 'Selenite') on activity and change observed on the earth's surface from the moon. Several aspects of the report are pertinent here. First, looking forward to Levi's fourth mode of shifting perspective, that of language, it is significant that a great deal of the humour and insight of the story derives from redescribing or remapping the workings of our world in the mock-technical, detached idiom of an experimental report. More significant still is the way in which distance alters the very shape of the most familiar aspects of our world. From the perspective of the moon—and indeed from a report which takes in almost a century of human history, since the previous report had been submitted in 1876 (time and space interwoven once more)—the observer is able to trace the growth in cities as a series of odd geometrical, crystalline growths on and above the planet surface and to observe the appearance of new pockets of local night-light from around 1905. The observer also investigates a form of ovoid, 'live' volcanic craters which seem particularly active on Sundays (a form of 'DSG' activity or 'Del Settimo Giorno'). And the story ends with a note on an anomalous period in the century, during the years 1939–45, when all the patterns and regularities otherwise observed were radically disrupted, ending with two intense light and energy emissions in Japan.

'Visto di lontano' has much in common with 'Caro Orazio' in what we might call its ironic procedure (see Chapter 12). The central device of the story is rather studied and forced and offers only a modicum of mystery (there are no prizes to be had for guessing that the craters are sports stadia, that the night-light is gas or electric lighting, that the emissions in Japan are from Hiroshima and Nagasaki, and so on). The interest lies rather in the ironic appeal to the reader to rethink his or her vision of their own world having made the relatively simple intellectual leap towards deciphering this half-decoded 'Selenitic Linear B'. The story invites the reader to carry on imagining and reimagining how aspects of the ordinary world and they would change when viewed from afar, from another perspective. As Levi puts it in *L'altrui mestiere*, when describing the contents of an otherwise quite frivolous book collecting odd, unexpected, and paradoxical data about the world, R. Houwink's *Il libro dei dati strani*: 'Non sono scienza, ma stimolo ad acquistarla' (II. 724; 'they are not science in themselves, but a spur to acquire it').

Once again, there are echoes here too of another far-off world, connected to ours by equally strange and difficult journeys, the world of Auschwitz. One of the founding moments of invitation to ethical enquiry in *Se questo è un uomo* is in effect just such an appeal to perspective: from the perspective of the barbed-wire compound, what remains of our own common world: 'Vorremmo ora invitare il lettore a riflettere . . . quanto del nostro comune mondo morale potesse sussistere al di qua del filo spinato' (I. 82; 'We would now like to invite the reader to reflect . . . on how much of our moral world could survive on this side of the barbed wire'). And both 'Visto di lontano' and that moment in *Se questo è un uomo* participate in another dynamic fundamental to Levi's moral universe, its appeal to a global humanism. The further Levi stands back from his world and the people in it, the more plausible it seems to talk generally of mankind, the human race, the world and universal laws, without necessarily slipping into bland or untenable generalization. Of course, the exact opposite—holding doggedly on to the humane and uncertain perspective of the individual—is at least as dear a principle to Levi. Watching the movement between the two allows him to sensitize the one to the other, to watch for points of where the individual collapses into solipsism and where the general lapses into the dogmatic and inhumane. In this context, the story 'Procacciatori d'affari' (*Vizio di forma*, I. 609–25) is particularly illuminating.

Some travelling salespeople in a somewhat strange world arrive at the home of the protagonist, S. It slowly becomes clear that what they are selling is human life and that our protagonist is a soul who has yet to be assigned a body and an identity within which to be born, live, and die. The sales pitch goes wrong, however, as the bland, whitewashed version of life offered to S. in brochures is

picked apart by the alert S. In the end the chief salesman admits to
him that a great deal is wrong with the world, that wars, famines,
poverty, and now the threat of nuclear destruction hang over
humankind and that in fact he and his colleagues are looking for
someone with 'la ragione, la pietà, la pazienza, il coraggio' (I. 624;
'the reason, pity, patience, courage') to help save the species. S. is
promised privilege, comfort, and all possible circumstantial aid to
smooth his passage in return. S. hesitates and then refuses, preferring the virtues of equality and perseverance to the heroic task
offered him:

Non vorrei partire con vantaggio. Temo che mi sentirei un profittatore,
e dovrei chinare la fronte per tutta la vita davanti a tutti i miei compagni
non privilegiati. Accetto, ma vorrei nascere a caso, come ognuno: fra i
miliardi di nascituri senza destino, fra i predestinati alla servitù o alla
contesa fin dalla culla, se pure avranno una culla. Preferisco nascere
negro, indiano, povero, senza indulgenze e senza condoni. Lei stesso lo
ha detto, che ogni uomo è artefice di se stesso: ebbene, è meglio esserlo
appieno, costruirsi dalle radici. (I. 625)
(I wouldn't want to start with an advantage. I'm afraid I would feel like
a profiteer, and I'd have to bow my head all my life before all my non-
privileged fellows. I accept, but I want to be born at random, like everyone else: one of the billions of newborns without destiny, or destined to
slavery or to struggle from cradle to grave (if there is even a cradle). I
prefer to be born black, Indian, poor, without special treatment or
amnesty. You said it yourself, every man is his own maker: well, it's
better to be so to the full, to build oneself from the very root.)

Aside from standing as a rhetorical flourish proclaiming a raft of
cardinal Levian virtues (equality, empathy, self-making, and a
sense of natural justice); and aside from containing yet further
echoes of camp trauma (S.'s fear of living in shame as a 'privile-
giato' comes directly from Levi's experience of the *Lager* and of
survival, even in its terminology), the passage and the story as a
whole mark an emblematic tension between a general view of the
world (which is distorting but also contains kernels of truth) and a
sensitivity to the suffering of individuals. Earlier in the dialogue
between S. and the salespeople, one of the latter tries to head off
S.'s continual, probing questions and his insistence on knowing
the fate of all the individuals whose images he is shown:

Lei non si deve lasciare impressionare da un caso singolo, di cui per di
più, lei è venuta a conoscenza in un modo tutt'altro che regolare. . . .

Ammetterà che per farsi un giudizio, è molto piú utile soffermarsi sulle situazioni generali, tipiche . . . (II. 618)
(You mustn't let yourself be scared by a single example, which in any case you found out about in a most irregular manner. . . . You must admit that to make a judgement, it's much more useful to dwell on the general, typical situation . . .)

As the story makes clear, the opposite is more likely to be the case, and if the general is useful, it is often as much for the errors it contains for the attentive observer as for its truths (see Chapter 6). Compare Levi's exasperated and wearily sarcastic reflection in the opening pages of *La tregua* when a Russian army barber greets him just days after liberation from Auschwitz as 'Italiano Mussolini': 'dove si vede quanto poco soccorranno le idee generali alla comprensione dei casi singoli' (I. 214; 'where it is clear how little general ideas help in the comprehension of individual cases'). It is, moreover, noteworthy that in 'Visto di lontano' and elsewhere, Levi plays continually on the errors brought about by distance and different languages: cities are not crystals, stadia are not volcanic, even if viewing them as such throws up compelling and useful new perspectives on them. In the Afterword to *Se questo è un uomo*, Levi explains why it is so profoundly wrong to ask why the Jews did not rebel against their fate—'rappresenta oltre a tutto un errore di prospettiva storica' (I. 184; 'beyond anything else, it represents a historical error of perspective').[9] Sensitivity to perspective is the best way to avoid errors of perspective.

SCALE

Distances in time and space are often closely bound up with, at times even indistinguishable from, the third mode of reshaping the world by perspective, difference in scale. Levi's scientific formation leaves him perennially fascinated by scales of existence beyond

---

[9] In *I sommersi e i salvati*, when Levi again addresses the question of rebellion and escape, he tells the story of the primary-school pupil who asks Levi to sketch the layout of the camp, before calmly explaining how he should have planned and executed his escape (I. 1115–16). Apart from illustrating a comic gap in perceptions the role of the sketch points up another form of perspective that fascinates Levi as part simplification and part explanation—the reading of reality as a map or a geometric model or schema (see the maps in *La tregua*, *Se non ora, quando?*, 'Mercurio' (*Il sistema periodico*); his use of chemical models including the periodic table itself; the schema at the start of *La ricerca delle radici*; and cf. Belpoliti, *Primo Levi*, 114–16).

the human and his humanistic formation leaves him mischievously imagining how he might anthropomorphize those micro- and macro-scales of existence. Indeed, the book which first turned him to science as a teenager, William Bragg's *The Architecture of Things*, did so through the excitement of using human scale models to understand both atoms and stars (*La ricerca della radici*, II. 1388–92 [1388]). In part, as with both of the previous categories, this is a linguistic problem, or more precisely, a problem of the limits of human language:

In un luogo dell'universo molto lontano di qui viveva un tempo una stella tranquilla. . . . Questa stella era molto grande, molto calda e il suo peso era enorme: e qui incominciano le nostre difficoltà di relatori. Abbiamo scritto 'molto lontano', 'grande', 'calda', 'enorme': L'Australia è molto lontano, un elefante è grande, stamattina ho fatto un bagno caldo e l'Everest è enorme. È chiaro che nel nostro lessico qualcosa non funziona.
   . . . Per discorrere di stelle il nostro linguaggio è inadeguato e appare risibile, come chi volesse arare con una piuma: è un linguaggio nato con noi, atto a descrivere oggetti grandi e duraturi press'a poco quanto noi; ha le nostre dimensioni, è umano. ('Una stella tranquilla', II. 77)
(In a place in the universe far away from here lived at one time a quiet star. . . . This star was very large, very hot, and its weight was immense: and here our troubles as narrator begin. We wrote 'far away', 'large', 'hot', and 'immense': Australia is far away, an elephant is large, this morning I had a hot bath, and Everest is immense. Clearly something in our vocabulary is awry.
   . . . To talk about stars our language is inadequate, risible, like trying to plough with a feather: it is a language born with us, apt for describing objects roughly as large and as durable as ourselves; it is our sort of size, human.)

We saw how important scale as measure was for Levi in Chapter 4, but there is also an issue of relative perspective in play here. He goes on to speculate that the language of mathematics—of 10s to the power x, y, and z—might capture something of the scale of the astral events he is describing: but, 'non sarebbe un racconto nel senso in cui questa storia desidera raccontare se stessa, cioè come una favola che ridesti echi, ed in cui ciascuno ravvisi lontani modelli propri e del genere umano' (II. 78; 'it wouldn't be a story in the sense that this story wishes to tell itself, that is like a fable that stirs up echoes, in which everyone can see distant models of their own and of humankind'). The balance between the grandeur of the universe and the recognizable humanity of the 'racconto' is crucial: Levi wants to imagine a dying star as an 'experience' in order to push and stretch the limits of his and our knowledge. So he tries out three distinct genres of narrative: first history (the Arabs—observant, patient, humble, and loving of knowledge—spotting and naming the dying star); then science fiction (the star dies as seen by a native of a planet as far from the star as the earth is from the sun); and finally, oddly, contemporary anecdote (a 34-year-old Peruvian astronomer and father-of-two spots an infinitesimal sign of the star's collapse from his observatory and is torn between excitement and guilt at leaving his family back at home in the lurch yet again). As in earlier instances, the key is in the ironic and fluid juxtaposition of scales.

The same ironic juxtaposition recurs in a number of other pieces. Two poems—'Nel principio' and 'Autobiografia' (II. 544, 558)—and one short story—'Il fabbro di se stesso' (*Vizio di forma*, I. 702–9)—all tell whimsical, anthropomorphized stories about the entire history of the universe, from the Big Bang until different stages of human evolution.[10] 'Il mondo invisibile' (in *L'altrui mestiere*, II. 800–4), by contrast, delves into the infinitesimal world of the microscopic: it tells of the sheer delight of the young Levi when his father presented him with a copy of an 1846 English book—G. A. Mantell's *Thoughts on Animalcules, or a Glimpse of the Invisible World Revealed by the Microscope*—followed, after much badgering, by an actual microscope. The experiments and discoveries that ensue are told with a brio that would not be out of place in *Il sistema periodico*; and indeed, perhaps the most accomplished and suggestive of all Levi's remappings of the world through different perspectives of scale is the extraordinary last chapter of that book, 'Carbonio' (I. 934–42), in which an atom of carbon, the very stuff of life itself, is given its own biographical narrative, over eons and continents, until it is finally imagined merging with the book itself by triggering in Levi's brain the movement to place its final full stop. Scales of life coexist and coincide, 'Carbonio' tells us, from the atomic to the human to the cosmic.

---

[10] All of these have much in common with Italo Calvino's mock-scientific tales *Le cosmicomiche* and *T con zero*, especially 'Il fabbro di se stesso' which is dedicated to Calvino.

LANGUAGE AND CULTURE

The fourth and final mode of shifting perspectives that character-izes Levi's work is the shifting of language and/or culture. In terms of language, we have already seen in 'Visto di lontano' how part of the yield of new understanding or fresh vision came from the ironic use of an unexpected language or idiom (of the technical report) to describe our familiar world. And the same could indeed have been said for 'Scacco al tempo', written in the formal language of patents, or the language of the sales pitch in 'Procacciatori d'affari'; or for the language of autobiography in charting the evolution of life in 'Autobiografia'. The same proce-dure characterizes the rich vein of science-fiction stories concern-ing the American inventor-cum-salesman Simpson, indefatigable employee of the mysterious corporation NATCA, where the language of commerce and bureaucracy sensitizes us to and mocks his extravagant inventions (see Chapter 8). Similarly, 'Il sesto giorno' rewrites the Creation story using the 'bureaucratese' of the expert committee ironically to recast the question 'what is a man?' All these examples show Levi intent on changing perspective by changing language, but not so much, say, by translating directly into a more accessible idiom, as by imagining other people's idioms and disturbing assumptions by shifting the tonal qualities of a given idiom.

In this context at least, Levi's interest in language is one element in a larger interest in other cultures that has been termed 'anthro-pological'.[11] *La chiave a stella* is in large part an exercise in creating and sustaining the voice of Faussone, and thereby representing the sub-culture of modern artisanal work he epitomizes.[12] We saw in Chapter 4 quite how far Levi was willing to go in adopting the voice of others, thinking himself into the most extreme positions of the Nazis in order to try and fathom their culture of 'useless violence' in *I sommersi e i salvati*. In both cases, the adoption of an

[11] See, e.g., D. Del Giudice, 'Introduzione', in Levi, *Opere*, pp. xiii–lxv [pp. lxii–xv]; Levi's most direct contact with anthropology came in his translations for Einaudi of three important works, two by Claude Lévi-Strauss (*Le Regard éloigné*, tr. 1984; *La Voie des masques*, tr. 1985) and one by Mary Douglas (*Natural Symbols*, tr. 1979).

[12] On Faussone's language, see G. L. Beccaria's preface and notes to the schools edition of P. Levi, *La chiave a stella*, ed. G. L. Beccaria (Turin: Einaudi, 'Letture per la scuola media', 1983); and C. Bura, 'Primo Levi: *La chiave a stella*', *Gli annali. Università per stranieri*, 8 (1987), 111–80.

idiom or a voice entails the adoption of a vision of the world also; difference in language swiftly turns into difference in culture. In a sense, 'Levi as anthropologist'—or (to make the link with ethics self-evident) 'Levi as ethologist'—is a natural endpoint to a discussion of Levi's search for knowledge and value through perspective, since the defining issues at the heart of anthropology (or ethology) as a practice and a discipline replay several of the issues we have discussed thus far: how to look from afar, at cultures and practices that are different; how to describe what you see; how to look close at home for the same as what you saw from afar; how to compare these data; and so on.

Claude Lévi-Strauss himself was quite enchanted by Levi's *La chiave a stella*, commenting that his insight into Faussone and his patterns of work made him 'un grande etnologo'.[13] Indeed, many of Levi's acute analyses of character and sub-culture and their mutual interdependence—of Sandro, Lorenzo, Rodmund (hero of the story 'Pimobo', *Il sistema periodico*, I. 809–21), the mysterious smuggler Levi meets in prison in Aosta ('Oro', I. 855–59), Mordo Nahum and Cesare of *La tregua*—could be reread as ethnological in this sense. In each case, there is both an intellectual and an emotional encounter with a different class, attitude, language, or culture, and also evidence of a mutual but restrained reciprocal influence between the two parties. Levi was also, however, interested in more strained encounters between cultures and in the strains in otherwise mutually transforming encounters. This is one of the several reasons why it is important, even if odd, for *La chiave a stella* that Faussone should be rather boring and inflexible in his everyday human interactions and in his storytelling, as well as strangely fascinating and alert in his pragmatic intelligence. It is also a key element in 'Verso occidente' (discussed above in Chapter 4), where Walter and Anna interfere with the self-aware and subtle culture of the Arunde, offering in effect to alter their values (i.e. their tendency to accept life's futility and take their own lives) through administration of a chemical substance. In passing, it is worth noting in 'Verso occidente' the equivalence that Levi sets up in the story structurally between anthropology and zoology or ethology—Walter and Anna work first on lemmings and then on the Arunde tribe—since it is also crucial to an understanding of

---

[13] Quoted in II. 1588.

Levi's anthropology and his shifting cultural perspectives that comparisons between peoples be a subset of an even greater potential pool of comparisons and contrasts, with animals and indeed minerals or inanimate matter.[14]

Finally we can point to a diptych of anthropological stories of cultural perspective in *Vizio di forma*, both entitled 'Recuenco' (I. 689–701). The first, subtitled 'la Nutrice', tells of a mythical, godly visitor to a tribe at Recuenco; the second, 'il rafter', of the visitor as in reality a vessel dropping emergency supplies of milk from the air. They tell the story from these two incompatible perspectives, allowing Levi to chronicle relations, work-habits, and customs in both environments whilst showing no mutual contact or understanding between them. The narratives turn on a wrench, 'la chiave' (certainly an image taken up in the 'chiave a stella' of the 1978 book), carelessly dropped by one of the rafter crew but taken up as a holy talisman by the tribe, a memorial of the visit of the 'Nutrice'.

VIRTUAL PERSPECTIVES

It will have become obvious in the course of the discussion that the engine behind much of Levi's enquiry into modes of perspective is one of transformation, and often, more specifically, of reversal. Levi himself notices his tendency to be drawn to reversal mid-way through his personal anthology *La ricerca delle radici*:

Mi sto accorgendo che in queste pagine si sono accumulate molti esempi di capovolgimento. Sinceramente: non era un assunto programmatico, è invece un risultato che non avevo previsto. Eppure, i pittori sanno bene che in un quadro messo a testa in giù si mettono in evidenza virtù e difetti che prima non si erano osservati. (II. 1491)

(I am coming to realize that in these pages there are many instances of

[14] The interplay between the animate and the inanimate has been labelled Levi's 'ilozoismo', by both Cesare Cases and Cesare Segre, now in E. Ferrero, ed., *Primo Levi: un'antologia della critica* (Turin: Einaudi, 1997), 12–14, 114–16: see also Del Giudice, 'Introduzione', pp. liii–lxi, especially on the combination in Levi of anthropology, zoology, and chemistry (epitomized by 'Verso occidente') that Del Giudice labels 'antropochemiozoologia' (p. liii). See also the many stories about animals or plants taking over human or machine tasks: e.g. 'Censura in Bitnia', ' "Cladonia rapita" ', 'L'amico dell'uomo', 'Pieno impiego' (*Storie naturali*, I. 409–12, 442–6, 456–9, 517–28); 'A fin di bene' and 'Ammuntinamento' (*Vizio di forma* I. 636–46, 718–24); and 'I costruttori di ponti', 'Self-control', and 'Tantalio' (*Lilìt*, II. 104–13, 136–41).

upturnings. I can sincerely say that this was not a deliberate project on my part, in fact it is a result I had not foreseen. And yet, painters know well that in a painting turned upside down, virtues and defects that had not been seen before jump at the eye.)

The image of the painter neatly captures the value of altered perspectives in Levi. Indeed, alteration, transformation, and reversal are dynamics that recur frequently in Levi's ethics. In a sense, the whole of Part I dealt in ethical transformations moving out of the camps into ordinary reality. Such dynamics are the means to an end of ethical flexibility and sensibility, to that form of malleable intelligence Levi treasures so greatly. They allow us to see differently and seeing differently affords us insights into how we and others live, into how others might see us live, and thus, crucially, into how we might live otherwise. The latter suggests a further avenue to explore in Levi's writing with perspective, and that is the way altered perspectives alter the self, for good or ill. One story in particular suggests itself to illustrate the point.

'Trattamento di quiescenza', the final story of Levi's first science-fiction collection, *Storie naturali* (I. 548–67), is a remarkable moral fable about technology and identity. It merits extended discussion here, because it stages the most elaborate and suggestive experiments in altered perspectives and the impact they might have on identity in Levi's entire *œuvre*. In it, the hapless Simpson, now nearing retirement from NATCA, convinces the narrator to try out his latest and most astonishing machine, the TOREC (for 'Total Recorder'). The TOREC is what we would call a virtual-reality device: it allows the viewer to experience in full first-person intensity someone else's pre-recorded actions and sensations, all somehow captured on tape. In other words, the TOREC is a machine for altering perspective, for temporarily transforming the self into another. This has an enriching effect first of all on the narrative itself, since the story becomes a sort of intricate anthology of narrative fragments as we are taken through each tape.

Simpson cajoles the narrator into trying out five exemplars of the tapes. Each represents a moment of both pleasurable and disturbing self-transformation. Initially, they are quite banal—the first has him scoring a goal for AC Milan—but they soon become more unsettling and alienating. With the second he is an Italo-American immigrant beaten unconscious by racist Americans. The third tape is the most alienating and unsettling of all: in error, Simpson gives the narrator a mildly pornographical tape about a model (for whom the narrator happens to harbour a secret desire), but worse still, Simpson fails to spot that the tape is recorded from the point of view of the model, not her lover. 'She' waits anxiously and desirously for an unfaithful lover, who arrives . . . but the furious narrator rips off his headset before the inevitable sexual encounter begins. Deeply hurt in his (somewhat homophobic) heterosexual masculinity, the narrator is furious with Simpson for what he assumes to be a trick; Simpson apologizes, mortified by his mistake.

The sex and gender transformation here represents an emblematic case of imagined seeing and feeling differently. Simpson touches on this when, in the midst of his embarrassment, he cannot help but speculate:

Eppure, non cosí di sorpresa ma sapendolo prima, sarebbe forse anche questa un'esperienza interessante. Unica: nessuno mai l'ha fatto, anche se i greci l'attribuivano a Tiresia. (I. 561)
(And yet, not as a surprise like that, but if you planned it first, perhaps it would be an interesting experience. Unique: no one has ever been through it, although the Greeks claimed Tiresias had.)

The reference to Tiresias is significant. More than once in Levi's *œuvre* he represents a double figure of ambivalent identification for Levi the survivor. Tiresias is the prophet, the cursed victim of the gods' anger, the changed man who has experienced what no one else has experienced, has been split in two; and each of these roles has also been thrust upon a reluctant, Job-like Levi. As the narrator of *La chiave a stella* explains to Faussone:

sí . . . un po' Tiresia mi sentivo, e non solo per la duplice esperienza [di chimico e scrittore]: in tempi lontani anch'io mi ero imbattuto negli déi in lite fra loro; anch'io avevo incontrato i serpenti sulla mia strada, e quell'incontro mi aveva fatto mutare condizione donandomi uno strano potere di parola: ma da allora . . . mi pareva di avere in corpo due anime, che sono troppe. (I. 988–9)
(yes . . . I felt a bit like Tiresias, and not only for my dual experience [as chemist and writer]: in a distant time I too had stumbled into gods fighting amongst themselves; I too had met serpents on my path and that meeting had changed my condition and given me a strange power of speech: since then . . . I felt as though I had two souls in my body, which are too many.)

The scene of transsexual desire in 'Trattamento di quiescenza' is thus an echo, modulated into a comic key, of a motif running throughout Levi's writing, of the dangerous and disquieting knowledge of having seen what he has seen. As we shall see, Simpson himself will fall victim to another variant of this motif at the end of the story.

The fourth tape is an anthology of seven different, fragmentary moments of extreme thirst followed by blissfully quenching.[15] Simpson explains that it comes from a series of tapes labelled 'Epic', which stands not for epic tales of war and action, but rather for 'effetto Epicuro' (I. 562), that is, founded on an Epicurean notion of happiness as the cessation of pain or suffering. The punning contrast is instructive, since it recalls that more general contrast in Levi's ethics between the heroic and its concomitant (epic) virtues, which he admires but somewhat takes his distance from, and his own more ordinary virtues, which are, in a sense, Epicurean, 'contro il dolore' (*L'altrui mestiere*, II. 673–5).

Lastly, Simpson offers the narrator one of the so-called 'fascia nera' of tapes (and it is interesting to note that, as Levi invents this new form of representation, he is careful also to invent its owners and marketing and also its inbuilt system of classification, regulation, and censorship). The black tapes are those that push the limits of the machine into identification with the non-human or the abnormal—with synthetic realities or from historical reality (e.g. the life of Socrates), with the mentally ill, or with animals. The last fascinates our (quite clearly autobiographical) narrator, who is given the only existing tape in this category to try out, that of a bird of prey soaring at two thousand metres before swooping in to kill a hare. The experience of seeing the world from on high, with the bird's heightened sensitivity and visual acuity, of feeling the workings of pre-rational animal instinct and knowledge and the natural ease of the kill is left unglossed in the story, but it represents a natural climax of the identification with altered perspectives, going beyond the self, reshaping its vision of the world through pleasure and through profound disturbance of the norm.

Before leaving, Simpson tells the narrator a cautionary tale of

---

[15] The narrative of this section has been shown to be a detailed reworking by Levi of elements of his own poetry on Auschwitz; see I. Rosato, 'Primo Levi: sondaggi intertestuali', *Autografo*, 6, NS 17 (June 1989), 31–43.

the tape of a parachute jump: at the start, the TOREC headset-wearer finds himself in pain, in a strange, crumpled position on the ground only to be dragged up vertiginously by the bulging parachute and sucked into the gaping door of the airplane, the parachute folding itself away on his back, at which point he suddenly begins to feel afraid. Of course, the tape has run backwards. The story might seem like a parting joke on Simpson's part, a harmless suggestion of how simply such an amazing invention can go wrong, but it is also a hint at something much more important. Reversal, as we saw above, represents something close to an essence of Levi's alteration of perspective. It is the mechanism behind the story 'Versamina', in which pain is turned into pleasure, and value and identity are turned upside down in the victims as a result (the story ends quoting *Macbeth*: 'fair is foul and foul is fair | Hover through the fog and filthy air'). Reversal is also the extreme (although not the only) configuration in Levi of the relation of the concentration-camp universe to our everyday universe—a configuration he does not present as true, since he is not so Manicheistic in his understanding of Auschwitz, but rather as a useful tool for understanding those different, contiguous, interpenetrating universes. Thus Simpson's story of the parachute jump foreshadows Martin Amis's remarkable Holocaust novella *Time's Arrow*, which uses the conceit of time running backwards to retell the story of a Nazi camp doctor in order to recover the ironies and subtleties of actions and responsibilities in the camps that are lost in linear narratives, in unaltered perspectives.[16]

Simpson's tale is not quite the last cautionary tale of the story. Before it ends, we learn that the TOREC proves catastrophic for Simpson himself, as he is all but devoured by a strange insatiable addiction to the ersatz experience of others' recorded sensations. As often happens when Levi reaches moments of high intensity, the language takes on a biblical, apocalyptic ring: Simpson's battle with the machine is likened to Jacob's with the Angel; his insatiable desire for its pleasures and the 'noia vasta come il mare' ('boredom as vast as the sea') that assails him whenever he is back in the real world only finds sense in Ecclesiastes:

> All the rivers flow into the sea, yet never the sea grows full . . . Eyes look on unsatisfied, ears listen ill content. Everything that shall be ever has

[16] M. Amis, *Time's Arrow* (London: Jonathan Cape, 1991).

been, that which happened once will happen again; there is nothing new under the sun . . . much wisdom, much woe; who adds to learning, adds to the load we bear. (1:7, 9, 18) (I. 567)

In the end, Simpson prematurely ages through his accelerated excess of pre-packaged experience, so that he seems like Solomon, with the wisdom of ages, but his is a fragile wisdom: 'la saggezza di Salomone era stata acquistata con dolore in una lunga vita piena di d'opere e di colpe; quella di Simpson è frutto di un complicato circuito elettronico e di nastri a otto piste, e lui lo sa e se ne vergogna' (ibid.; 'Solomon's wisdom had been won with pain over a long life of work and responsibilities; Simpson's is the product of a complicated electronic circuit and eight-track tapes, and he knows and is ashamed of it'). He now only waits for death, without fear, not through some knowledge or resignation fed by experience, but because he has already been through it, six times, on six different TOREC tapes. Simpson's 'noia'—he has seen so much and now waits only for death—is also not wholly unlike the numb passivity of the camp *Muselmann*, deprived of the will to live, to strive in any way, unafraid to die because he has seen it already. Both Simpson and the *Muselmänner* have crossed a threshold. As Giorgio Agamben has argued, the *Muselmann*'s perspective is one that in essence we cannot fathom. We cannot see from where they stand; they have no point of view.[17] They both represent the outer (and perhaps also the proper) limits of how malleable perspective can be.

'Trattamento di quiescenza' tells us that altered perspectives are pleasurable and useful because they are alienating. There is a natural and good fascination with new experience that the machine satisfies. But it is also a dangerous invention, because the knowledge thus acquired does not distil into substantial (useful) experience, into practical intelligence, into ethical knowledge. There is no process, there is no life ('dolore . . . opere . . . colpe') through which to etch the experiences into a memory or a reflection. 'Il Torec non dà assuefazione, purtroppo' (I. 566; 'Unfortunately, the TOREC is not habit-forming'): its mock-experiences cannot be integrated into the self, into identity and a

---

[17] See Agamben, *Quel che resta di Auschwitz*, 37–80.

mode of viewing the world (of 'good vision') because every new playing of the tape brings with it the necessary sensation that it is the first time the experience has been had. Thus there is a thin excess of ready-made, throwaway, technological experience that we might contrast to Levi's 'thick' ethical notion of working (thinking and imagining) his way through to other points of view (see Introduction) in a time-consuming, success- and failure-prone process. There may be limits to access to other perspectives, but the limits are vast and it is right to train ourselves to be aware of and expert in distance, difference, and the positions from which we look and look again at the world.

INVENTION, OR
FIRST THINGS

Did I request thee, Maker, from my clay
To mould me man? Did I solicit thee
From darkness to promote me?
(Milton, from Mary Shelley's *Frankenstein*)

In everything from its title to its structure to its ethical core, *Se questo è un uomo* concerns itself with dehumanization, the gradual, inexorable destruction of what is human, within Levi himself and those around him. The destruction is physical, emotional, moral; it is completed in stages of humiliation and degradation and is chronicled in all its awful intensity with Levi's typical complexity and clarity. The chronicle reaches an extraordinary climax at the end of the chapter 'L'ultimo' where Levi and Alberto look on at the execution of the 'last man' to resist the Nazi machine and realize that now all resistance is closed off, the very inner core of their sense of human worth has been worn away:

Distruggere l'uomo è difficile, quasi quanto crearlo: non è stato agevole, non è stato breve, ma ci siete riusciti, tedeschi. Eccoci docili sotto i vostri sguardi: da parte nostra nulla più avete da temere: non atti di rivolta, non parole di sfida, neppure uno sguardo giudice. (I. 146)
(To destroy a man is difficult, almost as much as to create one: it has not been easy, nor has it been swift, but you Germans have managed it. Here we are, subdued beneath your eyes: from our part you have nothing more to fear, no acts of revolt, no words of defiance, not even a judging look.)

This is Levi at his most eschatological, a chronicler of 'last things', of death and judgement. It is Levi at his most apocalyptic and abject. And yet, in a pattern with which we have come to be familiar, there is a chink of light even here. Hidden by Levi's

characteristic irony is the seed of one of his most fertile ethical itineraries, projected towards the very opposite of the eschatological:
'Distruggere l'uomo è difficile, *quasi quanto crearlo*: . . .' The incision ironizes and punctures the pretensions of the Nazi machine,
it tempers Levi's abjection even as it declares it, it makes careful,
witty judgement even as all such judgement is precluded ('neppure
uno sguardo giudice').

'L'ultimo' is followed by the horrific squalor of the book's coda,
'Storia di dieci giorni', and already here Levi is alive to the ethical
connections of such language. After two days, he and his companions are in terrible decline, but they have managed to find a stove
and, more importantly still, they have shared bread amongst themselves, an act so pregnant with humanity as to have been inconceivable, even a day earlier. At the end of this first day of tentative
ethical rebirth, Levi comments:

In mezzo alla sterminata pianura piena di gelo e di guerra, nelle cameretta
buia pullulante di germi, ci sentivamo in pace con noi e col mondo.
Eravamo rotti di fatica, ma ci pareva, dopo tanto tempo, di avere finalmente fatto qualcosa di utile; forse come Dio dopo il primo giorno della
creazione. (I. 157)
(In the middle of the boundless plain full of frost and war, in the small,
dark room swarming with germs, we felt at peace with ourselves and
with the world. We were broken with exhaustion, but, after so long, it
seemed that we had finally done something useful; perhaps like God after
the first day of creation)

The two turns of phrase in 'L'ultimo' and 'Storia di dieci giorni'
('quasi quanto crearlo'; 'forse come Dio . . .') introduce us, against
the black backdrop of last things, to Levi's equal and opposite
fascination with 'first things', with creation and genesis—indeed
with Creation and Genesis—and its apparently more mundane
cognate, invention.[1] This chapter investigates the questions of
invention and creation in Levi's work, as marked out in negative
in the barren terrain of the camps and then, through creative
inversion, transposition, and reshaping, turned elsewhere in the

[1] On Levi's reversal of Genesis, see W. Goldkorn, 'La memoria ambigua', *MicroMega*,
3 (July–Sept. 1989): 195–202 [200–2]. On 'naming' in Levi as a calque from Adam's naming
in Genesis, see G. Calcagno, 'Dante dolcissimo padre', in E. Mattioda, ed., *Al di qua del bene
e del male* (Milan: Franco Angeli, 2000), 169. On invention, see M. Belpoliti, *Primo Levi*
(Milan: Bruno Mondadori, 1998), 84–8; J. Usher, 'Primo Levi's Science Fiction and the
Humanoid', *Journal of the Institute of Romance Studies*, 4, 1996, 199–216.

œuvre into an enquiry regarding the potential and limits of human action or human making, into what we might call an ethics of the man-made.

As one might expect, Levi's treatment of this question of creation is typically less apocalyptic, more witty, light, and subdued than at the end of 'L'ultimo', where fine-tuned ethical enquiry is somewhat beside the point. A good case in point is a charming essay in *L'altrui mestiere* called 'Inventare un animale' (I. 711–15), where Levi wryly elaborates on the sheer difficulty of creation:

Inventare dal nulla un animale *che possa esistere* . . . è un compito pressoché impossibile. È una progettazione che supera di gran lunga le nostre capacità razionali . . . Tuttavia, l'esperienza di tremila anni di narrativa, di pittura e di scultura ci dimostra che anche inventare un animale a capriccio, un animale di cui non ci importa affatto che possa esistere . . . non è un compito facile. (II. 711; emphasis in the original)
(To invent from scratch an animal that could exist . . . is an almost impossible task. It requires a level of planning that outstrips by far our rational faculties . . . And yet, the experience of three thousand years of narrative, painting, and sculpture shows us that even the task of inventing an animal on a whim, whose possible existence has no importance at all . . . is not easy.)

The essay goes on, by way of centaur myths, science fiction, Borges, and others, to survey the fantastic inventions of some primary-school children. Both 'L'ultimo' and 'Inventare un animale' are strangely drawn to the same problem, of creation, invention, or the 'new', and the limits of these. And both, in their different ways, are drawn to a mythical idiom as a means to investigate them. Indeed, of all the virtues and values in this book, this one more than any other taps into the mythical, the universal, and the timeless, even as it is translated into a more pragmatic and realistically ethical device.

There are, first of all, the echoes of the Genesis creation story itself, a source Levi plays with again and again, not only in *Se questo è un uomo* but also in the title story of *Lilít e altri racconti*, which retells the Midrashic tale of Adam's first wife Lilith, whose existence is only hinted at between the lines of the text of Genesis (II. 18–23); or in the poem 'Nel principio' telling the story of the Big Bang by way of a calque of Genesis 1: 1 (II. 544); or in 'Il sesto giorno', an elaborate comic rewriting of the day of Man's creation told as the story of how a committee of bickering experts and bureaucrats fails to come up with a satisfactory model for the new species known as Man before the allotted deadline at the end of the sixth day (I. 529–47); or in 'L'ordine a buon mercato' where the weary narrator notes after days of excited experimentation ('Il primo giorno . . . il secondo giorno . . .' etc.): 'Il settimo giorno mi riposai' (I. 447–55 [453]; 'On the seventh day I rested').[2]

Beyond Creation itself, there is a series of high-flown models and sources in Levi who test the very outside limits of human creativity and capacity: one is the Tower of Babel, a product of human defiance of limits and subsequent punishment which recurs as a figure for the chaos of the *Lager* and the grotesque, useless tower of the Buna factory at Monowitz; another is Dante's Ulysses, falteringly recalled in 'Il canto di Ulisse', who stepped over divinely decreed boundaries of knowledge in his heroic 'last voyage' (more last things) and is both villain and hero in *Inferno* for this very transgression; or Icarus, a distant ancestor of 'Trattamento di quiescenza', with its fantasy of man flying as a bird; and finally, there is Prometheus and his modern progeny, Frankenstein,[3] who, as we shall see, haunt Levi's narrative explorations of the scientist as inventor and transgressor of dangerous limits. All of these figures—and Adam, the father of them all—are echoed in the course of the discussion here, which focuses especially on Levi's science-fiction stories and on the work narratives in *Il sistema periodico* and *La chiave a stella*, since it is in science and in work that the value of invention (and inventiveness) is at its most stimulating for Levi. But as with so many of Levi's ethical itineraries, we will also see it mapped onto an idea of writing, of literary invention.

A good starting point is a story from the late 1960s, 'Il servo' (*Vizio di forma*, I. 710–17), in which many of these threads are woven together in a relatively unusual narrative mode for Levi, the Talmudic parable.[4] 'Il servo' is Levi's version of the Talmudic

---

[2] On Levi's use of the Old Testament, see A. Cavaglion, 'La scelta di Gedeone: appunti su Primo Levi e l'ebraismo', *Journal of the Institute of Romance Studies*, 4 (1996), 187–98.

[3] M. Shelley, *Frankenstein, or the Modern Prometheus* (Harmondsworth: Penguin, 1985; 1st edition 1818). There is further interesting common ground between Levi and Shelley's *Frankenstein* in the influence on both of Coleridge's *Ancient Mariner* (see p. 32 of the Penguin edition); see Chapter 11 note 13 below.

[4] On 'Il servo', see M. Lollini, 'Golem', in M. Belpoliti, ed., *Primo Levi* (Milan: Marcos y Marcos, Riga 13, 1997), 348–60; E. Mattioda, *L'ordine del mondo* (Naples: Liguori, 1998), 79–83.

tale of the Golem. In reworking it, he binds the story of an ultimately disastrous man-made attempt at creation to several of his
own core motifs of identity and value, setting up the process of
invention as a deeply personal but also archetypal dynamic in his
meditation on human action and progress. His hero is Arié, a wise
and immensely strong 90-year-old Rabbi of Prague, distant ancestor of Marx, Kafka, Freud, and Einstein and thus also of the ideology and the science, the terrors and anxieties of modernity. Arié
makes his Golem using Kabbalistic lore as a strong, obedient
servant or 'robot'. The robot serves Arié and the community well,
labouring and when necessary fighting to defend them, despite an
eccentricity and wilfulness that seem all too human, until he is
destroyed, torn apart when ordered to work on the Sabbath as
forbidden in the very letters of the Torah that created him.

The story plays constantly on the Golem's affinities with the
human, whether with Adam or other Old Testament figures, with
Arié himself, or with a model of man in general. In order to judge
what is and is not human (if this is a man), it uses a sort of Platonic
scale of being, all cryptically contained in the letters of the Torah,
that rises from the lowest worm up to God's image in man. Arié's
task is to find the letters to bring his Golem close to but not beyond
the boundary of the human, which is also the boundary of dangerous pride variously transgressed by Adam, Ulysses, Prometheus, and
Frankenstein: 'Ora, Arié non era un bestemmiatore, e non si era
proposto di creare un secondo Adamo. Non intendeva costruire un
uomo . . . occorrevano dunque istruzioni . . . non altrettanto comp-
lesse di quelle che occorrono per "essere come Dio" ' (I. 711; 'Now
Arié was not a blasphemer, and he had not thought of creating a
second Adam. He did not mean to make a man . . . so instructions
were needed . . . that were not as complex as those for a creature "in
God's likeness" '). And yet, the task is all but impossible, since all
creatures on the scale are in some senses Golems:

Un Golem è poco piú che un nulla: è una porzione di materia, ossia di
chaos, racchiusa in una sembianza umana o bestiale, è insomma un simu-
lacro, e come tale non è buono a nulla; . . . Il Vitello d'Oro era un
Golem; lo era Adamo, ed anche noi lo siamo. (I. 710–11)
(A Golem is little more than nothing: a portion of matter or of chaos
enclosed in a human or animal semblance, a simulacrum in short, and as
such good for nothing; . . . the Golden Calf was a Golem; so was Adam
and so are we.)

Arié carefully chooses which qualities or virtues to allow his creature and which to deny: no to (ordinary virtues of) will, curiosity, and enterprise, to wit, wisdom, and prophetic understanding; yes to righteous anger, obedience, stubbornness, courage, and even a hint of rash folly (all qualities he finds in Old Testament figures or indeed in himself); no to Mind and Appetites, yes to some form of Spirit (I. 713). Despite his fear of aping God's Creation, he knowingly inserts elements of himself into his creature: its face is leonine to echo the meaning of Arié (lion); its hands are modelled on his own. And indeed the moment Arié's Golem is brought to life, it seems more an image of its maker than a dumb slave:

gli occhi del mostro si accesero e lo guardarono. Si attendeva che gli chiedesse: 'Che vuoi da me, o Signore?', ma udí invece un'altra domanda che non gli era nuova, e che gli suonò piena d'ira: 'Perché prospera l'empio?' Allora comprese che il Golem era suo figlio, e provò gioia, e insieme temette davanti al Signore; perché, come sta scritto, la gioia dell'ebreo è come un briciolo di spavento.' (I. 714)
(the eyes of the monster lit up and looked at him. He was expecting him to ask, 'What do you want of me, O Lord?' but instead he heard another familiar question, full of anger: 'Why does the sinner prosper?' And then he understood that the Golem was his son, and he felt joy and also fear before the Lord; because, as it is written, the joy of the Jew is like a crumb of terror.)

Later, when the Golem shows signs of laziness and reluctance to obey, Arié is at once both gratified and disturbed '. . . perché queste sono passioni umane, native; non lui gliele aveva inspirate, il colosso d'argilla le aveva concepite da solo: era piú umano di quanto lui lo avesse voluto' (I. 715; '. . . because these are native human passions; he had not inspired them in it, the clay colossus had conceived them alone: it was more human than he had wished'). It refuses to use a hatchet to cut wood, preferring instead to break it with its bare hands, and Arié understands after long reflection that this too is a marker of noble humanity, of self-defined destiny: the hatchet is a symbol of servility like the yoke for the ox, 'non cosí la mano, che è parte di te, e nel cui palmo è impresso il tuo destino' (I. 716; 'but not the hand, which is part of you, in whose palm your destiny is imprinted'). It is, of course, no coincidence that this human nobility resides in that very part of the creature that was modelled on Arié himself, the hands; nor that his long meditation on this matter is the very cause of the Golem's destruction, since the rabbi is so lost in thought about it that he fails to notice that the sun has set, Sabbath has begun and the Golem is still working. The profound difficulty of setting the boundaries of the human, of invention and knowledge, and the rewards and dangers of patrolling them, are neatly captured in this disastrous mistake which brings the story to an end.

'Il servo' is one of the most wholehearted and satisfying (as well as one of the earliest) applications on Levi's part of Ashkenazi Jewish culture.[5] Three aspects of it are particularly useful for questions of invention or creation, and each one, as if to underscore their importance, is also bound up with fundamental and recurrent features of Levi's own self-representations.

The first takes us to the core of Levi's understanding of science as an ordered and rational model for understanding the world, shot through with a sense of the mystery and unknowability of the world. The description of the Golem-like quality of all matter quoted above—'Un Golem è poco più che un nulla: è una porzione di materia, ossia di chaos, racchiusa in una sembianza umana o bestiale . . .'—is echoed at numerous moments in his work where he charts the tension between order and disorder within 'creation'; for example in 'Il rito e il riso'—'la vita è regola, è ordine che prevale sul Caos' (II. 798; 'life is rule, order which prevails over chaos'); or at several moments in *Il sistema periodico* at the time of Levi's youthful plunge into the world of scientific discovery, into chemistry as the battle of order, reason, and spirit against the formless chaos of matter, 'Hyle' (e.g. I. 767, 873).

At the same time, the transformation of brute matter into an all but human creature in 'Il servo' clearly recalls Levi's fascination with another miracle of metamorphosis—alchemy—and through it, his sense of science and knowledge as strangely transformative (see both Chapters 4 and 7 above), with the ethically charged potential for both renewal and destruction. As in Mary Shelley's *Frankenstein*, the struggle between order and chaos, between life and the void, is at the heart of Levi's meditation on science itself,

---

[5] 'Il servo' was written at some point between 1968 and 1970. In 1966, he had written a preface to the Italian edition of I. Katznelson's Yiddish poem *The Song of the Murdered Jewish People*, written in 1943 in the Warsaw ghetto and then buried under a tree (I. 1154–7). Later examples include 'Il rito e il riso' (*L'altrui mestiere*, II. 795–9) and much of *Se non ora, quando?*

filtered through the idiom of Talmudic and biblical Jewish story-telling in 'Il servo' as elsewhere he filters it through a wry, idiosyncratic version of the idiom of science fiction.[6] Throughout these modulations of idiom, however, one image or turn of phrase recurs almost obsessively as a marker of these transformations, the paradoxical image of extracting something from nothing, 'trarre dal nulla'. Tellingly, Levi uses the same phrase in the essay 'La vergogna' in *I sommersi e i salvati* when talking of the universal shame prompted by the Holocaust—the shame that mankind can create such pain, and that such immense pain 'è la sola forza che *si crea dal nulla*, senza spesa e senza fatica. Basta non vedere, non ascoltare, non fare' (II. 1058; emphasis added; 'is the only force that can be created from nothing, without cost or effort. Just don't look, don't listen, don't act'). And in the same essay, he returns us to the terrible source of the image of the void, Genesis 1: 2, ' "tòhu vavòhu", [l'] universo deserto e vuoto, schiacciato sotto lo spirito di Dio . . . l'uomo è assente: non ancora nato e già spento' (II. 1057; " 'tòhu vavòhu", [the] empty barren universe, crushed beneath God's spirit . . . man is absent: not yet born and already spent').

Secondly, there is the imagery of hands in 'Il servo'. The work of the rabbi, the work of the Golem, and even the 'genetic' bond of similarity between them are all, as we have seen, channelled through their hands. Their hands define their dignity, their capacity to invent or to make, their very autonomy as 'human' beings. It takes us to the core of Levi's pragmatism investigated in Chapter 6, and of his practice of science as applied 'life science'. In the essay 'Il segno del chimico' (II. 810–15), he talks of the ritual sign on the hands of chemists of a certain era, the residue of formative experiments and the symbol of the practical 'virtù del laboratorio' (II. 812; 'laboratory virtues').[7] This comes to richest fruition in *La chiave a stella*, whose hero Faussone is defined atavistically (his forebears were smiths), professionally (as an engineer), and morally (as

---

[6] On the links in Levi between science and Judaism, see V. De Luca, *Tra Giobbe e i buchi neri. Le radici ebraiche dell'opera di Primo Levi* (Naples: Istituto grafico editoriale italiano, 1991), 35–42; or the slightly more fanciful link made between Mendel, the protagonist of *Se non ora, quando?*, and Mendeleev, creator of the periodic table, by Giorgio Calcagno, 'Dante dolcissimo padre', 170.

[7] See interview with Paola Valabrega, in Levi, *The Voice of Memory*, 136–47 [139]; and Valabrega's 'Mano/Cervello' in Belpoliti, ed., *Primo Levi* (Riga 13), 380–92.

a pragmatist) by his status as a 'manual worker', and in its sister book, *Il sistema periodico*. To take only the founding instance in the latter, the chapter 'Idrogeno' contains a lament for the lost suppleness and sensitivity of Levi and his companion's atrophied hands:

Cosa sapevamo fare con le nostre mani? Niente, o quasi. Le donne sí: le nostre madri e nonne avevano mani vive ed agili, sapevano cucire e cucinare, alcune anche suonare il piano, dipingere con gli acquerelli, ricamare, intrecciarsi i capelli. Ma noi, e i nostri padri?

Le nostre mani erano rozze e deboli ad un tempo, regredite, insensibili: la parte meno educata dei nostri corpi. Compiute le prime fondamentali esperienze del gioco, avevamo imparato a scrivere e null'altro. Conoscevamo la stretta convulsa intorno ai rami degli alberi, su cui amavamo arrampicarsi per voglia naturale ed insieme (Enrico ed io) per confuso omaggio e ritorno all'origine della specie; ma ignoravamo il peso solenne e bilanciato del martello, la forza concentrata delle lame, troppo prudentemente proibite, la tessitura sapiente del legno, la cedevolezza simile e diversa del ferro, del piombo e del rame. Se l'uomo è artefice, non eravamo uomini: lo sapevamo e ne soffrivamo. (I. 759–60)

(What could we do with our hands? Nothing, or nearly nothing. Women, yes: our mothers and grandmothers had lively, agile hands, they knew how to sew and cook, some even played the piano, painted watercolours, did embroidery, plaited their hair. But us, and our fathers?

Our hands were rough and weak at once, a throwback, insensitive: the least educated part of our bodies. Once the first fundamental experiences of play were over, we had learned nothing except how to write. We knew the violent grip on tree branches that we (Enrico and I) loved to climb up, both out of a natural desire and in a muddled homage and return to the origin of our species: but we knew nothing of the solemn, balanced weight of the hammer, the concentrated force of blades (prohibited in an excess of prudence), the tangy texture of wood, the similar and yet distinct yield of iron, lead, and copper. If man is a maker, we were not men: we knew it and we suffered from it.)

Hands are the conduit for matter and experiment which come together to form the very purpose of invention. Hands make things, 'l'uomo è artefice'; to be human is to experiment, to forge from material, to invent, to construct or, as both narrator and hero of *La chiave a stella* put it in relation to their own work as rigger, chemist, writer, 'montare'. And in case Faussone's manual work stories seem too far removed from Rabbi Arié's mystical work in Prague, listen to Faussone's account of the moment when his troubled Alaskan sea-platform is finally set right in 'Off-shore':

... si è fermato netto, come un'isola, ma era un'isola che l'avevamo fatto noi; e io non so gli altri, magari non pensavano a niente, ma io ho pensato al Padreterno quando ha fatto il mondo, dato che sia stato proprio lui, e quanda ha separato il mare dall'asciutto, anche se non c'entrava poi tanto. (I. 1009)
(... it stopped dead, like an island, but it was an island we had made; and I don't know about the others, maybe they weren't thinking of anything, but I thought of God Almighty when he made the world, if it really was him, and when he set the sea apart from the dry land, although it didn't really have much to do with it.)

Elsewhere, Levi returns to the Dantesque-cum-Rabelaisian vocabulary of the forge, defining man as 'Il fabbro di se stesso', the title of the story immediately preceding 'Il servo' in *Vizio di forma*, which once again repeats the paean to hands as the culminating stage in the evolution of the species (I. 708–9). And this last bears interesting comparison to an essay in *Racconti e saggi*, 'Una bottiglia di sole', where Levi proposes to define the species Man as a 'costruttore di recipienti' (II. 958–62 [958]). Refining the sense of man as 'costruttore', 'montatore', or 'fabbro', where the quality of manuality is both necessary and sufficient to distinguish the human, the idea of man as a 'costruttore di recipienti' ('a maker of containers'), says Levi, takes us further still: it binds manual dexterity to a sense of future time that is unique to Man (containers imply preserving something for the future).[8]

The third aspect to note in 'Il servo' is the Golem's nature as split, hybrid in its make-up and ultimately doomed by contradictory imperatives. Indeed, the Golem is split not once but twice and more, even before its final quandary: first, in its material composition sculpted by the rabbi from a hybrid of matter ('d'argilla, di metallo e di vetro', I. 713, 'of clay, metal, and glass') and spirit; then in vertical halves:

aveva una figura umana dalla cintola in su ... la cintura è una frontiera, solo al di sopra della cintura l'uomo è fatto a immagine di Dio, mentre al di sotto è bestia; per questo l'uomo savio non deve dimenticare di cingerla. Al di sotto della cintura il Golem era veramente Golem ... (ibid.)

---

[8] This interest in futures and predictability connects back to a key feature of Levi's Popperian view of science and knowledge, based on unpredictable innovation and invention but then also future reproducibility: see 'Il rito e il riso', and also 'Roulette dei batteri' (II. 950–3) and 'Riprodurre i miracoli' (II. 966–9).

(he had a human figure from the waist up . . . the waist is a border, only above the waist is man made in God's image, below he is a beast: for this reason the wise man must not forget to bind it. Below the belt, the Golem really was a Golem.)

The image recalls Levi's self-mocking references to his unconscious or his desiring self as the 'tenant in the basement' or 'below the belt'.[9] It also points again to Levi's related fascination with syntheses of the animate and the inanimate.[10] Generally too, the notion of the split self goes to the heart of Levi's conception both of himself and of what it is to be human, contained in the recurrent image of the centaur—from Levi's declaration in a much-quoted interview of 1966 for *L'unità*, 'Io sono un anfibio, un centauro' ('I am an amphibian, a centaur'), to possibly his most ambitious short story of all, 'Quaestio de centauris' (I. 505–16).[11] This same defining quality emerges elevated to a universal plane in 'Argon' at the start of *Il sistema periodico*, where the comic contradictions of his Jewish ancestors' lives and languages reflect another, larger contrast, 'quello insito nella condizione umana, poiché l'uomo è centauro, groviglio di carne e di mente, di alito divino e di polvere' (I. 746; 'the contrast intrinsic to the human condition, for man is a centaur, a tangle of flesh and mind, of divine breath and dust').[12] And finally, this same image and some of the same vocabulary of 'Il servo' is to be found at a key juncture of *I sommersi e i salvati*, at the climax of the chapter 'La zona grigia' where the impossible moral complexity of the grey zone is read, again, as a given ambiguity of the creature that is man. Levi tries to explain the compelling and threatening power of the story of Chaim Rumkowski, the 'president'-collaborator of the Łódź ghetto: 'Forse il suo significato è più vasto: in Rumkowksi ci rispecchiamo tutti, la sua ambiguità è la nostra, connaturata, di

---

[9] For examples of such imagery, see Levi, *The Voice of Memory*, 157; 'A un giovane lettore' (*L'altrui mestiere*, II. 847); and 'Il segreto del ragno' (*Pagine sparse*, II. 1305).

[10] See Chapter 7 note 14; and cf. also the story 'I sintetici' (*Vizio di forma*, I. 588–99), about the 'racial' hostility to a young boy who is part synthetically made.

[11] See Levi, *The Voice of Memory*, 85; and also Marco Belpoliti's introduction to that collection, 'I am a Centaur', pp. xvii–xxv.

[12] According to Giovanni Tesio, 'Argon' was drafted as early as 1946 (G. Tesio, 'Primo Levi' (1979) in *Piemonte letterario dell'otto-novecento* (Rome: Bulzoni, 1991), 169); although Cavaglion, followed by Belpoliti, dates it to 1973 (A. Cavaglion 'Argon e la cultura ebraica piemontese', in *Primo Levi. Il presente del passato* (Milan: Franco Angeli, 1991), 169–96; and I. 1448).

ibridi impastati di argilla e di spirito . . .' (II. 1043; 'perhaps his importance is wider still: in Rumkowski we can all see part of ourselves, his ambiguity is ours, part of our nature as hybrid mixtures of clay and spirit . . .').

The image of Mankind as a synthesis of clay and its Creator's breath of life, an image shared by Levi's Golem, has its origin in the Book of Job, Levi's prime source for his poetry of suffering and confusion and the source of all four of his trajectories for understanding man and the world in the prefatory diagram of *La ricerca delle radici* (II. 1367–80):

> The spirit of God has made me,
> and the breath of the Almighty gives me life.
> .   .   .   .
> Behold, I am toward God as you are;
> I too was formed from a piece of clay. (Job 33: 4, 6)

The link to Job tells us finally that the fascination with creation is, among other things, a means of exploring the acts of moral choosing within the constraints set by our capacities, historical circumstances, or destiny. Acts such as Rabbi Arié's amount to acts of self-creation, carrying with them the terrible ambiguity—pride, ambition, risk of failure and of moral blindness—and the weight of responsibility and justice that any act of creation (any act) entails.

'Il servo' proves a useful hook on which to hang a first approach to Levi's concern with invention, but it is only one in a chain of stories, essays, and poems that probe and recast the question of the new, of 'first things'. Perhaps the fundamental feature that allows us to speak of invention in the context of ethics and ordinary virtues is the conjunction of invention as science and invention as imagination, myth, and fantasy, each variously embraced, ironized, contained, or dismantled as they rub up against each other. And as the terms themselves suggest, it is in his science fiction (in Italian, precisely, 'fantascienza') that the two poles of invention meet in the most interesting ways.

Of the fifteen stories in *Storie naturali*, all but one could be said to be about inventions, strange scientific discoveries, or adaptations. The exception is 'Quaestio de centauris' (I. 505–16) which in reality is no exception at all: we have already seen that the story has powerful subterranean links to Levi's conception of himself, of man and creation, through the hybrid nature of the centaur. We can take this further here, by noting that the story's own explanation for the creation of the centaur and of myriad other fantastical creatures most of which are now extinct derives from yet another 'creation' moment in Genesis, the story of the universal flood. After the flood, according to the centaur Trachi, there was a period known as the 'panspermía', of immense, spontaneous, and open fertility, during which species mated with other species, abolishing all boundaries of difference and distance: 'Fu questa seconda creazione la vera creazione' (I. 506; 'This second creation was the true creation'). This is one of several *loci* in Levi's work where, perhaps surprisingly for such a sober and modest writer, a form of polymorphous and vertiginous sexuality is the vehicle for creation and re-creation, for miscegenation and hybrid renewal.[13] Indeed, the story has some affinity with Levi's famous paean in *Il sistema periodico* to impurity—with explicit reference to absurd Fascist theorization about the 'purity' of the Italian race—as the very stuff and essence of life: 'Perché la ruota giri, perché la vita viva, ci vogliono le impurezze, e le impurezze delle impurezze: anche nel terreno, come è noto, se ha da essere fertile. Ci vuole il dissenso, il diverso, i grani di sale e di senape: il fascismo non li vuole, li vieta, e per questo tu non sei fascista' (I. 768; 'For the wheel to turn, for life to live, impurities are needed, and impurities in impurities: the same goes for soil, as is well known, if it is to be fertile. Dissent is necessary, an element of difference, grains of salt and mustard: Fascism does not want them, forbids them, and that is why you are not a fascist'). And alongside this, we might set a fascinating 1984 essay entitled 'L'asimmetria e la vita' (*Pagine sparse*, II. 1231–40),[14] where the origin of life itself, the true moment of 'creation', is ascribed to the remarkable quality of left–right asymmetry in molecular structure: this microcosmic geometric exception to patterned regularity allowed animate life to evolve from inanimate matter; 'tratta dal nulla', Levi would say.

'Quaestio de centauris' aside, *Storie naturali* is dominated by the

---

[13] See, for example, 'Erano fatti per stare insieme' and 'Il passa-muri' (both in *Racconti e saggi*, II. 866–7, 898–901) where sex and love challenge the Euclidean dimensions of reality; and 'Disfilassi' (in *Lilít*, II. 93–9) where science has inadvertently removed all obstacles to cross-fertilizations between humans, animals, and even plants.

[14] See A. Cavaglion, 'Asimmetrie', in Belpoliti, ed., *Primo Levi* (Riga 13), 222–9.

six stories revolving around Simpson, the idiosyncratic salesman-cum-inventor of the American firm NATCA of Fort Kiddiwanee. It is worth briefly summarizing them:

1. 'Il Versificatore' (I. 413–33)—after a series of tests and experiments, Simpson sells a verse-writing machine to a poet, who makes money writing occasional verse.
2. 'L'ordine a buon mercato' (I. 447–55)—the narrator experiments with Simpson's latest device, 'Il Mimete', which can replicate almost any object in exact 3-D material perfection. Simpson haughtily disapproves of the narrator's duplication of diamonds and of spiders.
3. 'Alcune applicazioni del Mimete' (I. 460–6)—the narrator's friend Gilberto takes the 'Mimete' one step further, adapting the machine to duplicate his wife Emma. This threatens to wreak havoc in his domestic life until he comes up with the ideal solution: he duplicates himself to provide a perfect partner for Emma II.
4. 'La misura della bellezza' (I. 495–504)—the narrator discovers Simpson voyeuristically observing women at the beach. In fact, he is testing and fine-tuning the 'Calometro' which measures the beauty of the person it is pointed at, relative to set standards (Elizabeth Taylor and Raf Vallone). The narrator's wife disapproves.
5. 'Pieno impiego' (I. 517–28)—bored with working for NATCA, Simpson develops his own commercial idea, learning how to talk to insects in order to take them on contractually as his workers. Despite an employee using them for drug-running he is confident he can use his 'invention' for good.
6. 'Trattamento di quiescenza' (I. 548–67)—adventures with the TOREC (see Chapter 7).

The Simpson stories replay in a different key many of the same chords found in 'Il servo', 'Quaestio de centauris', or elsewhere, even on the level of language alone. For instance, where 'Il servo' went to great lengths to pin down the technicalities of making a Golem, using the Torah and Talmudic or Midrashic commentary to make a sort of construction manual, so the Simpson stories often centre on the technical language required to explain the workings of Simpson's strange inventions. Similar linguistic-technical questions are thrown up, comically and seriously, elsewhere in the *œuvre* also: throughout both *La chiave a stella* and *Il sistema periodico* where the detail of the work described, in chemistry or in engineering, is part of Levi's self-consciously Conradian project to forge narrative from the particular idioms of these workplaces; in the tetchy debates between technicians over the specifications of Man in 'Il sesto giorno'; or in Levi's use of the language of patents as we saw in Chapter 5. Part and parcel of Levi's ubiquitous pleasure in language, this also reflects a key problem within the realm of invention, the problem of definition. What does one call and how does one explain something that is new? Does an invention stand without the description of it, the patent or equivalent that pins down the mechanism behind it? As with so many of Levi's ordinary virtues, the linguistic aspect of the question of invention has, among other things, a metaethical value, posing the question of how to articulate the processes and complexities of invention (and its cognates). It also necessarily suggests that need for precision and specificity and close distinction encountered earlier in Chapters 3 and 5.

The Simpson stories also retain, although as a dim, often comic echo, elements of the mythical side to invention and creation so prominent in 'Il servo' and 'Quaestio de centauris'. Over the sequence, Simpson evolves from a bland salesman with a good patter into a fully-fledged inventor in his own right and then into something akin to a superhuman figure with the doomed wisdom of ages, at the end of 'Trattamento di quiescenza'. As the former he is a figure of our second-rate, compromised modern world of commerce, science, and salaried slog (a world Levi worked in himself); as the latter a modern Prometheus, as he hints: 'Una vecchia storia, vero? Inventi il fuoco e lo doni agli uomini, poi un avvoltoio ti rode il fegato per l'eternità' ('Pieno impiego', I. 527; 'It's an old story, no? You invent fire and give it to man, and then a vulture gnaws at your liver for eternity'). Nor is Simpson alone in this: Simpson, Gilberto, the 'poeta', and indeed the narrator are, of course, among other things, figures for Levi himself, all with scientific, problem-solving minds, all with tendencies towards both the pragmatic and the poetic, all more or less able to judge the decent limits of what they are doing. Their stories drag us back and forth between a euphoric, if naive optimism over the timeless potential of human invention to change our world and an uneasy

anxiety over the risks (for Simpson the fatal risks) of giving too
much of ourselves over to our inventions. And the figure of
Prometheus returns again and again as both positive and negative
figure for the process:

Insistetti sul duplice aspetto delle sue virtù [del Mimete]: quello economico . . . e quello, dirò cosí, prometeico, di strumento nuovo e raffinato
per l'avanzamento delle nostre conoscenze sui meccanismi vitali.
('L'ordine a buon mercato', I. 454)
(I insisted on the double benefits it [the Mimete] could bring; economic
. . . and also, let me call it Promethean, the benefit of a new and refined
tool for the advancement of our understanding of living mechanisms.)

Questo è Gilberto, un uomo pericoloso, un piccolo prometeo nocivo:
ingegnoso e irresponsabile, superbo e sciocco. È un figlio del secolo,
come dicevo prima: anzi, è un simbolo del nostro secolo. Ho sempre
pensato che sarebbe stato capace, all'occorrenza, di costruire una bomba
atomica e di lasciarla cadere su Milano 'per vedere che effetto fa' ('Alcune
applicazioni del Mimete', I. 461)
(This is Gilberto, a dangerous man, a small-scale unwholesome
Prometheus: shrewd and irresponsible, proud and foolish. He is a child
of our century, as I said before: or rather a symbol of our century. I have
always thought that he would, if necessary, build an atomic bomb and
drop it on Milan 'just to see what would happen')

And not only in *Storie naturali*: in 'Sidereus nuncius', a poem in *Ad
ora incerta* dedicated to Galileo, another talismanic figure of the
scientist, writer, and searcher for knowledge against the scepticism
and dogmatism of the world around him, we find the same image
as that in 'Pieno impiego', of the punishment of Prometheus, to
evoke his punishment by the Church: 'L'avvoltoio che mi rode
ogni sera | Ha la faccia di ognuno' (II. 578; 'The vulture that
gnaws me every evening | has the face of everyman'). And in
'Cerio' in *Il sistema periodico*, Levi's companion in the *Lager*,
Alberto, becomes a Simpsonesque modern Prometheus because he
is intent on taking Primo's discovery of a supply of cerium and
exploiting it 'commercially' in the camp black market:

Prometeo era stato sciocco a donare il fuoco agli uomini invece di
venderlo: avrebbe fatto quattrini, placato Giove ed evitato il guaio
dell'avvoltoio. (I. 863)
(Prometheus had been a fool to make a gift of fire to man instead of selling it: he would have made money, placated Jove, and avoided all that
trouble with the vulture.)

The bridge to the camps and in particular to Alberto is crucial. On the same page of 'Cerio', Levi lays out one of the most moving and resonant eulogies of Alberto who stands like few others as a hero in the antiheroic camp world: for his constructive optimism, his resistance to the camp system, at once both reasoned and instinctive, for his strength and good will, for his freedom, and finally, for his shrewdness, 'la sua astuzia'—a common term in Levi, along with 'ingegno' for the practical wit that underpins all the virtues under discussion here in Part II. For all these qualities, Alberto is something of a protector for Levi in the camp, as Prometheus was a protector of Man from Zeus' wish to destroy him.[15]

The Simpson stories, then, retain an aura of the mythical or archetypal, allowing Simpson (and the others) to stand for the dubious modern Prometheus—striving for invention and renewal, working with a hybrid of technology, nature, and human nature, driven as much by economics as the search for knowledge, risking destruction or redundancy (in both senses of the word) at every turn. The risks are multiple—risks of exceeding the limits of human intelligence (Levi gives us a clue that this is a key concern by having the 'Versificatore' spew out two lyrical-philosophical, hendecasyllabic, 'seicento'-style terzinas on the topic 'Limiti dell'ingegno umano', I. 423–4); risks of technology producing conformity (the narrator's wife insists this would be the sole product of the 'Calometro' in 'La misura della bellezza'); and risks of the loss of body, self, and mind (as eloquently demonstrated by 'Trattamento di quiescenza').

The darker side to these Promethean risks comes into focus with considerable power in two stories in *Storie naturali* not about Simpson, 'Angelica farfalla' (I. 434–41) and 'Versamina' (I. 467–76), both of which draw us and the thematics of invention and destruction back towards the grim universe of Nazi Germany. Kleber, the inventor of the Versamina drug that transforms sensations of pain into pleasure, dies a death much like Simpson's in 'Trattamento di quiescenza', drained of life and selfhood by their extraordinary creations, spiralling towards the end, part conscious

---

[15] The figure of the self-destroying protector recalls another mythical counterpart, thrown up when the 'Versificatore' links Simpson to his etymological cousin Samson (I. 432); see also the poems 'Sansone' and 'Delila' (II. 617–18).

and part abandoned to their delusory new inverted or virtual realities. And Professor Leeb in 'Angelica farfalla' too, although not himself destroyed, is a symbol of the Icarus-like or Babel-like arrogance of the scientist-inventor, reaching for the heavens (in this case quite literally for the metamorphosis of humans into angels), without regard for the risks. In these stories both the Third Reich and the Hiroshima bomb are evoked, catastrophes that run parallel in much of Levi's *œuvre*, both characterized by utopian aspirations and disastrous dystopian realizations on the part of research scientists, once again cast as Frankenstein.

The Simpson stories further offer something of a compendium or taxonomy of modern invention or the modern inventor that can be summarized in five types: first, invention as a form of imitative reconfiguration or transposition of existing phenomena (the 'Mimete' is the obvious example, as is the TOREC which replays people's experiences to a second party); secondly, invention of a new language, a new code or channel of communication (as in the language of the insects in 'Pieno impiego'); thirdly, invention as the analysis of mechanisms, for which the inventor dismantles and rebuilds in order to analyse and perhaps adapt, to invent anew (Gilberto is described as someone who 'lima, sega, salda, incolla, smerglia . . . ripara . . . smonta e rimonta . . . modifica' (I. 460; 'files, saws, solders, glues, sands . . . repairs . . . takes apart and rebuilds . . . modifies'), making him among other things a cousin of Faussone; cf. *La chiave a stella*, I. 945).

The fourth and fifth modes of invention take us beyond technology into wider realms of the man-made, and thus provide a bridge from the technical to larger ethical questions. The fourth moves the short distance from 'invention' to its cognate 'inventiveness' and on towards that defining practice for Levi's ethical universe, wit ('ingegno' or 'astuzia' would be Levi's terms).

If to invent is to make it is also to do or to act (the terms are indistinguishable in Romance languages, of course); as Levi notes, 'avere "imparato a far una cosa" . . . è diverso dall'avere "imparato una cosa" ' (II. 814; 'to have "learned to do something" . . . is not the same as to have "learned something" '). Levi's most exuberant account of practical, active inventiveness is the joyous, witty, and good-hearted trickery of Cesare, his Roman companion for much of *La tregua*. Cesare is inventive, flexibly ingenious, and irrepressible: he is defined by his native wit ('le naturali qualità del suo ingegno', I. 262). And the term 'ingegno' is one that recurs again and again in the story of his companion, whether describing his fake strawberry-tasting in the market or his acquisition of a chicken with Primo, by way of an absurd mime of clucking and egg-laying, or, more glorious still, his picaresque and unlikely journey home told later in 'Il ritorno di Cesare' in *Lilìt* (II. 54–8). Cesare's inventiveness also comes accompanied by a sort of salutary naivety that makes him a source of joy and companionship for Levi:

> Cesare era un figlio del sole, un amico di tutto il mondo, non conosceva né odio né disprezzo, era vario come il cielo, festoso, furbo e ingenuo, temerario e cauto, molto ignorante, molto innocente e molto civile. . . . assistere alle imprese di Cesare, anche alle più modeste e triviali, costituiva una esperienza unica, uno spettacolo vivo e corroborante, che mi riconciliava col mondo, e riaccendeva in me la gioia di vivere che Auschwitz aveva spenta. (I. 270)
>
> (Cesare was a child of the sun, a friend to everyone, incapable of hatred or contempt, as varied as the sky, joyous, both cunning and innocent, rash and cautious, very ignorant, very innocent and very civilized . . . to watch Cesare's exploits, even the most modest and trivial, was a unique experience, a living, reassuring spectacle that reconciled me with the world and rekindled in me the joy for life that Auschwitz had snuffed out.)

Every 'hero' in Levi's world (the very opposite of the strong, soldierly hero of tradition) displays some version of Cesare's inventiveness; even flawed heroes such as Arié, Simpson, and Gilberto. They are all practically alert, the opposite of stupid. Indeed, stupidity is anathema in Levi's world-view, the very opposite of 'ingegno':

> Essere giudicati stupidi, e sentirselo dire, è più doloroso che sentirsi definiti golosi, bugiardi, violenti, lussuriosi, pigri, codardi: ogni debolezza, ogni vizio ha trovato i suoi difensori, la sua retorica, la sua riabilitazione ed esaltazione, ma la stupidità no. (II. 764–5)
>
> (To be adjudged stupid and to be told as much is more painful than to be called greedy, lying, violent, lascivious, lazy, or cowardly: every weakness, every vice has had its defenders, its rhetoric, its rehabilitation and exaltation; but not stupidity.)

The fifth and final mode of invention at work in the Simpson stories is invention as narrative or literary invention, as a site where technology and fiction, science and fantasy meet. 'Il Versificatore', for example, shows how a machine can create quite decent, if mediocre poetry—both are products of 'ingegno' of some kind. Even the TOREC shows how a machine can take or shape the narrative quality of experience in order to make it retransmittable. The bridge from science to fantasy to literature and the questions of creation and invention that hang over them all are developed most fully, however, in two stories in *Vizio di forma* which for all intents and purposes are 'posthumous' Simpson stories. The stories are Levi's Pirandellian literary experiments, 'Lavoro creativo' and 'Nel parco' (I. 651–60; 671–80).

In these two stories, the narrator—a writer called Antonio Casella—is visited by his own fictional creation James Collins (a renamed Simpson), created by Casella 'in his own image' perhaps (as the near-anagrammatic proximity of their names suggests). In the first story, Collins complains that Casella killed him off in a rather undignified fashion at the end of his previous book (cf. 'Trattamento di quiescenza'). The conceit—fictional characters revisit an author to contest the nature of their fictional existence—is strongly reminiscent of Pirandello's cycle of short stories and plays on the nature of fictional and dramatic creativity, culminating in *Sei personaggi in cerca d'autore* (1921).[16] Collins explains that all fictional characters live on together in an afterlife in a sort of holiday resort or park which Casella then visits in the second of the stories. The 'characters' sustain their existence there as long as they are remembered in the real world, as long as they retain a certain fame. As their fame fades so they fade, quite literally losing their physical consistency, until they are no longer there, forgotten (see Chapter 2).

Levi has lots of fun in these two stories, imagining the afterlives that famous fictional characters would get up to in the park. But he also plays games with and thinks quite subtly about all the questions of invention, creation, and creativity that we are interested in here.

---

[16] See A. Caesar, 'Pirandello and the Drama of Creativity', in P. Collier and J. Davies, eds., *Modernism and the European Unconscious* (Cambridge: Polity, 1990), 215–29. Levi mentions Pirandello in interviews when discussing problems of fiction: e.g. Levi, *The Voice of Memory*, 107, 149. Levi's park also recalls Pirandello's reworking of the classical notion of fame in his 1908 essay *L'umorismo*, where literary characters such as Dante's Paolo and Francesca are imagined as doomed to relive their torments in hell every time a reader reads *Inferno*. Finally, Levi is also fascinated by the Pirandellian theme of the mirror: in both 'Piombo' (*Il sistema periodico*, I. 809–21) and 'Il fabbricante di specchi' (*Racconti e saggi*, II. 894–7) the Levian archetype of the wandering artisan-alchemist-inventor is imagined as a maker of mirrors, and thus an inventor and transformer of (images of) selves.

His first means to this is to set up a symbiotic bond between Collins and Casella: both are inventors, Casella because he has created or invented Collins and Collins because he is, in effect, Simpson the inventor ('era un inventore, geniale ed un po' stravagante, che creava straordinarie macchine per conto di una società americana', I. 652; 'he was an inventor, brilliant and a little excessive, who created extraordinary machines on behalf of an American company'). But there is more: Casella speaks of his fictional invention using that talismanic phrase uttered by all Levi's inventors, mystical or mechanical—'tratto dal nulla' (I. 656).[17] And the reason Collins has left the park to come and browbeat Casella is that he, Collins, has been trying his hand at writing. Indeed Collins has been writing stories about Casella, thereby reversing the author–character relationship and perhaps propelling Casella into the park. And when Casella reads Collins's deficient version of himself, he turns to writing his own self-portrait in revenge. The inventor becomes a writer, the writer is an inventor (of inventors and a writer), the writer-inventor becomes the invented and then the self-inventor, and so on. Levi is suggesting more than loose equivalence here between different uses of the term invention, different forms of man's making: he is suggesting, precisely, a symbiotic merging of the two. Science and literature meet here not so much in respectful dialogue between 'Two Cultures' as in a magical, alchemical synthesis. We are back to the crucial passages in *La chiave a stella*, where the narrator and Faussone edge towards common ground between their three professions, rigging, chemistry, and writing.

Back in the park, we also find out that when Collins is inventing (not writing), he uses two assistants, Caliban and Frankenstein, two characters who mark the endpoints of the spectrum of invention as it moves from pure untamed nature or matter in Caliban to the hubristic, modern Promethean efforts of Frankenstein in creating his 'new man', both 'monsters' containing a germ of human dignity even in their unformed or untamed state.[18] And Collins

---

[17] The phrase also crops up in the Simpson stories in *Storie naturali*; e.g. I. 419, 449.
[18] For another use of the figure of Caliban, see Il Moro in *La tregua* (I. 288). On 'new men', see Usher (note 1 above). In an interesting parallel case, in *La tregua* Levi sees the different showers that beckon him and his fellow prisoners or survivors respectively into the worlds of the Germans, the Russians, and the Americans, as symbolic moments of branding, of making, precisely, 'new men' of them in their own image (I. 212–13).

takes us full circle, back to the very source of Levi's fascination with invention and first things: 'ho subito ricominciato a scrivere: è una storia un po' romanzata delle mie invenzioni; la loro Entstehungsgeschichte, la loro origine' (I. 671; 'I started writing again at once: it is the story of my inventions written in novel form, their Entstehungsgeschichte, their origin'). 'Entstehungs-geschichte', among other things, is the German term for Genesis.

Watching Levi indulge his fascination with the myths and metaphors of creation and invention may not seem at first sight to fit with our primary task of tracing patterns of 'ordinary virtues' in his work. And yet, there are bridges towards the ethical, both on the specific 'political' level of Levi's commitment to ethical science,[19] and a larger ethical concern with the nature of the human, its hybridity and impurity, the nature and limits of human artifice (including human art), how to live (well) through making and renewing, making something from nothing (making it useful). What makes up man can be told as a story of origins, an *Enstehungsgeschichte*, as an anthropological story of rituals and patterns of action and interaction, and as a story of what man makes, of the man-made (in Italian, variously 'fabbricato', 'artifi-ciale', 'manufatto'—all typically Levian terms). In this chapter we have seen Levi doing all three of these things. They have different vocabularies and patterns as forms of storytelling—between science, myth, magic, fantasy, and literature—but they all echo each other and ultimately ask similar questions, perhaps best encapsulated in the connection between man's making and his self-making, between man as 'fabbro' and man as 'fabbro di se stesso', ' "faber sui" ' (I. 702; II. 645).

---

[19] See, for example, his 1986 essay 'Covare il cobra' (II. 990–3).

PART III

COMMUNITY

Part I examined a number of centrifugal forces in Levi's work, pushing out from Auschwitz towards the world we recognize and the ethical questions of how to live in it. Part II saw Levi operating in that recognizable world (although the shadow of Auschwitz is never quite absent), applying himself to it through forms of malleable intelligence or wit. It dealt, in other words, with a cognitive dimension to Levi's ethics, with ways to interrogate and to know the world and the self, in practical terms. Part III now turns to another constitutive dimension to Levi's cognitive ethics, both in and beyond testimony; its recognition of others, of a shared ethical community as the best basis for asking questions about the world and the self. Community, commonality, or simply the dialogue between individuals refines knowledge, provides the means for testing it out, in a constant, shared, patient evolution towards better understanding and a Socratic acknowledgement of its limits. In his essay on falsity quoted at the start of Chapter 6, Umberto Eco uses C. S. Peirce to explain precisely how cognition and community go hand in hand in this way:

There exists a process of verification that is based on slow, collective, public performance by what Charles Sanders Peirce called 'the Community'. It is thanks to human faith in the work of this community that we can say, with some serenity, that the Donation of Constantine was false, that the world turns around the sun . . . At most, recognizing that our history was inspired by many tales we now recognize as false should make us alert, ready to call constantly into question the very tales we believe true, because the criterion of the wisdom of the community is based on constant awareness of the fallibility of our learning. . . .
    After all, the cultivated person's first duty is to be always prepared to rewrite the encyclopedia.[1]

Where Levi's communal ethics perhaps departs from Eco's reflections is in the latter's restriction of the communal process to 'the cultivated person'. Despite the constant shadow thrown over his work by corrupt and isolating anti-communities of Auschwitz, Levi is more interested in the ways in which we all communally interrogate the world and each other in the normal course of our lives—ordinarily—and can build communities by doing so. Part III looks in turn at three of the building-blocks of Levi's communitarian

1 U. Eco, *Serendipidies* (London: Weidenfeld and Nicolson, 1999), 19–21.

ethics; sharing knowledge about the world (common sense),
acknowledging and respecting others in it (friendship), and talking
to others about it, redescribing it flexibly and creatively (storytelling).

9

COMMON SENSE

knowledge grows in spots . . . and like grease-spots, the spots
spread . . . the novelty soaks in; it stains the ancient mass; but
it is also tinged by what absorbs it.

(William James)

Throughout his work, Levi persistently presents himself as unex-
ceptional, ordinary, as a normal man. He feels distinctly uncomfortable when others dress him in 'higher' garb, treating him, say,
like a prophet or a seer, for the mere fortune of having survived
Auschwitz: as he states in the preface to *Racconti e saggi*, 'Tale non
sono: *sono un uomo normale* di buona memoria che è incappato in
un vortice' (II. 859; emphasis added; 'I am none of these: I am a
normal man with a good memory who happened to get caught up
in a whirlwind').[1] Similarly, as we saw in Chapter 5, in the afterword to *Se questo è un uomo* he rejects the search for grand truths
and epiphanies, preferring to eke out more modest, hard-won
truths (I. 199). More portentously, but with the same undertow of
ordinariness, the preface to his poems explains how it is he has
written poetry when he is surely no poet by simply stating, 'Uomo
sono' (II. 517; 'I am human').

These declarations of normality are crucial to an understanding
of Levi's ethics. They represent a wholesale rejection not only of
the privilege and authority that naturally accrue to the survivor
(and the writer), but also of the sophisticated tools of the intellectual, the expert. In their place, Levi chooses to speak from a position of shared humanity and typical experience (even as he speaks
of the atypical *Lager*), to speak with insight not in spite of but
because of his normality. In doing so, he sets himself up in unusual

---

[1] As was seen in the Introduction above, he was profoundly disturbed by his religious
friend who believed that his survival must serve some higher purpose: see II. 1054-5.

counterpoint to the 'banality' of Eichmann and other functionaries of the Final Solution so famously analysed by Hannah Arendt,[2] making himself the voice of the 'banal' victim, the normal man who happened to be swept up in a whirlwind. The wisdom of shared humanity, the tools available to it to interrogate and understand the world, are what we might call 'common sense'; and the ways in which Levi uses and refines these tools of common sense, in the camps and beyond, are the subject of this chapter.

Before looking directly at the data of Levi's common sense, it is worth dwelling further on what he defines himself against when he declares himself as 'normal'. His work is peppered with negative declarations, with pleading or defiant rejections of labels that would tend to set him and his fellows apart, on a pedestal of any kind.[3] All three declarations of normality quoted above reject labels of this kind: 'il profeta, il vate, il veggente' ('the prophet, the vates, the seer') in *Racconti e saggi*; prophets again in the afterword to *Se questo è un uomo*; 'poet' in the preface to *Ad ora incerta*. In a series of texts concerning survival and return, the motif of abjuring the label of saint or martyr returns almost obsessively:

Il sopravvivere senza aver rinunciato a nulla del proprio mondo morale .
. . non è stato concesso che a pochissimi individui superiori, della stoffa dei martiri e dei santi. (*Se questo è un uomo*, I. 88)
(To survive without giving up on any part of one's moral world . . . was granted only to a tiny number of superior individuals, made of the stuff of martyrs and saints.)

> Fummo di nuovo soltanto giovani:
> Non martiri, non infami, non santi. ('Cantare', II. 522)
> (We became young people once more:
> Not martyrs, not evil, not saints.)

mi sentivo ridiventare uomo, uno come tutti, né martire, né infame, né santo, uno di quelli che si fanno una famiglia, e guardano al futuro anziché al passato. (*Il sistema periodico*, I. 871)[4]

---

[2] H. Arendt, *Eichmann in Jerusalem. A Report on the Banality of Evil* (Harmondsworth: Penguin, 1992; 1st edition 1963).
[3] Many first-hand accounts of the war and the camps, especially early accounts, laid claim to being non-literary and non-expert, as a means of reinforcing the immediacy and truth of what they had to tell. See A. Bravo and D. Jalla, eds., *Una misura onesta. Gli scritti di memoria della deportazione dall'Italia 1944–93* (Milan: Franco Angeli, 1994); and R. Gordon, 'Holocaust Writing in Context: Italy 1945–47', in A. Leak and G. Paizis, eds., *The Holocaust and the Text* (London: Macmillan, 1999), 32–50.
[4] Cf. Levi's preface to his own translation of J. Presser, *La notte dei Girondini* (Milan:

(I felt myself become human again, one like everyone, neither martyr nor evil nor saint, someone who raises a family and looks to the future not the past.)

These passages are, of course, in close relation to others we have seen in previous chapters, where Levi reluctantly or ironically accepts the unwanted and cruel destiny of the prophet, damned to question and to suffer: passages where he identifies with Tiresias or Job; passages where bitter experience does indeed lead to special wisdom (e.g. Mendel in *Se non ora quando?*, who learns to understand that justice pays more than revenge, II. 473). But even those passages underscore the messy human complication of the prophet's experience, not the pure myth of the saint. In a crucial passage from 'La zona grigia' in *I sommersi e i salvati*, Levi glosses his conception of sainthood as the very opposite of an intimate, difficult, shared humanity, and a proportionate, inclusive responsiveness to fellow human beings in real time and real individual experience, in a way that amounts to a credo of his communal ethics:

se dovessimo e potessimo soffrire le sofferenze di tutti, non potremmo vivere. Forse solo ai santi è concesso il terribile dono della pietà verso i molti . . . a noi tutti, non resta, nel migliore dei casi, che la pietà saltuaria indirizzata al singolo, al *Mitmensch*, al co-uomo: all'essere umano di carne e sangue che sta davanti a noi, alla portata dei nostri sensi provvidenzial-mente miopi. (II. 1034)
(if we had to and were able to feel the suffering of all, we would not survive. Perhaps only saints are given the terrible gift of pity for the many . . . to all the rest of us, there is only, at best, the intermittent pity directed to an individual, to the *Mitmensch*, our fellow-man: to a human being in flesh and blood, whom we see before us, within reach of our providentially short-sighted senses.)

Adelphi, 1976) in *Opere*, I. 1208–11: 'È ingenuo, assurdo e storicamente falso ritenere che un sistema demoniaco, qual era il nazionalsocilismo, santifichi le sue vittime: al contrario, esso le degrada e le sporca' (I. 1209; 'It is naive, absurd, and historically false to think that a devilish system, like National Socialism, sanctifies its victims: on the contrary, it degrades and defiles them'). These negations were clearly something of a philosophical and stylistic tic for Levi. It is striking to see them recurring, for instance, in Levi's descriptions of Müller, the camp chemist he encounters in his work years later: 'né infame né eroe . . . non era né un ignavo né un sordo né un cinico' (I. 931–2; 'neither a criminal nor a hero . . . he was neither a scoundrel nor deaf nor a cynic'). See P. V. Mengaldo, 'Lingua e scrittura in Levi', in E. Ferrero, ed., *Primo Levi. Un'antologia della critica* (Turin: Einaudi, 1997), 169–242. Todorov uses an instance, 'Ni héros ni saints', as a key phrase in his *Face à l'extrême* (Paris: Seuil, 1991), 51–66.

It is striking to note that the distancing from the rhetoric of tran-scendence here is also an embracing of dialogue between text and reader (see below).

These negative definitions, with their typically Levian antihero-ism and their embracing of human limit and weakness, bring Levi for once into contact with an element of the modernist tradition to which he otherwise seems so alien. His 'Non martiri, non infami, non santi' seems to echo, say, Eliot's 'No! I am not Prince Hamlet, nor was meant to be' or Montale's 'Codesto solo oggi possiamo dirti, | ciò che non siamo, ciò che non vogliamo' (This alone I can tell you today, | what we are not, what we do not want').[5] But the association is only momentary. Eliot's and Montale's metaphysical negativity, like Kafka's, have been taken as presages of that catastrophic post-Holocaust thought which sees 'the Event' as the insurmountable void of modernity, the nihilism seared into our consciousness by history. *Post hoc ergo propter hoc*: if our history contained the seeds of the Holocaust, then our history and its values are shattered and worthless, a debris of misplaced trust. Levi's negativity does not go so far, however. He sets the sense of void thrown up by the Holocaust into dialectic relation with the defects ('vizi di forma', we might say)[6] of the ordinary world that produced it. He does so by instigating a fluid process in which our common sense allows us to interrogate and chart the boundaries of the *univers concentrationnaire*, whilst at the same time, the *Lager* allows us to dismantle and reshape anew (although never quite abandon) that very common sense. The pay-off is twofold—facilitating a clearer and wider understanding of the Holocaust and removing some of the dead weight of certainty and dry authority that clings to common sense, replacing it with more fluid, evolv-ing paths of knowledge, built in dialogue, sensitive to historical and individual experience.

Levi achieves this fluidity by working with the dual meaning of common sense: on the one hand shared (common) and frequent

[5] T. S. Eliot, 'The Love Song of J. Alfred Prufrock' (1917), l. 111; E. Montale, 'Non chiederci la parola', ll. 11–12 in *Ossi di seppia* (1925). Cf. Bryan Cheyette's characterization of Levi's scepticism of systems as 'modernist' in a qualified sense (B. Cheyette, 'The Ethical Uncertainty of Primo Levi', in B. Cheyette and L. Marcus, *Modernity, Culture and 'the Jew'* (Cambridge: Polity, 1998), 271).

[6] The connection between the 'vizi di forma' of Levi's science fiction and the 'defect' of the Holocaust was made by Levi himself on the cover of the collection *Storie naturali*: see II. 1435.

(common) assumptions about the world; on the other hand, and more usually in modern usage, self-evidently good or sensible assumptions about the world, naturally shared by all right-thinking people. Italian has tended to observe the distinction more carefully, often using 'senso comune' for the former and 'buon senso' for the latter. Although the two might not seem drastically opposed, they are of course all too often precisely that, and there is a long-standing rather paternalistic tradition of pointing this out. In the Italian literary canon, the most notable voice of this kind is Alessandro Manzoni: observing the workings of mass psychology, public opinion, and common, wrong-headed prejudice in seventeenth-century Milan, Manzoni notes, 'il buon senso c'era: ma se ne stava nascosto, per paura del senso comune' ('there was good sense: but it was hidden away out of fear of common opinion').[7] Levi refers to this Manzonian distinction himself in *I sommersi e i salvati* (II. 1122; and cf. I. 194) and indeed, his practical interrogation of common sense, his deployment of it in writing about the non-sensical world of the *Lager* and later his science-fictional universe, is poised between the two meanings. It is all about interrogating the split and convergence between them, about building bridges towards and away from shared assumptions, and testing them through experience, even extreme and irrational experience, in order to render them 'sensible'.

Levi pushes the limits of common sense, but it remains accessible to the intelligent enquiry of the 'normal' person. Expertise is not necessary. Here we return to Levi's abjurations of privileged or specialist knowledge: again and again, he writes of himself as informed but proudly 'amateur', non-expert in some way: in *L'altrui mestiere*, he describes his culture as 'lacunosa e saputella' (II. 631; 'patchy and fake-learnèd'); in *I sommersi e i salvati*, he writes 'Non ho avuto intenzione, né sarei stato capace, di fare opera di storico . . .' (II. 1005; 'I had neither the intention nor the ability to write a work of history. . .') and 'non siamo né storici né filosofi' (II. 1110; 'we are neither historians nor philosophers'); his science is primitive, a mere technician's work when compared to pure

---

[7] A. Manzoni, *I promessi sposi* (1840), in *Opere*, ed. M. Barbi and F. Ghisalberti (Florence: Sansoni, 1942), I. 419. For a series of related distinctions and refinements of common sense, linking it to freedom and justice and the capacity to resist conditioning by the crowd or by those in power, see Raffaele La Capria's elegant essay *La mosca nella bottiglia. Elogio del senso comune* (Milan: Rizzoli, 1996).

scientific research (II. 951); his identity as a writer of literature highly ambivalent (he is 'Lo scrittore non scrittore', II. 1202–7); even his own Judaism is qualified and mocked (*Il sistema periodico*, I. 770). Most simply and resonantly of all, in the poem 'Delega', he pleads not to be looked upon as a teacher, 'Non chiamarci maestri' (II. 624). All this allows him to work away within the field of common sense, combining old and new knowledge about the world, to use it ethically but pre-philosophically, a crucial precondition to reading Levi as an ethical writer without ever reading him as a philosopher of ethics.[8]

What does this mean in concrete terms for Levi's writing? If we take *Se questo è un uomo* as the seedbed of this as so many other ordinary virtues in Levi, we can see him interrogating common sense at three levels; in the cumulative deployment of *sententiae*, aphorisms, nuggets of proverbial wisdom; in the local detail of narrative, style, even syntax; and in the structural composition of sequences and chapters. The second and third refine and complicate the first.

The basic currency of common sense in Levi is the data of aphoristic wisdom, a sort of dictionary of *idées reçues* recurring regularly throughout his work. *Se questo è un uomo*, for all its charting of the foreign and the alien, offers a rich seam of examples, several familiar to us by now, as the following selection shows:

'Ogni straniero è nemico' (I. 5)
('Every stranger is an enemy')

il primo ufficio dell'uomo è perseguire i propri scopi con mezzi idonei (I. 7)
(Man's first office is to pursue his own end with the proper means)

---

[8] There is a minor philosophical tradition that has tried to salvage common sense for philosophy in this way, with roots in the 18th-century thought of Thomas Reid and echoes in William James, G. E. Moore, even A. J. Ayer. See J. David Newell, ed., *Philosophy and Common Sense* (Washington: University Press of America, 1980); A. Musgrave, *Common Sense, Science and Scepticism* (Cambridge: Cambridge University Press, 1993). Perhaps the most useful, if surprising comparison to make here is with Antonio Gramsci, whose *Prison Notebooks* conceived of language, folklore, popular religion and morality, and common sense as all evidence of a universal, 'spontaneous' philosophical bent, of a capacity to embody a philosophical vision and understanding of the world without the rigid dogmas of Church or State or class ideology imposed from above. Part of the 'organic' intellectual's function, for Gramsci, was to articulate and bring to consciousness this 'first' philosophy. Gramsci's notes on the subject (mostly in his twenty-seventh notebook) have been collated in A. Gramsci, *Folclore e senso comune* (Rome: Editori Riuniti, 1992). For a different but related view see the chapter on 'The Ethics of Inarticulacy' in C. Taylor, *The Sources of the Self* (Cambridge: Cambridge University Press, 1989), 53–90.

come si può percuotere un uomo senza collera? (I. 11)
(how can you beat a man without anger?)

Tutti scoprono, piú o meno presto nella loro vita, che la felicità perfetta non è realizzabile, ma pochi si soffermano invece sulla considerazione opposta: che tale è anche una infelicità perfetta. . . . la nostra condizione umana . . . è nemica a ogni infinito. (I. 11)
(Everyone discovers sooner or later in life that perfect happiness is not achievable, but few pause to think also about the opposite consideration: that so too is perfect unhappiness. . . . our human condition . . . is hostile to all extremes.)

Pochi sono gli uomini che sanno andare a morte con dignità (I. 12)
(Few men are able to go to their deaths with dignity)

la nostra lingua manca di parole per esprimere questa offesa, la demolizione di un uomo (I. 20)
(our language has no words to express this offence, the demolition of a man)

accade facilmente a chi ha perso tutto, di perdere se stesso (I. 21)
(to one who has lost everything it is easy to lose oneself)

ragionevoli gli uomini sono assai raramente, quando è in gioco il loro proprio destino: essi preferiscono in ogni cosa le posizioni estreme (I. 30)
(people are very rarely reasonable when their own fate is at stake: they will prefer extremes in all things)

i privilegiati opprimono i non privilegiati: su questa legge umana si regge la struttura sociale del campo (I. 38)
(the privileged oppress the underprivileged: the social structure of the camp is built on this human law)

la facoltà umana di scavarsi una nicchia, di secernere un guscio, di erigersi intorno una tenue barriera di difesa, anche in circonstanze apparentemente disperate, è stupefacente (I. 50)
(the human capacity to carve out a niche, to secrete a protective shell, to build around themselves a flimsy defensive wall, even in the most apparently desperate circumstances, is astonishing)

La persuasione che la vita ha uno scopo è radicata in ogni fibra di uomo, è una proprietà della sostanza umana. (I. 66)
(The conviction that life has a purpose is rooted in our every human fibre, is a property of human matter)

Poiché tale è la natura umana, che le pene e i dolori simultaneamente sofferti non si sommano . . . ma si nascondono, i minori dietro i maggiori (I. 68)

(For human nature works so that afflictions and pain suffered all at once do not mount up together . . . but stay hidden, the smaller behind the larger)

Esistono fra gli uomini due categorie particolarmente ben distinte: i salvati e i sommersi (I. 83)
(There are two especially well-defined categories in human beings: the saved and the drowned)

l'uomo non è solo . . . è legato al destino dei suoi vicini (I. 84)
(man is not alone . . . he is bound up with the destiny of his neighbours)

una sensibile azione di smorzamento è esercitata dalla legge, e dal senso morale, che è legge interna (ibid.)
(a noticeable muffling effect is effected by laws and by our moral sense, which is an inner law)

una terza via [tra sommersi e salvati] esiste nella vita, dove è anzi la norma; non esiste in campo di concentramento (I. 86)
(there is a third way [between the drowned and the saved] in life, indeed it is the norm: it does not exist in concentration camps)

Moltissime sono state le vie da noi escogitate e attuate per non morire: tante quante sono i caratteri umani. (I. 88)
(Many, many ways have been thought up and put into practice to avoid death: as many ways as there are human characters.)

Per gli uomini vivi le unità del tempo hanno sempre un valore, il quale è tanto maggiore, quanto piú elevate sono le risorse interne di chi le percorre. (I. 113)
(For the living, units of time have a value that is greater the richer the inner resources of those experiencing them.)

strano, in qualche modo si ha sempre l'impressione di essere fortunati (I. 127)
(it's strange, but everyone always seems to think they are lucky)

ma l'ingegno non consiste forse nel trovare o creare relazioni fra ordini di idee apparentemente estranee? (I. 143)
(but doesn't wit perhaps consist in finding or making links between apparently extraneous orders of ideas?)

distruggere l'uomo è difficile, quasi quanto crearlo (I. 146)
(To destroy a man is difficult, almost as difficult as to create one)

È uomo chi uccide, è uomo chi fa o subisce ingiustizia; non è uomo chi, perso ogni ritegno, divide il letto con un cadavere (I. 168)
(A man who kills, or who inflicts or suffers injustice is still a man; someone who, all restraint lost, shares a bed with a corpse, is not a man)

Parte del nostro esistere ha sede nelle anime di chi ci accosta. (I. 168)
(Part of our existence resides in the souls of those around us)

Levi's *sententiae* address the question of what it is to be human and
what remains of the human at extremes, near death, when self and
society crumble. But it is striking that Levi is mobile in his modes
of comparison between 'normal' humanity and the camp. At
times, the camps confirm his assumptions (e.g. the powerful
oppress the weak), and at others they upturn them (e.g. the mean,
the 'terza via' of the outside world, is cut out in the camps). There
is even outright contradiction: first the human condition is the
enemy of all extremes, then, at a later stage, men are all too prone
to take up extreme positions. In other words, there is no system
behind the aphorisms; they are deployed as markers of a fallible
common law which opens up enquiry. Indeed, it is no coincidence that many of these statements occur at the beginning or
ending of chapters or sections of the book. They are more often
than not thrown out only in order to be questioned, reshaped,
rejected, or rehabilitated in the light of the new experience of
camp life and death. They act as a sort of counterpoint to the
narrative parts of the book.

As with the question of the language of morality, we are invited
to judge, to enter into a dialogue about what exactly remains of
the world of the everyday, of common sense, in this place where
they are stripped away:

Noi sappiamo che in questo difficilmente saremo compresi, ed è bene
che cosí sia. Ma consideri ognuno, quanto valore, quanto significato è
racchiuso anche nelle piú piccole nostre abitudini quotidiane, nei cento
oggetti nostri che il piú umile mendicante possiede: un fazzoletto, una
vecchia lettera, la fotografia di una persona cara. . . .
Si immagini ora un uomo a cui, insieme con le persone amate,
vengano tolti la sua casa, le sue abitudini, i suoi abiti, tutto infine, letteral-
mente tutto quanto possiede: sarà un uomo vuoto . . . (I. 21)
(We know that it will not be easy to understand us in this, and rightly
so. But let everyone reflect on how much value, how much meaning is
carried in the smallest of our everyday habits, in the hundred objects that
even the humblest beggar owns: a handkerchief, an old letter, the photo
of a loved one . . .
And now imagine a man who, along with his dearest, is deprived of
his home, his habits, his clothes, in short of literally everything he
possesses: he will be a shell of a man . . .)

Considering the absence of the minutiae of everyday life in the camps reawakens our awareness of their significance in our lives which in turn makes their absence all the more excruciating. We are resensitized to both here and there.

The accumulation of common-sense data in the aphoristic form illustrated above is only the baseline of Levi's ethics of common sense. As is typical of him, the close detail of his style and the turn of his thought themselves also sensitize his readers to the ethical questions at stake. Two examples, both once again from early on in *Se questo è un uomo*, one brief and intensely emotive, the other more complex and extended, make the point.

The first example is one of the most moving moments of the entire book. Levi is at Fossoli detention camp in central Italy, the night before being deported. Mothers are preparing suitcases, gathering clothes and toys, and feeding their children:

Non fareste anche voi altrettanto? Se dovessero uccidervi domani col vostro bambino, voi non gli dareste oggi da mangiare? (I. 9)
(Would you not do the same? If they were going to kill you tomorrow with your child, would you not give him food to eat today?)

In this simple appeal, at least three defining features of Levi's opening up to our common sense of humanity are apparent: the hanging rhetorical questions; the insistent use of second-person forms (six in two short sentences); and the juxtaposition of the everyday (mothers and babies, eating) with the horrifically extreme (the promise of imminent death).

The second example, following on less than two pages after the first, is taken up from the long list given earlier. The train is about to depart for its unknown destination in German-occupied Europe (the prisoners hear the name 'Auschwitz' for the first time immediately after this passage ends) as Levi reflects:

Tutti scoprono, piú o meno presto nella loro vita, che la felicità perfetta non è realizzabile, ma pochi si soffermano invece sulla considerazione opposta: che tale è anche una infelicità perfetta. I momenti che si oppongono alla realizzazaione di entrambi i due stati-limiti sono della stessa natura: conseguono dalla nostra condizione umana, che è nemica a ogni infinito. Vi si oppone la nostra sempre insufficiente conoscenza del futuro; e questo si chiama, in un caso, speranza, e nell'altro, incertezza del domani. Vi si oppone la sicurezza della morte, che si impone un limite a ogni gioia, ma anche a ogni dolore. Vi si oppongono le inevitabili cure materiali, che, come inquinano ogni felicità duratura, cosí distolgono assiduamente la nostra attenzione dalla sventura che ci sovrasta, e ne rendono frammentaria, e perciò sostenibile, la consapevolezza.

Sono stati proprio i disagi, le percosse, il freddo, la sete, che ci hanno tenuti a galla sul vuoto di una disperazione senza fondo, durante il viaggio e dopo. Non già la volontà di vivere, né una cosciente rassegnazione: ché pochi sono gli uomini capaci di questo, e noi non eravamo che un comune campione di umanità. (I. 11)

(Everyone discovers sooner or later in life that perfect happiness is not achievable, but few pause to think also about the opposite consideration: that so too is perfect unhappiness. The moments which prevent the realization of both these limit-states are of the same nature: they derive from our human condition which is hostile to all extremes. It is prevented by our ever inadequate knowledge of the future; and at times we call this hope, at others uncertainty about tomorrow. It is prevented by the certainty of death, which sets a limit to every joy, but also to every sorrow. It is prevented by inevitable material worries which, just as they pollute every lasting happiness, also consistently distract our attention from the misfortune overcoming us and make our consciousness of it fragmented and so bearable.

It was precisely the discomfort, the blows, the cold, the thirst that held us afloat above the void of bottomless despair, both during and after the journey. And not the will to live, nor open resignation, which few men are capable of; and we were merely a common sample of humanity.)

Levi's counterintuitive, but commonsensical point is quickly summarized: immediate physical suffering keeps absolute desperation at bay. The two paragraphs weave around that simple but important idea, projecting it onto different planes, qualifying it and reflecting on it. Indeed, it could be read as the seed of several lines of development in Levi's *œuvre*, such as his writing on suicide in *I sommersi e i salvati* or his rejection of 'sainthood', hinted at in the phrase 'pochi sono gli uomini capaci di questo'. We can point to three aspects of the passage as typical of Levi's probing manner.

First, the movement between narrative and discourse. The passage is framed at beginning and end by vivid narrative detail: 'Questa volta dentro [il treno] siamo noi . . . Gli sportelli eran stati chiusi subito, ma il treno non si mosse che a sera' (I. 11; 'This time *we* are inside [the train] . . . The doors had been shut at once, but the train only moved off in the evening'). It suspends narrative, just as the deportees are suspended, waiting for the train to move. It also, in its comments on common experiences of happiness and unhappiness, extremes and petty worries, gives us access to the patterns of thought of the deportees as they wait and worry. In other words, in moving between narrative and discourse, the particular and the general, the text builds both a temporal and experiential link between Levi and his companions, and his reader.

Secondly, there is a complex syntactical movement of persons and subjects in the passage.[9] The first paragraph moves from the universal 'tutti' and the impersonal 'vi si oppongono' to the exceptional 'pochi' (but we are now part of the few having read this), to a communal but universal 'we' ('la nostra condizione umana') to another 'we', 'la nostra attenzione', which sounds as though it is the 'we' of the train-occupants, of the 'questa volta dentro siamo noi'. The second paragraph inverts the movement of the first, starting with the 'we' of the train, and moving outwards towards both the exceptional ('ché pochi . . .') and the commonplace: the community of suffering on the train is reclaimed as normal, as a random and therefore ordinary sample of humanity, of the 'tutti' of the first paragraph. The 'common sample of humanity' that Levi includes himself in (and implicitly the reader also) thus begins and ends this ethical digression.[10]

Finally, there is a sort of sleight of hand at work in a sequence such as this, which shows us how Levi vivifies a somewhat deadening pontification on human nature. Levi slips triggers which, unnoticed at first, will later set off a sort of process of refinement, as the phrase 'durante il viaggio e dopo' hints. The specific narrative and the movement of syntax both gloss and qualify the opening, as we have seen. Larger issues of limits and extremes, of optimism and pessimism, run throughout Levi's work, as we saw in Chapter 5. The notion of the certainty of death, and the effect this has on our actions, takes on a very specific and fundamental weight in Auschwitz. All of these later moments or lines reflect back on this moment and mutually alter each other. And yet the

[9] On the significance of verb persons for *Se questo è un uomo*, see C. Segre, '*Se questo è un uomo* di Primo Levi', in A. Asor Rosa, ed., *Letteratura italiana. Le opere IV. Novecento. II. La ricerca letteraria* (Turin: Einaudi, 1996), 491–508 [502]. Todorov, echoing his structuralist past, pins his triangular model of everyday virtues on persons of the verb, 'je', 'tu', and 'ils' (*Face à l'extrême*, 111).

[10] On the problem of carving out a community by setting a meaning for the pronoun 'we', see Richard Rorty's discussion of what Wilfrid Sellars called 'we-intentions' and 'we-practices', as the basis for his ironist, pragmatic ethics, in *Contingency, Irony and Solidarity* (Cambridge: Cambridge University Press, 1989), 54–65 and *passim* (and see Introduction).

substantive point made here is that such large issues did *not* occur to Levi then and there. It is as though there is a complex interplay between the bald evocation of the moment and the web of generalities that surrounds it that acts as a sort of depth charge, resonating beneath the surface of the text and probing away at the assumptions we bring to it, here and afterwards.

A further example, from the one Holocaust-centred chapter of *Il sistema periodico*, makes Levi's sleight of hand clearer still. 'Cerio' (I. 860–6) is the story of Levi and Alberto's chance discovery of a hidden source of an iron-cerium alloy and their plan to make lighters out of it to sell. In retrospect Levi realizes that they risked their lives at every stage of their enterprise, with no guarantee of success:

Si esita sempre a giudicare le azioni temerarie, proprie od altrui, dopo che queste sono andate a buon fine: forse non erano dunque abbastanza temerarie? O forse è vero che esiste un Dio che protegge i bambini, gli stolti e gli ebbri? O forse...? Ma noi non ci ponemmo allora queste domande: il Lager ci aveva donato una folle famigliarità col pericolo e con la morte, e rischiare il capestro per mangiare di piú ci sembrava una scelta logica, anzi ovvia. (I. 865)
(We always hesitate to judge our own or others' actions rash once they have had a successful outcome: perhaps that means they were not rash enough? Or perhaps it's true that there's a God to protect babes, fools, and drunks? Or perhaps...? But back then we didn't think of such questions: the *Lager* had given us an insane intimacy with danger and death, and risking the gallows for some more food seemed to us the most logical, indeed obvious of choices.)

The questions here are posed and then removed ('Ma noi non ci ponemmo allora queste domande'), but their echo remains. They are built on almost folkloric or instinctual conceptions of cause and effect (echoes of Gramsci's link between folklore and common sense) which do not apply here. But their illogicality finds an echo in the unknown, macabre world of 'allora', with its own illogicality and upturned priorities.

The third, 'structural' process of refinement of common sense is little more than an extension of the second, in which the adjustments to the bare data of our earlier list take place over the course of a longer narrative sequence or chapter. Several chapters of *Se questo è un uomo* open aphoristically, move into a description of the present reality of the camp, and then work their way back to the terms of the opening in a way that ironizes and questions the reliability of those terms. One of the most direct examples of this comes in the seventh chapter, 'Una buona giornata', which opens as follows:

La persuasione che la vita ha uno scopo è radicata in ogni fibra di uomo, è una proprietà della sostanza umana. Gli uomini liberi danno a questo scopo molti nomi, e sulla sua natura molto pensano e discutono: ma per noi la questione è piú semplice.
   Oggi e qui, il nostro scopo è di arrivare a primavera. Di altro, ora, non ci curiamo. (I. 66)
(The conviction that life has a purpose is rooted in our every human fibre, is a property of human matter. Free men give this purpose many names and think and argue about its nature a great deal: but for us the issue is simpler.
   Here and now, our purpose is to reach spring. For now, we care about nothing else.)

The chapter goes on to relate a pause in the otherworldly suffering of normal days in the camp, as the sun shines and a store of fifty litres of extra soup is discovered. Levi carefully traces the partial resurfacing of the sensations of 'uomini liberi', of feelings of warmth, a sense of the future, however illusory, perhaps even a momentary happiness. The whole becomes a poignant meditation on human nature and its boundaries, by way of an implicit interrogation through narrative of the terms of the chapter's opening. And the threads of the chapter are tied together in its poignant final sentences, which confirm and amplify the reversals and profound ironies thrown up by the encounter of common assertions and unexpected moments of reprieve:

poiché siamo tutti, almeno per qualche ora, sazi, cosí non sorgono litigi, ci sentiamo buoni, il Kapo non si induce a picchiarci, e siamo capaci di pensare alle nostre madri e alle nostre mogli, il che di solito non accade. Per qualche ora, possiamo essere infelici alla maniera degli uomini liberi. (I. 72)
(since we are all, at least for a few hours, full, we do not argue, we feel good, the Kapo does not feel like beating us, and we are able to think of our mothers and our wives, which we usually cannot. For a few hours, we can be unhappy just like free men.)

Common sense is being rewritten before our eyes. At the end, however, there is no new 'thesis' to replace the old: there is only a series of open questions on freedom, happiness, and the meaning of life.

Both the questions and the terms of 'Una buona giornata' resonate forward throughout a whole swathe of Levi's work. The return of humanity in a moment of respite, marked by a return not of joy but of sorrow, mirrors precisely the workings of shame in the survivor chronicled in both *La tregua* and *I sommersi e i salvati*, as well as a number of other moments in *Se questo è un uomo*. More extensive still is a web of stories where Levi takes up the questions of life's purpose ('lo scopo della vita') and its relationship to happiness and freedom: as we saw in Chapter 4, the story 'Verso occidente' (I. 578–87) is in a sense an elaborate gloss on just this question, with both protagonists (Walter and Anna) and their experimental subjects (first lemmings and then a suicidal tribe) arguing for a different understanding of life's purpose; and the same terms are echoed in the last phrase of 'L'intellettuale ad Auschwitz', 'Gli scopi di vita sono difesa ottima contro la morte: non solo in Lager' (II. 1108; 'Life's aims are the best defence against death: not only in the *Lager*').[11] Indeed, this line of reflection quickly expands to take in all Levi's meditation on survival, on the human-animal and a conception of life as a (Darwinian) struggle (from Mordo Nahum's famous dictum in *La tregua*, ' "guerra è sempre" ', I. 242, ' "war is always" ' to the essay on Russell's *The Conquest of Happiness*, 'Lotta per la vita', II. 933–43). In other words, over the course of his *œuvre*, Levi excavates beneath the simplicities of his *idées reçues*, uncovering a profound complexity and a dialogue between different common-sense visions concerning the most fundamental aspects of how to live. This process of interrogation of our assumed knowledge about the world is itself, in Levi, a purpose in life, a shared, ordinary virtue.

The journey from static, knowing common sense to subtle and malleable judgement is, then, an epistemological journey from simplicity to complexity. In another aphoristic declaration, this time from 1968, this complexity is hooked up to fundamental aspects of Levi's thought and writing:

È proprio dell'uomo agire in modo estroso e complesso . . . partire per mete remote e verso scopi che sono giustificazioni a se stessi: agire per sfidare un segreto, per allargare il proprio confine, per esprimersi, per misurarsi. (II. 926)

---

[11] The phrasing also recurs in the prefaces to the 1961 and 1979 German editions of *Se questo è un uomo* (I. 1136–7, 1318–22).

(It is proper to man to be capricious and complex . . . to travel to far-off destinations and towards aims that are ends in themselves: to work to challenge a secret, to widen their horizons, to express themselves, to test themselves.)

Complexity here is not the impenetrable technical complexity of the 'expert': it is part of Ulysses' practical wit, part of the reaching for knowledge and self-knowledge that underpinned all the virtues of Part II. In other words, complexity grows dialectically out of, as well as against simplicity.[12] This dialectic is replayed in *I sommersi e i salvati*, in 'La zona grigia' and 'Stereotipi' (II. 1017–44, 1109–23). Both are interested in the complex multiplicity of human motivation and of historical circumstance ('i perché possono essere molti, confusi fra loro, o inconoscibili, se non addirittura inesistenti', II. 1110; 'why's can be many and confused amongst themselves, or unknowable, even non-existent'). In the later essay, he sees himself as shoring up the barriers against stereotypes and simplification ('vorrei porre qui un argine contro questo deriva [verso la semplificazione e lo stereotipo]', II. 1116; 'I'd like to set up here a barrier against this slippage [towards simplification and stereotypes]');[13] but he also half-acknowledges that stereotypes can be valid: 'non intendo dire che [lo stereotipo] non sia valido mai: dico che non è valido sempre' (II. 1117; 'I do not mean to say that a stereotype is never valid; only that it is not always so').[14] In 'La zona grigia', simplification plays an even stronger preliminary role to understanding complexity:

Senza una profonda semplificazione, il mondo intorno a noi sarebbe un groviglio infinito e indefinito, che sfiderebbe la nostra capacità di orientarsi e di decidere le nostre azioni. Siamo insomma costretti a ridurre il conoscibile a schema . . .
   Questo *desiderio* di semplificazione è giustificato, la semplificazione non sempre lo è. È un'ipotesi di lavoro, utile in quanto sia riconoscibile come tale e non scambiata per la realtà; . . . (II. 1017–18)

---

[12] On complexity, see G. Varchetta, *Ascoltando Primo Levi* (Milan: Guerini e Associati, 1991), 27–49.

[13] The image of building barriers or channels to guide action was one that fascinated Levi: he discusses its uses in 'Domum servavit' (*L'altrui mestiere*, II. 695–8) and elsewhere draws on a Talmudic phrase that describes a Jew's duty to 'far siepe alla legge' (e.g. I. 712; II. 796; 'to build a hedge around the law').

[14] On the ambivalences of stereotypes, see H. Bhabha, 'The Other Question: Stereotype, Discrimination and the Discourse of Colonialism', in *The Location of Culture* (London: Routledge, 1994), 66–84.

(Without profound simplification, the world around us would be an infinite and indefinite tangle that would defeat our ability to orient ourselves and decide what to do. In short, we are forced to make schemas of the knowable . . .
This *desire* for simplification is understandable, but simplification itself is not always so. It must be a working hypothesis, only useful if it is recognized as such and not mistaken for reality; . . .)

Again and again, Levi follows his own advice. Later in 'La zona grigia', for example, he will open a discussion of the nature of power first with a hypothetical universal—the domination of one man over another is part of, perhaps even a beneficial part of our genetic make-up as gregarious animals—only then to qualify—but in the camps the domination was so total and limitless as to be only ever harmful, almost totalitarian—and qualify again—'Ma questo "quasi" è importante' (II. 1025; 'but the "almost" is important'); and so on.

One final connection can usefully be made to conclude our discussion of common sense. The same pattern of using stereotypes or common sense as flawed starting points for the complex interrogation of the material of history and experience is repeated in the dialectic between the particular or individual and the general that we have seen at play more than once in previous chapters, a dialectic especially important for understanding the 'communal' side to Levi's common sense. Levi's suspicion of grand truths and deindividualization leads him to eschew generalizations, just as his storytelling bent—all his books are built on vignettes and anecdotes of individual characters—pushes him towards the local tale of one person's experience and away from the sweeping panorama. But his *sententiae* shows that there is also clearly a place for the general in his work. What emerges is a bridge between the two, a mid-point between the particular and the general that allows the former to qualify, correct, and analyse the latter: the individual character becomes an emblem or exemplum, a metonymic stand-in for the general. Perhaps the most powerfully drawn character-emblem of this kind in Levi's work is Hurbinek, the speechless, nameless, doomed child Levi encounters in the days after liberation and whom he rescues from oblivion by describing in his book, but who is emblematic precisely because he was never allowed to exist as a fully-fledged individual in this world (*La tregua* I. 215–16). But one could adduce any number of other characters in this regard. The individuals in Levi's world almost always have this metonymic potential, but they are not reduced to a metonym; they are partly representative, but representative precisely because each is unique. They exist in collective or communal groupings, but are not subsumed by them. We can read them out towards universals or in towards intimate humanity, or indeed in both directions at once.[15]

To illustrate the profound ethical impact of this movement, we can return to the passage quoted above from 'La zona grigia' about individual suffering and the suffering of all. It comes from a passage describing a horrifying episode amongst the Sonderkommandos told by a Hungarian doctor who worked in the camp, Miklos Nyiszli.[16] One young woman is found still alive after a gassing. Levi tells the story of how she is then put to death using an extraordinary style combining hesitation, generalization, and literary calque, rhetorical questions, free indirect speech, and historic presents, all to alert us to the complexities at stake. It is worth quoting at length, since the passage's circuitous style in itself enacts the ethical question—how to deal with the exception, the moment of discontinuity, the particular or individual; how to be 'noi', as victims or readers (as we saw above in the movement of syntax in passages from *Se questo è un uomo*), how to be a '*Mitmensch*':

... sul pavimento trovano una giovane ancora viva. L'evento è eccezionale, unico; forse i corpi umani le hanno fatto barriera intorno, hanno sequestrato un sacco d'aria che è rimasta respirabile. Gli uomini sono perplessi; la morte è il loro mestiere di ogni ora, la morte è una consuetudine, poiché, appunto, 'si impazzisce il primo giorno oppure ci si abitua', ma quella donna è viva. La nascondono, la riscaldano, le portano brodo di carne, la interrogano: la ragazza ha sedici anni, non si orienta nello spazio né nel tempo, non sa dov'è, ha percorso senza capire la trafila del treno sigillato, della brutale selezione preliminare, della spogliazione, dell'ingresso nella camera da cui nessuno è mai uscito vivo. Non ha capito, ma ha visto; perciò deve morire, e gli uomini della Squadra lo sanno, cosí come sanno di dover morire essi stessi e per la

---

[15] There is a possible further comparison to be drawn here between Levi's exempla and Levinas, whose notion of 'le tiers' is a means to extend his ethics from self-and-Other out into the realm of commonality and thus of justice and social responsibility (see C. Davis, *Levinas* (Cambridge: Polity, 1996), 52 f., 81 ff.).

[16] M. Nyiszli, *Auschwitz: A Doctor's Eyewitness Account*, trans. T. Kremer and R. Seaver (Greenwich, Conn.: Fawcett Crest, 1960).

stessa ragione. Ma questi schiavi abbrutiti dall'alcool e dalla strage quotidiana sono trasformati; davanti al loro non c'è piú la massa anonima, il fiume di gente spaventata, attonita, che scende dai vagoni; c'è una persona.

. . . Fatti come questi stupiscono, perché contrastano con l'immagine che alberghiamo in noi dell'uomo concorde con se stesso, coerente, monolitico; e non dovrebbe stupire, perché tale l'uomo non è. Pietà e brutalità possono coesistere, nello stesso individuo e nello stesso momento, contro ogni logica; e del resto, la pietà stessa sfugge alla logica. Non esiste proporzionalità tra la pietà che proviamo e l'estensione del dolore da cui la pietà è suscitata: una singola Anna Frank desta piú commozione delle miriadi che soffrirono come lei, ma la cui immagine è rimasta in ombra. Forse è necessario che sia cosí; se dovessimo e potessimo soffrire le sofferenze di tutti, non potremmo vivere. Forse solo ai santi è concesso il terribile dono della pietà verso i molti; ai monatti, a quelli della Squadra Speciale, ed a noi tutti, non resta, nel migliore dei casi, che la pietà saltuaria indirizzata al singolo, al *Mitmensch*, al co-uomo: all'essere umano di carne e sangue che sta davanti a noi, alla portata dei nostri sensi provvidenzialmente miopi.

Viene chiamato un medico. . . . sopraggiunge Muhsfeld, uno dei militi SS . . . esita, poi decide: no la ragazza deve morire . . . (II. 1033–4)[17]

(. . . on the floor they find a young woman who is still alive. The event is exceptional, unique; perhaps the other bodies made a barrier around her, stealing a pocket of still breathable air. The men are perplexed; death is their hourly business, a habit, since, precisely 'either you go mad on the first day, or you get used to it', but that woman is alive. They hide her, warm her up, bring her some meat stew, interrogate her: the girl is sixteen, she cannot get her bearings in space or time, she doesn't know where she is, she went through without understanding the sequence from the sealed train to the brutal first selection, the stripping down, entry into the chambers that no one has ever survived. She has not understood, but she has seen; and so she must die, and the men of the Squad know it, just as they know that they too must die, for the same reason. But these slaves, brutalized by alcohol and by the daily massacres, are now transformed: they have before them not the anonymous mass, the river of fearful, stunned people getting out of the carriages; this is a real person.

. . . Events like this surprise us, because they conflict with the image we have within of man in harmony with himself, coherent, monolithic; and it should not surprise us, because man is not like that. Pity and brutality can

---

[17] Levi first uses the term 'Mitmensch' in 'Vanadio' in *Il sistema periodico* (I. 927).

coexist, in the same individual and at the same instant, against all logic; and anyway, pity itself eludes logic. There is no proportion between the pity we feel and the extent of the suffering that stimulates it: a single Anne Frank stirs more emotion than the myriad that suffered like her, whose images have stayed in the shadows. Perhaps it has to be like that; if we had to and were able to feel the suffering of all, we would not survive. Perhaps only saints are given the terrible gift of pity for the many . . . to all the rest of us, there is only, at best, the intermittent pity directed to an individual, to the *Mitmensch*, our fellow-man: to a human being in flesh and blood, whom we see before us, within reach of our providentially short-sighted senses.

A doctor is called. . . . Muhsfeld, one of the SS soldiers, arrives . . . he hesitates and then decides: no, the girl must die . . .)

For Levi humanity exists and asserts itself within the individual in a sense of community, a common sense of being 'co-men'. The passage's complex syntax, tones, and style reflect the fundamental value of Levi's use of common sense as it has been understood in this chapter: a means to complexity that bypasses the pieties and the exclusivities of 'expert' discourses and also the certainties of systems; a way of using the experience and knowledge of others; a way towards proper (historical, measured, felt) response.

10

FRIENDSHIP

> For friendship is community and we are related to our
> friends as we are related to ourselves.
>
> (Aristotle)

Levi's narrative chronicles and creates communities. When he
turned for the one and only time in his writing career to the novel
form, in *Se non ora, quando?*, he built his entire narrative around
the difficult, dangerous, and intense small community of a Jewish
partisan band in hiding in the forests of central Europe, often
threatened as much by their 'fellow' partisans—Poles, Russians,
and Ukrainians—as by the Germans. The shifting allegiances,
alliances, loyalties, and loves within the band, and between it and
others, dramatically illustrate Levi's fascination with community,
and the circles of human experience it creates. Furthermore, in
this as in so many other ways, *Se non ora, quando?* is a reprise of the
boisterous moving feast of small communities that Levi had chronicled in *La tregua*. More than simply chronicling communities,
however, Levi works through his writing also to create a sense of
community with his own interlocutors, whether his characters,
fictional and non-fictional, or his real and imagined readers. This
web of affinities is one of the major means to ethical sensitization
and shared enquiry running through Levi's *œuvre*. And the key
vocabulary or metaphor in which his particular forms of community and affinity are given energy is that of friendship.

To talk of friendship and ethics in Levi is once again to mark
him down as 'old-fashioned', premodern, or at least premodernist
in his mindset. Friendship was of course a commonplace feature of
the Western philosophical tradition stretching from Plato and
Aristotle to Kierkegaard and Emerson, but fell into almost
complete disuse in the modern or modernist era, before a certain
revival in strands of recent philosophy and political theory. It was

a pillar in the foundations of both the Greek vision of ethics and politics (and especially where the two meet in Aristotle's *Nicomachean Ethics*, books 8 and 9), and the Christian notions of 'caritas' (in origin simply a translation from the Greek 'philia'), and 'agape', or unmotivated neighbourly love.[1] And there is an almost equally long-standing and equally disused tradition of treating books and their authors as friends: to look only at the Italian tradition, Dante does so in his declaration of 'friendship' with the vernacular tongue (*Convivio* I. xii–xiii), in his relations with Cavalcanti and the 'stilnovisti' generally ('Guido, io vorrei che tu e Lapo ed io . . .', *Rime* IX), and with Brunetto Latini (*Inferno* XV). Indeed, his portrait of Virgil in the *Commedia* is little more than a metaphorical embodiment of Virgil the author of the *Aeneid* as friend and guide, as 'vademecum' to Dante his reader.[2] Petrarch also, in his *Familiares* and *Seniles*, repeatedly turns to books and authors as friends: as Nicholas Mann puts it, 'he treated books as confidants and close companions, dear friends with whom he was constantly in conversation'.[3] Levi, without consciously drawing on this tradition, sets friendship as an ethical and literary vessel at the heart of his writing. It is the cement which binds together the communities he constructs in his writings. He re-explores, often in counterpoint to the weakened human relations in the camps or under strain as in *Se non ora, quando?*, a number of the issues which persistently troubled the tradition: for example, the possible typologies and initial conditions of friendship, the duties it involves, the degree of reciprocity, self-knowledge, and commitment to justice it requires, and its relation to wider or different

---

[1] For a useful anthology of the tradition of writings on friendship, see M. Pakaluk, ed., *Other Selves. Philosophers on Friendship* (Indianapolis: Hackett, 1991). For philosophical work on friendship since 1970, see N. Kapur Badhwar, *Friendship: A Philosophical Reader* (Ithaca, NY: Cornell University Press, 1993); and J. Derrida, *La Politique de l'amitié* (Paris: Galilée, 1994). See also F. Alberoni, *L'amicizia* (Milan: Garzanti, 1984); R. Pahl, *On Friendship* (Cambridge: Polity, 2000); R. Porter and S. Tomaselli, *The Dialectics of Friendship* (London: Routledge, 1989).

[2] See P. Armour, 'Dante and Friendship' (Oxford: Pagett Toynbee Lectures in Dante, 1995).

[3] N. Mann, *Petrarch* (Oxford: Oxford University Press, 1984), 10; see also pp. 98–100. On the tradition of treating texts and their authors as friends and its uses for a contemporary ethical reading of literature, see W. C. Booth, *The Company We Keep. An Ethics of Fiction* (Berkeley and Los Angeles: University of California Press, 1988), 169–224 [170–2] and *passim*; M. Nussbaum, *Love's Knowledge* (Oxford: Oxford University Press, 1990), 230–45.

social relations. It is the presence and characteristic features of the particular model of friendship which emerges from Levi's work that this chapter sets out to trace.

The vocabulary and imagery of friendship is everywhere in Levi's work, so much so that it is not uncommon to find it applied even to inanimate objects, say, metals or elements in *Il sistema periodico* ('ci sono metalli amici e metalli nemici', I. 898; 'there are friendly and hostile metals'). It makes its first appearance in 'Shemà', the epigraph to *Se questo è un uomo*, where it helps to define the ordinary world that is the antithesis of the *Lager* (and thereby set up the relation between here and there that is at the heart of his ethics):

> Voi che vivete sicuri
> Nelle vostre tiepide case,
> Voi che trovate tornando a sera
> Il cibo caldo e visi *amici*
> > Considerate se questo è un uomo . . .
> > > (I. 3; emphasis added)

(You who live secure | in your warm houses, | You who return in the evening to find | hot food and friendly faces | | Consider if this is a man . . .)

It permeates *Se non ora, quando?* and *La tregua* as has already been noted. Indeed the former could be reread entirely as the parabola of Mendel's friendships, from his hesitant and increasingly intense encounter with Leonid, to his arrival after many travails at the Austrian–Italian border with his group, where he reflects at length on each of his surviving companions and what they have meant to him:

si sentiva stanco e straniero. Solo, oramai; senza donne, senza meta, senza paese. Senza amici? No, questo non lo poteva dire; i compagni rimanevano, sarebbero rimasti: riempivano il suo vuoto. (II. 482)

(he felt tired and foreign. Alone now; no women, no destination, no country. No friends? No, he could not say that: his companions were still there, would still be there: they filled his void.)

Friendship also permeates the relations between Levi as writer and the characters of his texts, the readers of his texts, even books themselves. Each of these can be briefly illustrated.

Encounters with characters, whether fictional or real, dominate his narrative, and the defining characteristic of his narrative technique is its episodic, character-based nature. Almost all his works

are made up of anthologies of stories or essays built around character-sketches of those he encountered. Certain sequences of *La
tregua*, for example, pack in a vivid vignette on almost every page
(e.g. I. 216–24). And the strongest lines of continuity between
episodes and character-sketches, alongside the autobiographical
authorial voice, are invariably provided by the handful of his
longer-lasting and more intensely personal friendships, such as
those with Alberto and Lorenzo in *Se questo è un uomo* or Cesare
in *La tregua*.[4] Even the chemical conundrums of *Il sistema periodico*
are in part structured as a series of more or less fulfilled friendships
(with Enrico, Rita, Sandro, Giulia, his six Milan friends, Dora,
Emilio, and so on). Levi is particularly interested in the difficulties
of negotiating 'friendship', whether because of solitary character
(Rita and Sandro are both solitary), lifestyle (Faussone in *La chiave
a stella* is recalcitrant but also itinerant, so friendships are short or
non-existent; I. 967), or differences of opinion (such as several
with Simpson in *Storie naturali*). With characters like Faussone and
Simpson, the 'Levi'-narrator is intrigued by being not quite their
friend, but linked by a bond nevertheless: back in Turin, he visits
Faussone's old aunts:

'Cosí lei è un suo amico, non è vero?'
    Le ho spiegato che proprio amico no . . . ma ci eravamo trovati un
quei paesi lontani, avevamo passato insieme tante sere, insomma ci
eravamo fatta buona compagnia . . . (I. 1088)
('So you're a friend of his, is that right?'
    I explained that I was not quite a friend, no . . . but we'd met in those
far-off lands and spent many evenings together, in short we'd kept each
other company . . .)

Levi's affinity for these myriad characters, good and bad, give
his work its almost picaresque texture, and in an essay on Daudet
in *L'altrui mestiere*, he describes that affinity as a sort of love
('philia'): 'l'amore . . . è necessario alla creazione poetica. E' . . . un
amore disinteressato e puro, l'amore di Pigmalione, che lega il
creatore alla sua creatura perfetta, o in via di diventare perfetta; e
che non può mancare, perché senza amore non si crea' (II. 651–2;
'Love . . . is essential for poetic creation . . . The disinterested,

---

[4] On the link between friendship and survival, see C. Segre, '*Se questo è un uomo* di
Primo Levi', in A. Asor Rosa, ed., *Letteratura italiana. Le opere IV* (Turin: Einaudi, 1996),
497–8.

pure love, the love of Pygmalion that links the creator to his perfect, or nearly perfect creature; which cannot be lacking because without it creation is not possible').

This love or friendship for characters also has a metaliterary and metaethical dimension in Levi's use of telling and listening to stories as a means of communication in his episodic encounters (see Chapter 11). The same can be said in a handful of stories for the act of writing: in 'Lo zingaro' (*Lilít*, II. 32–6), for example, Levi forges an unlikely bond by agreeing to act as scribe for Grigo, the gypsy of the title, in exchange for some bread (the Nazis were staging the farcical letter-writing by inmates under the scrutiny of the Red Cross, although no letters ever reached their destination). Previously an irritant for Levi, Grigo forges an awkward but genuine bond as they struggle to make themselves understood.[5]

If we turn to his rapport with readers, a sense of intimacy is empirically observable with remarkable frequency from responses to his books: to give just two examples of many from English readers, 'Primo Levi seems to me to be one of that select band of writers with whom it is possible to sustain a lasting friendship. One can turn to him for advice and help'; 'When you read Levi, you feel like you have become friends with him.'[6] And Levi himself repeatedly insisted on the duty of the writer to show respect for and to communicate in good faith with the reader:

la scrittura serve a comunicare . . . il lettore di buona volontà deve essere rassicurato: se non intende un testo, la colpa è dell'autore, non sua. . . . Questo lettore, che ho la curiosa impressione di avere accanto quando scrivo, ammetto di averlo leggermente idealizzato. . . . Il mio lettore 'perfetto' non è un dotto ma neppure uno sprovveduto; legge non per obbligo né per passatempo, né per fare bella figura in società, ma perché è curioso di molte cose, vuole scegliere fra esse, e non vuole delegare questa scelta a nessuno; . . . nella fattispecie ha volonterosamente scelto i

[5] The episode is no doubt at the origin of a series of pieces about scribes, from ' "Cara mamma" ' (II. 126–30) to 'Lo scriba' (about the modern scribe, the computer; II. 841–4), and epistolary essays, from 'A un giovano lettore' (II. 845–7) to 'Caro Orazio' (II. 946–9).
[6] Respectively, P. Bailey, 'Introduction', to P. Levi, *The Drowned and the Saved*, tr. R. Rosenthal (London: Michael Joseph, 1988), p. x; John Turturro, star of Francesco Rosi's film of *La tregua*, quoted by H. Feinstein, 'Out of Auschwitz', *Guardian*, 29 Aug. 1996. And for similar comments, cf. D. Mendel, 'Un incontro con Primo Levi', *L'indice dei libri del mese* (*Liber* supplement), 11/5 (May 1994), 53–4 (first published in *Sunday Telegraph*, 8 Sept. 1991); A. Rudolf, *At an Uncertain Hour* (London: Menard Press, 1990), p. vii; and P. French, 'Books of the Year 1985', *Observer* (Dec. 1985).

miei libri, e proverebbe disagio o dolore se non capisse riga per riga
quello che io ho scritto, anzi, *gli* ho scritto: infatti scrivo per lui. ('Dello
scrivere oscuro', II. 678)[7]
(The function of writing is to communicate . . . a reader of good will
must be reassured: if he does not understand a text, it is the author's fault,
not his. . . . This reader, whom I have the strange impression of having
here beside me as I write, I confess I have slightly idealized him. . . . My
'perfect' reader is not erudite but nor is he totally unprepared; he reads
not for duty nor as a hobby, nor to look good in society, but because he
is curious about many things, wants to choose between them, and does
not want to delegate the choice to anyone else; . . . in particular he has
willingly chosen my books and he would feel uneasy or pained if he did
not understand each and every line of what I've written, or rather what
I have written *for him*: indeed, I write for him.)

Finally, the figuring of friendship in Levi's writing can be
extended to take in his own attitude to books and reading. In his
presentation of his anthology of favourite books, *La ricerca delle
radici*, he talks variously of books, authors, and people in terms of
companionship and friendship, of rich, varied and contingent
human contact:

le inimicizie sono inesplicabili quanto le amicizie: confesso di aver letto
Balzac e Dostoevskij per dovere, tardi. . . . In altri casi . . . non ho fatto
il passo decisivo per pigrizia, per pregiudizio o per mancanza di tempo.
Se lo avessi fatto, mi sarei forse procurato un nuovo amico. (II. 1364)
(enmities are as inexplicable as friendships: I confess I read Balzac and
Dostoevsky late and out of duty. . . . In other instances . . . I did not take
that decisive step out of laziness, prejudice, or lack of time. If I had done
so, perhaps I would have made a new friend.)

And, similarly, in an essay on Manzoni in *L'altrui mestiere*:

ho appetito sempre piú scarso per i libri nuovi, e tendo rileggere quelli
che già conosco. Allo stesso modo si attenua con gli anni il desiderio (o
la capacità?) di contrarre nuove amicizie, e si preferisce approfondire le
vecchie: magari notando qualche ruga in piú di cui prima non ci si era
accorti. (II. 699)
(my appetite for new books grows weaker and weaker and I tend to

---

[7] See also 'A un giovane lettore' (*L'altrui mestiere*, II. 845–7) where Levi advises the
aspiring writer to find a friend or spouse—'dotato di buon senso e di buon gusto, non
troppo indulgente: il/la coniuge, un amico/a' (II. 846; 'with the gift of common sense and
good taste, not too indulgent: your partner, a friend')—to be the first, private reader of their
work.

reread the books I already know. In the same way, the desire (or ability) to make new friendships diminishes with the years and we prefer to deepen those we already have; maybe noticing a few more wrinkles that we had not seen before.)

This range of examples is sufficient to establish a general and active presence of a vocabulary of friendship in Levi on levels of experience, narrative, and writing. To trace the contours of his particular understanding of friendship—its quality rather than its quantity—we can turn to a little-read poem published by Levi in *La stampa* on 31 December 1985, fourteen months before his death.[8] It is entitled 'Agli amici' and merits reading in full: it amounts to a measuring out of life in moments of friendship:

> Cari amici, qui dico amici
> Nel senso vasto della parola:
> Moglie, sorella, sodali, parenti,
> Compagne e compagni di scuola,
> Persone viste una volta sola   5
> O praticate per tutta la vita:
> Purché fra noi, per almeno un momento,
> Sia stato teso un segmento,
> Una corda ben definita.
>
> Dico per voi, compagni d'un cammino   10
> Folto, non privo di fatica,
> E per voi pure, che avete perduto
> L'anima, l'animo, la voglia di vita.
> O nessuno, o qualcuno, o forse un solo, o tu
> Che mi leggi: ricorda il tempo,   15
> Prima che s'indurisse la cera,
> Quando ognuno era come un sigillo.
> Di noi ciascuno reca l'impronta
> Dell'amico incontrato per via;
> In ognuno la traccia di ognuno.   20
> Per il bene od il male
> In saggezza o in follia
> Ognuno stampato da ognuno.

[8] The poem was later used as the general epigraph to the 1986 collection *Racconti e saggi*, but in *Opere* it is only in the poetry section (II. 623). Bianca Guidetti Serra, a friend of Levi's, described the poem shortly after his death as 'almost a farewell' (quoted by Cicioni, *Primo Levi* (Oxford: Berg, 1995), 152). Levi sent the poem privately to friends before its publication, as affirmed by Gina Lagorio, 'La memoria perenne e la poesia "Ad ora incerta" ', in P. Frassica, ed., *Primo Levi as Witness* (Florence: Casalini, 1990), 63–75 [74–5]).

Ora che il tempo urge da presso,
Che le imprese sono finite,   25
A voi tutti l'augurio sommesso
Che l'autunno sia lungo e mite.

(Dear friends, and here I say friends | in the vast sense of the word: |
Wife, sister, fellows, relatives, | Schoolfriends female and male, | People
seen only once | Or seen over a whole life: | As long as for at least a
moment | A segment has been drawn, | A well-defined chord. | | For
you I say, friends along the way | With its crowds, its struggles, | And
also for you who have lost | Your soul, your mind, your desire for life.
| Or no one, someone, perhaps only one, or you | Who is reading me:
remember the time, | Before the wax hardened, | When everyone was
like a seal. | Every one of us carries the imprint | Of the friend met along
the road; | In everyone the trace of everyone. | For good or ill | In
wisdom or in folly | Everyone imprinted by everyone. | | Now that
time pushes us closely, | That our exploits are over, | To all of you a
muted wish | That the autumn be long and mild.)

The poem makes four movements towards a possible redefinition
of friendship. The first is one of broadening: immediately after the
opening apostrophe to his friends, Levi pauses to qualify the term
'amici', and the qualification swamps the main proposition until as
far as l. 10, if not l. 15. These lines amount to a taxonomy of possible friends that takes in all bonds of human affection, from love
to family ties to childhood experience, until we reach the catch-
all *rejet* of l. 5, 'Persone . . .', which governs the remainder of the
first stanza. The second stanza continues to stress the neutral
universality of the addressee-friend—'o nessuno, o qualcuno'—
before turning tellingly to the emblematic addressee-reader as
friend—'tu | Che mi leggi' (ll. 14–15). As already noted, the turn
to the reader is a key step in the inscription of friendship in Levi's
œuvre. The poem becomes itself an appeal to its reader for a friendship built on this moment of mutual humane interaction shored up
in shared memory ('ricorda il tempo').

As the taxonomy evolves over fifteen lines, the second, complementary movement of the poem emerges. Friendship is loosened
in temporal terms as well as broadened in range, cast less as a fixed,
long-held bond of mutual relations between two people, and
more as an encounter, a moment of creation (and subsequent re-
creation) of such a bond.[9] The archetypal friend, as l. 19 indicates,

_____

[9] On friendship as encounter, see Alberoni, *L'amicizia*, 16–18. In the philosophical

is someone simply 'incontrato per via'; and ll. 5–7 are cast in precisely such temporal, momentary terms: 'viste una volta sola . . . praticate per tutta la vita . . . per almeno un momento . . .' Indeed, even the terms of ll. 4 and 10, 'compagni/e', suggest, in their etymology (*com* [with] + *panis* [bread], 'one who eats the same bread'), a mutually rewarding, partially symbolic, shared encounter. Companionship has vital resonance in Levi's Holocaust work, where bread—its bartering, exchange, and, on rare occasion, its sharing—determines both physical survival and the survival of human dignity in the camp world.[10] The turn to the reader in ll. 14–15 also has this temporally specific dimension—you who are reading me *now*.[11]

The moment of encounter is a necessary but not sufficient condition for creating a bond of friendship. The final three lines of the first stanza ('Purché . . .') open up the third movement of the poem with an image from geometry to define the minimum such condition: the encounter must fill out the moment with a connection, in the image of a line 'segment' ('segmento') or a 'chord' ('corda') which cuts a section out of a parabola intersecting it at two points. A line of friendship is drawn between two people at

tradition, much emphasis was laid on constancy and stability in friendship. Cicero, for example, thought it lasted even beyond death (*De amicitia*, 7.23), and his model was taken up in Montaigne's remarkable essay on his dead friend, Étienne de la Boëtie, 'De l'amitié' (*The Complete Essays*, tr. M. A. Screech (Harmondsworth: Penguin, 1991), 205–19). By contrast, the contemporary philosopher A. O. Rorty has underlined the 'historicity' or 'dynamic permeability' of friendship which is always open to alteration ('The Historicity of Psychological Attitudes: Love is not Love which Alters Not when it Alteration Finds', in Badhwar, *Friendship*, 73–88 [73–4, 77]. Levi draws on both these aspects in different ways.

[10] See e.g. the poem 'Buna' (II. 521) or *Se questo è un uomo*, I. 165–6; and G. P. Biasin, 'Our Daily Bread-pane-Brot-Broit-chleb-pain-lechem-kenyér', in Frassica, ed., *Primo Levi as Witness*, 1–20. The chain of words for bread (I. 33) echoes the multilingual first appearance of Panurge asking for food in Rabelais's *Pantagruel* (chapter IX) (see Chapters 12 and 13 below). Both the words 'compagno' and 'pane' have been identified as key words for *Se questo è un uomo* in a computer analysis of the text (J. Nystedt, *Le opere di Primo Levi viste al computer* (Stockholm: Almquist and Wiksell, 1993), 59–60). Companionship, and its etymology, also lie at the heart of the work of another 'moralist-writer', Ignazio Silone, for whom it encapsulates elements of his faded Marxism, his Christianity, and his liberalism: see R. W. B. Lewis, 'Ignazio Silone: The Politics of Charity', in *The Picaresque Saint. Representative Figures in Contemporary Fiction* (London: Gollancz, 1960), 109–78.

[11] As in Chapter 9, the syntactical movement of persons underlines this and other features of the poem: in the address to the reader, we find the only use in the poem of a second-person singular form ('tu . . . leggi'), and the second of only two first-person forms, marking the author's present voice ('mi leggi'; emphasis added; cf 'dico', ll. 1, 10). Throughout the poem, the addressee shifts around, from 'voi' (ll. 10, 12, 26), to 'noi' (ll. 7, 18), to 'tu' (ll. 14–15) and to 'ognuno' and cognates (ll. [14], 17, 18, 20, 23).

two points on the parabola of experience, and the line connects them for a moment and also cuts out an area whose form is unique to that encounter.[12] The image envisages a moment of clarity and precision, however brief, one of partial, shared experience or knowledge. These qualities are fundamental to Levi's vision of humanity and the humane throughout his work, as is the inclusiveness of the condition: such meaningful moments are possible with any other person, known or unknown, similar or different, at any point on the parabola. As he says in *La ricerca delle radici*: 'Io chimico, già esperto nelle affinità fra gli elementi, mi trovo sprovveduto davanti alle affinità tra individui; qui veramente tutto è possibile' (II. 1363; 'I, a chemist, and so expert in the affinities between elements, find myself at a loss in the face of affinities between individuals; where truly anything is possible'). The geometrical metaphor is modulated in ll. 10–11, and again in l. 19, into the vivid Dantesque metaphor of life as a journey of vicissitudes, contingencies, and suffering (ll. 10–14). These images mark the difficulty of carving out such encounters, the need to make offerings of friendship even when immediate problems block our vision of others, or our will to live. Indeed, human suffering, it is implied here, is almost a precondition for such a humane encounter.[13]

The fourth and final movement of the poem is provided by the extended metaphor of ll. 15–23, again drawn from Dante, of the stamp left in wax by a seal.[14] The key intuition here is that the moment of friendship is a mutually transformative process, a partial becoming of the other. Willy-nilly, an encounter leaves a mark, a

[12] A related metaphor of connection is to be found in Levi's fascination for bridges and frontiers, whence the highly apt subtitle of Mirna Cicioni's study, *Primo Levi. Bridges of Knowledge* (see pp. xi–xiii).

[13] On friendship and suffering, see Alberoni, *L'amicizia*, 81–4; cf. R. Rorty, *Contingency, Irony, and Solidarity* (Cambridge: Cambridge University Press, 1989), 198. A comparison suggests itself here with Elio Vittorini's *Conversazione in Sicilia* (1941–2) and *Uomini e no* (1945) on the congruence between suffering and the human: 'forse non ogni uomo è uomo . . . è piú uomo un malato, un affamato . . . dei morti di fame' (*Conversazione in Sicilia* (Milan: Rizzoli, 1988), 249 ff.; 'perhaps not every man is a man . . . an ill man, a hungry man, the dead starving . . . is more of a man'). Compare Levi's 'È uomo chi . . . è uomo chi . . .; non è uomo chi . . .' (I. 168). We know from a 1976 article that he read *Uomini e no* as he was writing *Se questo è un uomo* ('Piú realtà che letteratura', *Pagine sparse*, I. 1194–5). Vittorini also provides a further bridge from Levi to Robert Antelme; see Chapter 1 note 7.

[14] The metaphor recurs several times in the *Commedia*: see, for example, *Purgatorio*, X, 43–5; XVIII. 37–9; XXXIII. 79–81; *Paradiso* I. 41–2; VII. 67–9; VIII. 127–8; XIII. 67–8. Levi investigates the science of the seal in 'Domum servavit', *L'altrui mestiere*, II. 694–8.

trace, a print on the consciousness of both figures. It is a unique stamp of that encounter and a unique record of the other encountered. The metaphor sets out a dual, almost paradoxical quality of selfhood: on the one hand, a malleability, or openness to transformation—like soft wax (l. 16)—and, on the other hand, a distinctive individuality which marks the person encountered—like a seal (l. 17). In such an encounter, as in any act of communication, the two players constantly oscillate between 'I' and 'you', marker and marked, transformer and transformed; and thus also between permanent identity and contingent transformation. In this way a mutual immanence of the one in the other, through a form of memory, is created: 'In ognuno la traccia di ognuno . . . Ognuno stampato da ognuno' (ll. 20, 23).[15] Identity as selfhood coincides with identity as the sameness between self and other.[16] The metaphor is also one of reflection, in that the imprint of a seal is always a negative imprint, a trace which always leaves open the possibility of reconstructing the original marker of that trace.[17] Thus recognition and reconstruction after the encounter with the other, again most commonly through memory, is the last movement in Levi's open dynamic of friendship. It too resonates as a model for communication in language, since it suggests that the traces[18] of the self (or individual or writer) embodied in writing or speech can be used to reconstruct an encounter with that self. In

[15] The wax tablet is of course a traditional image for memory, as pointed out by S. Bartezzaghi, 'Cosmichimiche', in M. Belpoliti, ed., *Primo Levi* (Milan: Marcos y Marcos, Riga 13, 1997), 293. Levi also uses another art of memory, memory as space, as a house, in 'La mia casa', *L'altrui mestiere*, II. 633–6 (see Chapter 2).

[16] See P. Ricœur, 'Narrative Identity', in D. Wood, ed., *On Paul Ricœur. Narrative and Interpretation* (London: Routledge, 1989), 188–99. The issue of sameness and difference between friends was first crystallized by Aristotle's noted assertion 'the friend is another self' (*Ethics* 1166a30–32). See also comments on Levinas in Chapter 1 above.

[17] Similarly, Dante's use of the image most often plays on the perfectable repeatability or otherwise of the imprint transmitted from seal (i.e. God's will) to wax (i.e. man). An interesting, darker use of the same image is to be found in Philip Larkin's 'Continuing to Live' (in *Collected Poems*, ed. A. Thwaite (London: Marvell Press/Faber and Faber, 1988), 94): '. . . in time | We half-identify the blind impress | All our behavings bear, may trace it home. | | But to confess, | On that green evening when our death begins, | Just what it was, is hardly satisfying, | Since it applied only to one man once, | | And that man dying.' Here it is precisely the unrepeatable uniqueness of each of our 'impresses' which makes a mockery of life's learning: even if we can 'trace home' our own understanding of life, we cannot apply it to other lives. For Levi, because the uniqueness of the other is traceable in each of us through friendly encounter, life's learning is possible, bridges can be built. Larkin's poem is glossed in Rorty, *Contingency*, 23–43 [23–6].

[18] The title of 'Agli amici' when sent to Gina Lagorio (see note 8 above) was 'Tracce'.

other words, it all but explains the mechanics of the friendly encounter between writer and reader which pervades Levi's work.

'Agli amici' is by no means a systematic exploration of its theme, nor a palimpsest to be applied simplistically to Levi's work as a whole. It does, however, draw our attention to certain fundamental aspects of Levi the ethical writer, the builder of communities. One of these concerns time or duration. 'Agli amici' suggests that friendship can be struck up in the briefest of encounters. This simple, but striking insight has extensive implications for Levi's Holocaust writing in particular, since the very conditions of the concentration camps, and indeed of his long odyssey of return related in *La tregua* (but also the itinerant life of Faussone, in a certain sense), enforce rapid communication and truncated interaction. The reclaiming of the moment of any encounter as a potential vessel of friendship is then an important instance of Levi's reclamation of value from the 'useless' system of the camps. The value is enhanced still further by the mutually transformative potential of those encounters, suggested by the image of sealing-wax in 'Agli amici'. The moment is a vehicle for teaching and learning, for a sort of mutual guidance.[19] Indeed, Levi more than once used the image of Auschwitz as a university, a place of learning (I. 211).[20] Such moments of both cognitive and intensely experiential encounter are to be found in a number of stories also, such as the two encounters with enigmatic women in *Lilít*, 'La ragazza del libro' and 'Breve sogno' (I. 175–9; 200–5).

A further aspect figured by 'Agli amici' is a reciprocal openness to the other. Many of the most important encounters in Levi's work are with unfamiliar and diverse characters, and indeed often the narrative impulse derives precisely from the narrator's open curiosity for the way another mind copes with the world. He overcomes barriers of culture, class, language, or simply suffering

---

[19] Levi's encounters share this feature with Dante's encounters in the *Commedia*; indeed his most profoundly Dantesque quality is perhaps to be identified here, rather than in calques and citations or in the often strained analogy between Auschwitz and Dante's hell. On Levi and Dante, see L. Gunzberg, 'Down among the Dead Men: Levi and Dante in Hell', *Modern Language Studies*, 16 (1986), 10–28, and 'Nuotando altrimenti che nel Serchio: Dante as Vademecum for Primo Levi', in S. Tarrow, ed., *Reason and Light* (Ithaca, NY: Center for International Studies, 1990), 82–98.

[20] See, e.g., I. 200; or Levi, *The Voice of Memory*, 112, 234. (He invariably noted also that he borrowed the image from Lidia Beccaria Rolfi.)

to make contact.[21] Links are to be made here both with Levi's chemistry, which first taught him to mistrust apparent purity and identity and to cherish the impure and the different as the only trustworthy tokens of reality (*Il sistema periodico*, I. 768, 791); and with his tapping of Judaic culture, which in this instance provides him with moments of genuine illumination on the necessity of solidarity with any (suffering) fellow human. In *Se non ora, quando?*, Mendel recites a prayer to Piotr: ' "Benedetto sii Tu, Signore Iddio nostro, re dell' universo, che ha variato l'aspetto delle Tue creature" ' (II. 296–7; "Blessed are You, Lord our God, king of the universe, who has varied the aspect of your creatures" '); and the 1982 poem 'Pasqua' also draws on a prayer, here of the Passover festival:

> Di noi ciascuno è stato schiavo in Egitto,
> Ha intriso di sudore la paglia ed argilla
> Ed ha varcato il mare a piede asciutto:
> Anche tu, straniero.
> Quest'anno in paura e vergogna,
> L'anno venturo in virtù e giustizia. (II. 564)

(Each of us has been a slave in Egypt, | Has wetted straw and clay with our sweat | And has walked the sea with dry feet: | You too, stranger. | This year in fear and shame, | Next year in virtue and justice.)

It is openness to the other which also points to the nascent social dimension of friendship, to its role as a building-block for larger communities.[22] And, if friendship is built on a reciprocal and undetermined encounter between two strangers, it is necessarily contingent, singular, and malleable, inherently hostile to the categorical or the absolute.[23]

---

[21] The notion of guest- or stranger-friendship (*xenia*) was important in the Greek tradition: see P. Easterling, 'Friendship and the Greeks', in Porter and Tomaselli, eds., *The Dialectics of Friendship*, 11–25 [13–15]. In *Se non ora, quando?*, the initial encounters between Mendel and Leonid, between them and the Usbek Peiami and an old peasant couple, all play on the image of hospitality, the guest and host (II. 215, 230, 240–1). The problem of equality, difference, and reciprocity also exercised Aristotelians greatly (*Ethics* 8. 7–8; and cf. Levinas on reciprocity: see C. Davis, *Levinas* (Cambridge, Polity, 1996), 51).

[22] This was an important feature of Aristotle's view of friendship as one of the constituent elements of the *polis* (*Ethics* 8. 9). In this century, by contrast, C. S. Lewis and later feminist philosophers have suggested that friendship is secessive, a closed alternative relation to established communal institutions of family, Church, nation, and the like. See C. S. Lewis, 'Friendship: The Least Necessary Love' (from *The Four Loves* (London, Fount, 1977; 1st edition 1960), 55–84); M. Friedman, 'Feminism and Modern Friendship: Dislocating the Community', in Badhwar, *Friendship*, 285–302.

[23] Nussbaum (*Love's Knowledge*, 50, 76) notes that Kant, in contrast to Aristotle, rejected

The three concerns touched on thus far—temporality, openness to the other, and contingency—clearly lay a deal of emphasis on felt experience as the source of human knowledge and community. But this emphasis requires some qualification. Levi's model of friendship is never wholly emotive; it is rather poised between emotion and elucidation. It may well be a passion, a form of love or intimacy, as indeed were 'philia' and its cognates in the classical tradition, but for Levi it seems radically hostile to seduction or erotic love, since the latter mystifies and overwhelms and distances from clarity of mind.[24] In 'Uranio' in *Il sistema periodico*, Levi describes his dislike of working in the customer service department of his chemical company:

lo faccio malvolentieri, con esitazione, compunzione e scarso calore umano. . . . tutte le strategie e tattiche del SAC [Servizio Assistenza Clienti] si possono descrivere in termini di corteggiamento sessuale. (I. 905–6)
(I do it reluctantly, with hesitation, regret, and little human warmth . . . all the strategies and tactics of the SAC can be described in terms of sexual courtship.)

Only when he shifts the terrain of the interaction from this courting to one of tolerant listening does the narrator and narrative relax into the central story of the chapter. Similarly, in an essay in *Racconti e saggi*, Levi describes light-heartedly how a computer chess game 'seduced' him away from his serious task of writing (II. 970).[25] The unease with desire is another instance of Levi's conservative anti-modernism which was noted earlier, since modernism—at least since Freud—has tended to place desire and sexuality at the heart of its world-view.[26]

Instead of being built on seduction and impulse, friendship

love and friendship as criteria in moral judgement precisely because such passions are irrational and non-absolute. Kierkegaard takes a similar position: see Badhwar, *Friendship*, 1. The issue of singularity also evokes the debate in philosophies of friendship as to whether friendship with one precludes friendship with many or all (e.g. 'caritas'), echoed by Levi's conception of 'sainthood' as the (inhuman) capacity to respond to the suffering of the many (see Chapter 9). See also Derrida's reflections on Montaigne in *La Politique de l'amitié*, *passim*.

[24] Cf. Alberoni's description of friendship as 'la forma etica dell'eros' (*L'amicizia*, 33).
[25] Cf. the tense and intense chess match in *Se non ora, quando?*, II. 230–3.
[26] On the ambivalence and reticence of Levi's treatment of erotic love and women, see Cicioni, *Primo Levi*, 44–5, 78, 92–3. On his hostility to psychoanalysis, see II. 1026–7, where he criticizes Liliana Cavani's psycho-sexual account of fascism, *Il portiere di notte*.

involves a reasoned choice—hence its ethical weight—a willingness to criticize as well as to trust the second party, and to alter oneself in the give and take between trust and distance. In 'Il fabbricante di specchi' (II. 894–7), the 'Spemet' machine, a mirror that reflects back what others think of you, works as a sort of tester of the trustworthiness of a friendship: 'rinsaldava le amicizie antiche e serie, scioglieva rapidamente le amicizie d'abitudine o di convenzione' (II. 897; 'strengthened old and serious friendships, and quickly dissolved habitual or polite ones'). But perhaps the best way to understand the part-involved, part-detached relation is to return to an idiom noted as important to Levi in Chapter 4, the idiom of commerce. Friendship, between individuals and in turn as a basis for social mutuality, is a form of contract of benefit and recognition, the product of an ongoing process of negotiation. Sandro and Primo are friends not as equals but because 'la diversità delle origini ci rendeva ricchi di "merci" da scambiare, come due mercanti che s'incontrino provenendo da contrade remote e mutuamente sconosciute' (I. 773; 'the difference in our origins made us rich in "goods" to exchange, like the meeting of two merchants, from remote and mutually unknown lands'). And if we return again to *Se non ora, quando?*, we find bonds of friendship similarly built up through negotiations: 'i tre cenarono, legati dall'amicizia a fior di pelle che nasce dalle contrattazioni' (II. 226; 'the three dined, bonded by the edgy friendship forged in negotiations'). The same, of course, could be said for the Cesare–Mordo Nahum thread running through *La tregua*.

Friendship in Levi's work is only one element in the larger picture of his ethics of community. Its profound importance for his own negotiations between the Holocaust and the ordinary world is perhaps best encapsulated in one final line of enquiry growing out of 'Agli amici', that is, the self-evident difficulty of contracting and sustaining friendships, understood in that broad sense as meaningful human contact. What happens when friendly contact fails, when negotiations falter or break down? Levi comes up against this dilemma again and again when he encounters one group who, he tells us in *I sommersi e i salvati*, he has come to realize were the ideal readers, the 'destinatari veri' (II. 1125) of *Se questo è un uomo*: Germans.

Almost all Levi's contacts with Germans are difficult or

awkward, sometimes violently disturbing, but profoundly neces-sary. Some of the most angry passages in his Holocaust writing come when he sees himself or his fellow prisoners dragged into some sort of likeness, complicity, or brotherhood with the Germans: for example, in his fierce evocation of the 'satanic' foot-ball match between the SS and the Sonderkommandos; 'siete come noi . . . anche voi, come noi e come Caino, avete ucciso il fratello. Venite possiamo giocare insieme' (*I sommersi e i salvati*, II. 1032–3; 'you are like us . . . you too, like us and like Cain, have killed a brother. Come we can play together').[27] After liberation, Levi's first encounter with a German comes on the very first night, which he spends with a German political prisoner and former Kapo, Thylle, during which tears and then a difficult, confused dialogue emerge, shot through with the memory of Thylle's abuses of power only hours previously (*La tregua*, I. 207–9). Much later, in Levi's account of his correspondence with his German readers ('Lettere di tedeschi', *I sommersi e i salvati*, II. 1124–48), almost every exchange is awkward or faltering, more or less a dialogue of the deaf. The only exception, his friendship with Hety S. (II. 1142–8), proves the rule: Levi portrays her as, exceptionally, sharing many of his values, despite their starkly differing experi-ences, being naturally curious, and 'avida, addirittura famelica, di incontri umani' (II. 1146; 'avid, even greedy for human encoun-ters').

Awkwardness and embarrassment also mark encounters with Germans in the course of business, when, as Levi was wont to relate, he told them he had learned his German in Auschwitz (II. 1068). And a special case of just such a (near-)encounter is the intense exchange with the camp chemist Müller in 'Vanadio' (*Il sistema peri-odico*, I. 628–40). Levi's very real perplexity over how to deal with Müller is, strangely perhaps, expressed as careful debate over the nature of friendship, Christian love, and forgiveness: Müller had helped Levi a little in the camp, but hardly enough; he claims he had had with Levi 'un rapporto quasi di amicizia fra pari' (I. 930; 'a rapport almost of friendship between equals'); Levi cannot recall, but (echoing the Aristotelians) he doubts any such relation of equal-ity could have existed except in Müller's imagination; Müller

---

[27] Echoes of Cain and Abel return in *Se non ora, quando?* in the tortured rapport between Leonid and Mendel (e.g. II. 269).

congratulates him on his 'Christian' capacity to love his enemy; but Levi is not so sure—'no, nonostante i lontani privilegi che mi aveva riservati, e benché non fosse stato un nemico a rigore dei termini, non mi sentivo di amarlo . . . eppure provavo una certa misura di rispetto per lui' (I. 932; 'no, despite the distant privileges that he had reserved for me and although he was not strictly speaking an enemy, I did not feel I loved him . . . and yet I felt a certain measure of respect for him'); he is willing to forgive enemies, if and only if they have expressed regret and done penance, 'cioè quando cessino di essere nemici' (ibid.; 'that is when they stop being enemies');[28] in Müller's case, he acknowledges his help, but also notes that (some, very few) others did more.

All these charged exchanges with Germans are, ultimately, privileged testing grounds for a larger, anthropological–moral enquiry in Levi's work into the universal categories of friend and enemy. Indeed, as Levi states in the preface to *Se questo è un uomo*, the entire Holocaust can be read as the consequences of leaving unchecked the common sentiment that ' "ogni straniero è nemico" ' (I. 5; ' "Every stranger is an enemy" '). A 1981 poem puts it still more pessimistically, 'ognuno è nemico di ognuno . . . la guerra non è mai finita' (II. 561; 'everyone is the enemy of everyone . . . the war is never over'), echoing Mordo Nahum's 'guerra è sempre'; and in turn, *Se non ora, quando?* adjusts the phrase to make explicit the correlation between 'straniero', 'nemico', and Jew: 'ognuno è l'ebreo di qualcuno' (II. 427; 'everyone is the Jew of someone'). Finally, 'La zona grigia' states the general principle outright: 'è talmente forte in noi, forse per ragioni che risalgono alle nostre origini di animali sociali, l'esigenza di dividere il campo fra "noi" e "loro", che questo schema, la bipartizione amico-nemico, prevale su tutti gli altri' (II. 1017; 'the demand to divide the field between "us" and "them" is so strong in us, perhaps for reasons that go back to our origins as social animals, that this schema, the pairing friend–enenmy, prevails over any other'). In 'La zona grigia' this is presented as the most fundamental simplification of all in our tendency to read our world crudely and simplistically. Levi's multifaceted enquiry into friendship establishes a less schematic and more gradated model for

---

[28] Phrasing very close to this is also found in Levi's 1976 'Afterword' to *Se questo è un uomo*, I. 175.

human and humane contact, capable of serving as a vessel for navigating the difficult waters of moral grey zones and the question of how to live (together) with acuity, responsibility, and liberal receptiveness.

II

STORYTELLING

> traces of the storyteller cling to the story as the potter's hand-
> prints cling to the clay vessel.
>
> (Walter Benjamin)

Friends tell each other stories; by telling each other stories—of troubles overcome, 'ibergekumene tsores' (I. 739)—two interlocutors
become friends. The ethics of friendship and the ethics of storytelling are deeply intertwined. In Levi, stories real or invented—of
characters, episodes, curious facts or ideas, or fantastic possibilities—
are the basic currency of almost everything he wrote. His stories, in
the very human particularity and variety they present, provide the
raw material for his ethical universe, the individuals and the exempla that stimulate his flexible vision of how to live. They are his best
defence against reductive generalization and over-simplification, and
at the same time they foment his ethical enquiry, never stalling at
the merely anecdotal. They conform to Martha Nussbaum's understanding of a Jamesian narrative philosophy:

teaching and learning do not simply involve the learning of rules and
principles. A large part of learning takes place in the concrete. This experiential learning, in turn, requires the cultivation of perception and
responsiveness: the ability to read a situation, singling out what is relevant for thought and action. . . . [Henry] James plausibly suggests that
novels exemplify and offer such learning.[1]

In keeping with other ordinary virtues, storytelling is both
metaethical and ethical; not merely a good way to talk about and
interrogate ethical questions thrown up by experience; but also an
act of value in its own right. Also in keeping with other virtues,
the ethical status of storytelling is closely bound up with writing

---

[1] M. Nussbaum, *Love's Knowledge* (Oxford: Oxford University Press, 1990), 44.

both in and beyond testimony. Indeed, this relation is especially important here, since telling the story of the Event, of what 'has been', comes close to being a definition of testimony *tout court*, with all its cathartic and monumental power—'Mi pareva che mi sarei purificato raccontando', he says in *Il sistema periodico* (I. 870; 'I thought I would purify myself by telling my story')—, as well as opening up the possibility of a less solemn and tragic, more humane, witty, and flexible narrative of troubles overcome. This chapter examines Levi's ethics of storytelling in and beyond testimony, paying particular attention to the book apparently pitched furthest of all from concerns of testimony, *La chiave a stella*.[2]

La chiave a stella is a work apart in Levi's *œuvre*, *sui generis* in both subject matter and style. It is apparently neither testimonial, nor autobiographical (except incidentally), nor essayistic, nor fantastical in form. The fictional protagonist, Libertino Faussone,[3] is an industrial rigger who wanders the globe far from his native Piedmont, performing feats of engineering, solving enigmatic technical and human conundrums when constructions go awry. Faussone tells of his professional adventures in his strange hybrid language of technical jargon and workplace Piedmontese to an industrial chemist narrator—Levi in all but name—in an isolated Soviet town of the 1970s, where both have been sent on work.[4] Relations between Faussone and 'Levi', set in a sort of limbo as they wile away the evenings, act as a frame for the work narratives themselves, making of the text a sort of dour Decameron of the engineering and industrial-chemical worlds. Faussone is certainly by turns awkward, proud, stubborn, heroic and mock-heroic, and so on, but he is more archetype than psychological portrait (as the book's closing quotation from Conrad on his Captain MacWhirr declares, I. 1105), representative of that particular tradition of the journeyman-worker that fascinated Levi. In reality, the two principals are more defined by their dual roles as narrator and listener, by the substance of their stories and their responses, than they are constructed as characters.

From the very first words of the book, we are plunged into

---

[2] 'Raccontare' is another of the terms found in all Levi's books in J. Nystedt's computer analysis; *Le opere di Primo Levi viste al computer* (Stockholm: Almquist and Wiksell, 1993), 39.

[3] Levi was intrigued and gratified to be approached after the book's publication by a mechanical rigger actually called Faussone, who even seemed to share his fictional counterpart's stubborn Piedmontese temperament (see Levi, *The Voice of Memory*, 66–7).

[4] Levi made more than one work trip in the early 1970s to Togliattigrad.

questions of storytelling and writing, before we even learn who is speaking:

'Eh no: tutto non le posso dire. O che le dico il paese o che le racconto il fatto: io però, se fossi in lei, sceglierei il fatto, perché è un bel fatto. Lei poi, se proprio lo vuole raccontare, ci lavora sopra, lo rettifica, lo smeriglia, toglie le bavature, gli dà un po' di bombé e tira fuori una storia; e di storie, ben che sono più giovane di lei, me ne sono capitate diverse.' (I. 945) ('Oh no, I can't tell you everything. I can tell you either the place or the story: but if I were you, I'd choose the story, 'cos it's a good one. Then if you want to tell it, you can work on it, straighten it out, sand it down, get rid of the smears, give a bit of a finish and have yourself a story; and believe me, although I'm younger than you, I've run into more than a few stories in my time.')

Already here, the analogy between the work of construction ('montaggio', also editing or 'montage' in Italian), experience, and storytelling which characterizes the entire book is established. Faussone instructs his listener to work on a raw material to build and refine a finished object, a story. Here too is the first injunction or permission from Faussone for 'Levi' to write this book, which opens up the metanarrative dimension that also permeates the text. Furthermore, this metanarrative injunction is embedded in another dimension of the book, the personal meditation on the part of 'Levi' on a particular juncture in his own life, the prelude to retirement and the turn to full-time writing (or better, story-telling). As he explains later, the period in Russia marks:

la mia ultima avventura di chimica. Poi basta: con nostalgia, ma senza ripensamenti, avrei scelto l'altra strada, dal momento che ne avevo la facoltà ed ancora me ne sentivo la forza; la strada del narratore di storie. Storie mie finché ne avevo nel sacco, poi storie d'altri, rubate, rapinate, estorte o avute in dono, per esempio appunto le sue [di Faussone]; o anche storie di tutti e di nessuno, storie per aria, dipinte su un velo . . . (II. 1076)[5] (my last adventure as a chemist. Then that would be it: with some nostalgia but no regrets, I would set out on another road, since I still had the faculties and still felt strong enough to do it: the road of the storyteller. My own stories until the well ran dry, then other people's stories, stolen, robbed, extorted, or given away, like his [Faussone's] for example; or just stories of everyone and no one, stories in the air, painted on a veil . . .)

[5] Of course, just such a ludic gathering and retelling of other people's work stories defines the project of L'altrui mestiere, as well as parts of Il sistema periodico.

This decision is not a settled one as the book opens: it is rather one that matures over the course of the days and evenings spent in Russia. In the fifth chapter, 'Tiresia', the narrator tells Faussone that 'scrivere era il mio secondo mestiere, e che stavo meditando, proprio in quei giorni, se non sarebbe stato più bello farlo diventare il mestiere primo o unico' (I. 983; 'writing was my second métier, and that I was mulling over, in those very days, whether it wouldn't be better to make it my first and only job'). There follows the most extended comparison in the book between writing and rigging, and then writing, chemistry, and rigging, their different raw materials, tools, tests, checks and balances, pleasures and frustrations (I. 983–9). In passages such as these *La chiave a stella* is, among other things, a meditation on a new métier, on the formation of a storyteller.

Further links are created between work and stories: as discussed in Chapter 6, work, its successes and failures, and the pleasure of these, are the source of all the stories, including the two by the narrator ('Acciughe (I)' and 'Acciughe (II)'; I. 1076–86, 1094–105) which could have been part of *Il sistema periodico*. As Faussone opines, in full harmony with his listener:

'Insomma, bene o male siamo arrivati al giorno del collaudo. Più male che bene, come le ho detto; ma sul lavoro, e mica solo sul lavoro, se non ci fossero delle difficoltà ci sarebbe poi meno gusto dopo a raccontarle; e raccontare, lei lo sa, anzi, me lo ha perfino detto, è una delle gioie della vita' (I. 1071)

('So, for better or worse, we got to the day of the test. It was more for the worse than the better, as I said; but at work, and not only at work either, if there were no problems, there'd be less fun telling about them after; and telling stories, as you know, well, you were the one who told me, is one of life's joys')

As the typically Levian incision—'e mica solo sul lavoro'—makes clear, work and storytelling, their difficulties and joys, are fundamental and general analogues to and components of the interrogated, active life. In particular, they reflect the complexities and subtleties of the latter, without over-simplification, but they also envisage a form of learning and understanding. At the end of the book, as Levi begins a final story of his own, he notes that some stories, even those steeped in difficulty, offer none of that pleasure of storytelling: 'È stata piuttosto una storia stupida; non una di quelle che fa piacere raccontarle, perché a raccontarla uno si accorge che è stato stupido a non capire le cose prima' (I. 1095; 'It was quite a stupid story; not one of those that gives pleasure in the telling, because as you go along you realize that you were stupid not to realise sooner what was going on'). Faussone replies, correcting a rather disconsolate Levi: 'Non se la prenda tanto. . . . Le storie di lavoro sono quasi tutte cosí; anzi tutte le storie dove è questione di capire qualche cosa. . . . è che nella vita le cose non sono mai tanto semplici. Semplici sono i problemi che fanno fare a scuola' (ibid.; 'Don't get so upset. . . . Work stories are almost always like that; in fact any story that's about understanding something . . . it's just that in life, things are never quite that simple. Simple is what they make you do at school').[6]

The first key turn in the book towards its broader function as a meditation on the act and processes of storytelling comes in its third story, 'L'aiutante', where the narrator is on the point of interrupting Faussone's story. For us, the reader, he does indeed interrupt, but only to reflect on why he thinks twice about doing so at the scene of the narration itself:

ma mi sono trattenuto per non guastare il racconto. Infatti, come c'è un'arte di raccontare, solidamente codificata attraverso mille prove ed errori, cosí c'è pure un'arte dell'ascoltare, altrettanto antica e nobile, a cui tuttavia, che io sappia, non è stata mai data tanta norma. Eppure, ogni narratore sa per esperienza che ad ogni narrazione l'ascoltatore apporta un contributo decisivo: un pubblico distratto od ostile snerva qualsiasi conferenza o lezione, un pubblico amico la conforta; ma anche l'ascoltatore singolo porta una quota di responsabilità per quell'opera d'arte che è ogni narrazione: se ne accorge bene chi racconta al telefono, e si raggela, perché gli mancano le reazioni visibili dell'ascoltatore, che in questo caso è ridotto a manifestare il suo eventuale interesse con qualche monosillabo o grugnito saltuario. È anche questa la ragione principale per cui gli scrittori, ossia coloro che raccontano ad un pubblico incorporeo, sono pochi (I. 973)

(but I held back so as not to ruin his story. Indeed, just as there is an art of storytelling, solidly codified by a thousand trials and errors, so there is also an art of listening, just as ancient and noble, but which, to my knowledge, has never been set down in rules. And yet, every narrator knows from experience that the role of the listener is crucial to any narration: a distracted or hostile audience unnerves any lecture or lesson, a friendly audience encourages it; but even the individual listener carries

[6] Cf. Chapter 6 on stupidity and Chapter 9 on simplicity and complexity.

his quota of responsibility for the work of art that any narration represents: anyone who has told stories on the phone and frozen up because
they cannot see the reactions of their listener, who is limited in this case
to showing any interest with a monosyllable or an occasional grunt,
knows it all too well. This is the principal reason for which writers, that
is, those who tell stories to a disembodied audience, are so few and far
between.)

The art of listening is a crucial element in the dialogic value of
storytelling for Levi. Already in *Il sistema periodico*, he had, in
slightly different terms, formed a picture of himself as the natural
listener. In his first ever experience of professional work in 1941
('Nichel'), in a semi–clandestine isolation and anonymity not
unlike the setting of *La chiave*, Levi found himself bombarded with
gossip, with stories:

Mi vennero raccontate moltissime storie . . . ognuno conosceva la storia
di tutti. Non è chiaro perché queste vicende, spesso intricate e sempre
intime, le raccontassero con tanta facilità proprio a me . . . ma pare che
sia questo il mio pianeta (e non me ne lamento affatto): io sono uno a cui
molte cose vengono raccontate. (I. 798)
(I heard a great many stories . . . everyone knew everyone else's stories.
It is not clear why these events, often intricate and always intimate, were
related with such ease to me of all people . . . but it seems that this is my
star (and I'm not complaining): I am one to whom many things are told.)

Earlier, and in still more self-effacing terms, in *La tregua*, Levi
reflects in slightly bemused fashion on the willingness of the wily
Greek Mordo Nahum to share his experiences and deepest
thoughts with one so alien as himself:

Perché il greco raccontasse queste cose a me, perché si confessasse a me
non è chiaro. Forse davanti a me, cosí straniero, si sentiva ancora solo, e
il suo discorso era un monologo. (I. 243).
(Why the Greek told these things to me, why he confessed to me is not
clear. Perhaps before me, one so foreign, he felt still alone, and his tale
was in fact a monologue.)

As often with Levi, the quiet qualification 'perhaps' is fundamental, for the monologue he hears in Nahum's voice becomes something other through his own reflections: Levi forges a dialogue by
the act of listening. Similarly, in subordinating himself as narrator
for the larger part of *La chiave a stella*, Levi is not so much silenc-
ing himself and marking Faussone's discourse as a monologue, as

writing a manual on the art of listening, of letting monologue become dialogue (I. 983).[7]

At this point, an important parallel suggests itself. Several of Levi's Italian critics have noted in his narrative, with its restrained orality, affinities with the figure of Leskov described by Walter Benjamin in his remarkable essay 'The Storyteller'.[8] For Benjamin, the storyteller builds his craft (and his is an artisanal craft rather than an art) on the exchange of experiences with others ('The Storyteller', 83), just as Faussone and 'Levi' do. For Benjamin, there are two interpenetrating archetypes of the storyteller, 'someone who has come from afar' and 'the man who has stayed at home, making an honest living, and who knows the local tales and traditions' (p. 84). Thus the stories told are twofold: the lore of faraway places and that of the past (p. 85). Furthermore, tales contain what Benjamin calls 'counsel', 'something useful' (a moral, a maxim, advice); and 'counsel woven into the fabric of real life is wisdom' (pp. 86–7). Benjamin laments the loss of stories and the loss of the art of listening to stories about faraway things (in place or time), in order to repeat and transmit them in turn (p. 91). 'Levi' and Faussone echo Benjamin closely: they are both travellers, with stories to tell from their travels, and they both also have the local, more stationary wisdom of their trades, as well as of their land, Piedmont (for Levi, we might add his knowledge of Piedmontese-Jewish culture in 'Argon', *Il sistema periodico* (I. 741–56, and later Talmudic and Ashkenazi traditions in *Se non ora, quando?* and elsewhere).[9] They both share a distinctly practical

---

[7] Levi's fascination with dialogue and listening, and the chain of communality they create, can perhaps also be discerned in his half-mischievous, half-serious plan for a book on gossip ('Del pettegolezzo', *Racconti e saggi*, II. 982–5).

[8] W. Benjamin, 'The Storyteller. Reflections of the Works of Nikolai Leskov', in *Illuminations*, ed. H. Arendt, tr. H. Zohn (London: Jonathan Cape, 1970), 83–109. For parallels with Levi, see A. Bodrato, 'Nel racconto la verità di Auschwitz', *Humanitas*, 44, NS 1 (Feb. 1989), 51–73; G. Bertone, 'Italo Calvino e Primo Levi', in *Il castello della scrittura* (Turin: Einaudi, 1994), 191–8; D. Giglioli, 'Narratore', in M. Belpoliti, ed., *Primo Levi* (Milan: Marcos y Marcos, Riga 13, 1997), 397–408; and F. Moliterni, R. Ciccarelli, and A. Lattanzio, *Primo Levi. L'a-topia letteraria, il pensiero narrativo, la scrittura e l'assurdo* (Naples: Liguori, 2000). On Levi's orality, see A. Bravo and D. Jalla, eds., *La vita offesa* (Milan: Franco Angeli, 1986), 36–7; G. Poli and G. Calcagno, *Echi di una voce perduta* (Milan: Mursia, 1992), 128–9; but see also Chapter 12 note 17 below.

[9] On Levi and this Judaic tradition, see in particular P. Valabrega, 'Primo Levi e la tradizione ebraica-orientale', *Studi piemontesi*, 11/2 (1982) (now in E. Ferrero, ed., *Primo Levi: un'antologia della critica* (Turin: Einaudi, 1997), 263–88; cf. also ibid. 245–62, 289–99); V. De Luca, *Tra Giobbe e i buchi neri* (Naples: Istituto grafico editoriate italiano, 1991). On his

bent, both think in proverbial terms, drawing morals or maxims from their tales. And we have seen already how, here as in *Il sistema periodico*, Levi is the listener who then goes on (indeed has gone on) to narrate the tales in his turn.

But 'Levi' and Levi take on from Benjamin an even more striking resonance if we consider the latter's conjunction of storytelling and listening with memory (the listener's art is an art of remembering what he has heard and then repeating it to others) and with death. For Benjamin, the authority of the storyteller, the compulsion to listen, is a shadow of the authority of the dying man transmitting the meaning of his life, his 'testament' (pp. 93 ff.). The bridge to Levi as Holocaust writer is compelling: in those stories, the 'afar' from which Levi has returned is the void of Auschwitz, the memory and transmission of stories imbued with a moral duty, the death which authorizes narration in this case the shadow of six million, whose stories Levi has seen and listened to and now passes on.[10]

The parallel with Benjamin's storyteller suggests a rich avenue of exploration in Levi's entire *œuvre*. It also opens up further the apparently closed world of *La chiave a stella*, and through it, the dialectic between testimony and common lived experience transmitted through stories. It draws attention to a muted dimension of the text, a way in which it can be reread as truncated, as containing what we might call a Holocaust-shaped hole.

A clue to this beguiling incompleteness, if not yet to the substance of what might be missing, is already in the book's opening sentence quoted above: ' "Eh no: tutto non le posso dire" ' (I. 945). Stronger evidence comes in the various hints that a whole raft of stories told in the encounters between Faussone and 'Levi'

---

reading of writers from within it, such as Sholem Aleichem and I. B. Singer, see *La ricerca delle radici*, II. 1473–80 and *The Voice of Memory*, p. 269. Besides *Se non ora, quando?*, the most important examples of Levi's own attempts at tapping into this tradition are 'Il servo' (I. 710–17; see Chapter 8), 'Lilít', 'Il nostro sigillo', and 'Il cantore e il veterano' (II. 18–23, 28–31, 37–42); the essays 'Il rito e il riso', 'La miglior merce' (II. 795–9, 815–18); and the catalogue preface 'Ebrei dell'Europa orientale' (now at II. 1284–8).

[10] In the 1978 poem 'Huayna Capac', Levi adopts the voice of the dying Inca emperor in tones that tap into the same authority of the testamentary storyteller. In 'Dello scrivere oscuro', his critique of Celan's poetry is bound up with the terrible sense of death combined with solitude—'il rantolo di un moribondo' ('the rattle of a dying man')—that he finds there, a combination in contrast to the talking, shared death envisaged by Benjamin as the epitome of his storyteller (II. 676–81).

have been omitted from the book, the latter's own deportation stories: 'in altre sere io ho raccontato [a Faussone] tutte le mie storie' (I. 989; 'on other evenings I told [Faussone] all my stories'). The first of these hints comes at the opening of the second chapter, 'Clausura', a title that deliberately evokes the theme of imprisonment:

'. . . Beh, è roba da non crederci: lo capisco che queste cose le è venuto voglia di scriverle. Sí, qualche cosa ne sapevo anch'io, me le raccontava mio padre, che in Germania c'era stato anche lui, ma in un'altra maniera: ogni modo, guardi, io lavori in Germania non ne ho presi mai, sono terre che non mi sono mai piaciute, e mi arrangio a parlare tante lingue, perfino un poco di arabo e di giapponese, ma di tedesco non ne so neanche una parola. Un giorno o l'altro gliela voglio raccontare, la storia di mio padre prigioniero di guerra, ma non è come la sua, piuttosto da ridere. E neppure in prigione non ci sono mai stato, perché oggi come oggi per finire in prigione bisogna farla abbastanza grossa; eppure, vuol credere? una volta mi è successo un lavoro che per me è stato peggio che stare in prigione . . .' (I. 952)
('. . . Well, it's unbelievable: I can see that you wanted to write that stuff down. Sure I knew something about it, my father used to tell me about it, he'd been in Germany too, although not anywhere like that: anyway, look, I've never taken work in Germany, it's a place I've never liked, and I get by in lots of languages, even a bit of Arabic and Japanese, but I don't know a single word of German. One of these days I want to tell you the story of my father as prisoner of war, but his isn't like yours, it's a bit of a joke. And I've never even been in prison, 'cos the way things are these days you really need to mess things up to get yourself locked up; although, you know, once I had a job that was worse than a prison for me . . .')

This opening establishes a hidden exchange of Auschwitz stories for work stories in the book. The two central stories of the book, 'Off-shore' and 'Batter la lastra' (I. 990–1021), provide further resonance. They are steeped in Faussone's emotional and unresolved relationship with his father, a smith who seems to stand in complex counterpoint both to his son and to Levi himself. He was in a prison camp in Germany, as one of the 600,000 Italian military internees of the period 1943–5, echoing Levi's deportation;[11] and his experience in the snows of Russia during the war looks

[11] U. Dragoni, *La scelta degli I.M.I. Militari italiani prigionieri in Germania (1943–1945)* (Florence: Le Lettere, 1996).

forward to the Togliattigrad we are now in, but also to the snows
evoked by the story of Faussone's trip to Alaska in 'Off-shore',
with its explicit echoes of Jack London, one of Levi's favourite
literary reference points for narrating suffering in the camps and
elsewhere (see, e.g., 'Cerio', *Il sistema peridico*, I. 861). Further, the
father's doomed project for a local antiheroic monument to the
fallen in Russia, described in 'Batter la lastra', echoes in some
manner Levi's own antiheroic testimony.[12]

Faussone's genealogy links him to the camps in a literary sense
also: towards the end of *Se questo è un uomo*, just before the
Germans have evacuated the camp, Levi happens upon a French
novel, the first book he has seen since his arrest and deportation,
which helps return him to life from the threshold of death (I. 151).
In *La ricerca delle radici*, he tells us that the novel was Roger Vercel's
Remorques, which describes the adventures at sea of a tow-boat and
its captain Renaud. Levi draws parallels with Conrad, with the
millennial history of the rapport between man and machine, and
finally muses, 'la ricerca della paternità è sempre un'impresa
incerta, ma non mi stupirei se nel mio Libertino Faussone si
trovasse trapiantato qualche gene del capitano Renaud' (II. 1444;
'searching for ancestors is always an uncertain business, but I
would not be surprised to find some of the genes of captain
Renaud transplanted in my own Libertino Faussone').

The links from *La chiave a stella* to Levi's Holocaust writing do
not end there. The narrator's visit to Faussone's aunts back in
Turin, in 'Le zie' (I. 1087–93), recalls not only Levi's own eccentric extended family in 'Argon', but also, loosely and in a different
key, the visits of survivors, with more or less honest motives, to
the families of those presumed lost in the camps, such as Levi's
own awkward visits to Alberto's family related in *I sommersi e i
salvati* (I. 1014–15), or the criminal Cravero, who tried to extort
money from Levi's family and ended up stealing his sister's bicycle
(*La tregua*, I. 291–2). More telling still is the affinity between

---

[12] Levi himself wrote the text for the monument in the Italian national block at
Auschwitz (II. 1355–6; and cf. Poli and Calcagno, *Echi di una voce perduta*, 173–6). On the
important issue of Holocaust memorials, see J. Young, *The Texture of Memory. Holocaust
Memorials and Meaning* (New Haven: Yale University Press, 1993). On the issues of heroism, see the Introduction above and T. Todorov, *Face à l'extrême* (Paris: Seuil, 1991), 21,
who asks what new forms of narrative might reflect the pragmatic, non-heroic stories of the
Warsaw ghetto and elsewhere.

Faussone, with all his solitary, stubborn, taciturn, manual nobility (and for all his flaws), and the extraordinary figure of Sandro Delmastro in 'Ferro' whose strength and practical wit Levi felt with hindsight as a preparation for Auschwitz (see Chapter 5). Sandro, it should be noted, also read Jack London, as well as Kipling and Salgari (I. 775; for Faussone on Kipling, see I. 1036); and his family and ancestors were smiths just like Faussone's (I. 776). Even Faussone's father's monument seems to find a parallel in Levi's moving reflections on Sandro's death (itself an echo of Levi's memorial in words to Hurbinek, in *La tregua*):

[Sandro] non era uomo da raccontare né di fargli monumenti, lui che di monumenti rideva: stava tutto nelle azioni, e, finite quelle, di lui non resta nulla; nulla se non parole, appunto. (I. 781)
([Sandro] wasn't a man to tell about with stories nor to commemorate in monuments, he who laughed at monuments: he was all in his actions, and with them gone, nothing remains of him: nothing except words, precisely.)

A number of further connections to a testimonial subtext scattered through the book are worth noting. First, the setting itself recalls the 'other places' of Levi's deportation, as he points out: '. . . del resto, un curioso destino vuole che in quel paese grande e strano abbiano luogo le svolte della mia vita' (I. 1076; 'in any case, a strange destiny has meant that the turning points in my life have taken place in that great and strange land'). It also resonates metaphorically with the camps as a place of timeless suspension and waiting, 'senza tempo' (I. 1057–69), just as in Auschwitz, time and history had stood still (I. 113). In a key passage of 'Tiresia' referred to more than once in previous chapters, 'Levi' tells Faussone the myth of Tiresias—his double change of sex, his blinding and gift of prophecy—but Faussone loses the thread: 'Ma non ho capito bene cosa c'entra?: non vorrà mica venirmi a dire che Tiresia è lei?' (I. 988; 'But I don't quite see what you're getting at? You surely don't mean that you are Tiresias?'). Levi replies, connecting back to both his dual career and his deportation, beginning '. . . sí, forse me n'ero accorto *solo raccontandogli quella storia*, un po' Tiresia mi sentivo' (I. 989; emphasis added; '. . . yes, maybe I had only realized as I was telling him the story, I did feel a little like Tiresias'). The very processes of storytelling produce an oblique insight into both his ordinary and his Holocaust experience, and a link between the two.

Secondly, the nostalgic, retrospective relationship between storytelling and hard experience encapsulated in Faussone's phrase quoted above, 'se non ci fossero delle difficoltà ci sarebbe poi meno gusto dopo a raccontarle' (I. 1071; 'if there were no problems, there'd be less fun telling about them after'), contains strong echoes of the more general relationship between experience, memory, and narration in Levi's Holocaust work, best encapsulated in the Yiddish epigraph of *Il sistema periodico*—'Ibergekumene tsores iz gut tsu dertseyln', 'it is good to tell the story of past troubles' (I. 739). In *I sommersi e i salvati*, at the start of the essay on stereotypes, this same proverb lies at the centre of Levi's reflections on the two fundamentally different categories of survivors, 'quelli che tacciono e quelli che raccontano' (II. 1109; 'those who stay silent and those who tell their story'). The Yiddish proverb is inserted as an indicator of the human wealth and pleasures but also of the risks of deception and embellishment in the act of narration:

Parlano perché (recita un detto jiddisch) 'è bello raccontare i guai passati'; Francesca dice a Dante che non c'è 'nessun maggior dolore | che ricordarsi del tempo felice | nella miseria', ma è vero anche l'inverso, come sa ogni reduce: è bello sedere al caldo, davanti al cibo ed al vino, e ricordare a sé ed agli altri la fatica, il freddo e la fame: cosí subito cede all'urgenza del raccontare, davanti alla mensa imbandita, Ulisse alla corte del re dei Feaci. Parlano, magari esagerando, da 'soldati millantatori', descrivendo paura e coraggio, astuzie, offese, sconfitte e qualche vittoria (ibid)
(They speak because (as a Yiddish saying has it) 'it is good to tell the story of past troubles'; Francesca says to Dante, 'there is no greater pain | than to remember happy times | in sorrow', but the inverse is also true, as every survivor knows: it is good to sit in the heat, before food and wine, and to recall to oneself and to others tiredness, cold, and hunger: thus Ulysses gives in at once to the urgency of the story, before the sumptuously decked table of the king of the Phaeacians' court. They speak, perhaps even exaggerate, like the boastful soldier, describing fear and courage, tricks, offences, defeats and some victories.)

The lines emanating from this brief, dense evocation of the storyteller—lines back to Faussone, to Benjamin, and to several essential moments in Levi's *œuvre*—are manifold and important. The figure of Homer's Ulysses is the traveller-storyteller *par excellence*, as well as a figure of wit and patience as we saw above in Chapter 5. Just as compelling for Levi is the comparison with another, more tragic navigator-cum-storyteller at the heart of Levi's pantheon of self-defining archetypes, Coleridge's Ancient Mariner, whose 'ghastly tale' is told outside the wedding feast, as if cursed and exiled from 'the heat . . . food and wine' enjoyed by the narrator for whom the troubles are indeed in the past and narration is now only a pleasure.[13] The oscillation between narrative as curse and narrative as pleasure marks the storytelling of the survivor.

The Ancient Mariner's story is cursed because no one will listen, producing the pure pain ('dolore allo stato puro', I. 54) felt by Levi and others in the *Lager* when they dreamed of being ignored and disbelieved on their return. The failure to listen once again emerges as not simply a failure of courtesy, but also a betrayal of the act of mutual recognition contained within the processes of storytelling. In this it echoes strongly the ethics of looking charted in Chapter 1; and it evokes inevitably the other Ulysses, Dante's Ulisse (also echoed in the reference to Francesca in the quotation above) and the story of 'Il canto di Ulisse' in *Se questo è un uomo*. In 'Il canto di Ulisse', the true hero is neither Dante nor Ulisse nor Levi himself, but rather Jean il Pikolo, an intuitive master of the art of listening:

Jean è attentissimo, ed io comincio . . . mi suggerisce il termine appropriato per rendere 'antica' . . . Pikolo ha viaggiato per mare e sa cosa vuol dire . . . Ecco, attento Pikolo, apri gli orecchi e la mente, ho bisogno che tu capisca . . . Pikolo mi prega di ripetere. Come è buono Pikolo, si è accorto che mi sta facendo bene. . . . Pikolo attende e mi guarda . . . (I. 108–11)
(Jean is rapt with attention and I start . . . he suggests the best term to render 'antica' . . . Pikolo has travelled by sea and he knows what this means . . . Here, look Pikolo, open your ears and your mind, I need you to understand . . . Pikolo asks me to say it again. How good Pikolo is,

---

[13] For Levi's use of Coleridge's *The Rime of the Ancient Mariner*, see the poem 'Il superstite' (II. 576); the title of his collected poetry *Ad ora incerta*; the epigraph to *I sommersi e i salvati* (II. 995); the description of his state of mind immediately after his return, in 'Cromo' (*Il sistema periodico*, I. 870–1); and the appearance of the Mariner as a character in the fantastic literary theme-park of 'Nel parco' (*Vizio di forma*, I. 674). And compare his translation of the Scots sea ballad 'Sir Patrick Spens' (II. 585–7). It is worth noting that Coleridge's poem has been something of a key battleground in part of the debate over literature and ethics in recent work: see, for example, A. Z. Newton, *Narrative Ethics* (Cambridge, Mass.: Harvard University Press, 1995), 3–17 (and cf. pp. 71, 123–4 on Levi); D. P. Haney, 'Aesthetics and Ethics in Gadamer, Levinas, and Romanticism: Problems of Phronesis and Techne', *PMLA* 114/1 (Jan. 1999), 32–45.

he's realized that this is doing me good. . . . Pikolo waits and watches me
. . .)

The scene of Primo and Jean is the polar opposite of the dream of
failed storytelling; it is the primal scene of Levi's ethics of listening.
Faussone's formulation implied that past troubles serve as a
source of stories which are both pleasurable and useful. To a
degree, Levi subscribes to this, but with a caveat, as his reference
to the battle stories of bloodied soldiers suggests. Storytelling is
often among other things an art of embellishment, of fiction. Like
memory it is fallible, and like a fallible memory which supplements
with fictions that which it does not recall with precision, a story
rounds out with elegance and distortion that which does not fit.
Thus, stories are to be interrogated with knowledge and critical
intelligence, set in proper context using other stories and histories
as part of a longer process of understanding. But, beyond the truth
or otherwise of the story, the profound ethical weight of the act
of narrating and listening remains. In a famous passage of *Se questo
è un uomo*, Levi makes that weight sound mythical, even mystical:

. . . tutte le nostre storie, centinaia di migliaia di storie, tutte diverse e
tutte piene di una tragica sorprendente necessità. Ce le raccontiamo a
vicenda a sera, e sono avvenute in Norvegia, in Italia, in Algeria, in
Ucraina, e sono semplici e incomprensibili come le storie della Bibbia.
Ma non sono anch'esse storie di una nuova Bibbia? (I. 60)
(all our stories, hundreds of thousands of stories, all different and all full
of a tragic surprising necessity. We tell them to each other in turn in the
evenings, and they happened in Norway, in Italy, in Algeria, and in
Ukraine, and they are simple and incomprehensible like the stories of the
Bible. But are not these too stories of a new Bible?)

The resonant and open question that ends the passage is typical of
Levi's open ethical enquiry turned outwards towards the reader.
Less often noted, however, is that the immediate pretext for this
rhetorical and ethical crescendo is the story of Resnyk, which,
crucially, Levi has forgotten: 'Mi ha raccontato la sua storia, e oggi
l'ho dimenticata, ma era certo una storia dolorosa, crudele e
commovente: ché tali sono tutte le nostre storie . . .' (I. 59–60; 'He
told me his story and today I have forgotten it, but it was surely a
painful, cruel, and moving story: for such are all our stories . . .').
It is the act of Resnyk's telling his story, and the humanity
contained within it and within the multitude of stories, and within

the exchange of such stories in such a place—not the specifics of each story—that matter here.

The mystical thread of storytelling is picked up and developed in 'Lilít' (II. 18–23): Levi meets a certain Tischler (meaning carpenter; for Levi as for Benjamin, then, the craftsman-artisan is also the storyteller). Tischler knows Italian only from opera libretti but is a natural storyteller, performer, and singer, and the performative aspects of storytelling, at a given time and place about another time and place, are crucial to its yield of pleasure and good 'counsel' for Levi. Tischler manages to beguile him with terrifying and magical stories of Adam's first wife, Lilith. He puts on a show and Levi finds himself cast as Tischler's ignorant, incredulous, and impious straight-man, 'un gioco che mi piaceva' (II. 20; 'a game I enjoyed'). Now, as writer, he finds himself cast as Tischler, relaying to his incredulous reader the stories of Lilith told to him by the long-dead carpenter. The mystery lies in the strange passing on of stories and roles (Benjamin again):

è inesplicabile che il destino abbia scelto un epicureo per ripetere questa favola pia ed empia, intessuta di poesia, di ignoranza, di acutezza temeraria, e della tristezza non medicabile che cresce sulle rovine delle civiltà perdute (II. 23)
(it is inexplicable that destiny chose an epicurean to repeat this pious and impious fable, interwoven with poetry, ignorance, rash subtlety, and that incurable sadness that grows on the ruins of lost civilizations)

One final aspect of the figure of Faussone, declared from the outset and followed through stylistically to the end, seems to set a seal on the function of the book as a sort of experiment in the art and archetypes of storytelling and listening: the somewhat disquieting fact that Faussone, the teller of most of the book's stories, is not very good at storytelling:

Non è un gran raccontatore: è anzi piuttosto monotono, e tende alla diminuzione e all'ellissi come se temesse di apparire esagerato, ma spesso si lascia trascinare, ed allora esagera senza rendersene conto. Ha un vocabolario ridotto, e si esprime spesso attraverso luoghi comuni che forse gli sembrano arguti e nuovi; se chi ascolta non sorride, lui li ripete, come se avesse da fare con un tonto. (I. 945)[14]

---

[14] See also II. 957, 968, 970, 977–8, 1070. Faussone's insipid and simplistic use of commonplaces ('luoghi comuni') echoes several elements in the discussion of common sense in Chapter 9.

(He is not a great storyteller: on the contrary, he's rather boring, and tends to play things down and cut things out as if he were afraid of seeming excessive, but often he gets carried away, and then exaggerates without realizing it. He has a limited vocabulary, and he often speaks in commonplaces that maybe seem witty and new to him; if his listener doesn't smile at them, he repeats them, as though he were dealing with an idiot.)

A bad storyteller can tell us much about storytelling, as figures such as Tristram Shandy or Boccaccio's Madonna Oretta show in their different ways. And indeed, Faussone's technique, eschewing embellishment and revealing the mechanisms hidden by smoother practitioners of the art, has something of this negative lucidity.[15] But it is in the context of the ethics of storytelling that this bold decision by Levi to deprive his hero of the key tools of this second craft can best be read. Over the course of the text, the two characters clearly build a strange but nevertheless real bond; something like a friendship. Levi gets over his open irritation at Faussone's failures as a narrator, and one of the first steps in this direction is his decision not to interrupt the story of 'L'aiutante', indicated by the extended meditation on the art of listening quoted earlier. The decision indicates the need to listen at all costs, just as Jean il Pikolo listened and encouraged the confused, almost delirious half-memories of Levi in 'Il canto di Ulisse'. As is often the case with *La chiave a stella*, there is a close parallel to be found in *Il sistema periodico*. In the story 'Uranio', there is a much less likeable, physically somewhat repugnant character, Bonino, who is also a bad storyteller: 'Bonino non era un buon narratore: divagava, si ripeteva, faceva digressioni, e digressioni di digressioni' (I. 907; 'Bonino was not a good narrator: he drifted, repeated himself, went off at tangents, and then at tangents of tangents'). His story is confused, nebulous. Levi drifts in and out of listening to his war story, but he gives us a clue as to the function of the bad storyteller. With recourse to biblical language once more, he suggests the ethical imperative to listen even to a dull story is a sort of essence of the ethical imperative to listen, in particular to the stranger, the 'other':

Era chiaro che il racconto di Bonino non sarebbe stato tanto breve: ma

[15] A similar effect is to be found in Levi's parody of bad poetry, as written by a machine, in his science-fiction story 'Il Versificatore' (I. 413–33).

pazienza, ripensai a quanti lunghi racconti avevo inflitto io al mio prossimo, a chi voleva ed a chi non voleva ascoltare, ricordai che sta scritto (*Deut.* 10.19) 'Amerai lo straniero, poiché anche voi siete stati stranieri nel paese d'Egitto', e mi disposi comodo sulla sedia. (ibid.)
(It was clear that Bonino's story wasn't going to be brief: but never mind, I thought of how many long stories I had inflicted on my neighbour, whether they wanted to listen or not, and I remembered that it is written (Deut. 10: 19) 'You will love the stranger for you too were strangers in the land of Egypt', and I settled myself into the chair.)

Contrast this with the lapidary declaration of *Se questo è un uomo*, quoted in both Chapters 1 and 5 above: 'qui nessuno ha tempo, nessuno ha pazienza, nessuno dà ascolto' (I. 32; 'here no one has any time, no one has patience, no one listens).

When Bonino's story turns out to be fantasy in large part, Levi warms to him, seeing even in this boring and insensitive figure 'la libertà sconfinata dell'invenzione' (I. 911; 'the unbridled freedom of invention'). Levi, weighed down by a past which he cannot alter nor reinvent, by testimony in other words, envies the freedom of the narrator, even the poor one, and as a result, begins to see the human qualities of the fantasist which had been obscured in his, for once, discourteous and somewhat irritated half-listening to Bonino. An ominous note remains, however, since the processes of reinvention undertaken by Bonino—of a past falsified and narrated so often that the narrator himself forgets it is fiction— look forward to Levi's careful analysis of the denials and prevarications in the 'memories' of former Nazis in 'La memoria dell'offesa' (*I sommersi e i salvati*, II. 1006–16). Faussone is no falsifier, but he is a bad storyteller who is worth listening to. And indeed, perhaps the final confirmation that his stories are offerings of value in the ethical economy of human exchange is the very fact that, in exchange, 'Levi' offers him the stories of his darkest and deepest experiences.

La chiave a stella is, in all its strangeness, a crucial work for Levi's ethics—of work and wit, of friendship and storytelling. It is all the more important if, as this chapter has argued, its role as a sort of manual of storytelling is complemented by a hidden evocation of Levi's own Holocaust writings, making it a studiedly incomplete text. *La chiave a stella* then becomes a key moment in the journey through and beyond testimony that defines Levi's *œuvre* and his ethics within it. It is as though the book has been built in part on autobiography, memory, and testimony (echoing at a distance Judaic storytelling traditions), only for that element to be torn out, for the ladder to be thrown away. Something similar, if less subtle, had happened in the openly autobiographical *Il sistema periodico*, where the chapter 'Cerio' had opened 'Che io chimico . . . abbia vissuto una stagione diversa è stato raccontato altrove' (I. 860; 'That I, a chemist, . . . have lived another, different season has been related elsewhere'). The dynamic in *La chiave a stella* gives us a model for Levi's impulse to transcend the absolutes of testimony in order to tell stories of the ordinary. The very possibility of writing a book of stories about the experiences and techniques of rigging, the dilemmas of a manager nearing retirement, and the strange people and landscape of a Soviet industrial town of the 1970s is eloquent evidence of the impulse to the ordinary in Levi. Traces of the absolute remain, however, the memory of the offence is never and should never be quite thrown away, 'che poco lontano aspetta il treno' (II. 1044; 'for not far away, the train is waiting').

PART IV

DIVERSIONS

Common sense, friendship, wit, pragmatism, discretion, utility: many of the ordinary virtues discussed thus far as keys to Levi's ethics risk leaving us with the impression of a rather antique and conservative body of work, all reason and reasonableness, sobriety, detachment, and order. To some degree, the impression is not wrong.[1] We have seen Levi apparently keeping a certain distance from aspects and assumptions of modernism. We have seen how he taps into an often unknowing mix of values of humanist, Enlightenment, or positivist origin, tested to their limits but somehow retained in the face of the collapse of value concomitant with the Holocaust. Indeed the very notions of value or virtue themselves carry with them, as we saw in the Introduction, a return to disused, prescriptive models of how to live and how to talk about how to live. But just as virtue in Levi is in reality a more flexible, pragmatic, and fluid mechanism than that more static prescriptive tradition would suggest (is 'world-guided and action-guiding'), so Levi's apparent conservatism of style and outlook provides only a partial picture of his ethics. Inbuilt and integral to his ethics, the exception that proves the rule, the asymmetrical twist to his ordered patterns of understanding, is an impulse towards the very opposite of order, sobriety, and utility. Part IV investigates this other Levi, the diversions from his grounded enquiries into value as seen in Parts I to III, towards a complementary realm of pleasure, paradox, and play, a realm which nevertheless contains essential virtues of its own. Chapter 12 looks at Levi's ironic humour, in and beyond testimony, as a mechanism that shares both the cognitive and communal dimensions running through his ethics and therefore acts as a bridge between his sober and his more exuberant sides. And Chapter 13 tackles the exuberance head on, looking at curiosity and play as keys to a sort of ethics of freedom in Levi that is perhaps the most profound and persistent value of all underpinning his work.

---

[1] It is interesting to note that the same criticism has been levelled at some of the work on literature and ethics discussed in the Introduction: thus Martha Nussbaum has been criticized for reading literature without any sense of reverie or playfulness in her search for ethical paths (see J. Adamson, 'Against Tidiness: Literature and/versus Moral Philosophy', in J. Adamson, R. Freadman, and D. Parker, eds., *Renegotiating Ethics in Literature, Philosophy and Theory* (Cambridge: Cambridge University Press, 1998), 84–110 [94–9]).

IRONY, OR WIT REVISITED

> Mieulx est de ris que de larmes escrire.
>
> (Rabelais)

As was noted at the outset of Part II, wit has a double meaning that perfectly fits Levi's *forma mentis*. In Levi as in Boccaccio, wit in the sense of shrewd, practical intelligence overlaps and coincides with a taste for wit in the sense of incisive, clear, light-handed humour. Indeed, each gains ethical value by association with the other. In particular, certain forms of humour in Levi serve as a means to sharpen the insights offered by intelligent application, to complicate and delimit the possibilities of response, whilst at the same time reinforcing the bonds of community through a shared smile or laugh.

Levi's sense of humour seems to start out as a form of ribald pastiche, without this ethical, intelligent dimension: in 'Fosforo' (*Il sistema periodico*, I. 835), he counts among his most precious possessions the burlesque 'Macaroneae';[1] in 'Oro' (I. 850), he describes the vapid intellectual games of his group of friends in Milan in 1942–3, which included satires on literary classics and mock-crepuscular poems, and which marked their naive irresponsibility as Europe collapsed around them (they called themselves the 'Orchestra on the Titanic').[2] Only later does laughter seem to acquire a sense of value, as if here as elsewhere the camps acted as teacher for Levi, darkening and also heightening his humour. Thus when we reach *La tregua* there is a sort of bitter, grotesque humour

[1] The list of precious possessions also includes a bicycle, Rabelais, Pavese's translation of *Moby Dick*, mountaineering rope and hooks, a slide-rule, and a recorder. Giovanni Tesio sees the list as defining 'the features of a sure moral physiognomy . . . which in Levi's literature never fades' (*Piemonte letterario dell'otto-novecento* (Rome: Bulzoni, 1991), 143).

[2] Some of the group's drawings and satires, now owned by one of them, Eugenio Gentili Tedechi, are reproduced in A. Guadagni, 'Prima del grande buio', *Diario*, 2/13 (2–8 Apr. 1997), 52–7.

to Mordo Nahum's pithy 'guerra è sempre'; and a warm appreci-
ation of the humane confusions of the Russian army contrasted
with the Germans (and later the Americans). Even open comedy,
such as the set-piece scene of miming a chicken in 'Una curizetta'
(I. 315–23), takes on, as we will see in the next chapter, profound
ethical resonance, as borne out in the 'macaronic' line of Levi's
humour in *La ricerca delle radici*, which starts from Rabelais and
takes in Porta and Belli.

Other sides to his humour emerge in the course of his writing
from the 1960s onwards: comedies of error make up large parts of
both his science fiction and his writing on chemistry and work; we
saw in Chapter 8 a Pirandellian thread to his stories about character and identity, which includes elements of Pirandello's literary-
philosophical notions of 'umorismo';[3] and, most importantly of all,
later in his career, Levi found in Judaic traditions of storytelling
and Talmudic debate a form of humour which chimed loudly with
the cerebral-cum-magical elements of his own humour. Passages
in *Se non ora, quando?* illustrate the point explicitly, even didactic-
ally. Levi's rather forced display of his acquired Jewish culture in
the novel[4] includes set-piece examples of Jewish jokes, stories, and
angels-on-pinhead debates, often witnessed by a non-Jew to
whom all is patiently explained (or explained away). So, Pavel gets
carried away one evening telling story after story, joke after joke:

. . . attingendo al corpus sterminato dell'autoironia ebraica, surreale e
sottile, giusto contrappeso al rituale che è altrettanto surreale e sottile:
forse il frutto piú raffinato della civiltà che attraverso i secoli si è distillata
dal mondo stralunato dell'ebraismo orientale. (II. 299)[5]

---

3. These were formulated in his 1908 essay 'L'umorismo', where he theorized and traced
a literary history of a form of ironic humour based on the perception of contradiction in
reality and identity and a certain perplexed, sympathetic response to it.

4. Levi was criticized for this in America, where much less of Jewish lore and habit
needed to be explained to the average reader (F. Eberstadt, 'Reading Primo Levi',
Commentary (Oct. 1985), 41–7; R. Angress, 'Primo Levi in English', *Simon Wiesenthal Center
Annual*, 3 (1988), 317–30). One example of several is: ' "Kòscher-schmòscher," . . . l'ingegnoso modo jiddisch di sminuire l'oggetto di cui si parla ripetendolo distorto' (II. 364;
' "Kosher-smosher" . . . the ingenious Yiddish method for diminishing what is being talked
about by repeating it in a distorted form').

5. The same bond between ritual and laughter is made in the closing paragraph of 'Il rito
e il riso' (*L'altrui mestiere*, II. 795–9 [798–9]), where Levi imagines his own laughter echoing the laughter of the rabbis as they use all their ingenuity to complete the mind-
bogglingly detailed rules of the *Shulkan Arukh*. Once again wit as laughter and wit as
ingenuity are as one.

(. . . drawing on the endless corpus of self-mocking Jewish irony, surreal and subtle, an apt counterbalance to its equally surreal and subtle rituals: perhaps the most refined product of the civilization that was distilled over centuries out of the wide-eyed world of Eastern European Judaism.)

Or the Russian non-Jew Piotr is turned in circles, variously 'sbalordit[o]', 'matto', 'in cerca di una aiuto', 'mezzo spaventato e mezzo incuriosito', and 'attonito' (II. 364–8; 'dumbfounded' 'mad', 'looking for help', 'half scared and half curious', 'amazed'), in the face of a group display of Talmudic debate. Along the way, Gedale explains the strange combination that characterizes the Jews and their absurd cavilling about the law: the Jews are mad reasoners—'Tutti gli ebrei sono matti . . . Noi [ebrei] siamo bravi a fare le distinzioni' (II. 364; 'All Jews are mad . . . We are good at making distinctions'). Not for the last time here, we see in Levi's humour a leavened, comic version of a more sober ordinary virtue already encountered, the virtue of careful distinction or discretion seen in Chapter 3. However, the most significant element to take from these moments in *Se non ora, quando?* is their pointer towards perhaps the most characteristic form of all in Levi's wit-led humour, so prevalent that it acts as a sort of stylistic and tonal signature throughout his work: his irony.

The tone of open, but subtle irony is set at the very start of Levi's work, in the preface to *Se questo è un uomo*, by two remarks tinged with a studied and strange humour. Following on from the blunt admonitory power of the poem-epigraph that precedes it, the preface opens on a perplexing note: '*Per mia fortuna*, sono stato deportato ad Auschwitz solo nel 1944 . . .' (I. 5; emphasis added; 'It was my good fortune to be deported to Auschwitz only in 1944 . . .'). The literal truth of the statement is unimpeachable, since, as Levi goes on to explain, the shortage of manpower in Germany at the time led the Nazis to extend the average life of camp inmates, and hence gave young prisoners like Levi at least a slim chance of survival. However, the boldness of the opening—what fortune is it to be deported to Auschwitz?—immediately has an effect that goes well beyond the literal. It begins a process of dismantling the narrow assumptions that might (for good or bad reasons) govern a reading of a work of testimony of this kind. The irony of the phrase 'per mia fortuna' nudges us towards rebuilding our expectations and perceptions of the experience of deportation by undermining our tendency to conflate or generalize individual experiences of suffering. Within a given context, even the system of the Final Solution, there are positions of greater and lesser fortune, not simply a 'lump sum' of five or six million dead. Our sensitivity is heightened towards the subtle gradations of the individual's position within the camps and within historical events in general. In the space of three words, we are already in the grey zone which Levi will explore with such acuity decades later in *I sommersi e i salvati*. And other threads develop out of this beginning also: as we saw in Chapter 6, there is a careful meditation running throughout Levi's work on the nature of luck, fortune, and its relation to the vicissitudes of experience and history (success and failure), a meditation inaugurated in the ironic turn of this phrase. And, again, *I sommersi e i salvati* will replay the same concerns and the same touch of irony more than once: for example, 'Per nostra paradossale fortuna (ma esito a scrivere quella parola in questo contesto) . . .' (II. 1078; 'By a paradoxical stroke of fortune (but I hesitate to write this word in this context) . . .'; and cf. II. 998,1096, 1102).

The preface to *Se questo è un uomo* ends with a second touch of irony, more playful and more ambiguous than the first, but just as much pointed towards a sharpening of distinctions in the reader, an awareness of boundaries and definitions, this time of something akin to genre: 'Mi pare superfluo aggiungere che nessuno dei fatti è inventato' (I. 6; 'It is, I think, superfluous to add that none of the events is invented').[6] Poised somewhere between rhetorical conventions of 'true story' fiction and copyright disclaimers ('any resemblance to real persons living or dead . . .'), the statement is also an ironic *a priori* reflection on testimony itself and its claims to self-evident truth-telling and its anxieties about being believed (with perhaps even a distant echo of the juridical witness's oath to tell the truth, the whole truth . . .). At the same time, the statement has substantial literal validity: this is indeed a true story.

The opening and closing of the preface give us something of a sketch of the possible mechanisms and uses of irony which condition

---

[6] A. Cavaglion, *Primo Levi e 'Se questo è un uomo'* (Turin: Loescher, 1993), 20–1, sees in this formula a veiled reference to literary debates in 1940s Italy surrounding the neo-realist movement and reportage. Links might be made with Levi's own interest in invention, discussed in Chapter 8.

our reading of both preface and book[7] and point forward to persistent features of Levi's humour. It gives us a range of ironic tone, from the disquieting to the playful; it shows how irony can be produced by playing with expectations and conventions, offered and then checked back; it demands effort and response on the part of the reader, pushing us to take more care in our reading; it works for a gradated, complex understanding of the facts and the problems at stake; and it carefully refrains from pitching itself in a way that distorts out of all recognition the primary substance of what is being said.

Although irony is notoriously difficult to classify and wide-ranging in its potential application, something of the pattern of these first two ironies can be found underpinning large parts of Levi's writing, and providing his humour with its ethical undertow. His work is shot through with rhetorical checks and balances, self-conscious interruptions, and nods and winks to the reader, or to some larger outside force such as fate or history which he sometimes does and sometimes does not believe in fully; and all these are built on irony. A good example—one that links his irony to his common sense, by way of a Gramscian detour into folk wisdom (see Chapter 9)—is his whimsical evocation of myths of guardian angels and the like: 'O forse è vero che esiste un Dio che protegge i bambini, gli stolti e gli ebbri?' ('Cerio', I. 865; 'Or perhaps it's true that there's a God to protect babes, fools, and drunks?'), he muses as he tries to explain the oddity of Alberto's and his machinations, without any real conviction of the truth of what he is saying but with a sense of how such musings can ironically highlight the confusions, idiocies, and turns of luck that milled and muddled together in his *Lager* existence.

To describe the particular qualities and dynamic of Levi's irony and to position him in the spectrum of ironists, we might first look at his favoured models. As noted already, in *La ricerca della radici*, one of the lines he traces through his selections is what he calls 'la salvazione del riso' (II. 1367; 'the salvation of laughter'), which moves from Job to Black Holes (as do all four of his lines

---

[7] Levi's own notes to the 1973 schools edition of *Se questo è un uomo* are peppered with the vocabulary of irony (e.g. pp. 70, 98, 125, 136); and cf. his comment on *Il sistema periodico* that the analogy between chemistry and life governing the book is 'always subtly ironic' ('Itinerario di uno scrittore ebreo' (1984), now at II. 1213–29 [1216]).

of navigation through his reading) via Rabelais, Porta, Belli, and Sholem Aleichem; but these four are models for Levi's humane, 'naive' comedy more than for his more cerebral irony. Within the anthology, however, examples of the latter are to be found in a small group who might in different ways be characterized as ironists: Parini, Swift, and Thomas Mann. In so far as connections can be drawn, all three use forms of irony or satire to strip down what is self-evident into what is, perhaps, true: Parini's *Il giorno* punctures the pomposity and idiocy of a young aristocrat (II. 1396–400); Swift's *Gulliver's Travels* turns the world on its head to reveal its hypocrisies (Levi chooses passages about the Struldbruggs and the Houyhnhnms; II. 1408–13);[8] Mann, in the first part of *Joseph and his Brothers*, retells the story of Jacob and Esau in what Levi calls a mixture of 'la poesia, la sapienza e l'ironia, in modulazioni sempre nuove' (II. 1435; 'poetry, wisdom, and irony, in constantly renewed forms').[9] All three bind irony to morals, rather than to formal experiment and dissolving play, in a way Levi clearly deeply admires (he treats Parini as a close friend, imagining spending an evening in conversation with him; and praises Mann's book as the greatest of the century). In a broad sense, Job and the chronicler of Black Holes are ironists also, in that they both have an acute, self-limiting awareness of the discrepancies between man's will and his place in the universe, an irony that is quite genuinely 'cosmic'.

Levi's own position, forged in the wake of the ironies of Parini, Swift, Mann, and others, can be elucidated using the descriptive model given in one of the most sober and meticulous modern (but not modernist) accounts of irony, Wayne Booth's *A Rhetoric of Irony*.[10] Booth's particular voice in the extensive field of theories of irony chimes well with Levi's own instinct for sobriety, wit, and the impulse towards the moral. In particular, Levi would seem to share Booth's reservations about the over-enthusiastic excesses of modernist ironists and theorists of irony, who see all irony as

---

[8] M. Cicioni, *Primo Levi* (Oxford: Berg, 1995), 62 suggests another intriguing parallel close to Swift's satires, in Voltaire's 'contes philosophiques'.

[9] We know from *Il sistema periodico* how important other works by Mann were for the young Levi, especially *The Magic Mountain*, itself a work of extraordinary analytical and oblique irony (I. 769).

[10] Wayne C. Booth, *A Rhetoric of Irony* (Chicago: University of Chicago Press, 1974). See also Douglas Muecke, *The Compass of Irony* (London: Methuen, 1969).

somehow subversive, ambiguous, endlessly deferring meaning and resolution, 'opening out vistas of chaos'.[11] For Booth, irony has most often been 'intended, but covert, stable and localized' (p. 7). It serves most often to dismantle one literal meaning in order then to rebuild another meaning in place of the first: 'once a reconstruction of meaning has been made [after the literal meaning has been demolished], the reader is not then invited to undermine it with further demolitions and reconstructions . . . It does not say, "There is no truth" ' (p. 6). And the process is none the less sophisticated for having an identifiable endpoint, a truth to convey. Levi too is insistent that his irony does not leave him with nothing firm to say: on the contrary, the former alerts his reader to the latter, whilst marking the latter as difficult, open to further stable adjustments.

Booth sets great store by two consequences of this stable process, both of which are powerfully applicable to Levi also. First, it can produce a particular form of knowledge, based on a Socratic acknowledgement of the limits of the knowable (pp. 274–5), and also on the potential falsifiability of the ironic speech acts at its source (pp. 14–19). As we have seen in other contexts, Levi's ethics are also closely bound up with notions of both limit (Chapter 5) and falsifiability (Chapter 6). Secondly, and as a consequence of the first, it creates strong bonds of community through the process of 'reconstructing' out of irony.[12] And once again, we know from Part III above that Levi too invests heavily in commonality and community in his ethics. Describing his own working model of the reconstructive processes of irony (pp. 10–12), Booth notes:

I see that it completes a more astonishing communal achievement than most accounts have recognized. Its complexities are, after all, shared: the whole thing cannot work at all unless both parties to the exchange have confidence that they are moving together in identical patterns. The

[11] Booth, *A Rhetoric of Irony*, p. ix.

[12] Irony and community in the form of friendship are closely linked in Booth's work, as his later book *The Company We Keep* (Berkeley and Los Angeles: University of California Press, 1988; referred to in Chapter 10) makes clear. Guido Almansi makes the same link between irony and friendship in *L'amica ironia* (Milan: Garzanti, 1986), but Almansi is a reveller in irony's infinite, ludic ambiguity: his hostility to Manzoni's irony as flat and pedantically moralistic, would, I suspect, be applied to Levi as well.

wonder of it is not that it should go awry as often as it does, but that it should ever succeed. (p. 13)[13]

But the general flexibility and adaptability of Levi's fluid inter-rogation of his world means that in a crucial sense he is less narrow than Booth, whose irony depends for its effectiveness on tightly shared assumptions ('identical patterns') between reader and writer. For Levi, by contrast, the very core focus of his ironic enquiry is the tenability and adjustability of such common assumptions (Chapter 9) when confronted with the experience of Auschwitz. In other words, he ironizes one of the key preconditions of irony itself, loosening the consonance neces-sary for it to work its cognitive and communal modulations. Thus Levi not only creates community through irony and uses community to create irony, but also uses irony to set out a trajectory of change, of shared ethical evolution. This turning of irony in on itself as a means to doubt and self-questioning is a feature Levi picks out in a review of a book by the science-writer Roberto Vacca,[14] whom Levi compares to Swift and Butler:

è tipico della migliore ironia ironizzare su se stessa, cancellando o sfumando impercettibilmente i propri confini, in modo da suscitare nel lettore un dubbio persistente e salutare (I. 1225)
(it's typical of the best irony to ironize on itself, erasing or imperceptibly blurring its own boundaries, so as to evoke in the reader a persistent, healthy doubt)

And its communal aspect, the shared evolution between writer/text and reader, is neatly captured in an image that Levi uses in the preface to *L'altrui mestiere* to describe the symbiotic

---

[13] On reconstruction see also Booth, *A Rhetoric of Irony*, 33–47, 233–76. On irony and knowledge, see ibid. 14–19. There has been a significant return in theoretical work on irony to the potential for ethical communities created by and creating irony. See, for exam-ple, Gary Handwerk, *Irony and Ethics in Narrative. From Schlegel to Lacan* (New Haven: Yale University Press, 1985); Linda Hutcheon, *Irony's Edge. The Theory and Politics of Irony* (London: Routledge, 1995), who echoes Booth on community in her chapter 'The Miracle of Ironic Communication' (pp. 89–101; and see also pp. 44–56); and Richard Rorty, *Contingency, Irony, and Solidarity* (Cambridge: Cambridge University Press, 1989).

[14] Vacca, a friend of Levi's and a working engineer, had been the author of a best-sell-ing book on the grim future of technological societies, *Medioevo prossimo venturo* (Milan: Mondadori, 1971). Levi is here reviewing Vacca's book on Italo-English, *Parliamo itangliano*, published under the mock-pseudonym Giacomo Elliot (Milan: Rizzoli, 1978).

give-and-take possible between literature and science: 'un mutuo trascinamento' (II. 632; 'a mutual carrying along').[15]

Concrete instances of Levi's irony are not hard to find in the *œuvre*, well beyond the preface to *Se questo è un uomo*. Indeed, many of the instances adduced in previous chapters to illustrate the workings of other ordinary virtues enter the considered, challenging realm of the ethical by way of irony. To recall a handful: in Chapter 3, it was noted how the title of the crucial chapter of *Se questo è un uomo*, 'Al di qua del bene e del male', was ironic, echoing and reversing Nietzsche and thereby setting the chapter (and the *Lager*) on an enigmatic borderline between moral and amoral worlds, questioning the nature of the boundary between them. In Chapter 6, as an important corollary to Levi's reflections on grand themes of trial and error, victory and defeat, it was noted how he carefully deflated his own at times grandiose or pious tone, for example through Sandro's native ironic wit (which sounds highly Boothian in nature):

Sandro mi ascoltava, con attenzione ironica, sempre pronto a smontarmi con due parole garbate e asciutte quando sconfinavo nella retorica (I. 775) (Sandro listened to me, with ironic attention, always quick to deflate me with two graceful, terse words whenever I spilled over into rhetoric)

Chapters 7 and 9 both relied heavily on a pattern of juxtaposition of different scales or idioms, the dismantling and reassembling of assumptions, values, points of view by way of a more or less comic deflation of expectation. Thus we saw how 'Il sesto giorno', by rewriting Genesis in a bureaucratic key, comically and ironically rewrote the question 'what is a man?'; how 'Una buona giornata', through a set of rather melancholic ironies on the nature of unhappiness and suffering, adjusted the datum of common sense that had been thrown out at the start of the chapter; or how Levi rejected the label of prophet, whilst also reluctantly and ironically accepting it in order to show its limitations, to dismantle its privileges (reflecting a larger, probing scepticism about certainty and system in general). And so on.

It is no coincidence to find irony working away just beneath the surface at the *loci* of other ordinary virtues. For it seems to be

[15] The phrase brings to mind the crucial process of ethical evolution towards judging between text and reader that Booth calls 'coduction' (*The Company We Keep*, 70–5).

part and parcel of irony's efficacy to work metaethically, as a device through which other ethical questions are opened up, made resonant for others, and pondered, by making us realize that he is talking about something other than, or larger than seems apparent at first. And for this reason, as well as for reasons of Levi's extraordinarily rich fascination with language, the seedbed of his irony needs to be searched out in words, turns of phrase, images, and idioms, in the microtextual humus of his writing. Modulating the language in which something is said creates comedy, but it also, in the shift of attitude and in the defamiliarization that it brings, ironizes. And it does so with concision and brevity (a precondition of wit). Thus Simpson is rendered both a comic fool and an ironic symbol of the dangers and pretensions of both commerce and science when he talks as a mock-modern Prometheus, as we saw in Chapter 8: 'Una vecchia storia, vero? Inventi il fuoco e lo doni agli uomini, poi un avvoltoio ti rode il fegato per l'eternità' ('Pieno impiego', I. 527; 'It's an old story, no? You invent fire and give it to man, and then a vulture gnaws at your liver for eternity'). On foundations such as these the larger ironies and, with them, several other virtues are built.

Perhaps the best 'open' illustration of all of the way in which the microtextual level sets up the possibility of larger ironic reflection is a particular stylistic tic of Levi's used to great effect throughout his work, especially (but not exclusively) at moments of high narrative or moral tension: the incision. Here is a sample from a range of works, some of which we have already encountered in earlier chapters:

È anche lui un Doktor: non in chimica bensí (ne pas chercher à comprendre) in glottologia; tuttavia è lui il capolaboratorio (*Se questo è un uomo*, I. 136)
(He is a Doktor too: not of chemistry but (ne pas chercher à comprendre) in linguistics; yet he is the head of the lab)

Distruggere l'uomo è difficile, quasi quanto crearlo: non è stato agevole . . . ma ci siete riusciti, tedeschi (*Se questo è un uomo*, I. 146)
(To destroy a man is difficult, almost as much as to create one: it has not been easy . . . but you Germans have managed it)

Forse me lo raccontò in buona fede (Gilberto è sempre in buona fede), . . . ('Alcune applicazioni del Mimete', *Storie naturali*, I. 462)
(Maybe he told me in good faith (Gilberto is always in good faith), . . .)

P. era uñ vecchio scettico e ironico, nemico di tutte le retoriche (per questo, e solo per questo, era anche antifascista), intelligente, ostinato, ed arguto . . . (*Il sistema periodico*, I. 764)

(P. was an old man, sceptical and ironic, an enemy of all forms of rhetoric (for this reason, and this reason only, he was also an anti-Fascist), intelligent, obstinate, and cunning . . .)

'. . . ma sul lavoro, e mica solo sul lavoro, se non ci fossero delle difficoltà ci sarebbe poi meno gusto dopo a raccontare . . .' (*La chiave a stella*, I. 1071)

('. . . at work, and not only at work either, if there were no problems there'd be less fun telling about them after . . .')

l'intera umanità d'oggi [è] condannata e abituata a vivere in un mondo in cui tutto sembra stabile e non è, in cui spaventose energie (non parlo solo degli arsenali nucleari) dormono un sonno leggero. ('Stabile/instabile', *L'altrui mestiere*, II. 781)

(today the whole of humanity [is] doomed, inured to living in a world in which everything seems stable and it is not, in which terrifying powers (and I am not only talking about nuclear arsenals) are sleeping lightly.)

L'assedio della violenza e della turpitudine esiste, e si fa sempre piú stretto. Chi non ha buone difese ne viene contagiato già oggi, e non solo nei sogni ('I nostri sogni', *Racconti e saggi*, II. 932)

(We are besieged by violence and baseness, and the siege grows ever tighter. Those without good defences are already contaminated by it today, and not only in their dreams)

Al ricercatore (e chi non è ricercatore?) il mondo si presenta come un vasto intrico di simboli: sta a lui ritrovarne l'interpretazione ('Roulette dei batteri', *Racconti e saggi*, II. 951)

(To the researcher (and which of us is not a researcher) the world presents itself as a vast web of symbols: it is up to him to find the correct interpretation)

Il discorso sul privilegio (non solo in Lager!) è delicato . . . (*I sommersi e i salvati*, II. 1002)

(The issue of privilege (and not only in the camps!) is a delicate one . . .)

Gli scopi della vita sono la difesa ottima contro la morte: non solo in Lager. (*I sommersi e i salvati*, II. 1108)[16]

(The aims of life are the best defence against death: and not only in the Lager.)

---

[16] Cf. Levi's 1949 letter to the Trieste-Jewish poet Umberto Saba, praising his book *Scorciatoie* (Milan: Mondadori, 1946): 'vi ho ritrovato molto del mondo. Non del Lager, voglio dire: meglio, non solo del Lager' (quoted in Cavaglion, *Primo Levi*, 18; 'I found much of my world in it. Not of the *Lager*, I mean: or rather, not only of the *Lager*').

This sample gives us a good indication of the range of tone available to Levi in the use of this simple device: the last two instances alone have the same phrase used first with exclamatory emphasis and then with solemn reflectiveness; and there is also sarcasm, mockery, admonition, and self-consciousness on display. Several are explicit models of Booth's dismantling and reconstructing irony: thus, in the quotation from 'Alcune applicazioni del Mimete' in *Storie naturali*, the incision seems literally to confirm and amplify the main clause—Gilberto speaks in good faith—but the very redundancy of the confirmation (why say it twice?) tells us that this is not meant literally, and thus inverts our reading of both parts of the sentence. Of course, this circling around contributes to Gilberto's status in the story as comic but also complex antihero, both ingenious amateur scientist and arrogant breaker of boundaries. Others use irony as a way to make us pause and question, and so reinforce rather than dismantle the initial statement: thus in the first example from *Se questo è un uomo*, the incision 'ne pas chercher à comprendre' picks up on a terrible lesson from earlier in the book, tells us not to question why a linguistician should be in charge of the lab, but of course in doing so forces us precisely to question, to note the perversity and connect it to other systemic absurdities in the camp world.

The most consistent and most consistently ethical effect of these incisions is to act as bridges between different worlds or different scales, as points of ethical suture. Thus 'Roulette dei batteri' connects Levi's specific interest in science and the patterns of research within it to a possible virtue of any life, that of 'research', of probing enquiry into the world and others. Or the description of P. in *Il sistema periodico* connects the closed world of the lab to the outside world of the Fascist regime, but in a way that underlines the complex multiplicity of often banal motivations and character quirks, as much as ideologies, that divided Fascists and anti-Fascists. But most importantly, the larger number of these incisions allows us to move back and forth in two particular directions, between the *Lager* and the everyday world of experience on the one hand, and between the specific and the general on the other. Both extracts from *I sommersi e i salvati* project large questions—power, suicide, and life's purpose—out from the strange specificities of the camp to more recognizable worlds, insisting that the two are connected, although refusing to simplify the connection. The

extract from *L'altrui mestiere* and even the one from *La chiave a stella*
move surreptitiously perhaps in the other direction, marking
echoes of the camps in the outside world. And as we saw in Chapter 8, the ironic incision at the climax of 'L'ultimo' ('... quasi
quanto crearlo ...'), in moving from the scene of an execution to
a parodic evocation of Genesis and creation myths and back again,
is powerfully resonant for a dense line of ethical enquiry in Levi
which moves nimbly between science, myth, religion, and responsibility. Indeed, this function of the incision amounts to a sort of
'degree zero' dynamic for our entire investigation of Levi as ethical writer, since the positing of a bond of a dense, but active kind
between the extraordinary *univers concentrationnaire* and the ordinary world of Levi's here and now is the first building-block of
this study. The sudden moments of transition offered by these
ironic incisions open up vistas of comprehension, later filled out in
ways we have seen throughout this book.

One further aspect of this device is worth noting as part and
parcel of the efficacy of ironic moves for facilitating ethical moves,
and that is its oral quality. We saw in Chapter 11 how there was a
link between the oral storytelling traditions tapped into and
analysed by Walter Benjamin and the rather unusual spoken quality of Levi's storytelling. As several of his most acute critics have
noted, there is in Levi's writing (and indeed even in the style and
syntax of his speaking, in interviews and the like) a strange mix of
formality and restraint on the one hand and a direct, clear orality
on the other.[17] Incisions, in their quick change of direction and
subject matter and in their frequent suspension of grammatical
sequence, are often also markers of the oral side to Levi's language;
and indeed ironic moves in general tend in that direction, as they
implicitly step out from the surface of the text to nod to the reader
and nudge us in new directions (hence the extension of irony into
the sphere of dramatic irony). Both the assumption of an alert,
listening reader and the appeal to the latter in an oral idiom root
the ironic turn of phrase in dialogue, another cardinal feature of
Levi's ethical writing. And if we return to the example given

---

[17] See Chapter 11. On the formality or writerliness of Levi's apparently oral style, see C.
Cases, 'L'ordine delle cose e l'ordine delle parole', in E. Ferrero, ed., *Primo Levi: un'antologia della critica* (Turin: Einaudi, 1997), 5–33 [5–14]; and M. Belpoliti, 'Animali e fantasmi',
in P. Levi, *L'ultimo natale di guerra* (Turin: Einaudi, 2000), 129–41 [133].

above from *Il sistema periodico* of the character-sketch of Professor
P., we can extend the oral aspect of Levi (and by association also
the ironic aspect) still further. The description of P. shares a quality often found in Levi's initial presentation of characters, that is a
rolling, rhythmic, continually self-adjusting movement of adjectives and adjectival phrases, often mutually contradictory, as if
homing in on the best epithets to capture his individual human
qualities. Another rich example comes in the following description
of Cesare in *La tregua* quoted above in Chapter 8:

Cesare era un figlio del sole, un amico di tutto il mondo, non conosceva
né odio né disprezzo, era vario come il cielo, festoso, furbo e ingenuo,
temerario e cauto, molto ignorante, molto innocente e molto civile. (I.
270)
(Cesare was a child of the sun, a friend to everyone, incapable of hatred
or contempt, as varied as the sky, joyous, both cunning and innocent,
rash and cautious, very ignorant, very innocent, and very civilized.)

The exuberance on display here moves us closer to the matter of
Chapter 13 below, but it also has echoes of the ironic-oral quality
of Levi's incisions, as every new clause cuts in a new direction,
adds something new, qualifies or distinguishes, climaxing in a
series of outright oxymorons, which leave us spinning at the
contradictory and multifaceted nature of (the best) human character.[18]

The epigraph to this chapter, taken by Levi from Rabelais as the
key to the latter's wise humanism (the quotation continues, 'Pour
ce que rire est le propre de l'homme'), should perhaps have stood
as the epigraph to the following chapter, given Rabelais's status as
the master of pure joyous excess and voracious curiosity. But it
stands just as well here because the wit it displays through its
knowledge of human nature is, of course, also tinged with dark
irony. For both Levi and Rabelais know what is missing here, that
tears too are proper to man; and both know that the poignant,
'medicinal' value of laughter, of irony itself (Levi calls Rabelais
'buon medico anche quando scrive', II. 1426; 'a good doctor even
when he writes'), lies precisely in the humane intuition that wit in

[18] On these aspects of Levi's style, see P. V. Mengaldo, 'Lingua e scrittura in Levi', in
E. Ferrero, ed., *Primo Levi: un'antologia della critica*, 179–84 (on his adjectives as 'abbondante,
a festoni', p. 180), 233–7 (on oxymoronic pairs or other series).

both senses serves as a defence against and a window onto the literal, flat, heavy hand of suffering. As the beleaguered old Jewish commander Dov says of the Talmud in *Se non ora, quando?*, with all its ironic humour, absurdity, and wisdom, 'è come una minestra con dentro tutte le cose che un uomo può mangiare . . . Non è tanto buona, ma nutre' (II. 367; 'it's like a soup containing everything a man can eat . . . It doesn't taste that good, but it is nourishing').

PLAY

è filo teso per siti strani.
(Primo Levi)

In Chapter 6, a swathe of Levi's ethics was described, in the
Pavesian vocabulary he was fond of, as an 'ethics of maturity'.
Practical intelligence and the acknowledgement of its limits, openness and responsiveness to others, knowledge about the world, and
other virtues were all characterized as both cause and symptom of
growth into a sort of moral maturity. But as was also suggested
there, prior to this maturity, and in many ways a prerequisite of it,
was a certain child-like sense of unguided discovery and accident,
best summed up in the phrase 'la libertà di sbagliare' ('the freedom
to make mistakes'), used to capture the much-missed youthful
excitement of Levi and Sandro's rash mountain-climbing expedi-
tions 'to taste bear's meat'. In reality, however, the sequence from
childish play to adult virtue is as much ideal or imaginary as real,
as the latter never entirely supersedes the former. A powerful
residue of the child remains and flourishes in Levi, alongside his
more sober, mature virtues, alongside his reason and reasonableness and alongside his darkest meditations on the horrors of the
Holocaust, acting as a yeast without which the latter could seem
all too dry and flat. So important is this element of play in Levi that
it not only constitutes a further 'ordinary' virtue, but it also has
some claim to be the final such virtue, source of the single most
characteristic and resonant virtue of all in his work, a disposition
towards freedom. Through it, all the others can become light,
flexible vessels of reflection rather than heavy-handed prescriptions
or proscriptions. This chapter examines Levi's ethics of play.

The key text for charting this other Levi, the Levi of diversion
and pleasure, is undoubtedly the 1986 collection *L'altrui mestiere*,
an extraordinarily rich display of Levi's culturally and intellectually

eclectic curiosity.[1] Four essays in particular give us the contours
we need: they are (in the order they are treated here) 'Il rito e il
riso', 'Le parole fossili', 'François Rabelais', and 'La *Cosmogonia* di
Queneau' (II. 795–9, 819–22, 644–7, 766–9).

'Il rito e il riso' is a good place to start, not this time for its
immersion in Judaic lore or humour but instead for its paean to a
certain restrained disorder at large in the world:

. . . le contraddizioni [sono] un ingrediente immancabile della vita; e la
vita è regola, è ordine che prevale sul Caos, ma la regola ha pieghe,
sacche inesplorate di eccezione, licenza, indulgenza e disordine. Guai a
cancellarle, forse contengono il germe di tutti i nostri domani (II. 798)
(. . . contradictions [are] an unfailing ingredient of life; and life is rule,
order that prevails over Chaos, but the rule has weaknesses, unexplored
corners of exception, licence, indulgence, and disorder. Woe betide
attempts to cancel them, they contain perhaps the seeds of all our tomor-
rows)

The pattern Levi sketches here is worth underlining since it recurs
persistently in other spheres of his work also: a predominant sense
of rule and regularity made more complex and more rich by a
margin of disorder. At the margin, the point of transition, a harder,
higher clarity is to be found. It is the same pattern as subtends
much of his science-fiction (with echoes of the *Lager*), the rule of
scientific or social progress complicated by the blip, the defect, the
'vizio di forma' which reveals the deeper dangers and truths of
science or society; or the rule encountered in *Il sistema periodico* of
material properties rendered wild and unpredictable, but all the
more instructive, by the slightest molecular difference or impurity;
or, sticking with molecules, the rooting of the predictable, stable
structures of matter in the strange asymmetry that is the prime
cause of the evolution of life itself ('L'asimmetria e la vita', II.
1231–41); or again, in Levi's thinking about the Holocaust and
communication, the rule of language and its communicability
complicated by the challenges of communicating the contradictory extremes of the *Lager* which then reveal unknown sides to
language and unfathomed levels of understanding of the camps. In
all these instances, there is in some necessarily unpredictable way a

---

[1] On curiosity in Levi, see G. Poli and G. Calcagno, *Echi di una voce perduta* (Milan:
Mursia, 1992), 63–4; and Italo Calvino's remarkable review of *L'altrui mestiere*, 'I due
mestieri di Primo Levi', *La repubblica*, 6 Mar. 1985.

pay-off to be had from experimenting with stories, elements, languages at the point where they spill over into complexity or contradiction. And precisely because this eventual ethical-cognitive pay-off is something of a item of faith for Levi, he can indulge in the sheer pleasure of teasing out the contradictions, training the mind to encompass complexities, enjoying the mastery of both order and disorder, confident that it will yield results in due course. 'Il rito e il riso' celebrates that phase of pleasurable enigma, 'il fascino della *subtilitas*, del gioco disinteressato dell'ingegno' (ibid.; 'the fascination of *subtilitas*, of the unmotivated play of wit'). In a sense, then, this undirected, eclectic pleasure reclaims the (apparently) 'useless'—which in Chapter 4 was so darkly negative, an essence of Nazi anti-ethics—for the good.

'Le parole fossili' adds further layers to Levi's indulgence in the pleasurably useless. Levi is delighted to discover that a linguistic connection he had made in passing decades earlier between a word in Hebrew and a word in Piedmontese dialect (they seem to share the same word for 'house') is confirmed and explained in an etymological dictionary. Two pleasures converge here: the pleasure of rummaging through the disordered mental 'storeroom' of useless curios and curiosities—'per decenni mi sono tenuta in corpo questa curiosità frammista a innumerevoli altre, nel grande serbatoio dei perché senza risposta' (II. 819; 'for decades I have kept this curiosity to myself, mixed in with innumerable others, in the large reservoir of questions without answers')—and the pleasure of the chance resolution, by serendipity we might say echoing Chapter 5, of one of those 'perché'—'mi sono sentito pervadere da un'allegrezza altrettanto puerile' (ibid.; 'I felt pervaded by an equally boyish happiness'). The pleasure is in the first instance one of connection, between the two words and between that near-forgotten connection and the leafing through of the etymological dictionary. In Chapter 10, we saw an image of geometrical connection (a chord cutting between two points of a parabola) as a metaphor for human encounter and friendship in Levi; and here we can see a parallel idea of arbitrary connection (connectivity) as a source of play and pleasure. The same image produces the most elaborate of all Levi's games with words, the bilingual pseudo-palindrome that crowns the virtuoso palindromic story 'Calore vorticoso': '*in arts it is repose to life: è filo teso per siti strani*' (II. 103). The English is shaky, but Levi's meaning is clear:

strange, serendipitous connections are art's means to 'repose', to diversion from the travails of life.[2]

'Le parole fossili' goes on to expand on the child–like curiosity which is so important for Levi, coming close to a definition (and a confession) of pure diversion ('puro divertimento: il diletto incontaminato dei dilettanti', I. 820; 'pure diversion: the uncontaminated delight of amateurs'), espied from the margins, at an oblique angle to central, ordered reality:

preferisco orecchiare che ascoltare, spiare dai buchi di serratura invece di spaziare sui panorami vasti e solenni; preferisco rigirare tra le dita una singola tessera invece di contemplare il mosaico nella sua interezza. . . .

È certamente un vizio, ma tra i meno nocivi; al di fuori della lettura, si manifesta nella tendenza a fare le cose che non si sanno fare; cosí operando, può anche capitare che si impari a farle, ma questo è un accidente, un sottoprodotto: il fine principale è il tentativo in sé, il libertinaggio, l'esplorazione. (ibid.)

(I prefer eavesdropping to listening, spying through keyholes to ranging over vast, solemn panoramas; I prefer turning over a single tile in my hand to looking over the mosaic in its entirety. . . .

It is certainly a failing, but a harmless one; beyond my reading, it manifests itself in a tendency to do things I don't know how to do; in this way, I might just learn how to, but that would be an accident, a side-effect. The principal end is the attempt in itself, the libertinage, the exploration.)

Of course, there are echoes here of the observer's curiosity which more than once Levi noted as a contributor to his survival in Auschwitz: 'Può stupire che in Lager uno degli stati d'animo piú frequente fosse la curiosità' (II. 873; 'It might come as something of a surprise that one of the most common states of mind in the

---

[2] For this and all Levi's wordplay, see S. Bartezzaghi, 'Cosmichimiche', in M. Belpoliti, ed., *Primo Levi* (Milan: Marcos y Marcos, Riga 13, 1997), 267–314; and G. Dossena, *La zia era assatanata* (Rome: Theoria, 1988). The palindrome is, of course, a ludic version of the ethical reversals of perspective seen in Chapter 7. There and here, reversal is an essentially comic, carnivalesque device (linking Levi back to Bakhtin's Rabelais (*Rabelais and his World* (Cambridge, Mass.: MIT Press, 1968): cf. his comments on Belli in *La ricerca delle radici*, II. 1481). The wordplay also links Levi to Georges Perec (although A. Cavaglion, 'Asimmetrie', in Belpoliti, ed., *Primo Levi* (Riga 13), 228, is not convinced by the comparison). Perec and Levi share a fascination with language games, systems of classification, and apparently rational, mechanical systems which have flaws, gaps, and therefore hidden resonances (cf. Perec's *W ou le souvenir d'enfance, La Disparition, La Vie mode d'emploi*); resonances which for both authors connect in some way to the trauma of the Holocaust (see D. Bellos, *Georges Perec. A Life in Words* (London: Harvill, 1993)).

Lager was curiosity'). And there are other signs in 'Le parole fossili' of Levi replaying in upbeat rhythm some of his more minor, 'sober' virtues. In more than one chapter above, for example, the preference for the small-scale and particular over the general and systematic (and the careful, dialectical contraposition of the two) was marked down as a cardinal feature of his ethics. Here that microcosmic tendency is replayed as a source of pure and child-like diversion, playing with the tiny mosaic fragment, naughtily playing hide-and-seek with the world. Similarly, the amateur ('a fare le cose che non si sanno fare'), chance-driven ('un accidente') nature of these pleasures both echoes and reverses Levi's ethics of intelligence and the useful, and his enquiries into luck that we have encountered elsewhere. And the economy, the measured restraint and lack of excess of other virtues seems reversed in the meandering, inefficient, studiedly eclectic shape of this 'vice': this is what here (and again in the preface to *Racconti e saggi*, II. 859) he calls his 'libertinaggio' or, in the preface to *L'altrui mestiere*, his 'via serpeggiante' ('meandering way'), his 'cultura disordinata, lacunosa e saputella' ('disordered, patchy, and fake-learnèd culture'), his 'vagabondaggio di dilettante curioso' ('curious amateur's wander-ing') (all II. 631). Furthermore, there is a connection to be made between this intellectual 'vagabondaggio' and the picaresque geographical wanderings of both *La tregua* and *Se non ora, quando?*, two key texts for certain forms of exuberant humour as will be seen below. The link is made in passing in a mock-Manzonian end of one chapter of *La tregua*, where Primo and Cesare make plans: 'decidemmo per i giorni successivi un programma di massima, in cui avremmo unito l'utile al dilettevole, vale a dire gli affari al vagabondaggio' (I. 260; 'we decided on a general plan for the next few days, which would unite utility and pleasure, that is business and wandering'). The virtues of economy and play are here twinned and complementary opposites.

The third essay from *L'altrui mestiere*, on Rabelais, takes us deeper still into the realm of exuberance, lack of restraint, and excess.[3] Rabelais strikes us as so different in temperament from

---

[3] For other examples of Levi's fascination with excess and extremes see the contrast between the larger-than-life, unrestrained Gedale and his serious, sober woman Bella in *Se non ora, quando?* (II. 431); his narratology of animals, 'Romanzi dettati dai grilli' (II. 689–93); or the inclusion of Melville and the immense modern Italian novel *Horcynus Orca* by Stefano D'Arrigo in *La ricerca delle radici* (II. 1452–4, 1496–503).

Levi and yet few authors could compete with him for the intensity of Levi's attachment to both him, ' "mon maître" ' (II. 644),
and his colossal work, 'per metà buffonata epico-popolare, per
metà intriso della vigorosa e vigile consapevolezza morale di un
grande spirito del Rinascimento (ibid.; 'half epic-popular buffoon-
ery, half shot through with the vigorous, alert moral awareness of
a great Renaissance spirit'). Levi is paradoxically drawn to the very
excess and carnivalesque transgression in Rabelais that he eschews
elsewhere: 'siamo all'opposto della sapienza stoica del giusto
mezzo. L'insegnamemto rabelaisiano è estremistico, è la virtù
dell'eccesso' (II. 646; 'this is the very opposite of the stoic wisdom
of the just mean. Rabelais teaches extremism, the virtue of
excess'); his is a 'smisurata e lussureggiante epica' (II. 647; 'uncon-
tained and lascivious epic').[4] But within the larger-than-life canvas
of excesses, Levi teases out elements that are more familiar to us:
the rejection of the grand themes of epic poetry (love, death, God,
and destiny) for the tricks and tones of the fairground improviser
or the inventor (II. 645) echoes both Levi's abjuration of grand
truths and his fascination with the figure of the inventor. And in
the warm sketch of Panurge—the 'eroe a rovescio' ('the up-turned
hero'), the flawed, at times fraudulent alter ego of Rabelais and
Levi himself—we can hear echoes of several of Levi's consistent
ethical concerns: Panurge as complex and contradictory modern
man, with all his weaknesses, not the exemplary symbol but rather
the peculiar exemplum of mankind: 'non è esemplare, non è la
"perfection", ma è l'umanità in quanto cerca, pecca, gode e
conosce' (II. 646; 'he is not exemplary, he is not perfect, but he is
humanity in all its searching, sinning, enjoying, and knowing').
Hence the robust, secular, but universal conviction Levi finds in
Rabelais and adapts as a linchpin of his ethics that mankind, warts
and all, can reach 'virtue and knowledge' in the here and now:
'Dio esiste, ma nei cieli: l'uomo è libero, non predestinato, è
"faber sui" ' (II. 645; 'God exists but he is in the heavens: man is
free, not predestined, he is "faber sui" '). And the pure and impure
pleasures of Rabelais are constituent parts of the freedom envisaged in this pregnant dictum.

[4] Levi is as attracted to the scatological and sexual side of Rabelais as he is to the cerebral wordplay. For Levi's rather intense forays into stories of trangressive sexual desire, see
Chapter 8 note 13 above.

280   *Diversions*

Finally, we can turn to 'La *Cosmogonia* di Queneau', Levi's astonished reaction to Queneau's *Piccola cosmogonia portatile* (*Petite Cosmogonie portative*),[5] in which Levi finds the voice of a modern Lucretius, in the scientific vision, and a modern Rabelais, in the joyous, linguistically hyper-elaborate and ludic display of knowledge as poetry. Levi is left reeling—'attonito, rallegrato e con un po' di capogiro' (II. 766; 'amazed, cheered, and a little dizzy')— a puzzle in every line and inventive turn of phrase, 'un enigma, ora arguto, ora futile, ora denso di significati' (II. 767; 'an enigma, at times sharp, at others futile, at others heavy with meaning'). He sees both the translator (Sergio Solmi) and the interpreter (Italo Calvino) of the Italian edition as immersing themselves in the same world of games as the author, and the reader, if he or she is lucky, can do the same: 'alcuni [enigmi], l'autore stesso aveva amesso di non saperli piú spiegare, erano stati illuminazioni di un istante: ebbene, tanto meglio per il lettore amante del gioco, potrà magari venirne a capo lui' (II. 768; 'for some [of the mysteries] even the author admitted he no longer remembered the explanations, they had been instantaneous illuminations: well, so much the better for the game-loving reader, maybe he can work them out'). As in Rabelais, the play is never quite whimsy, however. It is always projected towards a cognitive dimension: comedy obliquely breaks down barriers of specialist knowledge between the two cultures in ways that direct explication cannot. Thus the poem is always both serious and comic, 'eterodosso, barocco, ma fondamentalmente serio', 'insieme solenne e buffone' (ibid.; 'heterodox, baroque, but basically serious', 'both solemn and clownish'). And this oblique, meandering path to knowledge gives a very particular gloss to the role and authority of the author, linking back to Levi's own reservations about the aura of the writer (and the survivor), to his Socratic acknowledgement of the limits of knowledge, and to his investment in flexibility above all. He translates some lines from Queneau:

'costui [l'autore] non ha nulla di didattico | che cosa didatterebbe dal momento che non sa quasi nulla?' È una delle chiavi dell'opera. Non la

---

[5] See also 'Calvino, Queneau e le scienze', II. 1344–6. Levi helped Calvino with some of the difficulties and puzzles of revising the translation of Queneau's work, as Calvino acknowledged (*Piccola cosmogonia portatile* (Turin: Einaudi, 1982), 162). See G. Bertone, 'Italo Calvino e Primo Levi', in *Il castello della scrittura* (Turin: Einaudi, 1999), 177–84.

scienza è incompatibile con la poesia, ma la didattica, cioè la cattedra sulla pedana, l'intento dogmatico-programmatico-edificante. (II. 769) ('he [the author] has nothing of the didactic | what could he didact given he knows almost nothing?' It is one of the keys of the work. It is not science that is incompatible with poetry, but didacticism, preaching *ex cathedra*, on a pedestal, the dogmatic-programmatic-edifying effect.)

This is a key to Levi's work and to his ordinary virtues as much as to Queneau. And that he takes it from Queneau, like Rabelais so different from himself temperamentally, is itself eloquent evidence of his own flexibility and responsiveness, as the opening of his essay suggests:

Ho sempre pensato che si deve scrivere con ordine e chiarezza; che scrivere è diffondere un messaggio, e che se il messaggio non è compreso la colpa è del suo autore . . . Dopo aver letto la *Piccola cosmogonia portatile* di Queneau (Einaudi: Torino 1982) mi vedo costretto a rivedere questi principî. (II. 766)

(I have always thought that it is a duty to write with order and clarity; that writing means spreading a message and that if the message is not understood, the fault is the author's . . . Having read Queneau's *Piccola cosmogonia portatile* I find I am forced to adjust these principles.)

The four essays from *L'altrui mestiere* give us a raft of features of Levi at play that can serve as a guide to the rest of his *œuvre*. Disorder, trangression, contradiction, serendipitous connection, meandering curiosity, childish joy, oblique and microcosmic spying, excess, exuberance, extremes: it is a strange and surprising gamut to run for a figure such as Levi, so apparently rooted (as he himself would often insist) in reason, calm, and clarity. A cluster of three further aspects of the realm of play, present but not predominant in the pieces from *L'altrui mestiere*, is worth following up briefly, for the clues they offer to the impact all this vitality might have on a way of looking at the world in Levi, itself a step towards the founding ethical question of how to act in the world, how to live. The three are games, theatre, and magic.

Games take us back to the child-rooted aspect of play. Stefano Bartezzaghi has carefully charted Levi's 'musa giocosa' ('playful muse')[6] in a series of stories and essays from *La tregua*, where some

---

[6] S. Bartezzaghi, 'Primo Levi giocatore', in E. Mattioda, ed., *Al di qua del bene e del male* (Milan: Franco Angeli, 2000), 129–42.

Italian children teach Russian soldiers a game modelled on the cycle-race, the 'giro d'Italia' (I. 371), through to his 1980s articles about chess (e.g. 'Gli scacchisti irritabili', II. 763–5, centred on the Karpov–Korchnoi world championship match). A group of stories in *L'altrui mestiere* and *Racconti e saggi* take Levi back to his or to an imagined childhood, where playing at or indeed watching others play games, traditional or invented, or sports is a means to playing out rivalries and forming friendships, initiation, learning about the world and creating formal matrices (the rules of the game) for understanding it. In both 'Un lungo duello' (II. 831–6) and 'Meccano d'amore' (II. 882–5), Levi recalls strange adolescent friendships which were in reality tense rivalries played out in sport, invented games (Levi proves hopeless at the striptease-in-class game invented by his burly friend Guido), and love. In other stories, childhood games are an early instance of the anthropological-zoological tendency in Levi: in 'Ranocchi sulla luna' (II. 890–3), summers in the country are filled with fascinated games with nature, including watching tadpoles grow into frogs, replaying puberty as the young Levi is living it; in 'L'internazionale dei bambini', he is intrigued by a survey of children's games which shows how their rules and rituals recur across cultures with astonishing regularity, even when they have no apparent 'primitive' purpose (training for hunting, and the like). And in 'Tornare a scuola' (II. 655–8), Levi the adult goes back to school, to learn formally the German that he knows informally from other circumstances: in the 'useless' game of learning for its own sake, Levi feels a return to the innocent games and social instincts of childhood:

[tornare a scuola] è anche gioco, teatro e lusso. Il gioco, cioè l'esercizio fine a se stesso, ma regolato e ordinato, è proprio da bambino; ma giocando a tornare a scuola si ritrova un sapore d'infanzia, delicato e dimenticato. (II. 658)[7]

([to go back to school] is also a game, a performance, a luxury. Playing, that is practising something as an end in itself, but in a regular, ordered way, is part of being a child; and playing at going back to school, the taste of childhood returns, delicate and long forgotten.)

---

[7] More than one of these games stories have connections to the Holocaust (the German of the language-learning; games learned in the Ukraine). There are parallels to be drawn here with Roberto Benigni's interesting, if deeply flawed replaying of the concentration camp as a child's game (as a mechanism for the child's survival) in his 1997 film *La vita è bella*.

As 'Tornare a scuola' suggests, childhood games are, among other things, exercises in role-play, in theatre. And another line in Levi's work sees him evoking the mysteries and pleasures of performance of various kinds as a source of pleasure. We saw above the element of the fairground performer that Levi taps into in Rabelais. The 'ventriloquism' of many of his later, comic poems and of a group of dialogues written near the end of his life, in all of which he adopts the voice or point of view of animals and plants, is strong evidence of this performative impulse.[8] The same could be said for aspects of storytelling in Levi, since the oral performance of the story with an audience of one or many is crucial to realizing its ethical, humane dimension, as we saw in Chapter 11 with the example of Tischler ('Lilít', II. 18–23), the opera-loving singer and performer who tells Levi the story of Adam's first wife with such verve, casting Levi in the role of incredulous listener. Indeed, there is a strong histrionic element to Levi's portrayal of Ashkenazi and Talmudic styles of dialogue and learning. He describes Gedale, the Chagallian, violin-playing partisan leader of *Se non ora, quando?*, in just such terms, contrasting him with the grim Russian Ulybin:

Dove Ulybin calcolava, Gedale si gettava come in un gioco. Mendel riconosceva in lui, ben fusi come in una lega pregiata, metalli eterogenei: la logica e la fantasia temeraria dei talmudisti; la sensitività dei musici e dei bambini; la forza comica dei teatranti girovaghi; la vitalità che si assorbe dalla terra russa. (II. 339)[9]

(Where Ulybin calculated Gedale threw himself into things like in a game. Mendel recognized in him, fused together as in a precious alloy, several different metals: the logic and fantasy of the Talmudists; the sensitivity of the musician and the child; the comic force of the wandering player; the vitality drunk in from the Russian soil.)

The contrast echoes that between Cesare and Mordo Nahum in *La tregua*, also set in that strange Russian-centred world. And indeed, several striking moments of *La tregua* are scenes of theatre

---

[8] See, for example, the poems 'I gabbiani di Settimo', 'Aracne', 'Vecchia talpa', 'Un topo', 'Agave', 'Meleagrina', 'La chiocciola', 'L'elefante', 'La mosca', 'Il dromedario' (II. 551, 562, 566, 569, 571–3, 577, 626–7), and also their origin in two much darker earlier poems, both entitled 'Il canto del corvo' (II. 524, 538). For the animal dialogues, see II. 1325–7, 1332–43.

[9] For Chagall's influence, see Poli and Calcagno, *Echi di una voce perduta*, 273; M. Cicioni, *Primo Levi* (Oxford: Berg, 1995), 124.

and performance, whether Cesare's mimes (I. 272, 322–3), the improvised, amateurish, but intensely joyful and liberating theatrical celebration of Victory Day (I. 280–1), or the climactic, spectacular variety review ('Teatro', I. 359–67), crowned by the announcement of the inmates' long-awaited repatriation and the extraordinary appearance of the great Bolshevik Timoshenko in a Fiat 500. Once again, throughout these scenes, there is a strong association of theatre with renewal and innocence (even in Cesare's use of mime for his dubious deals), and thus directly or indirectly with a rediscovery of childhood. And whilst this is in part escape from the horrors of recent experience—the truce of the book's title, or the 'vacanza' of one of its chapter titles—it is also a core part of the return to life that *La tregua* narrates.[10]

Childhood vitality also pervades the third and final element of play to trace through Levi's work, the element of magic and wonder. Days before the first moon-landings in 1969, Levi writes an interesting article ('La luna e noi', later in *L'altrui mestiere*, II. 648–50) in which he both celebrates the extraordinary scientific and human achievement and laments the loss of the moon as 'other world', as a site of fantasy, to be replaced by the moon as an end to be reached, a tool to be used (and indeed misused): 'siamo ormai assuefatti, come bambini viziati: il rapido susseguirsi dei portenti spaziali sta spegnendo in noi la facoltà di meraviglia, che pure è proprio dell'uomo, indispensabile per sentirci vivi' (II. 649; 'we are used to it all now, like spoiled children: the rapid sequence of messages from space is extinguishing in us the capacity for wonder, which is part of what it is to be human, indispensable to feel we are alive'). Later in the article, the sense of wonder is synonymous with poetry, as if Levi saw one of the tasks of writing as to revive the sense of awe (positive and negative, wonder and fear)[11] at the world. In a sense, all Levi's imaginings of science, invention, and transformation are, among other things, attempts to transmit or create wonder. As we saw in Chapters 4 and 8 above, the language of alchemy is crucial to Levi and to an understanding of his ethics, and here we can gloss the image a little further by

[10] On Levi's involvement with theatre and theatrical versions of his work, see L. Scarlini, 'Teatro', in Belpoliti, ed., *Primo Levi* (Riga 13), 485–99.

[11] There is an interesting line of meditation in Levi, as so often both ethical and zoological, on the workings and uses of fear: see especially 'Paura dei ragni', 'Bisogna di paura', and 'Eclissi dei profeti' (*L'altrui mestiere*, II. 755–8, 848–56).

linking it to wonder and to a sense of the miraculous or the magical. In doing so, we are once again witnessing Levi replaying another of his virtues, but almost stripping it of its direct utilitarian function; in this case, setting aside the imperative to trace, experiment with, and understand the modes of transformation and simply enjoying and seeing the virtue in the extraordinary surprise of the transformation. A good instance is Doctor Gottlieb in *La tregua* (I. 284–7, 299–305), who is surrounded by an aura of mystery as to his origins and how he survived Auschwitz (given his crippled arm), and who seems to heal Levi from a near-fatal bout of fever more as miracle-worker ('taumaturgo', I. 286) than as medic. Or, keeping the link with childhood, we could point to the shortest and most unassuming of all the stories in *Il sistema periodico*, 'Titanio' (I. 882–4). The plot is simple and fabulous and quite inconsequential: Felice draws a circle of chalk around the child Maria to stop her from getting near his wet paint; Maria is stuck in the circle as if by magic until Felice rubs it out. The self-evidence of the magic—'il cerchio era palesemente magico' (I. 883; 'the circle was quite clearly magical')—puts us neatly into the awestruck, creative, transformative world of the child, bound to the magic of chemistry by Maria's misunderstanding of the word 'Titanio' as a magician's promise 'ti taglio' ('I cut you'). Or, finally, we could note Levi's comment in the preface to *La ricerca delle radici*, as he looks over and stands back from his choices: 'Non avrei previsto, accingendomi al lavoro, che fra gli autori preferiti . . . i magici dovessero prevalere sui moralisti, e questi sui logici' (II. 1362–3; 'I would never have predicted when I started working on it that amongst my favourite authors, the magicians would win out over the moralists and the moralists over the logicians'). From what we have seen, we could perhaps qualify this observation by saying that, for Levi, the magic, the child-like, and the wondrous are themselves part of the foundations of the moral, just as they are of the 'logical' or scientific.

For all the exuberance on display thus far, the final step that makes play such a fundamental virtue still needs elucidating. The ethical core of play and the source of its status as a founding site for Levi's ethics becomes clearer when we see the virtue it expresses as not only one of pleasure (although pleasure for its own sake is one of its primary means) but also one of freedom.

As so often in Levi, the association of play to freedom is best made by way of a chain of language. In both *L'altrui mestiere* and *Racconti e saggi*, as quoted above, Levi describes his intellectual eclecticism as 'libertinaggio', a term which evokes licentiousness and vice, but which Levi uses more neutrally (although with an ironic tinge of transgression) to mean free- and flexible-thinking. It is not used casually, however: in *La chiave a stella* Levi paints a portrait of another libertine, *Libertino* Faussone, and Faussone, never one to leave anything implicit, explains to his listener at digressive length how he got his name:

'Lo sa qual è il mio nome di battesimo? Tino, come tanti altri: ma il mio Tino vuol dire Libertino. Mio padre veramente quando ha fatto la denuncia mi voleva chiamare Libero . . . ma col segretario comunale non c'è stato verso. . . . morale della favola, mio padre ha ripiegato su Libertino perché pover'uomo non si rendeva conto, si credeva che fosse lo stesso, che Libertino fosse come quando uno si chiama Giovanni e lo chiamano Giovannino; ma intanto Libertino io sono rimasto . . . Anche perché, passa un anno passa l'altro, a girare il mondo cosí come faccio io un po' libertino lo sono poi diventato sul serio. . . . Mio padre voleva chiamarmi Libero perché voleva che io fossi libero . . . di non lavorare sotto padrone . . .' ('Batter la lastra', I. 1016)[12]

('Do you know what I was christened? I'm called Tino, like a lot of people, but my Tino is short for Libertino. My father really wanted to call me Libero [Free] when he went to the register . . . but the local official was unbending . . . and the moral of the story, my father fell back on Libertino, because the poor man didn't realize, thought it was like when you're called Giovanni and you get called Giovannino; but anyway, Libertino stuck . . . And it's true that as the years have gone by, travelling round the world as I do, I suppose I really have become something of a libertine. . . . My father wanted to call me Libero because he wanted me to be free . . . not working for a boss . . .')

For all Faussone's laughing at his father's expense for confusing libertinage with liberty, he knows that he is indeed both free and libertine in his work, that it was in the end not so absurd to have had one stand for the other on his birth certificate. And Levi quite deliberately embraces the same 'confusion': his libertinage, his

---

[12] On Faussone's name, see G. Calcagno, 'Dante dolcissimo padre', in Mattioda, ed., *Al di qua del bene e del male*, 173; Cicioni, *Primo Levi*, 86. And cf. the contrast between real freedom and a freedom which is merely licence drawn by Leo Strauss in *Persecution and the Art of Writing* (see Chapter 3 note 13 above).

'vagabondaggio' is also a form of freedom. The 'libertà di sbagliare' from 'Ferro' which is so important and resonant for Levi's youth, for his celebration of Sandro and therefore of an entire set of values that he takes with him into adulthood, is one of a series of freedoms, almost a sort of decalogue of human rights, that turn up in his *œuvre*. The single, purest, and most powerful declaration of freedom in Levi is one we came across above, forged in the wise pleasures and transgressions of Rabelais's work: 'l'uomo è libero, non predestinato, è "faber sui" ' (II. 645). Freedom is here learned from play and forged in choice and self-determination, and the moment of choice is, of course, the ethical moment *par excellence*. It is the same freedom, the same ethical right of self-determination claimed by the Arunde in 'Verso occidente': 'preferiamo la libertà alla droga, e la morte all'illusione' (I. 587; 'we prefer freedom to drugs, death to illusion'). Bearing this in mind, we can feed other freedoms into the same ethical dimension.

Much of *La chiave a stella* is something of a celebration of the right or freedom to work, but also, through this, of freedom generally, as 'Levi' the narrator hypothesizes openly:

Il termine 'libertà' ha notoriamente molti sensi, ma forse il tipo di libertà piú accessibile, piú goduto soggettivamente, e piú utile al consorzio umano, coincide con l'essere competenti nel proprio lavoro, e quindi nel provare piacere a svolgerlo. (I. 1074)

(The term 'freedom' notoriously has many meanings, but perhaps the type of freedom that is most accessible, most personally enjoyed, and most useful to human society is the type that comes from being good at one's own work and so taking pleasure in carrying it out.)

As in Chapter 6, we can see here a rather strait-laced Levi, praising work for its socially useful aspect, but also, through work, a Levi reaching for a sense of freedom as subjective enjoyment, autonomy, and intelligent pleasure, open to all. The hypothesis also underlines the breadth of meaning that Levi sees in the term 'libertà', the underlying consistency across its many usages. In *Il sistema periodico* alone, alongside the youthful freedom to err, we come across 'la libertà sconfinata dell'invenzione' ('Uranio', I. 911; 'the boundless freedom of invention'), which Levi sees in the dull and fanciful storyteller Bonino, and which subtends both his own work on invention and his understanding of memory in *I sommersi e i salvati*. And in 'Oro' (I. 849–59), in the story of Levi's imprisonment in Aosta after his ill-fated efforts as a partisan, there is a powerful evocation of freedoms of landscape, nature, work (again), and, more loosely, of identity and family. Seeing Levi in prison, we are immediately reminded of Faussone's father in 'Batter la lastra' whose notions of freedom and autonomy for his son precede the story of his own time as a forced labourer in Germany. Levi in prison dreams, of course, of freedom: 'le cento cose splendide che se fossi tornato libero avrei potuto fare' (I. 855; 'the hundred splendid things I could do if I was ever free again'). He is put in a cell with a smuggler and gold-digger who comes to stand excruciatingly for those forms of freedom noted above: very much Faussone *avant la lettre*, he works at several jobs, smuggling, working the land, sifting the river for gold, 'nessuno sotto padrone . . . a me importa vivere libero' ('never working for anyone . . . I need to be free'); his skills are handed on from his father and fore-fathers, 'gente libera' ('free people'); and the memory of him, for Levi stuck in prison, is one of 'la sua vita precaria ma mostruoa-mente libera' (I. 857–9; 'his precarious but monstrously free life').

'Oro' inevitably propels us back to Levi in his other prison, in Auschwitz. The bridge is provided by the single Auschwitz story in *Il sistema periodico* (which follows on immediately after 'Oro'), 'Cerio', centred on Alberto who is a vessel for so many of Levi's ordinary humane virtues, even in the camps. The epithet Levi uses to capture his vital force is once again 'free', with a strong dose of wonder to echo the child-like freedoms we have been looking at above: 'Era un uomo di volontà buona e forte, ed era miracolosa-mente rimasto libero, e libere erano le sue parole e i suoi atti: non aveva abbassato il capo, non aveva piegato la schiena' (I. 863; 'He was a man of good, strong will and he had miraculously remained free, free in both his words and his acts: he had not lowered his head nor bent his back').

From several moments in *Se questo è un uomo*, we know, as if it needed guessing, that memories and dreams of freedom were extraordinarily powerful talismans, positive and negative, through-out Levi's eleven months in Auschwitz. And each moment under-lines how freedom is not only the literal freedom of survival, of leaving the camp: it is also a complex and weighty key to retain-ing humanity and to understanding the Final Solution. Three examples, all noted in previous chapters, touching respectively on classic Levian questions of happiness, dignity, and language, make the point:

poiché siamo tutti, almeno per qualche ora, sazi, cosí non sorgono litigi, ci sentiamo buoni, il Kapo non si induce a picchiarci, e siamo capaci di pensare alle nostre madri e alle nostre mogli, il che di solito non accade. Per qualche ora, possiamo essere infelici *alla maniera degli uomini liberi.* (I. 72, emphasis added; see Chapter 9)
(since we are all, at least for a few hours, full, we do not argue, we feel good, the Kapo does not feel like beating us, and we are able to think of our mothers and our wives, which we usually cannot. For a few hours, we can be unhappy just like free men.)

Da quel giorno, io ho pensato al Doktor Pannwitz molte volte e in molti modi. Mi sono domandato quale fosse il suo intimo funzionamento di uomo. . . . soprattutto, *quando io sono stato di nuovo un uomo libero, ho desiderato di incontrarlo ancora,* e non già per vendetta, ma solo per una mia curiosità umana.

Perché quello sguardo non corse fra due uomini; e se io sapessi spiegare a fondo la natura di quello sguardo, scambiato come attraverso la parete di vetro di un acquario tra due esseri che abitano mezzi diversi, avrei anche spiegato l'essenza della grande follia della terza Germania. (I. 101–2, emphasis added; see Chapter 1)
(From that day, I have thought of Dr Pannwitz many times and in many different ways. I have wondered about his innermost workings as a man . . . above all, once I had regained my freedom, I wished to meet him again, not for revenge but just out of human curiosity.

Because that look did not run from one man to another; and if I could get to the bottom of that look, exchanged as if across the glass of an aquarium between two beings living in two different worlds, I would have found also the essence of the great folly of the Third Germany.)

Noi diciamo 'fame', diciamo 'stanchezza', 'paura', e 'dolore', diciamo 'inverno', e sono altre cose. *Sono parole libere, create e usate da uomini liberi* che vivevano, godendo e soffrendo nelle loro case. (I. 119, emphasis added; see Chapter 3)
(We say 'hunger', we say 'tiredness', 'fear', and 'pain', but they are something different. They are free words, created and used by free men who lived in their own homes, in happiness and in suffering.)

In each case, the recourse to the terminology of freedom goes a long way beyond a simple desire to escape from a terrible prison. Freedom is imagined in turn as a thick spectrum between poles of happiness and unhappiness, as an engaged self-changing encounter with another on equal terms, and as a richly textured, self-defining mixture of pleasure and pain transmitted in language. And the wealth and complexity behind the term means that, potentially at least, freedom as a virtuous, but also messy, contingent end might contain all the evolving, self-doubting, intelligently analytical and childishly playful virtues that we have seen operating throughout this book.

To end on an etymological note would doubtless have pleased Levi: so if we return to what has emerged as the governing term of this chapter, 'libertinaggio', encompassing both the child-like curiosity and play of *L'altrui mestiere* and the autonomy and dignity of a chain of figures leading from Faussone and his father to the smuggler, Sandro, Levi in prison, Levi in Auschwitz, Alberto, and others, it is apposite to note that its Latin roots lie not only in 'liber' (free) but also and more closely in 'libertinus', the freedman, the former slave now enfranchised. Levi's ethics, as this book has argued throughout, are an ethics of the former slave, ever mindful of his experience of slavery and of its continued dangers, but fully enfranchised, attuned as a liberal citizen of the world. In other words, freedom is the ordinariness to which his ordinary virtues aspire.

BIBLIOGRAPHY

1. WORKS BY LEVI

(a) *Levi's collected works*

Opere, vols. I–II. ed. Marco Belpoliti (Turin: Einaudi, 1997). The fullest available bibliography of Levi's writings is at I. pp. ciii–cxv. Uncollected pieces are included in the miscellany sections ('Pagine sparse' and 'Appendici', I. 1107–372; II. 1155–527). Belpoliti describes some unpublished work in his notes, including the epistolary novel Levi was working on at his death (*Chimica per signore* or *Il doppio legame*), but none of this has been published as yet. (There is a radio-play, *Intervista aziendale* (Turin: RAI radiodramma, [1968?]), by P. Levi and C. Quartucci, which is not included in the miscellany by Belpoliti as Levi provided only the initial plot outline for the piece.)

(b) *Levi's published works*

For details on the publication of all Levi's books see the notes to *Opere* I and II.

In his lifetime Levi published the following books (first editions only, except where substantially new material was published for the first time in later editions):

Se questo è un uomo (Turin: De Silva, 1947; 2nd edition, Turin: Einaudi, 1958; with 'Appendice' from 1976; and in a theatrical version, co-authored by P. Marché, Turin: Einaudi, 1966).
La tregua (Turin: Einaudi, 1963) [published in some editions together with *Se questo è un uomo* after 1972].
Storie naturali (Turin: Einaudi, 1966) [until 1979 under the pseudonym Damiano Malabaila].
Vizio di forma (Turin: Einaudi, 1971).
L'osteria di Brema (Milan: Scheiwiller, 1975).
Il sistema periodico (Turin: Einaudi, 1975).
La chiave a stella (Turin: Einaudi, 1978).
Lilìt e altri racconti (Turin: Einaudi, 1981).

La ricerca della radici (Turin: Einaudi, 1981).
Se non ora, quando? (Turin: Einaudi, 1982).
Ad ora incerta (Milan: Garzanti, 1984) [incorporating *L'osteria di Brema*].
L'altrui mestiere (Turin: Einaudi, 1985).
I sommersi e i salvati (Turin: Einaudi, 1986).
Racconti e saggi (Turin: Editrice La Stampa, 1986) [republished and enlarged in 1997 as *Il fabbricante di specchi*].

Since his death, the following collections or collations have been published:

Opere, vols. I–III (Turin: Einaudi, 1987–9; introductory essays by Cesare Cases, Cesare Segre, and P. V. Mengaldo, all now in Ferrero, ed., *Primo Levi: un'antologia della critica*).
I racconti (*Storie naturali. Vizio di forma. Lilít e altri racconti*), ed. E. Ferrero (Turin: Einaudi, 1996).
L'ultimo natale di guerra, ed. M. Belpoliti (Turin: Einaudi, 2000) [containing stories written between 1977 and 1987, including those from *Racconti e saggi*].

Einaudi also published schools editions of several of Levi's books:

Se questo è un uomo, ed. with notes by P. Levi (1973).
La tregua, ed. with notes by P. Levi (1965).
Il sistema periodico, ed. N. Ginzburg, with notes by P. Levi (1979).
La chiave a stella, ed. G. L. Beccaria (1983); ed. G. Tesio (1992).

(c) *Books translated by Levi*

Chimica organica superiore, vols. I–IV, tr. P. Levi and G. Anglesio (Turin: Edizioni scientifiche Einaudi, 1955).
Douglas, M., *I simboli naturali. Sistema cosmologico e struttura sociale* (Turin: Einaudi, 1979).
Kafka, F., *Il processo* (Turin: Scrittori tradotti da scrittori, Einaudi, 1983).
Lévi-Strauss, C., *Lo sguardo da lontano. Antropologia, cultura, scienza a raffronto* (Turin: Einaudi, 1984).
——— *La via delle maschere* (Turin: Einaudi, 1985).
Presser, J., *La notte dei Girondini* (Milan: Adelphi, 1976).

(Levi also translated several poems for *Ad ora incerta* and extracts for *La ricerca della radici*; see II. 1582–9.)

(d) *Interviews with Levi*

The fullest available bibliography of Levi's interviews is at I. pp. cxvii–cxxvi. The following book-length interviews or collections of interviews have been published:

Single interviews

Camon, F., *Autoritratto di Primo Levi* (Padua: Nord-Est, 1987; later Milan: Garzanti, 1991).

Levi, P., *Le Devoir de mémoire* (Paris: Mille et une nuits, 1995) (in *The Voice of Memory*, 218–49).

—— and Regge, T., *Dialogo* (Milan: Edizioni di comunità, 1984; later Turin: Einaudi, 1987).

Spadi, M., *Le parole di un uomo. Incontro con Primo Levi* (Rome: Di Renzo, 1997).

Collections

Levi, P., *Conversazioni e interviste 1963–1987*, ed. M. Belpoliti (Turin: Einaudi, 1997): rev. and tr. as P. Levi, *The Voice of Memory. Interviews 1961–87*, ed. M. Belpoliti and R. Gordon (Cambridge: Polity, 2001).

Poli, G., and Calcagno, G., *Echi di una voce perduta. Incontri, interviste e conversazioni con Primo Levi* (Milan: Mursia, 1992).

(e) *Levi in English*

The first British editions of Levi's books appeared as follows (dates of American editions varied slightly in some instances):

If This is a Man, tr. Stuart Woolf (London: Orion Press, 1959).

The Truce, tr. Stuart Woolf (London: Bodley Head, 1965).

Shema. Collected Poems, tr. Ruth Feldman and Brian Swann (London: Menard Press, 1976).

The Periodic Table, tr. Raymond Rosenthal (London: Michael Joseph, 1985).

If Not Now, When?, tr. William Weaver (London: Michael Joseph, 1986).

Moments of Reprieve, tr. Ruth Feldman (London: Michael Joseph, 1986).

The Wrench, tr. William Weaver (London: Michael Joseph, 1987).

Collected Poems, tr. Ruth Feldman and Brian Swann (London: Faber and Faber, 1988).

The Drowned and the Saved, tr. Raymond Rosenthal (London: Michael Joseph, 1988).

Other People's Trades, tr. Raymond Rosenthal (London: Michael Joseph, 1989).

The Mirror Maker, tr. Raymond Rosenthal (London: Methuen, 1990).

The Sixth Day, tr. Raymond Rosenthal (London: Michael Joseph, 1990) (selections from *Storie naturali* and *Vizio di forma*).

The Search for Roots, tr. Peter Forbes (Harmondsworth: Penguin, 2001).

2. OTHER WORKS

The following Bibliography includes a number of entries not referred to in the body of the book but which are nevertheless pertinent to it.

Adamson, J., 'Against Tidiness: Literature and/versus Moral Philosophy', in Adamson, Freadman, and Parker, eds., *Renegotiating Ethics in Literature, Philosophy and Theory*, 84–110.

—— Freadman, R., and Parker, D., eds., *Renegotiating Ethics in Literature, Philosophy and Theory* (Cambridge: Cambridge University Press, 1998).

Adorno, T. and Horkheimer, M., *Dialectic of Enlightenment* (London: Verso, 1997; 1st edition 1947).

Agamben, G., *Quel che resta di Auschwitz. L'archivio e il testimone* (Turin: Bollati Boringhieri, 1998).

Alberoni, F., *L'amicizia* (Milan: Garzanti, 1984).

Almansi, G., *L'amica ironia* (Milan: Garzanti, 1986).

Améry, J., *At the Mind's Limits* (London: Granta, 1999; 1st German edition 1966).

Amis, M., *Time's Arrow. Or The Nature of the Offence* (London: Jonathan Cape, 1991).

Amsallem, D., 'Illuminista', in Belpoliti, ed., *Primo Levi* (Riga 13), 361–71.

Angress, R., 'Primo Levi in English', *Simon Wiesenthal Center Annual*, 3 (1988), 317–30.

Anissimov, M., *Primo Levi, ou la tragédie d'un optimiste* (Paris: Lattès, 1996), tr. and rev. as *Primo Levi. Tragedy of an Optimist* (London: Aurum Press, 1998).

Antelme, R., *L'Espèce humaine* (Paris: Gallimard, 1978; 1st edition 1947), in Italian as *La specie umana* (Turin: Einaudi, 1997).

Arendt, H., *Eichmann in Jerusalem. A Report on the Banality of Evil* (Harmondsworth: Penguin, 1992; 1st edition 1963).

Armour, P., 'Dante and Friendship' (Oxford: Pagett Toynbee Lectures in Dante, 1995).

Badhwar, N. Kapur, *Friendship: A Philosophical Reader* (Ithaca, NY: Cornell University Press, 1993).

Bailey, P., 'Introduction' to P. Levi, *The Drowned and the Saved*, tr. R. Rosenthal (London: Michael Joseph, 1988), pp. ix–xvii.

Bakhtin, M., *Rabelais and his World* (Cambridge, Mass.: MIT Press, 1968).

Baldissone, G., 'Primo Levi. Les camps, les lettres', *Études* (Oct. 1995), 385–96.

Baranski, Z., 'Comedia: Notes on Dante, the Epistle to Cangrande and Medieval Comedy', *Lectura Dantis*, 8 (Spring 1991), 26–55.

Bartezzaghi, S., 'Cosmichimiche', in Belpoliti, ed., *Primo Levi* (Riga 13), 267–314.

—— 'Primo Levi giocatore', in E. Mattioda, ed., *Al di qua del bene e del male*, 129–42.

G. Bassani, *Il giardino dei Finzi Contini* (Milan: Mondadori, 1980; 1st edition 1962).

Bauman, Z., *Modernity and the Holocaust* (Cambridge: Polity, 1989).

—— *Postmodern Ethics* (Oxford: Blackwell, 1993).

Baumgarten, M., 'Primo Levi's Periodic Art: *Survival in Auschwitz* and the Meaningfulness of Everyday Life', in R. Rohrlich, ed., *Resisting the Holocaust* (Oxford: Berg, 1998), 115–32.

Beckett, S., and Duthuit, G., 'Three Dialogues' (1949), in M. Esslin, ed., *Samuel Beckett* (Englewood Cliffs, NJ: Prentice Hall, 1965).

Bellos, D., *Georges Perec. A Life in Words* (London: Harvill, 1993).

Belpoliti, M., ed., *Primo Levi* (Milan: Marcos y Marcos, Riga 13, 1997).

—— 'Animali', in Belpoliti, ed., *Primo Levi* (Riga 13), 157–209.

—— *Primo Levi* (Milan: Bruno Mondadori, 1998).

—— 'Animali e fantasmi', in P. Levi, *L'ultimo natale di guerra* (Turin: Einaudi, 2000), 129–41.

—— 'Il falso scandalo', *La rivista dei libri*, 10 (1 Jan. 2000), 25–7.

Benjamin, W., 'The Storyteller. Reflections of the Works of Nikolai Leskov', in *Illuminations*, ed. H. Arendt, tr. H. Zohn (London: Jonathan Cape, 1970), 83–109; in Italian as 'Il narratore. Considerazioni sull'opera di Nikolai Leskov', in *Angelus Novus*, ed. R. Solmi (Turin: Einaudi, 1995), 247–74.

Bentham, J., *An Introduction to the Principles of Morals and Legislation* (Oxford: Oxford University Press, 1996; 1st edition 1789).

Berkowitz, P., *Virtue and the Making of Modern Liberalism* (Princeton: Princeton University Press, 1999).

Bernstein, M. A., *Foregone Conclusions. Against Apocalyptic History* (Berkeley and Los Angeles: University of California Press, 1994).

—— 'A Yes or a No' [review of M. Anissimov, *Primo Levi. Tragedy of an Optimist*], *New Republic*, 27 Sept. 1999 (consulted online).

—— 'Unspeakable no more', *Times Literary Supplement*, 5061 (3 Mar. 2000), 7–8.

Bertone, G., 'Italo Calvino e Primo Levi', in *Il castello della scrittura* (Turin: Einaudi, 1994), 177–211.

Bettelheim, B., *Surviving and Other Essays* (New York: Knopf, 1979).

Bhabha, H., 'The Other Question: Stereotype, Discrimination and the Discourse of Colonialism', in *The Location of Culture* (London: Routledge, 1994), 66–84.

Biasin, G., 'Our Daily Bread-pane-Brot-Broit-chleb-pain-lechem-kenyér', in Frassica, ed., *Primo Levi as Witness*, 1–20.

296   *Bibliography*

Bibliografia della deportazione (Milan: Aned/Mondadori, 1982).

Blanchot, M., *L'Amitié* (Paris: Gallimard, 1971).

—— *L'Écriture du désastre* (Paris: Gallimard, 1980).

Bobbio, N., *Trent'anni di storia della cultura a Torino (1920–1950)* (Turin: Cassa di Risparmio di Torino, 1977).

—— 'Addio a Primo Levi', *Nuova antologia*, 122/557/2162 (Apr.–June 1987), 202–4.

—— 'Primo Levi, perché', *Nuova antologia*, 123/559/2166 (Apr.–June 1988), 108–10.

—— *L'elogio della mitezza e altri scritti morali* (Milan: Pratiche, 1998).

Bodrato, A., 'Nel racconto la verità di Auschwitz', *Humanitas*, 44, NS 1 (Feb. 1989), 51–73.

Booth, W. C., *The Rhetoric of Fiction* (Chicago: University of Chicago Press, 1961).

—— *A Rhetoric of Irony* (Chicago: University of Chicago Press, 1974).

—— *The Company We Keep. An Ethics of Fiction* (Berkeley and Los Angeles: University of California Press, 1988).

Borges, J. L., 'Funes el memorioso', in *Prosa completa*, vol. II (Barcelona: Bruguera, 1985), 177–84.

Borri, G., *Le divine impurità. Primo Levi tra scienza e letteratura* (Rimini: Luisé, 1992).

Branca, V., *Boccaccio medievale* (Florence: Sansoni, 1991).

Bravo, A., and Jalla, D., eds., *La vita offesa. Storia e memoria dei Lager nazisti nei racconti di duecento sopravvissuti* (Milan: Franco Angeli, 1986).

—— —— 'Primo Levi: un uomo normale di buona memoria', *Passato e presente*, 18 (Sept.–Dec. 1988), 99–108.

—— —— eds., *Una misura onesta. Gli scritti di memoria della deportazione dall'Italia 1944–93* (Milan: Franco Angeli, 1994).

Brunazzi, M., and Fubini, A. M., *Gli ebrei dell'Europa orientale dall'utopia alla rivolta* (Milan: Edizioni di Comunità, 1985).

Buell, L., ed., *Ethics and Literary Study*, special issue of *PMLA* 114/1 (Jan. 1999), 7–96.

Bura, C., 'Primo Levi: *La chiave a stella*', *Gli annali. Università per stranieri*, 8 (1987), 111–80.

Caesar, A., 'Pirandello and the Drama of Creativity', in P. Collier and J. Davies, eds., *Modernism and the European Unconscious* (Cambridge: Polity, 1990), 215–29.

Caffaz, U., ed., *La difesa della razza*, monographic issue of *Il ponte* 34/11–12 (30 Nov.–31 Dec. 1978).

Cagliotti, L., *I due volti della chimica. Benefici e rischi* (Milan: Mondadori, 1979).

Calcagno, G., 'Dante dolcissimo padre', in Mattioda, ed., *Al di qua del bene e del male*, 167–74.

Calvino, I., 'I due mestieri di Primo Levi', *La repubblica*, 6 Mar. 1985.

Cannon, J., 'Canon-Formation and Reception in Contemporary Italy: The Case of Primo Levi', *Italica*, 69/1 (Spring 1992), 30–44.

Carasso, F., *Primo Levi. Le parti pris de la clarté* ([Paris?]: Belin, 1997).

Cases, C., 'Levi ripensa l'assurdo', *L'Indice dei libri del mese*, 3/7 (July 1986), 6–7.

—— 'L'ordine delle cose e l'ordine delle parole', *L'indice dei libri del mese*, 4/10 (Dec. 1987), 25–31 (later in Ferrero, ed., *Primo Levi: un'antologia della critica*, 5–33).

—— *Patrie lettere* (Turin: Einaudi, 1987), 137–50.

—— 'Ricordo di Primo Levi', in G. Folena, *Tre narratori: Calvino, Primo Levi, Parise* (Padua: Liviana, 1989), 99–103.

Cavaglion, A., ' "Argon" e la cultura ebraica piemontese', *Belfagor*, 43/5 (Sept. 1988), 541–62.

—— 'Il termitaio', *Asino d'oro*, 4 (1991) (now in Ferrero, ed., *Primo Levi: un'antologia della critica*, 76–90).

—— ed., *Primo Levi: Il presente del passato* (Milan: Franco Angeli, 1991).

—— *Primo Levi e 'Se questo è un uomo'* (Turin: Loescher, 1993).

—— ed., *Il ritorno dai Lager* (Milan: Franco Angeli, 1993).

—— 'La scelta di Gedeone: appunti su Primo Levi e l'ebraismo', *Journal of the Institute of Romance Studies*, 4 (1996), 187–98.

—— 'Asimmetrie', in Belpoliti, ed., *Primo Levi* (Riga 13), 222–9.

—— ed., *Primo Levi per l'ANED. L'ANED per Primo Levi* (Milan: Franco Angeli, 1997).

Cavell, S., 'Knowing and Acknowledging', in Mulhall, ed., *The Cavell Reader*, 46–71.

Celan, P., *Selected Poems*, tr. M. Hamburger (Harmondsworth: Penguin, 1990).

Cereja, F., 'Contre l'oubli', in P. Levi, *Le Devoir de mémoire* (Paris: Éditions Mille et une nuits, 1995), 73–81.

—— and Mantelli, B., *La deportazione nei campi di sterminio nazisti* (Milan: Franco Angeli, 1986).

Cesari, S., *Colloquio con Giulio Einaudi* (Rome: Theoria, 1991).

Cheyette, B., 'The Ethical Uncertainty of Primo Levi', in Cheyette and Marcus, eds., *Modernity, Culture and 'the Jew'*, 268–81.

—— and Marcus, L., eds., *Modernity, Culture and 'the Jew'* (Cambridge: Polity, 1998).

Cicioni, M. 'Bridges of Knowledge: Re-reading Primo Levi', *Spunti e ricerche*, 3 (1987), 54–94.

—— ' "Different Springs and Different Airs" : Primo Levi's Multiple Autography', *Menorah*, 3/2 (Dec. 1989), 20–31.

—— *Primo Levi. Bridges of Knowledge* (Oxford: Berg, 1995).

Cicioni, M. (as M. Risk), 'Razionalità e coscienza etica di Primo Levi', *Italian Studies*, 34 (1979), 122–31.

Clendinnen, I., *Reading the Holocaust* (Cambridge: Cambridge University Press, 1999).

Collotti, E., 'Leggendo il revisionismo di Primo Levi', *Belfagor*, 44/1 (31 Jan. 1989), 98–102.

Colombo, F., 'Primo Levi: chi parla, chi ascolta', in *Il destino del libro e altri destini* (Turin: Bollati Boringhieri, 1990), 122–8.

Comollo, G., 'Lo sterminio del senso. I "sommersi e i salvati" di Primo Levi', *Aut Aut*, NS 216 (Nov.–Dec. 1986), 11–21.

Critchley, S., *The Ethics of Deconstruction* (Oxford: Blackwell, 1992).

Dante, *La commedia*, in English as *The Divine Comedy*, tr. A. Mandelbaum (London: Everyman, 1992).

Davidowicz, L., *The Holocaust and the Historians* (Cambridge, Mass.: Harvard University Press, 1981).

Davis, C., *Levinas* (Cambridge: Polity, 1996).

——— 'Reviewing Memory: Wiesel, Testimony and Self-Reading', in H. Peitsch, C. Burdett, and C. Gorrara, eds., *European Memories of the Second World War* (Oxford: Berghahn, 1999), 131–40.

Debenedetti, G., *16 ottobre 1943* (Rome: Edizioni del Secolo, 1945).

De Ceccatty, R., 'Primo Levi: ne jugez pas', *Nouvelle Revue française*, 429 (Oct. 1988), 68–74.

Deguy, M., 'Primo Levi ou la banalité du bien', *Les Temps modernes*, 44/516 (July 1989), 158–70.

De Luca, V., *Tra Giobbe e i buchi neri. Le radici ebraiche dell'opera di Primo Levi* (Naples: Istituto grafico editoriale italiano, 1991).

De Marco, G., 'Primo Levi o la tentazione della poesia', *Testo*, 25 (1988), 95–104, later in *Pretesti dell'invenzione. Dall'ultimo Montale a Primo Levi* (Pisa: Giardini, 1995), 103–13.

Derrida, J., *La Politique de l'amitié* (Paris: Galilée, 1994).

Des Pres, T., *The Survivor* (New York: Oxford University Press, 1976).

Devoto, A., *Bibliografia dell'oppressione nazista fino al 1962* (Florence: Olschki, 1964).

——— *L'oppressione nazista. Considerazioni e bibliografia 1963–1981* (Florence: Olschki, 1983).

——— *Il comportamento umano in condizioni estreme. Lo psicologo sociale e il lager nazista* (Milan: Franco Angeli, 1985).

Dini, M., and Jesurum, S., *Primo Levi. Le opere e i giorni* (Milan: Rizzoli, 1992).

Dolza, D., *Essere figlie di Lombroso* (Milan: Franco Angeli, 1990).

D'Orsi, A., *La cultura a Torino tra le due guerre* (Turin: Einaudi, 2000).

Dossena, G., *La zia era assatanata* (Rome: Theoria, 1988).

Dragoni, U., *La scelta degli I.M.I. Militari italiani prigionieri in Germania (1943–1945)* (Florence: Le Lettere, 1996).

Ducci, T., ed., *I Lager nazisti. Per distruggere l'uomo nell'uomo* (Milan: Aned/Mondadori, 1983).

Easterling, P., 'Friendship and the Greeks', in Porter and Tomaselli, eds., *The Dialectics of Friendship*, 11–25.

Eberstradt, F., 'Reading Primo Levi', *Commentary* (Oct. 1985), 41–7.

Eco, U., *Serendipities* (London: Weidenfeld and Nicolson, 1999).

Epstein, A., 'Primo Levi and the Language of Atrocity', *Bulletin for the Society for Italian Studies*, 20 (1987), 31–8.

Farinelli, G., 'Primo Levi e la difesa dell'uomo umano: quale insegnamento?', *Otto/Novecento*, 19/1 (Jan.–Feb. 1995), 147–66.

Feinstein, H., 'Out of Auschwitz', *Guardian*, 29 Aug. 1996.

Feldman, R., 'Moments of Reprieve', *Rassegna meusile di Israel*, 55/2–3 (May–Dec. 1989), 205–14.

Felman, S., and Laub, D., *Testimony. Crises of Witnessing in Literature, Psychoanalysis and History* (London: Routledge, 1992).

Felstiner, J., *Paul Celan: Poet, Survivor, Jew* (New Haven: Yale University Press, 1995).

Ferrero, E., 'Introduzione', in P. Levi, *I racconti* (Turin: Einaudi, 1996), pp. vii–xx.

—— ed., *Primo Levi: un'antologia della critica* (Turin: Einaudi, 1997).

Finkelstein, N., *The Holocaust Industry. Reflections on the Exploitation of Jewish Suffering* (London: Verso, 2000).

Foa, V., *Il cavallo e la torre. Riflessioni su una vita* (Turin: Einaudi, 1991).

Forti, M., '*I sommersi e i salvati* di Primo Levi, dieci anni dopo', *Nuova antologia*, 131/2197 (Jan.–Mar. 1996), 203–17.

Foucault, M., *Discipline and Punish* (Harmondsworth: Penguin, 1979).

—— *Ethics. Subjectivity and Truth*, ed. P. Rabinow (Harmondsworth: Allen Lane, 1994).

Frankl, V., *Man's Search for Meaning* (New York: Washington Square Press, 1985; 1st edition 1946).

Frassica, P., 'Aspetti della narrativa postbellica (Beppe Fenoglio e Primo Levi)', *Forum italicum*, 8/3 (Sept. 1974), 365–80.

—— ed., *Primo Levi as Witness* (Florence: Casalini, 1990).

French, P., 'Books of the Year 1985', *Observer* (Dec. 1985).

Freschi, M., 'La fortuna italiana della letteratura ebraico-orientale (1960–1991)', in *La cultura ebraica nell'editoria italiana (1955–1990)* (Rome: Ministero per i beni culturali e ambientali, Quaderni di libri e riviste d'Italia 27, 1992), 105–13.

Friedlander, S., ed., *Probing the Limits of Representation. Nazism and the Final Solution* (Cambridge, Mass.: Harvard University Press, 1992).

Friedman, M., 'Feminism and Modern Friendship: Dislocating the Community', in Badhwar, *Friendship*, 285–302.

Galante Garrone, A., 'Il grido di Primo Levi', *Nuova antologia*, 122/2163 (July–Sept. 1987), 212–27.

Garin, E., 'Conseguenze culturali delle leggi razziali del 1938: l'emarginazione degli intellettuali ebrei dalle università, dalla ricerca, dalla vita del paese', in *La cultura ebraica nell'editoria italiana (1955–1990)* (Rome: Ministero per i beni culturali e ambientali, Quaderni di libri e riviste d'Italia 27, 1992), 79–88.

Garosci, A., 'Se questo è un uomo...' (1947), *Rassegna mensile di Israel*, 55/2–3 (May–Dec. 1989), 229–32.

Geertz, C., *The Interpretation of Cultures* (London: Fontana, 1993; 1st edition 1973).

Giglioli, D., 'Narratore', in Belpoliti, ed., *Primo Levi* (Riga 13), 397–408.

Gilbert, P., 'A Letter for Primo Levi', *Jewish Quarterly*, 34/3/127 (Autumn 1987), 10–12.

—— 'Darkness Illuminated', *Jewish Quarterly*, 35/4/132 (Winter 1988–9), 59–62.

Gilman, S., 'To Quote Primo Levi: "If You Don't Speak Yiddish, You're Not a Jew" ', in *Inscribing the Other* (Lincoln: University of Nebraska Press, 1991), 293–316.

Ginzburg, C., 'Unus testis. Lo sterminio degli Ebrei e il principio della realtà', *Quaderni storici*, 27/80/2 (Aug. 1992), 529–48 (also in Friedlander, ed., *Probing the Limits of Representation*, 82–96).

—— *Occhiacci di legno. Nove riflessioni sulla distanza* (Milan: Feltrinelli, 1998).

Gioanola, E., 'Diversità della letteratura. Letteratura della diversità', in Momigliano Levi and Gorris, eds., *Primo Levi testimone e scrittore della storia*, 1–17.

Giuntella, V., 'Il ritorno dai Lager: considerazioni introduttive', in Cavaglion, ed., *Il ritorno dai Lager*, 85–118.

Goldberg, S. L., *Agents and Lives. Moral Thinking in Literature* (Cambridge: Cambridge University Press, 1993).

Goldkorn, W., 'La memoria ambigua', *MicroMega*, 3 (July–Sept. 1989), 195–202.

Gordon, R., 'Primo Levi: Storyteller', *European Judaism*, 23/1 (Spring 1990), 11–20.

—— 'Etica', in Belpoliti, ed., *Primo Levi* (Riga 13), 315–30.

—— '*Per mia fortuna*...: Irony and Ethics in Primo Levi's Writing', *Modern Language Review*, 92/2 (Apr. 1997), 337–47.

—— 'Primo Levi: On Friendship', in G. Bedani et al, eds., *Sguardi sull'Italia* (Leeds: W. S. Maney/Society for Italian Studies Occasional Papers 3, 1997), 284–94.

—— 'Primo Levi: The Duty of Memory', in H. Peitsch, C. Burdett, and C. Gorrara, eds., *European Memories of the Second World War* (Oxford: Berghahn, 1999), 131–40.

—— 'Holocaust Writing in Context: Italy 1945–47', in Leak and Paizis, eds., *The Holocaust and the Text*, 32–50.

—— 'The Art of Listening: Primo Levi's Ethics of Storytelling', *Jewish Culture and History*, 3/1 (Summer 2000), 1–22.

—— 'Per un'etica comune: le virtù quotidiane di Primo Levi', in Mattioda, ed., *Al di qua del bene e del male*, 87–108.

Gould, S. J., *The Mismeasure of Man* (Harmondsworth: Penguin, 1997; revised edition).

Gramsci, A., *Folclore e senso comune* (Rome: Editori Riuniti, 1992).

Grassano, G., *Primo Levi* (Florence: La Nuova Italia, 1981).

Greppi, C., 'Una figura nella poesia di Primo Levi', in Ioli, ed., *Primo Levi: memoria e invenzione*, 147–51.

Guadagni, A., 'La memoria del bene: Luciana Nissim', *Diario*, 2/8 (26 Feb.–4 Mar. 1997), 14–19.

—— 'Prima del grande buio', *Diario*, 2/13 (2–8 Apr. 1997), 52–7.

Guidetti Serra, B., 'Minima personalia', *Belfagor*, 46/4 (31 July 1991), 449–56.

Gunzberg, L., 'Down among the Dead Men: Levi and Dante in Hell', *Modern Language Studies*, 16 (1986), 10–28.

—— 'Nuotando altrimenti che nel Serchio: Dante as Vademecum for Primo Levi', in S. Tarrow, ed., *Reason and Light* (Ithaca, NY: Center for International Studies, 1990), 82–98.

—— *Strangers at Home. Jews in the Italian Literary Imagination* (Berkeley and Los Angeles: University of California Press, 1992).

Haidu, P., 'The Dialectics of Unspeakability: Language, Silence and the Narratives of Desubjectification', in Friedlander, ed., *Probing the Limits of Representation*, 277–99.

Halbwachs, M., *On Collective Memory* (Chicago: Chicago University Press, 1992; 1st edition 1950).

Hand, S., ed., *The Levinas Reader* (Oxford: Blackwell, 1989).

Handwerk, G., *Irony and Ethics in Narrative. From Schlegel to Lacan* (New Haven: Yale University Press, 1985).

Haney, D. P., 'Aesthetics and Ethics in Gadamer, Levinas, and Romanticism: Problems of Phronesis and Techne', *PMLA* 114/1 (Jan. 1999), 32–45.

Harpham, G., *Getting it Right. Language, Literature, and Ethics* (Chicago: Chicago University Press, 1992).

—— 'Ethics', in Frank Lentricchia and Thomas McLaughlin, *Critical Terms for Literary Study* (Chicago: Chicago University Press, 1995; 2nd edition), 387–405.

Hartman, G., ed., *Holocaust Remembrance. The Shapes of Memory* (Oxford: Blackwell, 1994).

Hastings R., *Nature and Reason in the Decameron* (Manchester: Manchester University Press, 1975).

Hawkins, P., and Howland Schotter, A., eds., *Ineffability. Naming the Unnamable from Dante to Beckett* (New York: AMS Press, 1984).

Herman, M., *Diario di un ragazzo ebreo* (Cuneo: L'Arciere, 1984).

Hillis Miller, J., *The Ethics of Reading* (New York: Columbia University Press, 1987).

Höss, R., *Comandante ad Auschwitz. Memoriale autobiografico* (Turin: Einaudi, 1985).

Hughes, H. Stuart, *Prisoners of Hope. The Silver Age of the Italian Jews 1924–1974* (Cambridge, Mass.: Harvard University Press, 1983).

Hutcheon, L., *Irony's Edge. The Theory and Politics of Irony* (London: Routledge, 1995).

Ioli, G., ed., *Primo Levi: memoria e invenzione* (San Salvatore Monferrato: Edizione della Biennale 'Piemonte e letteratura', 1995).

James, C., 'Last Will and Testament', *New Yorker* (23 May 1988), 86–92.

Jesurum, S., *Essere ebrei in Italia* (Milan: Longanesi, 1987).

Jowett's Dictionary of English Law, 2nd edition ed. J. Burke, vols. I–II (London: Sweet and Maxwell, 1977).

Judt, T., 'The Courage of the Elementary', *New York Review of Books*, 46/9 (20 May 1999), 31–8.

Kaplan, C. A., *Scroll of Agony. The Warsaw Diary of Chaim A. Kaplan*, tr. and ed. A. I. Katsh (London: Hamilton, 1966).

Katz, A., 'On "Maelstroms Large and Small, Metaphorical and Actual": "Gray Zones" in the Writings of Primo Levi', *Cultural Studies*, 13/3 (July 1999), 423–47.

Katzenelson, Y., *Il canto del popolo ebraico massacrato* (Florence: La Giutina, 1995; 1st edition 1948; in English as *The Song of the Murdered Jewish People* (Tel Aviv: Hakibbutz Hameuchad, 1980)).

Kermode, F., *The Uses of Error* (London: Collins, 1990).

König, J., *Sfuggito alle reti del nazismo* (Milan: Mursia, 1973).

Kushner, T., *The Holocaust and the Liberal Imagination* (Oxford: Blackwell, 1994).

LaCapra, D., *Representing the Holocaust. History, Theory, Trauma* (Ithaca, NY: Cornell University Press, 1994).

La Capria, R., *La mosca nella bottiglia. Elogio del senso comune* (Milan: Rizzoli, 1996).

Lagorio, G., 'La memoria perenne e la poesia "Ad ora incerta" ', in Frassica, ed., *Primo Levi as Witness*, 63–75.

Lang, B., *Act and Idea in the Nazi Genocide* (Chicago: Chicago University Press, 1990).

Langbein, H., *Uomini ad Auschwitz. Storia del più famigerato campo di sterminio nazista*, tr. Daniela Ambroset (Milan: Mursia, 1984; 1st German edition 1972).

Langer, L., *The Holocaust and the Literary Imagination* (New Haven: Yale University Press, 1975).

—— *Admitting the Holocaust* (Oxford: Oxford University Press, 1995).

—— *Preempting the Holocaust* (New Haven: Yale University Press, 1998).

Larkin, P., *Collected Poems*, ed. A. Thwaite (London: Marvell Press/Faber and Faber, 1988).

Leak, A., and Paizis, G., eds., *The Holocaust and the Text: Speaking the Unspeakable* (London: Macmillan, 1999).

Lerner, G., 'I legionati dell'ex città-fabbrica', *La stampa*, 3 Nov. 1997.

Levi, A., 'Primo Levi e la scienza', *Rassegna mensile di Israel*, 55/2–3 (May–Dec. 1989), 271–80.

Levi, F., ed., *L'ebreo in oggetto. L'applicazione della normativa antiebraica a Torino 1938–1943* (Turin: Silvio Zamorani, 1991).

Levi Della Torre, S., ed., *Scritti in memoria di Primo Levi*, monographic issue of *Rassegna mensile di Israel*, 55/2–3 (May–Dec. 1989), 191–346.

Levi Montalcini, R., *Elogio dell'imperfezione* (Milan: Garzanti, 1987).

—— *Senz'olio contro vento* (Milan: Baldini and Castoldi, 1996).

Levinas, E., *Totalité et infini. Essai sur l'extériorité* (The Hague: Martinus Nijhoff, 1971; 1st edition 1961).

Levra, U., and Tranfaglia, N., eds., *Torino fra liberalismo e fascismo* (Milan: Franco Angeli, 1987).

Lewis, C. S., *The Four Loves* (London: Harper Collins/Fount, 1977; 1st edition 1960).

Lewis, R. W. B., *The Picaresque Saint. Representative Figures in Contemporary Fiction* (London: Gollancz, 1960).

Loftus, E., *Eyewitness Testimony* (Cambridge, Mass.: Harvard University Press, 1979).

Lollini, M., 'Il caso Primo Levi e il problema della testimonianza', *Il piccolo Hans*, 72 (Winter 1991–2), 193–210.

Lopez, G., 'Primo Levi: l'opera, gli avvenimenti, l'umanità', *Rassegna mensile di Israel*, 55/2–3 (May–Dec. 1989), 215–28.

—— 'Ebraismo e editoria in Italia. Tendenze e sviluppi dagli anni trenta agli anni novanta', in *La cultura ebraica nell'editoria italiana (1955–1990)* (Rome: Ministero per i beni culturali e ambientali, Quaderni di libri e riviste d'Italia 27, 1992), 23–47.

Luria, S., *A Slot Machine, a Broken Test-Tube* (New York: Harper and Row, 1984).

Lyotard, J.-F., *Le Différend* (Paris: Éditions de Minuit, 1983).

—— *Discussion, or Phrasing 'After Auschwitz' (Working Paper No. 2)* (Madison: Center for Twentieth Century Studies, 1986).

Macchia, G., ed., *I moralisti classici. Da Machiavelli a La Bruyère* (Milan: Garzanti, 1978).

MacIntyre, A., *After Virtue* (London: Duckworth, 1985; 1st edition 1981).

Magris, C., *Lontano da dove. Joseph Roth e la tradizione ebraico-orientale* (Turin: Einaudi, 1971).

Maida, B., 'Dopo "la tregua": gli ex-deportati nella società italiana del dopoguerra', in Cavaglion, ed., *Il ritorno dai Lager*, 189–200.

Mann, N., *Petrarch* (Oxford: Oxford University Press, 1984).

Manzoni, A., *Opere*, vols. I–III. ed. M. Barbi and F. Ghisalberti (Florence: Sansoni, 1942).

Margalit, A., *The Decent Society* (Cambridge, Mass.: Harvard University Press, 1996).

——— and Motzkin, G., 'The Uniqueness of the Holocaust', *Philosophy and Public Affairs*, 23/1 (Winter 1996), 65–83.

Marrus, M., *The Holocaust in History* (New York: New American Library, 1987).

Martini, M., *Il trauma della deportazione. Ricerca psicologica sui sopravvissuti italiani ai campi di concentramento nazisti* (Milan: Mondadori, 1983).

Massano, R., 'Moralità e stile di Augusto Monti. Resistenza senza era: la sua scuola dal carcere', in G. Tesio, ed., *Augusto Monti nel centenario della nascita,* conference proceedings (Turin: Centro studi piemontesi, 1982).

Mattioda, E., *L'ordine del mondo. Saggio su Primo Levi* (Naples: Liguori, 1998).

——— ed., *Al di qua del bene e del male. La visione del mondo di Primo Levi* (Milan: Franco Angeli, 2000).

Mauro, W., and Mondo, L., 'Primo Levi', in G. Grana, ed., *Letteratura italiana. Novecento,* vol. VII (Milan: Marzorati, 1979), 6885–901.

Mendel, D., 'Un incontro con Primo Levi', *L'indice dei libri del mese* (*Liber* supplement), 11/5 (May 1994), 53–4 (first published in *Sunday Telegraph,* 8 Sept. 1991).

Mengaldo, P. V., 'Ciò che dobbiamo a Primo Levi', in G. Folena, *Tre narratori: Calvino, Primo Levi, Parise* (Padua: Liviana, 1989), 89–98.

——— 'Lingua e scrittura in Levi', in Ferrero, ed., *Primo Levi: un'antologia della critica,* 169–242.

Michaelis, M., *Mussolini and the Jews* (Oxford: Oxford University Press, 1978).

Millu, L., *Il fume di Birkenau* (Florence: La Giuntina, 1986).

Molino Signorini, F., ' "Uomini fummo"...: Riflessioni su Primo Levi e Jean Améry', *Rassegna mensile di Israel,* 57/3 (Sept.–Dec. 1991), 463–78.

Moliterni, F., Ciccarelli, R., and Lattanzio, A., *Primo Levi. L'a-topia letteraria, il pensiero narrativo, la scrittura e l'assurdo* (Naples: Liguori, 2000).

Momigliano, A., *Pagine ebraiche* (Turin: Einaudi, 1987).

Momigliano Levi, P., and Gorris, E., eds., *Primo Levi testimone e scrittore della storia* (Florence: La Giuntina, 1999).

Montaigne, M. de, *The Complete Essays*, tr. M. A. Screech (Harmondsworth: Penguin, 1991).

Morgan, M., ed., *A Holocaust Reader* (Oxford: Oxford University Press, 2000).

Mortara di Veroli, E., 'La biblioteca di Babele', in *La cultura ebraica nell'editoria italiana (1955–1990)* (Rome: Ministero per i beni culturali e ambientali, Quaderni di libri e riviste d'Italia 27, 1992), 89–103.

Motola, G., 'The Varnish-Maker's Dreams', *Sewanee Review*, 98/3 (Summer 1990), 506–14.

Muecke, D., *The Compass of Irony* (London: Methuen, 1969).

Mulhall, S., ed., *The Cavell Reader* (Oxford: Blackwell, 1996).

Murdoch, I., *The Sovereignty of Good* (London: Routledge and Kegan Paul, 1970).

Musgrave, A., *Common Sense, Science and Scepticism* (Cambridge: Cambridge University Press, 1993).

Neppi, E., 'Sopravvivenza e vergogna in Primo Levi', *Strumenti critici*, NS 11/82 (Sept. 1996), 479–500.

Newell, J. David, ed., *Philosophy and Common Sense* (Washington: University Press of America, 1980).

Newton, A. Z., *Narrative Ethics* (Cambridge, Mass.: Harvard University Press, 1995).

Nissim, L., 'Ricordi della casa dei morti', in L. Nissim and P. Lewinska, *Donne contro il mostro* (Turin: Vincenzo Ramella Editore, 1946), 18–58; later in *Diario*, 4/14 (7–13 Apr. 1999) and 15 (14–20 Apr. 1999).

Novick, P., *The Holocaust and Collective Memory* (London: Bloomsbury, 1999).

Nussbaum, M., *Love's Knowledge* (Oxford: Oxford University Press, 1990).

Nyiszli, M., *Auschwitz: A Doctor's Eyewitness Account*, tr. T. Kremer and R. Seaver (Greenwich, Conn.: Fawcett Crest, 1960).

Nystedt, J., *Le opere di Primo Levi viste al computer. Osservazioni stilolinguistiche* (Stockholm: Acta Universitatis Stockholmiensis/Almquist and Wiksell, 1993).

Ossola, C., 'Pensare all'ordinario', in G. Barbieri and P. Vidali, eds., *La ragione possibile. Per una geografia della cultura* (Milan: Feltrinelli, 1988), 207–23.

Ozick, C., 'Primo Levi's Suicide Note', in *Metaphor and Memory* (New York: Knopf, 1989), 34–48.

Pahl, R., *On Friendship* (Cambridge: Polity, 2000).

Pakaluk, M., ed., *Other Selves. Philosophers on Friendship* (Indianapolis: Hackett, 1991).

Parker, D., *Ethics, Theory and the Novel* (Cambridge: Cambridge University Press, 1994).

Patruno, N., *Understanding Primo Levi* (Columbia: University of South Carolina Press, 1995).

Pauletto, P., 'Frontiere', in Belpoliti, ed., *Primo Levi* (Riga 13), 336–47.

Pavese, C., *Il mestiere di vivere* (Turin: Einaudi, 1981; 1st edition 1952).

—— *La luna e i falò* (Turin: Einaudi, 1990; 1st edition 1950).

Pecora, V., 'Habermas, Enlightenment and Antisemitism', in Friedlander, ed., *Probing the Limits of Representation*, 155–70.

Petrucciani, M., 'Tra algebra e metafora: la scienza nella cultura letteraria italiana 1945–1975', in V. Branca et al., eds., *Letteratura e scienza nella storia della cultura italiana* (Palermo: Manfredi, 1978), 273–330.

Phelan, J., ed., *Reading Narrative. Form, Ethics, Ideology* (Columbus: Ohio State University Press, 1989).

Picciotto Fargion, L., 'Le informazioni sulla "soluzione finale" circolanti in Italia nel 1942–1943', *Rassegna mensile di Israel*, 55/2–3 (May–Dec. 1989), 351–6.

—— *Il libro della memoria. Gli ebrei deportati dall'Italia (1943–1945)* (Milan: Mursia, 1991).

Pintore, E., 'Il ritorno dei deportati nella memorialistica italiana', in Cavaglion, ed., *Il ritorno dai Lager*, 201–12.

Pirandello, L., *L'umorismo* (Milan: Mondadori, 1986; 1st edition 1908).

Poliakov, L., *Auschwitz*, tr. Betty Foà (Rome: Veltro, 1968).

Popper, K., *The Logic of Scientific Discovery* (London: Hutchinson, 1959).

Porro, M., 'Scienza', in Belpoliti, ed., *Primo Levi* (Riga 13), 434–75.

Porter, R., and Tomaselli, S., *The Dialectics of Friendship* (London: Routledge, 1989).

Queneau, R., *Piccola cosmogonia portatile*, by S. Solmi, ed. I. Calvino (Turin: Einaudi, 1982).

Riatsch, G., and Gorgé, V., 'Né sistema né periodico: appunti per la lettura di "Il sistema periodico" di Primo Levi', *Esperienze letterarie*, 16/4 (Oct.–Dec. 1991), 65–81.

Ricœur, P., 'Narrative Identity', in D. Wood, ed., *On Paul Ricœur. Narrative and Interpretation* (London: Routledge, 1989).

Roditi, E., 'The Jewish Contribution to Post-war Italian Literature', *Jewish Quarterly*, 28/1/102 (Spring 1980), 20–3.

Rorty, A. O., 'The Historicity of Psychological Attitudes: Love is not Love which Alters Not when it Alteration Finds', in Badhwar, *Friendship*, 73–88.

Rorty, R., *Contingency, Irony, and Solidarity* (Cambridge: Cambridge University Press, 1989).

Rosato, I., 'Primo Levi: sondaggi intertestuali', *Autografo*, 6, NS 17 (June 1989), 31–43.

Rose, G., *Mourning Becomes the Law. Philosophy and Representation* (Cambridge: Cambridge University Press, 1996).

Rosenfeld, A., *A Double Dying. Reflections on Holocaust Literature* (Bloomington: Indiana University Press, 1980).

—— and Greenberg, I., eds., *Confronting the Holocaust: The Impact of Elie Wiesel* (Bloomington: Indiana University Press, 1978).

Rubinstein, R., and Roth, J., *Approaches to Auschwitz* (Atlanta: John Knox, 1987).

Rudolf, A., *At an Uncertain Hour. Primo Levi's War against Oblivion* (London: Menard Press, 1990).

—— 'Pikolo, Three Great Poems and Primo Levi's "The Mensch" ', *PN Review*, 19/6 (July–Aug. 1993), 12–13.

Russell, B., *The Conquest of Happiness* (London: Allen and Unwin, 1930).

Saba, U., *Scorciatoie e raccontini* (Milan: Mondadori, 1946).

Santagostino, G., 'Primo Levi e le facce nascoste del tempo', in Ioli, ed., *Primo Levi: memoria e invenzione*, 190–206.

—— *Shoah, mémoire et écriture: Primo Levi, et le dialogue des savoirs* (Paris: L'Harmattan, 1997).

Sarfatti, M., *Gli ebrei nell'Italia fascista. Vicende, identità, persecuzione* (Turin: Einaudi, 2000).

Scarlini, L., 'Teatro', in Belpoliti, ed., *Primo Levi* (Riga 13), 485–99.

Scarpa, D., 'La specie umana negli anni del silenzio', *L'indice dei libri del mese*, 7/14 (July 1997), 31–2.

—— ' "Tutto si confessa". Primo Levi e il grigiore del passato', in Mattioda, ed., *Al di qua del bene e del male*, 47–58.

Schwarz-Bart, A., *Le Dernier des justes* (Paris: Seuil, 1959).

Scurani, A., 'Primo Levi', in *Scrittori italiani*, 9th series (Milan: Edizioni 'Letture', 1983), 35–58.

Segre, C., '*Se questo è un uomo* di Primo Levi', in A. Asor Rosa, ed., *Letteratura italiana. Le opere IV. Novecento. II. La ricerca letteraria* (Turin: Einaudi, 1996), 491–508.

—— 'I romanzi e le poesie', in Ferrero, ed., *Primo Levi: un'antologia della critica*, 91–116.

Semprun, J., *L'Écriture ou la vie* (Paris: Gallimard, 1994).

—— and Wiesel, E., *Se taire est impossible* (Paris: Arte/Mille et une nuits, 1995).

Sereny, G., *Into that Darkness* (London: Deutsch, 1974).

—— *Albert Speer: His Battle with Truth* (London: Macmillan, 1995).

Shelley, M., *Frankenstein, or the Modern Prometheus* (Harmondsworth: Penguin, 1985; 1st edition 1818).

Shklar, J., *Ordinary Vices* (Cambridge, Mass.: Bellknap Press, 1984).

Siebers, T., *The Ethics of Criticism* (Ithaca, NY: Cornell University Press, 1988).

Singer, P., ed., *A Companion to Ethics* (Oxford: Blackwell, 1991).

Sodi, R., 'The Memory of Justice: Primo Levi and Auschwitz', *Holocaust and Genocide Studies*, 4/1 (1989), 89–104.

——— *A Dante of our Time: Primo Levi and Auschwitz* (New York: Peter Lang, 1990).

Steinberg, J., *All or Nothing. The Axis and the Holocaust 1941–43* (London: Routledge, 1990).

Steiner, G., *Language and Silence* (London: Faber and Faber, 1985; 1st edition 1967).

Stille, A., 'Introduction', in J. Améry, *At the Mind's Limits* (New York: Schocken, 1990), pp. vii–xv.

——— *Benevolence and Betrayal. Five Italian Jewish Families under Fascism* (London: Jonathan Cape, 1992).

Storia vissuta. Dal dovere di testimoniare alle testimonianze orali nell'insegnamento della storia della seconda guerra mondiale (Milan: Franco Angeli, 1988).

Strata, M., 'Primo Levi: un uomo al lavoro', *Critica letteraria*, 20/11/75 (1992), 369–84.

Strauss, L., *Persecution and the Art of Writing* (Glencoe, Ill.: Free Press, 1952).

Sullam Calimani, A.-V., 'A Name for Extermination (Hurban, Auschwitz, Genocide, Holocaust, Shoah)', *Modern Language Review*, 94/4 (Oct. 1999), 978–99.

Tadini, E., *La distanza* (Turin: Einaudi, 1998).

Tarrow, S., ed., *Reason and Light* (Ithaca, NY: Center for International Studies, 1990).

Taylor, C., *Sources of the Self. The Making of Modern Identity* (Cambridge: Cambridge University Press, 1989).

Tedeschi, G., *Questo povero corpo* (Milan: EdIt, 1946).

——— *C'è un punto della terra...: una donna del Lager di Birkenau* (Turin: Loescher, 1989).

Tesio, G., *Piemonte letterario dell'otto-novecento. Da Giovanni Faldella a Primo Levi* (Rome: Bulzoni, 1991).

Todorov, T., *Face à l'extrême* (Paris: Seuil, 1991).

Tracy, D., 'Christian Witness and the Shoah', in Hartman, ed., *Holocaust Remembrance*, 81–9.

Usher, J., 'Primo Levi's Science Fiction and the Humanoid', *Journal of the Institute of Romance Studies*, 4 (1996), 199–216.

Vacca, R., *Medioevo prossimo venturo* (Milan: Mondadori, 1971).

——— *Parliamo itangliano*, [pub. under pseudonym Giacomo Elliot] (Milan: Rizzoli, 1978).

Valabrega, P., 'Primo Levi e la tradizione ebraico-orientale', *Studi piemontesi*, 11/2 (Nov. 1982), 296–310.
—— '*Il segreto del cerchio*: la percezione del tempo nell'opera di Primo Levi', *Rassegna mensile di Israel*, 55/2–3 (May–Dec. 1989), 281–8.
—— 'Mano/Cervello', in Belpoliti, ed., *Primo Levi* (Riga 13), 380–92.
Varchetta, G., *Ascoltando Primo Levi. Organizzazione, narrazione, etica* (Milan: Guerini e Associati, 1991).
Vidal-Nacquet, P., *Assassins of Memory. Essays on the Denial of the Holocaust* (New York: Columbia University Press, 1992; 1st French edition 1987).
Vincenti, F., *Invito alla lettura di Primo Levi* (Milan: Mursia, 1987).
Vittorini, E., *Conversazione in Sicilia* (Milan: Rizzoli, 1988; 1st edition 1941–2).
Volpato, C., and Contarello, A., *Psicologia sociale e situazioni estreme. Relazioni interpersonali e intergruppi in* Se questo è un uomo *di Primo Levi* (Bologna: Patron Editore, Quaderni di psicologia 20, 1999).
von Alphen, E., *Caught by History. Holocaust Effects in Contemporary Art, Literature and Theory* (Stanford, Calif.: Stanford University Press, 1997).
Weisberg, R., *Poethics, and Other Strategies of Law and Literature* (New York: Columbia University Press, 1992).
Wiesel, E., *La Nuit* (Paris: Éditions de Minuit, 1958).
—— 'The Holocaust as Literary Inspiration', in E. Wiesel et al., *Dimensions of the Holocaust. Lectures at NorthWestern University* (Evanston, Ill.: The University, 1977), 4–19.
—— 'Io e Primo Levi', *Nuova antologia*, 127 (Apr.–June 1992), 204–8.
Wieviorka, A., *Déportation et génocide* (Paris: Plon, 1992).
Williams, B., *Morality* (Cambridge: Cambridge University Press, 1993; 1st edition 1972).
—— *Ethics and the Limits of Philosophy* (London: Fontana, 1993; 1st edition 1985).
Winter, J., *Site of Memory, Sites of Mourning. The Great War in European Cultural History* (Cambridge: Cambridge University Press, 1995).
Wood, N., 'The Victim's Resentments', in Cheyette and Marcus, eds., *Modernity, Culture and 'the Jew'*, 257–67.
Woolf, J., *The Memory of the Offence. Primo Levi's 'If This is a Man'* (Market Harborough: University Texts/Hull Italian Texts, 1996).
Woolf, S., 'Primo Levi, Drowning and Surviving', *Jewish Quarterly*, 34/3/127 (1987), 6–9.
Yerushalmi, Y., *Zakhor* (Seattle: University of Washington Press, 1982).
Young, J., *Writing and Rewriting the Holocaust: Narrative and the Consequences of Interpretation* (Bloomington: Indiana University Press, 1990).

Young, J., *The Texture of Memory. Holocaust Memorials and Meaning* (New Haven: Yale University Press, 1993).

Zucotti, S., *The Italians and the Holocaust. Persecution, Rescue and Survival* (London: Peter Halban, 1987).

INDEX

To avoid elaborate sub-entries, there are no main entries for ethics, the Holocaust, or Levi. Levi's works—whether book titles or the separate titles of smaller pieces—appear in their alphabetical positions.

314   *Index*